Redisco

Rediscovering Palestine

Merchants and Peasants in
Jabal Nablus, 1700–1900

BESHARA DOUMANI

University of California Press

BERKELEY   LOS ANGELES   LONDON

University of California Press
Berkeley and Los Angeles, California

University of California Press, Ltd.
London, England

©1995 by
The Regents of the University of California

Library of Congress Cataloging-in-Publication Data
Doumani, Beshara, 1957–
   Rediscovering Palestine : merchants and peasants in
Jabal Nablus, 1700–1900 / Beshara Doumani
      p. cm.
   Includes bibliographical references and index.
   ISBN 0-520-08895-6
   1. Nablus Region—Economic conditions. 2. Nablus Region—Politics
and government. 3. Nablus Region—Commerce—History. 4. Peas-
antry—Palestine—History. 5. Palestine—History—638-1917. I. Title.
HC415.25.D68 1995
330.95695'3—dc20   94-30401
CIP

Printed in the United States of America

The paper used in this publication is both acid-free and totally chlorine-
free (TCF). It meets the minimum requirements of ANSI/ NISO Z39.48-
1992 (R 1997) (*Permanence of Paper*). ∞

To my parents,
Hanna Doumani and Mounifa Barakat

and to my lifelong friend,
Halim

Errata:

In chapter 2, several backnotes are incorrectly numbered. Note number 79 in the text corresponds to
endnote 80, and so on through note 128. Note number
129 is superfluous. Notes 130 and 131 are correctly
numbered.

p. 74: The text of note 84 should read: NICR 13A:222.
See also ibid., 13A: 191, 237, 258.

Contents

Maps, Plates, and Tables

Preface

This book attempts to write the inhabitants of Palestine into history. Using the documents they generated during the eighteenth and nineteenth centuries, I have tried to make their society and its inner workings come alive by listening to their voices and by gazing at the world through their eyes. This book also seeks to make a small contribution to a rethinking of Ottoman history by foregrounding the dynamics of provincial life in the vast Ottoman interior, especially the role of merchants and peasants in the shaping of urban-rural relations.

Considering that the historiography of Palestine is dominated by nationalist discourses on both sides of the Palestinian-Israeli divide, and that these discourses are built on the premise of a sharp discontinuity from the past caused by outside intervention, there is no shortage of assumptions to be revised and new issues to introduce. This book calls for a rediscovery of Ottoman Palestine by drawing attention to long-term processes and by highlighting the agency of the inhabitants in the molding of their own history.

The first, formative period of research, 1986–1988, was made possible by an International Doctoral Research Fellowship granted by the Joint Committee on the Near and Middle East of the Social Science Research Council and the American Council of Learned Societies, with funds provided by the William and Flora Hewlett Foundation. The University of Pennsylvania Research Foundation funded further forays into the archives in 1991. Much of the writing was done in 1993 while I was on leave from the University of Pennsylvania School of Arts and Sciences.

I owe a special debt of gratitude to the employees of the Nablus Islamic Court who shared their crowded office with me, for there was no separate room for researchers. Nazih al-Sayih's calm authority, humor, and sensitivity made the court feel like home and kept us focused despite the all-too-frequent distractions of nearby gunfire and the biting wafts of tear gas that seeped through the windows. Jawwad Imran, always with a smile in his heart, shared his desk with me six hours a day, six days a week, for more than two and a half years. All answered my never-ending questions and posed a few of their own.

A network of people helped me gain access to private family papers. The late Ihsan Nimr, whenever he was asked to share his extensive collection of private family papers, always referred researchers to his book instead. Husam al-Sharif, in addition to kindling my interest in soap factories, arranged for me to photocopy this collection, thus making it publicly accessible for the first time. When Lubna Abd al-Hadi showed me a loosely bound collection of old papers, neither she nor I could have imagined that I would spend years examining what turned out to be the remarkably rich records of the Nablus Advisory Council (*majlis al-shura*). *Hajj* Khalil Atireh, Adala Atireh, Saba Arafat, and Naseer Arafat are but a few of the many people who made it possible for me to tap into the collective memory of Nabulsis by facilitating my access to people, places, and papers.

Judith Tucker introduced me to the world of court records and the field of social history. As a graduate student I also learned from (and was humbled by) the rigorous scholarly work of Hanna Batatu, and I sharpened my theoretical tools with the help of Hisham Sharabi. Notes on an earlier version of the manuscript by Roger Owen, Edmund Burke III, and Ken Cuno considerably strengthened the final product, as did the valuable comments of Leila Fawaz, Zachary Lockman, Abdul-Karim Rafeq, Linda Schilcher, Bruce Masters, David Ludden, Lee Cassanelli, Salim Tamari, and Joe Stork. Andrew Todd prepared the city and regional maps of Jabal Nablus, and Bridget O'Rourke designed the family tree (Plate 5). That this book has seen the light of day is due largely to the love, patience, and support of Ismat Atireh.

Abbreviations

AAS	*African and Asian Studies* (Jerusalem)
IJMES	*International Journal of Middle East Studies*
IJTS	*International Journal of Turkish Studies*
JESHO	*Journal of the Economic and Social History of the Orient*
JICR	Jerusalem Islamic Court Records
JPOS	*Journal of the Palestine Oriental Society*
JPS	*Journal of Palestine Studies*
MES	*Middle Eastern Studies*
NICR	Nablus Islamic Court Records
NIMR	Ihsan Nimr, *Tarikh Jabal Nablus wa al-Balqa,* (4 vols.; Nablus, 1936–1961).
NMSR	Nablus *majlis al-shura* Records

Note on Translation
and Transliteration

I wrote this book in a language that I hoped would prove both accessible and interesting to first-time students of the Middle East and that would impart a live and intimate portrait of the people of Palestine during the Ottoman period. In translating the numerous documents which carry their voices, I tried to avoid the technical jargon so common in Ottoman Studies. Whenever possible, I used English instead of Arabic or Turkish terms. When Arabic and Arabized words do appear (usually in parentheses), I transliterated them according to the system of the *International Journal of Middle East Studies*. All diacritical marks were omitted except for the *ayn* (') and *hamza* ('), and these were used only when they occur in the middle of a word or name. Definitions of Arabic terms are provided in the text the first time they are used. A glossary of the most frequently used terms can be found in the back of the book.

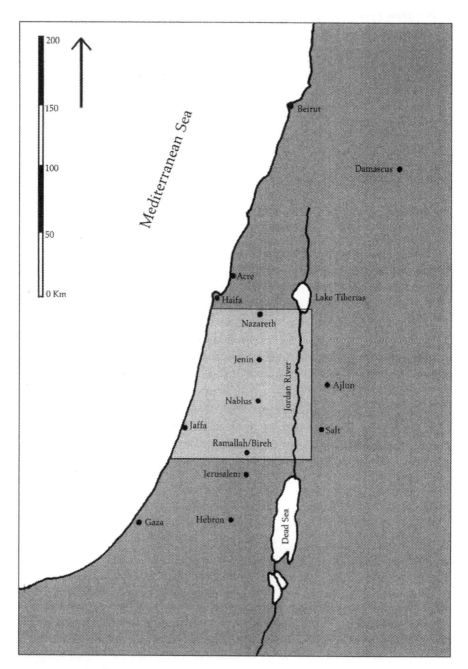

Map 1.　Southern Syria

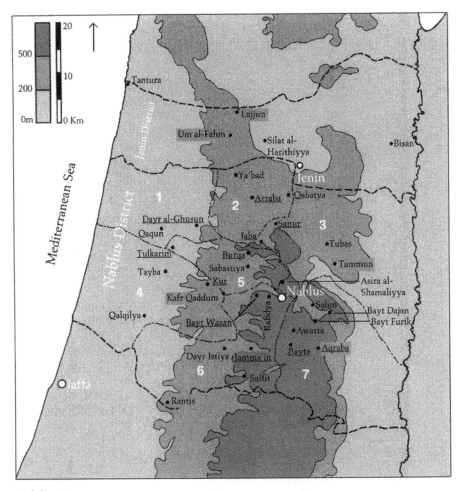

Subdistricts:

1. Sha`rawiyya al-Gharbiyya
2. Sha`rawiyya al-Sharqiyya
3. Mashariq al-Jarrar
4. Bani Sa`b
5. Wadi al-Sha`ir
6. Jamma`in
7. Mashariq Nablus
(<u>Kursi</u> villages are underlined)

Jabal Nablus, circa 1850

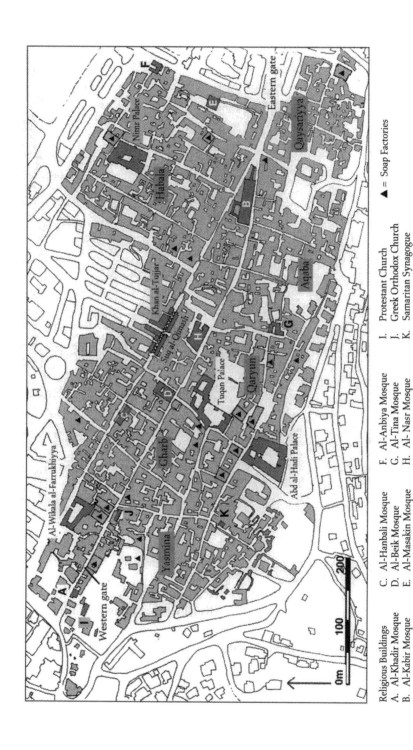

Nablus Old City, showing the positions of key buildings in the late nineteenth century (base map, Nablus Principality 1987).

Religious Buildings
A. Al-Khadir Mosque
B. Al-Kabir Mosque
C. Al-Hanbali Mosque
D. Al-Beik Mosque
E. Al-Masakin Mosque
F. Al-Anbiya Mosque
G. Al-Tina Mosque
H. Al- Nasr Mosque
I. Protestant Church
J. Greek Orthodox Church
K. Samaritan Synagogue

▲ = Soap Factories

Introduction
Palestine and the Ottoman Interior

During the eighteenth and most of the nineteenth centuries, the city of Nablus was Palestine's principal trade and manufacturing center.[1] It also anchored dozens of villages located in the middle of the hill regions which stretched north–south from the Galilee to Hebron and which were home to the largest and most stable peasant settlements in Palestine since ancient times. This study unpacks the social history of Nabulsi merchants and peasants by exploring the relationship among culture, politics, and trade. It investigates how merchants built and reproduced local and regional networks, organized agricultural production for overseas trade, and gained access to political office and to the major means of agricultural and industrial production (land and soap factories). It also examines the ways in which they competed with foreign and regional merchants based in the coastal cities, as well as their discourse with Ottoman officials who were keen on securing the state's share of the rural surplus.

Peasants left far fewer clues for the historian to assemble than merchants did. This study attempts to discern their role in the construction of urban-rural commercial networks and to outline how growing urban domination over the rural sphere complicated the peasants' relations with each other and with their rural chiefs. It also traces the coming of age of a middle peasantry and details their efforts to reproduce urban economic and cultural practices on the village level. Finally, peasant initiatives, ranging from petitions to violent confrontations, are mined for clues about how they defined their identity, understood their connection to the land, and formulated their notions of justice and political authority.

I undertook this study with two goals in mind: first, to contribute to a bottom-up view of Ottoman history by investigating the ways in which urban-rural dynamics in a provincial setting appropriated and gave meaning to the larger forces of Ottoman rule and European economic expansion; and second, to invite a rethinking of the modern history of Palestine by writing its inhabitants into the historical narrative, a task largely neglected by the predominantly nationalist (re)constructions of its Ottoman past.

TOWARD A HISTORY OF PROVINCIAL LIFE
IN THE OTTOMAN INTERIOR

As a single unit, Nablus and its hinterland constituted a discrete region known for centuries as Jabal Nablus.[2] Scores of roughly similar regions filled the interior of the vast and multiethnic Ottoman Empire and surrounded each of its few large international trading cities like a sea around an island. Home to the majority of Ottoman subjects, these discrete regions were located at one and the same time at the material core and the political periphery of the Ottoman world. The opinions of their inhabitants did not carry much weight in determining the political course of the central government in Istanbul, but their combined human resources and productive capacity were absolutely crucial to the empire's tax base and to the provisioning of its metropolitan centers and military forces. An indepth look at the changing political economy of these provincial regions can provide a valuable and fresh perspective on the deep undercurrents of change in the Ottoman domains.

The need for such a perspective has been made clear by the two dominant trends in the growing field of Ottoman Studies. The first has relied mostly on mining the central Ottoman archives and has used the state as the key unit of analysis. The invaluable research in these archives has demonstrated the dynamic character of the Ottoman Empire and has shown that its remarkable longevity was due largely to the energetic, flexible, and thoroughly pragmatic policies of its central administration.[3] The second (more recent) trend, has focused on the capital cities of the provinces—such as Cairo, Damascus, Aleppo, or Beirut—as the point of departure. Using a wide range of sources, including records of the local Islamic courts, these studies have brought to the fore the realities of daily life in large urban settings and have elucidated the diverse historical trajectories possible under the umbrella of Ottoman rule.[4]

Both vantage points have also made painfully clear that the survival of both the Ottoman Empire and its international trading cities was predicated, first and foremost, on their ability to gain access to and control the agricultural surplus of the peasants and the trading activities of the merchants in the interior. Indeed, it is around these two key issues, access and control, that much of the debate on the history of the Ottoman Empire revolves. Precisely because the discrete building blocks of the Ottoman world, interior market towns and their hinterlands, were not passive spectators in these struggles for access and control, the frontiers of research must be pushed to their doorsteps and their experiences must be integrated into the larger discourse of Ottoman history.

When it comes to the modern period, this discourse has been dominated by a single overarching narrative: the piecemeal incorporation or integration of the Ottoman Empire into the European economic and political orbits. This narrative is a central one because it deals directly with the problematics of capitalism, imperialism, and colonialism and because it has implications for current debates on development strategies, international relations, regional conflicts, state formation, and the social bases of nationalist movements. A variety of approaches have been used to frame this narrative,[5] but the same underlying set of economic and political issues continues to be hotly debated: the commercialization of agriculture and the patterns of trade with Europe; the impact of European machine-produced imports on local manufacturing; the growth of coastal trade cities and the rise of minority merchant communities which served as go-betweens; the commoditization of land and the emergence of a large landowning class; the Ottoman government's program of reforms; and the rise of nationalist movements, to name but a few.[6]

In discussions of these key issues the Ottoman Empire was, until fairly recently, usually portrayed as a stagnant, peripheral, and passive spectator in the process of integration. The decline thesis, as it has come to be called, has been persuasively challenged since the early 1970s,[7] but the very thrust of the integration narrative, regardless of the theoretical approach used, tends to relegate the interior regions of the Ottoman Empire, such as Jabal Nablus, to the status of a periphery's periphery. Hence, despite the rapidly growing number of studies, little is known about provincial life, albeit with some important exceptions.[8]

In the case of Palestine it has long been assumed, for example, that transformations in agrarian relations usually associated with so-called modernization did not begin until the first wave of European Jewish immigration in 1882. According to Gabriel Baer, "Arab agriculture did not change its traditional character throughout the nineteenth century. German and Jewish settlers introduced some innovations, but subsistence farming continued to be the predominant type of agriculture in the country, and the growing of cash crops was rare."[9]

Baer seems to have confused traditional methods of farming with subsistence agriculture. Methods and technology remained largely unchanged, it is true, but they were eminently suited to the thin topsoil and rocky ground of the hill regions, the heartland of Palestinian peasantry. Indeed, it was with these traditional means that Palestine, as later shown in a pioneering study by Alexander Schölch, produced large agricultural surpluses and was integrated into the world capitalist economy as an exporter of wheat, barley, sesame, olive oil, soap, and cotton during the 1856–1882 period.[10] In addition, through a detailed study of Western sources, especially consular reports on imports and exports through the ports of Jaffa, Acre, and Haifa, Schölch showed that exports not only closely shadowed shifting European demand but also exceeded imports of European machine-manufactured goods, which meant that Palestine helped the rest of Greater Syria minimize its overall negative balance of trade with Europe.[11]

Schölch chose the Crimean War as a starting point because of the strong demand it generated for grains and because of the new political environment created by Ottoman reforms (*Tanzimat*).[12] But the qualitative leap in trade with Europe between 1856 and 1882, it seems to me, could only have taken place given an already commercialized agricultural sector, a monetized economy, an integrated peasantry, and a group of investors willing to sink large amounts of capital into the production of cash crops. Pushing the process of integration further back in time would help explain the massive and quick "response" of Palestinian peasants and merchants to the increase in European demand and would bring the experience of Palestine into line with the rest of the Ottoman domains. More important, what is now called the Middle East was not a stranger to commercial agriculture, protoindustrial production, and sophisticated credit relations and commercial networks.[13] The same has been shown for other regions, especially for South Asia.[14] In other words, many of the institutions and practices assumed to be the products of an externally imposed capitalist transformation existed before European hegemony and may in fact have helped pave the way for both European economic expansion and Ottoman government reforms. It is critical, therefore, to examine the local contexts in which the processes of Ottoman reform and European expansion played themselves out and to explore how these processes were perceived and shaped by the inhabitants of the Ottoman interior.

Because each market town and its hinterland had its own deeply rooted and locally specific social formation and cultural identity, the question becomes: how to conceptualize the relationship between this bewildering diversity of largely semiautonomous regions and the central government in Istanbul? A complicating factor is that Ottoman administrators, long faced with the same dilemma, neither set out to nor could impose a uniform set of policies, at least not until the 1860s. Rather, different and sometimes contradictory fiscal and administrative arrangements were introduced over the centuries, and they often coexisted and overlapped for long periods of time. In addition, the implementation of government policies was usually channeled indirectly through local elites, as a result of which the policies were constantly reformulated and redefined.

Ever since the publication in 1968 of Albert Hourani's article on the "politics of notables,"[15] historians of the Ottoman provinces in general and of Greater Syria in particular have had access to an insightful framework which explains how native elites mediated between the local inhabitants and the central government authorities.[16] Yet to emerge is an equally persuasive framework which situates the political role of notables within the material, social, and cultural contexts in which they operated, on the one hand, and which allows an agency for those outside public office, particularly merchants and peasants, in the molding of their own history, on the other.

In Greater Syria during most of the Ottoman period, local and regional commerce was every bit as important, if not more so in terms of daily life, as trade with Europe.[17] The merchants of the interior dominated commercial, social, and cultural networks that, so to speak, were linchpins which connected the peasants who produced agricultural commodities with the artisans who processed them and with the ruling families who facilitated the appropriation and movement of goods.[18] These networks also connected the interior regions to each other and, in the process, made it possible for European businessmen and the Ottoman government to gain access to the surplus of these regions. Access and control depended, in other words, on making use of the interior merchants' knowledge of the productive relations on the village level, their credit advances to peasants, their organization of local production for overseas exports, their management of regional markets and trade routes, and their domination of local retail venues and small-scale manufacturing. Merchants of the interior, therefore, occupied a crucial mediating position that could be seen as the underlying basis or economic and cultural counterpart to Hourani's "politics of notables." This book pays special attention to merchant life and to the changing relations between merchants, peasants, and the central Ottoman government.

RETHINKING OTTOMAN PALESTINE

The contours of inquiry into the modern history of Palestine have been and continue to be shaped by two factors that set this region apart from most of the other Ottoman domains: its symbolic and religious significance to Muslims, Christians, and Jews all over the world and the century-long Palestinian-Israeli conflict, an intense political drama that pits two nationalist forces in a struggle over the same land.[19] The combination of these factors has resulted in a voluminous but highly skewed output of historical literature. On the one hand, thousands of books and articles have focused high-powered beams on particular periods, subjects, and themes deemed worthy of study. On the other hand, entire centuries, whole social groups, and a wide range of fundamental issues remain obscure.

The dominant image in the West of Palestine as the Holy Land has concentrated the output of historical texts on the Biblical, Crusader, and modern periods (especially after the British occupation in 1917), because they were perceived as directly linked to European history. Meanwhile, hundreds of years of Arab/Muslim rule have largely been ignored.[20] As the site of the Arab-Israeli conflict, Palestine's past has been used by both nationalist forces to construct a legitimizing national historical charter. Yet, although each camp reaches opposite conclusions and passionately promotes its own particular set of historical villains and heroes, when it comes to the Ottoman period (1516–1917), they share the same underlying set of assumptions.

Generally speaking, most Arab nationalists view the entire Ottoman era as a period of oppressive Turkish rule which stifled Arab culture and socioeconomic development and paved the way for European colonial control and the Zionist takeover of Palestine.[21] Similarly, many Zionist historians represent Ottoman Palestine before European Jewish immigration as an economically devastated, politically chaotic, and sparsely populated region.[22] The intellectual foundation for this shared image can be traced to the extensive literature published during the nineteenth and early twentieth centuries by Westerners bent on "discovering," hence reclaiming, the Holy Land from what they believed was a stagnant and declining Ottoman Empire. This literature detailed the landscape in excruciating detail but turned a blind eye to the native inhabitants who, at best, were portrayed as nostalgic icons of Biblical times or, at worst, as obstacles to modernization.[23] Even Islamicist historians, who argue for a golden age of Islamic justice shattered by Western intervention in the nineteenth century, invoke the same dichotomy, which effectively partitions the history of Ottoman Palestine into two disconnected stages: traditional and modern.[24] The perception of discontinuity was so powerful that, as of this writing, only two monographs that deal specifically with Palestine during the eighteenth century have been published in English, and none covers the seventeenth century.[25] One wonders how it is possible to understand the social structure, cultural life, and economic development of Palestinian society during the Mandate period (1922–1948) on the basis of such scanty knowledge about the preceding four hundred years.

Another widely shared set of assumptions concerns the dichotomy between active and passive forces of change. Periodization reflects the assumption that change is an externally imposed, top-down process: most books on the modern history of Palestine, regardless of the nationality of their author, begin with the year 1882. The rest almost always begin with the Egyptian invasion in 1831, which is said to have initiated a process of so-called modernization that was haltingly continued by the *Tanzimat* in 1839 and 1856, then sealed by the arrival of European Jewish settlers in 1882. Although each of these events was of crucial significance, the implicit corollary is that the indigenous inhabitants played little or no role in the shaping of their history.

The resulting boundaries in time betray the deep concern of nationalist historians on both sides with the political legacy of the last phase of Ottoman rule to twentieth-century developments, hence the heavy emphasis in the literature on patterns of government and administration. Also, political history has been largely limited to those social groups that had direct contact with the West or were key to Ottoman administration. Similarly, far more attention was paid to those urban centers that were beachheads for Western expansion and Ottoman centralization—Jaffa, Haifa, and Jerusalem—than to the interior hill regions, where the majority of inhabitants lived until the late nineteenth century. The combined result is a general neglect of underlying socioeconomic and cultural processes and, more important, the exclusion of the native population from the historical narrative. This holds especially true for those groups that did not enjoy easy access to political position, wealth, and status: peasants, workers, artisans, women, bedouin, and the majority of retailers and merchants.[26]

The subject matter of this book was conceived, partly at least, in response to the state of the art in the field. Jabal Nablus is located in the heart of Ottoman Palestine. During the eighteenth and nineteenth centuries Nablus was the most important of the interior cities in terms of continuous settlement, density of population, economic activity, leadership role, and degree of autonomy within Ottoman rule. It was also Palestine's primary center for regional trade and local manufacture and was organically linked to its hinterland through deeply rooted local networks of trade. The dynamics of change experienced by its homogeneous Sunni Muslim population approximated the overall trends in Palestinian society and culture to a greater degree than did those of either the coastal cities or Jerusalem.

The focus on merchants and peasants is designed to highlight the importance of urban-rural relations to the political economy and cultural life of Palestine, as well as to take advantage of the fact that merchants are an ideal subject for researchers. The well-to-do merchant families that dominated the top ranks of the local trading community constituted a fairly cohesive and remarkably resilient group, whose engagement in this profession spanned generations. By virtue of their ownership of urban properties and the very nature of their occupation, they generated more documents than did any other social group. Consequently, it is possible to track specific families over relatively long periods and to impart an intimacy and immediacy to otherwise abstract undercurrents of change. The focus on merchants also allows researchers to examine this social group in a setting partly of its own creation: in Jabal Nablus, as in most market towns of the interior, the merchant community's influence on the local socioeconomic and cultural life was a preponderant one.

Finally, this study begins in the early eighteenth century in order to bridge the two artificially disconnected stages of Palestine's Ottoman past. Features usually associated with so-called modernization—such as commercial agriculture, a money economy in the rural areas, differentiation within the peasantry, commoditization of land, and ties to the world market—were present in Jabal Nablus before they were supposedly introduced by the Egyptian occupation (1831–1840), the Ottoman *Tanzimat*, or Jewish colonization. Similarly, so called traditional forms of social and economic organization survived well into the twentieth century. The point here is not to minimize the importance of nineteenth-century developments. Rather, it is to recognize that the regions of Greater Syria, including Jabal Nablus, had a great deal in common with the rest of the Mediterranean world and were not simply standing still until awakened by an expanding Europe and a centralizing empire. In the words of Fernand Braudel, "The Turkish Mediterranean [in the sixteenth century] lived and breathed with the same rhythms as the Christian . . . with identical problems and general trends if not the same consequences."[27] No doubt Braudel's insight holds less true for the eighteenth and nineteenth centuries. Still, it clearly points out that a lively pulse beat everywhere in the Mediterranean, and our knowledge of the past cannot be advanced by essentializing difference, much less eliminating the agency of the "Orient" by subjecting its history to the dichotomies of traditional/modern, active/passive, and internal/external.

SOURCES

In order to bring the voices of inhabitants to the fore and to impart a flavor of their world, I have drawn most heavily on local sources, which are detailed in Appendix 2. Hitherto, our understanding of Ottoman Palestine has been largely a product of a heavy reliance by historians on the central Ottoman archives and European consular reports and travel accounts. Although these sources were used in this study, their primary limitation is that they portray the inhabitants of Palestine as *objects* to be ordered, organized, taxed, conscripted, counted, ruled, observed, and coopted. A refreshing aspect of local sources, in contrast, is that the inhabitants come across as *subjects* who take an active role in the construction of their own history: they voluntarily appeared before the judge in the Islamic court, petitioned the Advisory Council (*majlis al-shura*), and entered into private contracts. The voices in these documents are largely their own, and their perceived priorities take precedence.

The advantages of local sources are multiplied several fold in the case of Jabal Nablus, because of the paucity of literary, consular, and central government sources on the one hand, and the fortuitous combination of local sources on the other. As a relatively small interior city whose economy was based on local and regional trade and manufacture, Nablus was of little interest to Western government officials and was, consequently, neglected in their dispatches—especially when compared with the voluminous reporting on Jerusalem and the commercial activities of the coastal cities. Lacking in great religious significance for the outside world except for the small Samaritan community, it was also of little interest to Western travelers, who invariably perceived Nablus as a temporary resting place between Jerusalem and Damascus.[28] According to James Finn, the British consul in Jerusalem during the mid-nineteenth century, "With these two exceptions [Reverend Bowen and Reverend Mills, who spent 12 months and 3 months, respectively, in Nablus] no one from our land has remained, even a few days, in this most interesting district, visited and passed through by hundreds of British travellers, for pleasure, but cared for by none."[29] Finally, as the capital of a hill region which enjoyed a significant degree of autonomy and self-rule and in which there were no "foreigners" who held military or bureaucratic posts, Nablus remained outside the detailed supervision of the Ottoman government, at least until the mid-nineteenth century. Thus the bureaucratic documentation generated by the central bureaucracy was usually not grounded in a thorough and timely knowledge of actual developments.

Happily, this study benefits from a unique combination of local sources. The Islamic Court records of Nablus provide a wealth of detail on social life, especially in the urban sphere, and on urban-rural relations. These records, in turn, are supplemented by the correspondence of the Nablus Advisory Council and by a wide range of private family papers. Both were kindly made available to me by dozens of individuals and are used here for the first time. The Advisory Council records, which span the years 1848–1853, have greatly increased the scope and depth of our knowledge about Jabal Nablus, for they contain information on precisely those areas—political, administrative, and fiscal—which lay outside the scope of the Islamic court.[30] The most important private family papers— business contracts between merchants, artisans, and peasants, account-books, *waqf* endowments, personal correspondence, and property disputes—make it possible to trace the transformations in business practices, patterns of investment, and use of properties over a long period of time. They also add much-needed depth and local color to the issues discussed.

The vantage point of the central government is far from absent in these local sources. Private family papers include many original letters of appointments, land grants, and imperial edicts (*firmans*). The records of the Advisory Council, by their very nature, contain copies of the detailed correspondence between Nabulsi public officials and their superiors on a wide range of issues. The most important source of central government documents, however, is the Nablus Islamic Court, which also functioned as a public-records office. Hundreds of letters generated by the central bureaucracy in Istanbul, as well as by military commanders and governors of Damascus, Acre, Sidon, and Jerusalem, were copied into the court registers. Indeed, the Nablus court records probably contain the largest concentration of official correspondence dealing with this region to be found anywhere.

A few words of caution are in order. Records of the Islamic court and the Advisory Council, like those in any other archive, are products of social institutions and, consequently, are encoded with the language or discourse of these institutions. The Islamic court was, above all else, the guardian of (mostly urban) property. Aside from the administrative correspondence received and copied, all cases brought before the court—whether lawsuits, purchases and sales of immovable properties, *waqf* endowments and exchanges, inheritance estates, rent contracts, or matters of personal status—involved the movement, registration, or right of access to property. The Islamic court, in short, was a clearinghouse which channeled, gave legal sanction to, and legitimated the transfer of property. Consequently, the Islamic Court of Nablus served mostly the needs of the propertied urban middle class of merchants, well-to-do artisans, and religious leaders. Before the 1860s, for example, peasants were greatly underrepresented. I have used these sources mostly as literary texts; that is, as self-conscious representations reflecting the agendas of particular individuals, groups, and institutions.[31] I have often found them valuable less for what they were designed to record and more for unintended bits of information that were generally irrelevant to the outcome of each specific case. Indeed, the assumptions that underlay them and the types of information they leave out usually provided the most important clues to their significance. In addition, most disputes and inheritance cases, to name but two types of cases, were not brought before the court. Thus these records do not easily lend themselves to statistical analysis, at least not to the same degree as those of Jerusalem (where the court was a more powerful institution because of the high rank of the judges who presided over it) and of Damascus (a provincial capital). I have, for the most part, avoided the temptation of quantifying them.

The Advisory Council records pose their own sets of interpretative problems. The letters of the council, as texts, were far less predictable and standardized than were those of the Islamic court: they did not need to conform to a strict formulaic set of legal rules governing the presentation and outcome of each case. Rather, they were careful constructions—subtle, complex, evasive, probing, contingent—that reflected all the tensions of a correspondence between heads of competing bureaucratic departments who were forced to cooperate. As the appointed mediators between the central government and the local population, members of the council presented to their superiors a carefully edited image of Jabal Nablus's political economy and cultural life, on the one hand, and creatively interpreted the demands of the central government to the local inhabitants, on the other. I have attempted to interpret them with this context in mind.

Finally, the reader will also note that I have occasionally made use of two other valuable but problematic local sources: published autobiographies and oral history. Both, of course, present difficulties stemming from the use of memory in the writing of history. My own skepticism about the usefulness of such sources for understanding the period under study was so ingrained that it was not until six years after I had started this project that I seriously considered probing them, and then only within narrow and carefully laid out limits. To my delight, they proved to be very useful. Still, I avoided treating these sources as definitive records of events that took place prior to the beginning of the twentieth century. Rather, I mined them for information on specific cultural and work-related practices and cross-checked the information against available contemporary evidence and accounts from unrelated informants.

APPROACH AND METHODOLOGY

A common methodological challenge for social historians is how to organize the extremely fragmented information available. This particular project involved thousands of documents, each of them a closed world. This challenge is made all the more difficult by the paucity of studies on the social history of Ottoman Palestine: even the most basic demographic and economic data are in the very early stages of being unearthed for the period before the 1850s.

Although the more traditional chronological or thematic approaches have their virtues, they often achieve narrative clarity and cohesiveness by either downplaying some dimensions of the human experience or erecting artificial boundaries between these dimensions. In order to organize the details into a format which gives primacy to process and which, at the same time, relates the specific history of Jabal Nablus to the larger, more familiar themes of social history, this study has adopted a somewhat unconventional approach. I have organized the chapters around the "social lives" of four commodities,[32] the production and circulation of which were central to the livelihoods of Jabal Nablus's inhabitants: textiles, cotton, olive oil, and soap.[33]

The phrase "social life" and the word "story" are used strictly for heuristic purposes. By the former I mean the social relations embedded in the production, exchange, and consumption of commodities. Specifically, I am referring to the linkages among economic, political, and cultural factors that determined both the meaning(s) of a particular commodity to different social groups and its trajectory through space and time. The word "story" is used in two ways: first, to emphasize that this study seeks to interpret social relations, not to expose so-called facts; and second, as an heuristic tool to express the attempt I have made in the narrative to combine cultural analysis with the language of political economy. Thus the story of the social life of each commodity becomes a vehicle for raising a number of central themes with a greater degree of complexity and, I hope, nuance than could usually done through the language of a single discipline.

These stories, I must quickly add, do not cover identical temporal spans: different commodities had different career patterns and turning points. The defining moments in the story of cotton, for example, took place during the eighteenth and early nineteenth centuries, whereas that of soap unfolded between 1820 and the early twentieth century. That is why this book covers two entire centuries. Using such an approach is bound to create a significant degree of overlap, especially for the 1760–1860 period, which is subjected to the greatest degree of scrutiny. Each story, therefore, is not covered from all possible angles. Rather, it is used to open a window on a discrete set of relations and dynamics that complements those of other stories. The chapters are arranged the way transparencies might be overlaid to progressively add detail, color, and depth to the final image.

The story of textiles (Chapter 2) is mostly about the relationships between culture and trade and between the city and its hinterland. Textiles were the backbone of merchant communities in much of Asia as well as key markers of social status and self-identification. The majority of Nabulsi merchants dealt in this commodity, and their trading activities occupied the central physical, social, and cultural spaces of Nablus. The social life of textiles sheds light on how merchants constructed and reproduced regional and local trade networks in the context of a decentralized political structure and on how they used them to knit the rural and urban populations into one social formation. In order to elucidate the transformation of these networks over time, the bulk of this chapter is devoted to a case study of the Arafat family (no relation to Yasir Arafat), which produced nearly a dozen generations of successful textile merchants.

The story of cotton (Chapter 3) explores the connections between politics and trade, especially the points of tension between Nabulsi merchants and their regional and international competitors, in the context of the changing political landscape during the *Tanzimat* era. The commercial production of cotton for export has long been a feature of Palestine's economic history, and during the eighteenth century the trade in cotton undergirded Palestine's integration into the European-dominated world capitalist economy. Hitherto, the role of Jabal Nablus in cotton production and trade has not been detailed, even though it was the largest producer of cotton in the Fertile Crescent by the early nineteenth century. Because cotton lived on as textiles, this chapter also examines the impact of European competition on the textile industry in Nablus.

Olive oil was the most important product of the hinterland of Nablus, and soap made from olive oil was the most important manufactured commodity of the city. The social lives of olive oil and soap, therefore, can tell us a great deal about the changing political economy of Jabal Nablus, especially during the nineteenth century. It was during this period that the olive-based villages in the core hill areas of Jabal Nablus were fully integrated into the networks of urban merchants and that the soap industry underwent a remarkable expansion.

The large number of issues raised by the careers of these two commodities can be grouped under four discrete but related questions. First, how and under what conditions was olive oil transferred from the hands of peasants to those of merchants? Put differently, what were the mechanisms through which merchants appropriated the olive-oil surplus? In this regard, private family papers provide a fascinating look at how the *salam* (advance purchase) moneylending system was used in order to secure agricultural commodities for the purposes of manufacturing and investment. Chapter 4 also contains a discussion of the impact of moneylending on the commoditization of land, the urbanization of the rural sphere, and the rise of a middle peasantry.

Second, how was this system of surplus appropriation enforced? In the last section of Chapter 4, peasant petitions and the responses to them by both the central government and the local leaders are used to shed light on how an alliance between merchants and ruling families had taken shape by the mid-nineteenth century, especially when it came to dealing with peasant resistance to the established order. These petitions also detail peasant notions of identity, state justice, and sources of political authority and reveal the role they played in dragging the central government into the affairs of Jabal Nablus over the heads of their local leaders.

Third, how was the transformation of olive oil into soap organized economically and politically? Chapter 5 focuses on partnerships between factory owners and oil merchants who pooled their resources in order to finance this capital-intensive industry. A case study of the Yusufiyya soap factory and the estates of soap merchants from the Bishtawi family traces the reasons behind the expansion of this industry and the ways in which it was reorganized. Fourth, what was the social basis of soap production? In addressing this question in Chapter 5, special attention is given to the changing social composition of soap-factory owners. The detailed correspondence between the Nablus Advisory Council members (all of whom were involved in soap production and trade) and the central government concerning taxes on soap and the disposal of olive oil collected as taxes-in-kind allows for an in-depth look at how Ottoman reforms were perceived and molded from below.

Taken together, the stories of the social lives of these commodities shed light on the long and convoluted journey of Jabal Nablus from a semiautonomous existence under the umbrella of Ottoman rule to a more integrated and centralized one on four spatial levels. Locally, the city integrated its hinterlands into its legal, political, economic, and cultural spheres of influence to a far greater degree than ever before. Regionally, new networks of trade emanating from Beirut, Damascus, and Jaffa reoriented Jabal Nablus's economic relations with the outside world. On the level of the empire as a whole, a centralizing Ottoman state slowly but steadily consolidated its grip on Jabal Nablus. Finally, on the international level, all of Palestine, including Jabal Nablus, was incorporated into the capitalist world economy dominated by Europe, as well as subjected to an onslaught of political and cultural incursions by foreign merchants, missionaries, settlers, and government officials.

Before tracing this journey, we need to set the stage by investigating the meanings of autonomy as experienced by the people of Jabal Nablus during the eighteenth and nineteenth centuries. We also need to explore the political history of Jabal Nablus and the tensions arising from the differences between the central government's bureaucratic construction of this region as an administrative unit and its actual political and economic boundaries as a discrete social space.

1 The Meanings of Autonomy

The inhabitants of Nablus are governed by their own chiefs. . . .
They are a restless people, continually in dispute with each other,
and frequently in insurrection against the Pasha [governor of
Damascus]. Djezzar never succeeded in completely subduing them,
and Junot, with a corps of fifteen hundred French soldiers, was
defeated by them.

> John Lewis Burckhardt, *Travels in Syria and the Holy Land*, 1822

Nablus, being the center of a rich district, and, as of old, the
gateway of the trade between the northern and southern parts of the
country, as also between Jaffa and Beirut on the one hand, and the
trans-Jordanic districts on the other, becomes, of necessity, the mart
of an active traffic. The consequence is that the inhabitants enjoy a
greater amount of the comforts of life than those of any other town
in Palestine.

> Reverend John Mills, *Three Months' Residence at Nablus
> and an Account of the Modern Samaritans*, 1864

Napoleon's brief military adventure in Palestine in 1799 ended in failure
and did not carry in its wake any significant repercussions. But the military and cultural mobilization that took place in response reveals the
meanings of the autonomy in Palestine within the context of Ottoman
rule. That year Shaykh Yusuf Jarrar, the *mutasallim* of Jenin District
(*sanjaq*),[1] wrote a poem in which he exhorted his fellow leaders in Jabal
Nablus to unite under one banner against the French forces, which were
then laying siege to Acre.

Shaykh Yusuf's poem unwittingly exposes the two major sets of tensions that informed the political life of Jabal Nablus at the turn of the
nineteenth century. The first was the bureaucratic construction of Jabal
Nablus from above by the central Ottoman government in Istanbul versus
the dynamics of self-rule developed from below. The second was the cohesiveness of this region's social formation and the shared sense of identity
among its inhabitants versus the factionalism of multiple territorially
based centers of power.

Shaykh Yusuf began his poem by expressing how the letters he re-

16

ceived bearing the news of the invasion have brought fire to his heart and tears to his eyes. "The infidel *millet* [non-Muslim religious community]," he exclaimed, "are storming our way, intending to obliterate the mosques." He then located the ruling urban households and rural clans of Jabal Nablus at that time by praising the courage and military prowess of the Tuqan, Nimr, Rayyan, Qasim, Jayyusi, At'ut, Hajj Muhammad, Ghazi, Jaradat, and Abd al-Hadi families (in that order), beginning:

> House of Tuqan, draw your swords
>> and mount your precious saddles.
> House of Nimr, you mighty tigers,
>> straighten your courageous lines.
> Muhammad Uthman, mobilize your men,
>> mobilize the heroes from all directions.
> Ahmad al-Qasim, you bold lion,
>> prow of the advancing lines.[2]

The most striking aspect of this poem is what it does not say. Not once in its twenty-one verses does it mention Ottoman rule, much less the need to protect the empire or the glory and honor of serving the sultan. Rather, Shaykh Yusuf casts the impending danger entirely in terms of the threat to Islam and to women, and his appeal stresses local identification above all else ("Oh! you Nabulsis . . . advance together on Acre"). Even though all the leaders of Jabal Nablus, including Shaykh Yusuf, were inundated with *firmans* from Istanbul announcing the invasion and calling for soldiers and money,[3] the poem leaves the origin of the letters intentionally vague, saying only that they came "from afar."

"From afar" aptly describes the relationship between Palestine and the central government, which, except for token garrisons in Jerusalem and some of the coastal towns such as Jaffa, did not maintain a permanent military presence in this area.[4] It is not difficult to understand why. Although Palestine constituted a natural land bridge connecting Asia and Africa—and hence had strategic value, as clearly demonstrated by the 1799 invasion—it was of no exceptional material importance. Palestine did not contain any large cities that were entrepôts for international trade, such as Cairo, Damascus, or Aleppo, and its size, population, and productive capacity were all relatively small. True, Palestine, especially Jerusalem, was of special religious and symbolic significance; but Palestine was also a "frontier" region difficult to control because of its terrain and its location; it served as a buffer zone against bedouin migration from the deserts in the east. Indeed, the Ottoman authorities had such a troublesome time collecting taxes in this area that a tax-collection practice (somewhat similar to ones in North Africa) came into existence: the tour (*da-wra*).[5] Every year starting in the early eighteenth century, the governor of Damascus Province or his deputy would, a few weeks before the holy month of Ramadan, personally lead a contingent of troops into a number of predetermined points as an aggressive physical reminder of the inhabitants' annual fiscal obligations to the Ottoman state. Even then, taxes were rarely paid fully or on time.

Within Palestine the extent of autonomy differed from one region to another. Soon after the onset of Ottoman rule, Jabal Nablus developed a reputation for being the most difficult region to control.[6] One need only compare the divergent responses to the sultan's *firmans* requesting assistance. Heeding the call for soldiers (the first *firman*, dated December 21, 1798, claimed that "the number of men and heroes in the mountains of Nablus and Jerusalem and their outlying parts is estimated to be 100,000 fighters"[7]), the leaders of Jabal al-Quds and Jabal al-Khalil trekked to the premises of the Islamic Court in Jerusalem. Facing the judge, each leader personally pledged a certain number of fighters, under pain of paying a large fine if he failed to deliver.[8]

In contrast, the leaders of Jabal Nablus treated the *firmans* as opening bids in a lengthy negotiation. Instead of dispatching fighters, they sent consecutive petitions requesting that Jabal Nablus's share, including that of Jenin District, be reduced: first to 4,000, then 3,000, then 2,000, and finally 1,000.[9] Almost two years later the matter had still not been settled. In mid-November 1800, a *firman* was sent to the leaders of Jabal Nablus reminding them of the "atrocities" of the "infidel" French and, more to the point, setting a clear deadline for their contribution:

> Previously we sent a . . . *firman* . . . asking for 2,000 men from the districts of Nablus and Jenin to join our victorious soldiers . . . in a Holy War. Then you signed a petition excusing yourselves, saying that it was impossible to send 2,000 men due to [the need for] planting and plowing. You begged that we forgive you 1,000 men . . . and in our mercy we forgave you 1,000 men. But until now, not one of the remaining 1,000 has come forward . . . and since the armies had to depart quickly [to Egypt] . . . we will accept instead the sum of 110,000 piasters. . . . As soon as this order is received, you have until Shawwal 8 [February 22, 1801] to deliver the sum of 40,000 piasters . . . and to mid-Shawwal for paying the rest. . . . If you show any hesitation . . . you will be severely punished.[10]

Despite repeated threats that the Ottoman armies upon their return from Egypt would punish them for their "insubordination," "corruption," and "stupidity," as another angry missive from Istanbul put it, the leaders of Jabal Nablus never sent the money, at least not in full.[11] Quite the contrary, some of them looted and burned three caravansaries along the Damascus–Cairo highway—Khan Jaljulya, Qalanswa, and Ayn al-Asawir—in which supplies were stored by the *mutasallim* of Nablus by the orders of the central authorities, in anticipation of the Ottoman armies' march back from Egypt.[12]

These actions, about which more will be said below, were not meant as a challenge to Ottoman rule: all of the leaders operated willingly within the framework of the Ottoman political system. An important element of their power was the legitimacy conferred on them by the central government, which annually renewed their appointments as subdistrict chiefs and district governors. Nor did they welcome the French invasion or fail to take it seriously: Nabulsi fighters handed French troops their first defeat in Palestine during one of several skirmishes. According to Nimr, they also sneaked through the enemy lines surrounding Acre and entered the besieged city, to the loud cheers of the local population and Ahmad Pasha al-Jazzar's soldiers.[13] Rather, they interpreted the invasion and the Ottoman response in terms of their own local dynamics and behaved within the boundaries of the wide autonomy they had enjoyed for generations. The Nabulsi leaders had no intention of handing their fighters over to Ottoman military commanders or of joining the expedition to Egypt: their primary concern was to protect Jabal Nablus. As Shaykh Yusuf's poem indicates, Jabal Nablus had a cohesive economic, social, and cultural identity which claimed the loyalties of its inhabitants in the face of external threats.

At the same time, however, there were political divisions and rivalries within Jabal Nablus. Power was shared by a number of territorially based rural and urban families, each of which controlled a section of the hinterland and was capable of mobilizing a peasant militia. In 1799 Jabal Nablus was also embroiled in an escalating internal power struggle between two well-defined camps, one led by the urban Tuqan household and the other by the rural Jarrar clan. The burning and looting of supplies was not a protest against Ottoman rule but a calculated act designed to embarrass and undermine the power of the current Nablus *mutasallim*, Khalil *Beik* Tuqan.[14]

It was within this local context that Shaykh Yusuf Jarrar wrote his poem. In it, he presented a constructed version of reality that best fit his purposes. By initiating the call to action, Shaykh Yusuf projected himself as first among equals and claimed local leadership in the fight against external forces that threatened Jabal Nablus and its way of life. As the leader of the faction that violently opposed the Tuqan's drive for centralization of political power in Jabal Nablus, his poem pointedly celebrated political decentralization by giving equal praise (though in ranked order) to a large number of factions, even though some of them had little actual power. His poem also advanced an alternative framework to centralization: unity through cultural solidarity and local identification, not through political hegemony—especially not that of an urban family.

The Jarrars' concerns were not unfounded. Since the second half of the seventeenth century, Jabal Nablus had been undergoing internal integration characterized by the city's creeping domination over its hinterland economically, culturally, and politically. This process was driven largely by the increased importance of commercial agriculture as the primary source of wealth and upward mobility in Jabal Nablus. Accompanying changes, such as the proliferation of a money economy and credit relations, as well as commoditization of land in the countryside were, in turn, outcomes of two larger economic dynamics. The first was the flourishing of local, intraregional, and interregional trade networks emanating from Nablus under the umbrella of Ottoman rule. The second dynamic, which began during the eighteenth century, was the incremental incorporation of Palestine, including Jabal Nablus, into the European economic orbit as expressed in the commercial production of cotton for export to France.

By the time Napoleon set foot in Palestine, therefore, Jabal Nablus was already in the midst of slow and uneven transformation from a politically fragmented and economically segmented cultural unit into an increasingly integrated one internally, regionally, and internationally. The timing, causes, and inner workings of this transformation are detailed in the following chapters. But at this point, it is necessary to set the stage by exploring the structural and political contexts that defined the meanings of autonomy under Ottoman rule. The first section of this chapter sketches the basic topographical, demographic, and economic features that imparted to Jabal Nablus its autonomy and distinctiveness as a discrete social space. The second section analyzes the watershed events in the political development of Jabal Nablus from the sixteenth to the late nineteenth century; that is, the critical junctures that helped shape this region's internal political configuration and its relationship to regional powers and the central Ottoman government. This section also contrasts the official administrative boundaries and status of Jabal Nablus with its actual development as a social space.

JABAL NABLUS AS A SOCIAL SPACE

Ever since its origins as a Canaanite settlement, the city of Nablus has been locked into a permanent embrace with its hinterland. Over the centuries the multilayered and complex interactions between these two organically linked but distinct parts generated a cohesive and dynamic social space: Jabal Nablus. The material foundations of the autonomy of Jabal Nablus were the deeply rooted economic networks between the city and its surrounding villages; and the cultural fountains of its identity were the social and political dynamics of urban-rural relations, especially between merchants and peasants. It was this combination of material and cultural transactions that made Jabal Nablus recognizable to outsiders as a discrete entity and, more important, made it feel like home to its residents by inculcating in them a sense of regional loyalty. In the words of Reverend John Mills, "The inhabitants [of Nablus] are most proud of it, and think there is no place in the world equal to it."[15]

In this general sense, Jabal Nablus was similar to many others that existed under the umbrella of Ottoman rule, and the centuries-long existence of these social spaces explains the strong regional identifications that are still an important part of popular culture in Greater Syria.[16] For example, one can talk about Jabal Lubnan (Mount Lebanon), Jabal Amil (also known as Bilad Bishara), in what is today southern Lebanon; Jabal al-Druze (Hauran), in today's Syria; and Jabal al-Khalil and Jabal al-Quds, whose urban centers were Hebron and Jerusalem, respectively.

This is not to say that these social spaces had clear and unchanging borders, nor that the nature of interaction between city and hinterland was everywhere the same. For instance, the urban centers of Jabal Nablus, Jabal al-Quds, and Jabal al-Khalil occupied different points along the spectrum of possibilities during the Ottoman period. Hebron was largely an extension of its hinterland, its economic life for the most part focused on agricultural pursuits and on providing essential services to the surrounding villages. Jerusalem, in contrast, stood somewhat aloof from its hinterland primarily because of the external infusions of economic and political capital that its religious, symbolic, and administrative significance attracted. Nablus lay somewhere between the two: its connections to the hinterland were absolutely vital, but it also contained a large manufacturing base and was a nexus for substantial networks of regional trade. Its hinterland, moreover, contained some of the richest agricultural lands in Palestine, as well as the largest and most stable concentration of villages and people. The city of Nablus did not possess the glamour or drama of

Jerusalem; nor did it suffer from the relative sleepiness and obscurity of Hebron. Rather, it served, at least during much of the eighteenth and the first half of the nineteenth century, as the economic and, occasionally, political center of Palestine. Not surprisingly, Jabal Nablus—often referred to as *jabal al-nar* (mountain of fire)—played a leading role in the 1834 revolt against the Egyptian forces, in the 1936–1939 rebellion against British rule, and in the Palestinian uprising (*intifada*) against Israeli occupation that exploded in 1987.

The City of Nablus

"The immediate vicinity of Nabloos is remarkable for the number of its trees, and its luxuriant vegetation; it is, indeed, one of the most beautiful and fertile spots in all Palestine."[17] Practically every visitor to Nablus— from Muslim travelers in the Middle Ages to young Englishmen in search of adventure in the nineteenth century—described the appearance of the city in similarly flattering terms.[18] Embedded between two steep mountains in a narrow but lush valley and surrounded by a wide belt of olive groves, vineyards, fruit orchards, and a sprinkle of palm trees, the ancient city of Nablus has long been described as resembling, in the words of Shams al-Din al-Ansari (d. A.H. 727, A.D. 1326–1327), a "palace in a garden" (see Plates 1–3).[19]

The secret was water—the primary reason why Nablus was able to support a large population and a wide range of manufacturing establishments. Its twenty-two gushing springs were channeled into the city's public fountains, mosque courtyards, gardens, tanneries, and dye and pottery establishments, as well as the private homes of the rich.[20] Water was also carried down into the 1,220-meter-long valley that widened westward via aqueducts that fed irrigation canals and powered the large, round stones of grain mills. In the summer heat, evaporated water formed a thin blue mist that enveloped the city and accentuated its charms: "Its beauty can hardly be exaggerated. . . . Clusters of white-roofed houses nestling in the bosom of a mass of trees, olive, palm, orange, apricot, and many another varying the carpet with every shade of green. . . . Everything fresh, green, soft, and picturesque, with verdure, shade, and water everywhere. There is a softness in the colouring, a rich blue haze from the many springs and streamlets, which mellows every hard outline."[21]

The phrase "Little Damascus," which its inhabitants commonly use to describe Nablus, sums up the look, feel, and essence of the city. The similarities between the two were, in fact, striking. Both were blessed with water and surrounded by greenery, both were "dry ports" located in the interior of Greater Syria, both had strong manufacturing sectors, and both functioned as the commercial hubs for numerous surrounding villages. Finally, in both cities cultural life was dominated by conservative and entrenched merchant communities and characterized by the persistence of family politics.

Of course, Nablus differed from Damascus in some important respects. In contrast to the religious and ethnic diversity of the latter's population, that of Nablus, like that of Hebron, was homogeneous. Except for the small Christian and Samaritan communities, which together numbered no more than a few hundred, virtually all the inhabitants were Sunni Muslims.[22] The largest minority were Christians; most worked as artisans and merchants.[23] Most of the Christians were Greek Orthodox. The rest became Protestants around the mid-nineteenth century in response to the evangelical activities of Reverend Bowen from the Church Missionary Society, who, over a twelve-month period, opened a day school and initiated a number of other projects, such as the purchase of a modern loom and an iron oil press.[24]

The Samaritans numbered 150 to 200 throughout the nineteenth century. Unlike the Christians, they were a tightly knit community living in their own neighborhood in the Yasmina quarter. A few worked as scribes and accountants to the governors of Nablus and some of its rich merchants, but most were relatively poor retailers or artisans.[25] Because the Samaritan community was virtually nonexistent outside Nablus, it became an object of great curiosity for European visitors and scholars, especially during the nineteenth century.

Also unlike Damascus, Nablus was neither a large metropole nor the administrative capital of a province. The difficult, hilly terrain and its geographical location helped preserve its autonomy and protect it from imperial armies, but at the expense of making it unsuitable for international trade.[26] Historically, however, intraregional and interregional trade were far more important to the economy of Palestine, and Nablus was ideally situated for both. The narrow valley which bisects the central highlands and connects the desert with the fertile western plains was a natural corridor for goods heading in all four directions. Droves of Nabulsi merchants regularly traveled to nearby localities such as Jaffa, Haifa, Acre, and Gaza along the coast; to southern Lebanon, Nazareth, Safad, Jerusalem, and Hebron in the hill areas; and to Salt, Jabal Ajlun, and Hauran to the east and northeast.[27]

As for interregional trade, Cairo and Damascus were by far the most important destinations for Nabulsi merchants. This trade involved mostly bulk goods, not luxury items. During the Ottoman period, roughly three-quarters of Nablus's soap was shipped to Cairo overland through Gaza and the Sinai Desert and by sea through the ports of Jaffa and Gaza (see Chapter 5). From Egypt, especially Cairo and Damietta (Dimyat), Nabulsi merchants imported, among other things, rice, sugar, and spices, as well as linen, cotton, and woolen textiles.[28] To Damascus they exported a large variety of products, the most important of which were cotton, soap, olive oil, and medium-grade textiles. From Damascus, they mostly imported silks, textiles of all kinds, copper, and some luxury items (see Chapter 2).

The longevity and relative stability of Ottoman rule, as well as the large political space it created, enhanced the advantages of Nablus's fortuitous geographical location. Beginning in the early sixteenth century, the networks connecting Nablus to Damascus and Cairo were supplemented by the establishment of secure trading posts in the Hijaz and Gulf regions to the south and east, as well as in the Anatolian Peninsula and the Mediterranean islands to the north and west. Nablus also developed steady trade relations with Aleppo, Mosul, and Baghdad (see Chapter 3).

Closer to home, the constant and vigorous efforts by the Ottoman government to ensure adequate safety and funding for the annual pilgrimage caravan (*qafilat al-hajj*) from Damascus to the Holy Cities of Mecca and Medina also benefited Nablus politically and economically.[29] Almost from the very beginning of Ottoman rule, pilgrimage caravans became the key variable in the fiscal and political relationship between Jabal Nablus and the central government. Indeed, for a brief period in the early seventeenth century, the governor of Nablus, Farrukh Pasha Ibn Abdullah, was appointed leader of the pilgrimage caravan (*amir al-hajj*).[30] He built an impressive commercial compound in Nablus for that purpose. The Wikala al-Farrukhiyya, as it was still called in the mid-nineteenth century, became one of the city's prime commercial properties (see Map 1).[31]

More important, the taxes levied on Jabal Nablus and on most of Palestine were specifically earmarked for meeting the costs of the caravans.[32] Jabal Nablus, for example, contributed more than did any other Palestinian region to the financing of pilgrimage caravans during the first half of the eighteenth century.[33] These moneys filtered back to the merchants and artisans of Nablus in the form of payments for locally produced provisions for the pilgrims, as well as for armed escorts and transport. Part of the taxes from the peasants of Jabal Nablus, therefore, never left the city's treasury. Instead, as receipts registered in the Islamic court show, these moneys were used to pay the leaders of the various artisan guilds who produced provisions on commission.[34] From this perspective, Nablus's relationship with pilgrimage caravans established a fairly routine transfer of rural surplus into the city's manufacturing, trade, and transportation sectors.

For example, the leather water-pouch makers (*qirabiyyin*) of Nablus and Hebron received commissions for thousands of leather pouches (*qirab*) annually from the water officer (*saqa bashi*) of the caravan.[35] These pouches, like the other types of supplies, were purchased, not collected as taxes-in-kind. That this business was fully subject to market forces is demonstrated by an exchange in 1853. At that time, the Nablus Advisory Council, in a letter to the governor of Jerusalem, noted that the *qirabiyyin* of Nablus were united in their demands that the price of each pouch be raised from 16 to 21 piasters. The reason, they continued, was that "there was heavy demand from Egypt for leather pouches, causing a healthy rise in the price of leather in these territories."[36]

The advantages of Ottoman rule—an enlarged regional trading area and consistent attention to the pilgrimage caravan—were never wholly contingent on the strength of the central Ottoman government. Nablus was ruled by a relatively stable group of leading families from the late seventeenth century to the late nineteenth century, and it was home to an entrenched and influential merchant community that was reinforced by a strong socioreligious leadership. All were native sons.[37] This autonomy, when combined with the weakness of the central government (especially during the eighteenth century), probably encouraged rather than hindered economic growth because much of the surplus was reinvested into the local economy. In fact, it was precisely during the period of so-called Ottoman decline—that is, from the late sixteenth century to the early nineteenth century—that Nablus emerged as Palestine's key center for regional trade, manufacturing, and the local organization of commercial agriculture. It also played a leading role in the growing trade with Europe, especially the export of cotton.

The city's economic growth was most evident in the impressive increase of its population. According to Ottoman population counts (which constitute the best evidence available), the inhabitants of this ancient city multiplied from approximately 5,000–7,000 people in the mid-sixteenth century to more than 20,000 in 1850, making it the possibly the largest city in Palestine at the time.[38] The size of the city's population during the seventeenth and eighteenth centuries is not known, but it is almost certain that growth took place steadily rather than in dramatic waves. This is because the demographic pattern of the hill regions, especially Jabal

Nablus, was one of stability and of only incremental and sluggish response to the more volatile regional trends.[39]

Even more important than intraregional and interregional trade for the prosperity of Nablus was the core area of local trade and manufacturing. The essential character of Nablus remains defined by its role as the commercial, manufacturing, administrative, and cultural capital of the surrounding villages, and its economic health depended largely on its access to the rural surplus. Nablus's dependence on its hinterland for most of its needs was most eloquently symbolized by the city's vulnerable physical position. It lay at the mercy of two imposing mountains that pressed on either side, and it had no natural defenses to speak of. Its simple wall provided less protection than did the compact buildings and the large compounds of the leading families. Most often, it was the armed peasants and the fortified villages of powerful rural clans that bore the brunt of the fighting whenever the Nablus region was invaded by an external force or became mired in internal conflict.

The rhythms of urban life reflected the agricultural calendar of the peasant community. The hustle and bustle of tons of oil being deposited in the underground wells of huge soap-factory buildings after the olive harvest in the fall, for instance, were perhaps only surpassed by the commotion of raw cotton arriving in the city to be ginned and spun in the summer. Thus there were no sharp dividing lines between city and country. Indeed, Nablus was, in some ways, akin to a very large village: at sunrise many Nabulsis exited the city gates to work on the extensive olive groves, vineyards, and orchards that covered the terraced slopes, as well as in the fields, vegetable gardens, and grain mills that were scattered across the valley.

In a reverse flow, peasants poured into the city to sell their goods and to search for wedding clothes, work tools, cooking utensils, rice, coffee, and a host of other items.[40] For them, as for their urban counterparts, Nablus was (to use a common metaphor) the beating heart of the surrounding hinterland. Monitored by customs officials during the day and closed at night, the two largest "valves" were the eastern and western gates, through which long lines of peasants and traveling merchants entered, along with their pack animals. Many remained in the city for a few days and used the extra time to become further acquainted with the city. Most likely, visitors first walked along one of the two roughly parallel thoroughfares that stretched east–west (see Map 1). Hundreds of shops lined each artery and spilled over into smaller streets and alleys, which connected them with each other and with the six major quarters of the city: Yasmina, Gharb, Qaryun, Aqaba, Qaysariyya and Habala.[41] In the southern thoroughfare were the covered market of textile merchants (Khan al-Tujjar) and the Wikala al-Farrukhiyya, which constituted the key commercial spaces of the city. Interspersed throughout were the five central mosques; the large, fortresslike compounds of the ruling urban households, such as those of the Nimrs, Tuqans, and Abd al-Hadis; as well as the numerous soap factories, baths, leather tanneries, and pottery and textile workshops.

Most peasants must have also been impressed by the tall three- and four-storied residential buildings, if only because they reminded them of the grand compounds of their subdistrict chiefs. As Suad Amiry has shown, the dwellings of subdistrict chiefs—usually built in the seat (*kursi*) village of each subdistrict—were arranged in such a way that they created distance from the normal peasant quarters in the rest of the village, both spatially and aesthetically.[42] These dwellings, constructed by master-builders from Nablus, consciously imitated urban architectural forms in order to project the status and power of these chiefs, to allow them to lead an urban lifestyle even in the village, and to reinforce their image as the natural bridge for urban-rural interaction. The difference, of course, was that of scale: Nablus's massive stone buildings—tightly packed and looming large above the heads of pedestrians—were the norm, not the exception, hence adding immensely to the city's authority and grandeur.

The Hinterland of Nablus

Palestine's small size, remarkably diverse geographical terrain, and dependence on rain-fed agriculture precluded large-scale farming and the development of a monocrop economy. Peasants, approximately 80 percent of the total population, developed varied sources of income by learning how to utilize every topographical feature. Fields were sown with grains, legumes, and vegetables; hills were terraced and planted with trees; and higher-up stony lands were used for grazing. Until the last decades of Ottoman rule, most peasants were small landholders concentrated in the interior hill regions where horticulture, especially the tending of olive groves, was a way of life.

The peasants of the hill regions lived in close-knit village communities that varied in size from a few dozen to a few hundred inhabitants. Most had an average of two to four constituent clans and some large extended families. The basis of collective solidarity was the organization of peasant society into clans (*hamulas*): patrilineal descent groups related by the fifth degree from a common ancestor. The clan system provided a safety net which supported individual families at times of difficulty, and it was well suited to the vagaries of rain-fed agriculture and the poor soil of hill regions. Clans were also responsible for defending their members in times of trouble, negotiating settlements or taking revenge for bodily harm. These duties were organized and directed mostly by the clan elders. They settled internal disputes according to commonly accepted legal and cultural norms embodied in a deeply rooted system of unwritten customary practices, known as *urf*, which spelled out rights and responsibilities and elucidated the mechanisms for conflict resolution, compensation, and punishment.[43]

This set of norms differed significantly from the application of Islamic law (*shari'a*) that was prevalent in the urban centers and reflected the "tribalization" of peasant society, in that *urf* drew a great deal on concepts originally articulated in bedouin communities. In this respect, therefore, peasant society had its own internal cultural and legal autonomy. Consequently, and as detailed in Chapter 5, before the mid-nineteenth century peasants rarely went to the urban-based Islamic court to settle disputes, form partnerships, buy property, contract loans, or conduct a host of matters relating to personal status, such as marriage, divorce, or inheritance.[44]

This relative autonomy even extended to criminal matters as late as the mid-nineteenth century. In a revealing letter to the governor of Sidon province dated February 18, 1853, the Nablus council members cited peasant *urf* traditions and what they called "stupid customs" to explain why some suspects from Jamma'in village could not be released from prison despite a lack of proof of their guilt. Briefly, the council members emphasized that the obstacle to the extension of the state's legal codes to individual peasants was that they were not simply individuals but members of clans that insisted on overall collective rights. Until the real culprits could be identified, they argued, the release of the suspects would only inflame the situation and cause problems on an even wider scale.[45]

Clans varied in size and power. The number of adult males in each clan, the internal cohesion in their ranks, the size of the lands they controlled, and the efficacy of their political alliances determined their overall power and prestige. Because each village was usually home for the same clans for generations, Palestinian peasants—like their counterparts in Syria, Lebanon, and communities all over the rim of the Mediterranean Basin— developed a strong sense of local identification, which still survives.[46] Communal belonging and solidarity were expressed in a variety of cultural, social, and economic ways. For example, the peasants of each village usually paid their taxes and even contracted their loans on a collective basis (see Chapter 4). It was also common practice to build new homes collectively and to render mutual assistance during the harvest season.

Wedding rituals included all of these elements of village solidarity. It was not unusual for the elders of a village's various clans to be consulted prior to a village member's marriage to an outsider (meaning someone from another village). Once their blessing was obtained, the village elders could receive gifts, and they, in turn, were expected to mobilize their constituents to participate fully in the preparations. Some wedding practices combined local identification with the patriarchal character of clan organization in strikingly revealing ways. Certain villages in the Galilee, for example, had a heavy rock which was set aside for the purpose of competition prior to marriage ceremonies. For an outsider to be allowed to marry one of the village women, the strongest man in the groom-to-be's village had to be able to lift the host village's "marriage rock"—assuming that the host village had someone who could lift this rock also.[47] This ritual carried within it a gendered symbolism of power relations between villages and clans: the bride's village agreed to submit—or, more accurately, to lose one of its women because the wife relocated to the husband's home—on the condition that the groom's village passed a test of virility (physical strength).

This is not to say that each village constituted an autonomous and self-sufficient community. Villages were knit together into a variety of economic, political, social, and cultural networks (see Chapter 2).[48] The larger and more powerful clans, for example, had branches in a number of villages, and many clans were connected to each other through marriage, political alliance, and patronage networks. Many villages specialized in particular varieties of sought-after crops and artisanal products, such as watermelon, pottery, or baskets. Urban merchants, meanwhile, carved geographical spheres of influence in the hinterland through social connections that were passed from father to son. Religious Sufi orders, such as the Qadriyya order, also had branches in some of the larger villages. Furthermore, each village was part of a larger cluster of neighboring villages, and several of these constituted a subdistrict (*nahiya*). Each subdistrict had one or more central villages, larger in population size as well as landholdings—which functioned as political, economic, and social hubs of smaller villages. These central villages were often the administrative headquarters (seat or *kursi*) for the dominant clan of each subdistrict.

In the mid-nineteenth century, the social space of Jabal Nablus encompassed close to 300 villages, whose economic, social and, to a lesser extent, political life was more closely tied to the city of Nablus than to other urban centers. These villages filled a space stretching along the coastal plains from Haifa and Jaffa in the west to the Ajlun and Balqa regions beyond the River Jordan in the east and from the Galilee in the north to the hills of Ramallah and al-Bireh in the south (see Map 2).[49] The peasants of these villages farmed some of the richest agricultural lands in Palestine.

Not all of Jabal Nablus is equally well endowed, however. Rather, one can speak of three discrete zones: the western slopes, the central highlands, and the eastern slopes. The eastern slopes descend rapidly to below sea level, have precipitous crags, very narrow valleys, and little topsoil, and catch less of the rain that blows in from the Mediterranean Sea. Still, this zone receives adequate rain for the cultivation of wheat and barley, and it enjoys the advantage of a hotter climate and lower altitude, which allow agricultural crops to mature approximately a month earlier than they do in the rest of the region. In addition, Palestinian peasants and urban entrepreneurs have taken advantage of the steeply sloped eastern hills by channeling the rushing streams to power grain mills and to irrigate large parcels of land in valleys of Wadi al-Badhan and Wadi al-Far'a.[50] Beginning in the 1820s, this region witnessed large investments by merchants and leading families who were eager to acquire mills and lands in order to meet the increased demand for grain.[51]

The eastern slopes contained the smallest number of villages because the terrain, on the whole, lent itself more to the raising of livestock than to cultivation. As a transitional zone between nomadic and settled life, its inhabitants, both villagers and bedouins, led a hybrid existence: many bedouins engaged in seasonal agriculture, and many peasants left their homes for long periods of time as they led their livestock through the surrounding grazing lands. For example, most of the men in the northeastern village of Tammun, one of the largest villages in the subdistrict of Mashariq al-Jarrar, moved around the grazing lands in the Ghur (Jordan Valley), while the women made cheese, clarified butter, woolen rugs, tents, ropes, and cloth bags.[52] That their primary source of income was livestock, not agriculture, was indicated in a petition addressed to the Nablus Advisory Council, in which they asked for relief from the collection of clarified butter (*samn*) as taxes-in-kind.[53]

The most fertile lands in Jabal Nablus tend to be concentrated in the western slopes. This zone receives much of the rainfall coming in from the Mediterranean because the clouds are trapped by the hills that divide the coast from the desert. The low angle of gradations makes for a thicker and less stony topsoil, especially where the hills give way to large fertile plains. Well suited for the planting of grain, legumes, cotton, fruits and vegetables—the best of these plains are concentrated in what is known today as the Jenin–Tulkarem–Qalqilya triangle. Consequently, this zone contained some of the largest villages in Jabal Nablus.

The best lands in this triangle are the hinterland of the town of Jenin (including the Marj Ibn Amir plain); the plain of Arraba; and the area southwest of the latter where the villages of Dayr al-Ghusun, Attil, Quffin, Shwayka, Bal'a, and Anabta are located. Marj Ibn Amir, the most fertile plain in all of Palestine, was famous for its plentiful grain harvests as well as for the quality of its tobacco, watermelons, and cotton. This wide plain also had a strategic importance: it constituted the broadest expanse connecting the coast with the interior, and astride it ran one of the main trade routes to Damascus. On its soil numerous famous battles were fought from the time of the pharaohs to World War I, including the battle of Hitten (1187), during which Salah al-Din dealt a decisive blow to the Crusader armies. In the eighteenth century this plain became a bone of contention between the rulers of Jabal Nablus and Zahir al-Umar, the strong man of the Galilee; and in the nineteenth century its wide stretches of land not only produced large amounts of grains for the world market but also became concentrated in the hands of a few large landowners.[54]

The market town of Jenin, which guards the entrance to this large plain, was and remains one whose economy is predominantly agricultural. The storehouses for taxes collected in kind, for example, were located both in Nablus and in Jenin.[55] It is no coincidence that the Jarrar clan, long the most powerful of the subdistrict chiefs, was based in this area. The smaller Arraba plain (11 kilometers long and 4 kilometers wide) contained some of the largest villages in Jabal Nablus, including Arraba, Qabatya, and Ya'bad. Parts of this area were forests, which were ideal for livestock and were an important source of charcoal. The most prized cheese in Jabal Nablus, for example, came from the village of Ya'bad. The village of Arraba, it is worth noting, was home to the most important leading family in Jabal Nablus to emerge during the nineteenth century: the Abd al-Hadis.

Closer to the coast, the seasonally alternating humid and hot weather allowed intensive cotton cultivation. The commercial production of this commodity helped pave the way for the eventual integration of Palestine into the capitalist world economy. Jabal Nablus played a leading role in this trade: its cotton was considered the best in Greater Syria, and it was this region's largest producer. The amount of production far exceeded local demand, and most of the cotton was exported to France, Egypt, or Damascus (see Chapter 3). Consequently, this zone was the first to experience the socioeconomic changes associated with the intensification of commercial agriculture: peasant differentiation, commoditization of land, and expansion of moneylending practices, among other things (see Chapter 4).

Even though the coastal plains had greater agricultural potential than did the hill areas, most peasants were partial to life in the highland villages. The coastal areas were more vulnerable to attack and within easy reach of the government tax collector. They were also exposed to malaria and other diseases: much of the water that streamed from the hills failed to reach the sea, forming swamps instead. The hill villages, in contrast, provided protection from both political and physical dangers: the mountain air was healthier, and the rugged hills formed a natural barrier because the complexity of the folds allowed easy escape from and attack on conventional military forces. This zone included the largest number of villages and exhibited the steadiest level of population density in Palestine over the centuries, and its rough terrain and entrenched peasantry made it the backbone of Nablus's autonomy.

The central zone was also home to the oldest continuously inhabited settlements. Due to population growth and increased pressure on the land, especially during the nineteenth century, it was quite common for "mother" villages in the hills to spawn "daughter" villages in the plains.[56] Peasants built temporary structures on the farthest lands under their control so that they would not have to travel back to the village during the harvest season. Called *khirba* (ruins), they were often mistaken by western travelers as remnants of once prosperous villages and cited as examples of agricultural decline in Palestine. In fact, the opposite was true, for many of these satellite settlements or offshoots became permanent villages in the nineteenth century.[57]

Interspersed among the hill villages were many small but fertile valleys, in which a variety of rain-fed crops, especially wheat, was grown.[58] Horticulture, however, was the most important agricultural pursuit in terms of time, effort, and income. The limited agricultural potential of the hill areas was conserved through the centuries by terracing, which protected the thin topsoil from erosion. Terracing is a strenuous, time-consuming task because the walls, made out of loosely stacked stones, have to be repaired annually after the winter rains. Even now the prosperity of a village is most easily judged by how well its terraces are maintained.

Most of the terraced hills were and still are covered with a variety of fruit-bearing trees and vines, mainly olives. Olive trees are especially well suited to the Mediterranean climate and, more important, to the high limestone base that is inhospitable to a wide variety of plant life. This is why olive trees and vines dominate the hill areas along most of the Mediterranean Basin from Spain, Italy, and Greece to the Syrian highlands and to parts of North Africa.[59] In the words of Fernand Braudel, "Everywhere [in the Mediterranean rim] can be found the same eternal trinity: wheat, olives, and vines, born of the climate and history; in other words an identical agricultural civilization, identical ways of dominating the environment" (see Plate 4).[60]

Nowhere in Palestine was the centrality of the olive tree more in evidence than in Jabal Nablus. Since ancient times this area has produced the largest olive-oil harvests in Palestine, a significant proportion of which, as in North Africa, was exported both regionally and internationally (see Chapter 4).[61] This tree's central importance was evident in the many ways it was used. Its wood became fuel and was carved into small implements and decorative items. Its fruit was cracked, pickled, and eaten or pressed for oil. The oil remains a staple item in Palestinian cuisine. Olive oil was also used to make soap at home and in large factories and as fuel for lamps. In addition, olive oil has a variety of special purposes such as medicinal ointments. The dried, crushed pits of pressed olives (*jift*), when burned, proved ideal as a long-lasting source of heat. Large amounts of *jift* were consumed every winter as fuel for braziers, and it was used throughout the year as fuel for cooking the large vats of soap in factories.

Olive oil was literally liquid capital, and it often served in lieu of money. Because it could easily be stored for at least one year, it was "deposited" in oil wells dug deep into the ground, both in the city and in many of the villages. Peasants, merchants, and others could then "draw" on these accounts or take money instead. Its status as a marker of wealth is the subtext of stories about how rich rural *shaykhs* supposedly used olive oil instead of water to mix the mortar which held together the stones of their fortresslike residential compounds.[62]

BOUNDARIES IN TIME AND SPACE

Compared to economic, social, and cultural processes which slowly undulate like hidden deep-sea currents, political developments move rapidly across the surface like weather fronts that have visible boundaries in time and space. Because political history is not the main concern of this book, it will be sufficient to briefly consider four turning points that introduced new political dynamics.[63] At the same time, we shall compare the Ottoman government's bureaucratic and somewhat static construction of Jabal Nablus's administrative boundaries with its actual and dynamic social space, especially as reflected in its relations with regional powers, particularly the rulers of Acre.

The first of the four dramatic and rather violent moments was the 1657 Ottoman military campaign, which sought to restore central control in southern Syria. This campaign introduced a new and stable group of ruling families to Jabal Nablus, families that came to dominate the region's political life well into the nineteenth century. The second was the sieges of Nablus in 1771 and 1773 by Zahir al-Umar, which reflected the rise of Acre as the political capital of Palestine during a period of weak central control, on the one hand, and marked the beginning of the Tuqan household's bid for hegemony over Jabal Nablus, on the other. The third was the military occupation of Greater Syria in 1831 by the forces of Muhammad Ali Pasha, the ruler of Egypt. Although of short duration (nine years), Egyptian rule accelerated ongoing socioeconomic trends and restructured the local and regional configurations of political power. It also brought to the fore a new leading family, Abd al-Hadi, after the failed 1834 revolt led by Nabulsi subdistrict chiefs. The fourth was the destruction in 1859 of the village of Arraba, headquarters of the Abd al-Hadi family, by a resurgent Ottoman government. This event marked the official end of rule by native sons and the fruition of a major Ottoman campaign of centralization and administrative reforms that was initiated in 1839.

The cumulative effect of these watershed events was twofold: it reduced the autonomy of the hinterland in relation to the city, as well as the autonomy of Jabal Nablus and of Palestine in general vis-à-vis the Ottoman state. Put differently, these turning points marked the temporal boundaries of a slow and multilayered process of political centralization on the local, regional, and international levels.

The 1657 Campaign

After their victory over the Mamluks in the battle of Marj Dabiq on August 23, 1516, the Ottoman rulers chose not to undertake a fundamental administrative and political reorganization of Greater Syria. Palestine was divided into five districts (sing. *liwa*, later called *sanjaq*) that closely reflected the administrative arrangement under the Mamluks: Safad,

Nablus, Jerusalem (Quds al-Sharif), Gaza, Ajlun, and Lajjun. All were attached, as in Mamluk times, to the province (*wilaya*) of Damascus.[64] Nor did the Ottoman rulers attempt to restructure the political configuration on the local level. Jabal Nablus was divided into four subdistricts (sing. *nahiya*), in addition to the city itself: Jabal Qubla (south mountain), Jabal Shami (north mountain), Qaqun, and Bani Sa'b—all of which reflected long-standing divisions.[65] For instance, the Jayyusi clan, which ruled the area of Bani Sa'b in the fifteenth century, was reconfirmed in its position and further entrusted in the late sixteenth century with safeguarding the section of the Damascus–Cairo highway between the fortresses of Qaqun and Ras al-Ayn.[66] As these official administrative divisions on the local level suggest, political power in Jabal Nablus did not emanate solely from the city, nor was it centralized in the hands of one household. Rather, the city of Nablus was only one among a number of local centers of power within Jabal Nablus, and its relations with the surrounding villages were partially mediated by the rural-based subdistrict chiefs (sing. *shaykh al-nahiya*), such as the Jayyusis.

The power of rural chiefs was ultimately based on violence or the threat thereof. These chiefs lived in strategic fortresslike compounds located in seat (*kursi*) villages which served as their political and military headquarters.[67] Using their quickly mobilized peasant militia and their command of the hilly terrain, they could project their forces to control the villages in their area and the approaches to Nablus. In effect, they could restrict or relax the arteries of local and regional trade and, in the process, reward or punish particular clans and/or urban trading families. They rarely had to resort to force, however, because they operated tightly knit patronage networks in which peasants traded loyalty for protection. They also commanded allegiance by inserting themselves into the social fabric: they lived among the peasants, married into the key clans of their subdistricts, and transplanted their own clan members into a number of strategic villages. The subdistrict chiefs reinforced their authority by arbitrating disputes and dispensing justice according to the unwritten rules of customary law called *urf*. Their actions, therefore, were circumscribed by social and cultural boundaries that defined ideals for accepted behavior, notions of justice, and levels of accountability to the collective community. Developed over the centuries, it was this nexus of rural relations that constituted the building blocks of rural autonomy and accounted for the deeply rooted yet decentralized power relations.

The Ottoman bureaucracy, honed by generations of imperial expansion in Anatolia and eastern Europe, was both skillful and pragmatic in absorbing such semiautonomous regions. From the very beginning, local leaders were coopted into becoming the representatives of the Ottoman government. This is why the official administrative divisions constructed on the subdistrict level were not primarily meant to be effective grids for the organization of political hierarchies emanating from the center. Rather, they were flexible fiscal shells designed to maximize revenue at the least political cost. The government, in other words, read the existing local political map and then drew boundaries around the actual relations of power. In addition, the government did not attempt to rule the hinterland of Nablus through the city. Rather, each subdistrict chief was directly appointed by the governor of Damascus and invested with the authority to collect taxes and to maintain law and order. These appointments, made annually, were largely ceremonial in nature: in practice, the post of *shaykh al-nahiya* became hereditary in each subdistrict as it was passed down within the same family for generations.[68]

Still, a certain level of control was exercised by playing local leaders off against each other and, when circumstance left no other choice, by punitive expeditions against the whole region. Such an expedition was sent in 1657 as part of a larger campaign by the Ottoman government to reassert central control after decades of social upheavals and economic crises that rocked the empire as a whole. Palestine was a key target because of its importance to land communications with Egypt as well as to the safety and financing of the Damascus pilgrimage caravan.

The Ottoman military expedition consisted primarily of Arab local militia (*yerliyya*) from central Syria.[69] In lieu of salaries for the pacification of Jabal Nablus and, subsequently, for annual military service as escorts for pilgrimage caravans, the cavalry officers (*sipahis*) were granted revenues of some agricultural lands. These land grants, called *timar* or *za'ama*, depending on their size, were carved out from specific villages in Jabal Nablus.[70] To prevent grant holders from establishing independent bases of power, the Ottoman government dispersed the lands and villages of each holder to separate and distant parts of Jabal Nablus. They also assigned the key village of each *za'ama* as a separate *timar* to another grant holder.[71] Furthermore, they made these grants subject to annual renewal in order to forestall privatization through inheritance.

The expedition succeeded in pacifying Jabal Nablus, but the Ottoman government failed in its efforts to prevent the military officers from establishing a strong local base of power. The expedition leaders settled in the city of Nablus and managed to pass their *timar* and *za'ama* holdings on to their descendants.[72] They also consolidated local alliances by selling and renting their rights to these *timars*,[73] as well as by farming them out to middlemen who paid out the revenues in advance, then collected as much as they could from the peasants.[74] In addition to their control of village lands, they quickly diversified their material base by training their sons in a variety of occupations and by investing in manufacture, trade, and urban real estate. According to Ihsan Nimr, a local historian, "Their properties, of all different kinds, were the symbol of their power and princely status. . . . They were careful to acquire all types of properties so that they would need no one nor to purchase anything from others: theirs were the soap factor[ies], bath-house[s], vegetable gardens, pottery factories, mills, bakeries, olive and sesame presses, shops, and lands for planting various crops."[75]

Over time the expedition leaders slowly melted into the local population[76] and became more concerned with running their business affairs than with military service to the Ottoman state.[77] The most powerful of them built large, fortresslike homes with high walls, within which there were stables, water wells, gardens, storage rooms, and quarters for armed retainers and servants. Many of these houses are still standing today. Of this group, the Nimrs, originally subdistrict chiefs in the hinterlands of Homs and Hama, north of Damascus, were the most important, for they received the lion's share of the land grants. They quickly gained control of the posts of *mutasallim* and of *mir alay* (or chief of the *alay*, as the company of local *sipahis* was called). They also intermarried with rich merchant and leading religious (ulama) families and entered into business partnerships with them.

Aside from the Nimrs, the two most important leading families to emerge soon after the 1657 campaign were the Tuqans and the Jarrars. The Jarrar clan moved from the al-Balqa region on the east bank of the River Jordan to the plain of Marj Ibn Amir in Lajjun district sometime around 1670.[78] The economic power of the Jarrars was based on their hold over what eventually became known as the Jenin district (*sanjaq*) around the turn of the nineteenth century. Their political power stemmed from their peasant militia and their possession of a formidable fortress in Sanur village, which controlled the access to the city from the north. They were the only subdistrict chiefs until the 1820s to achieve the post of *mutasallim*, albeit briefly.[79]

The Tuqans, originally from northern Syria,[80] emerged as strong competitors of the Nimrs around the turn of the eighteenth century. They were the only household that ever came close to centralizing all of Jabal Nablus under their rule, and their members held the post of *mutasallim* longer than did any other family in the eighteenth and nineteenth centuries, albeit inconsistently. Their most prominent member in the eighteenth century was *Hajj* Salih Pasha Tuqan (d. 1742). Descended from a family that was wealthy and politically prominent before it came to Jabal Nablus,[81] Salih Pasha began his political career by serving in the military contingent of the pilgrimage caravan. In 1709 he was appointed *mutasallim* of Jerusalem, and later on he filled the same post in the district of Tarabzon near the Black Sea. He returned to Jabal Nablus in 1723, when he was appointed governor of the districts of Gaza, Nablus, and Lajjun.[82] Salih Pasha and some of his descendants intermarried with the Nimrs,[83] but it was not long before internal competition, exacerbated by political interference from the governors of Damascus and the rulers of Acre, caused a serious rift between them that was not mended until the 1820s.

The 1657 expedition heralded a period of relative stability and prosperity for Jabal Nablus. The infusion of a powerful new urban elite also increased the authority and power of the city over its hinterland and reasserted the primacy of Ottoman rule. These developments, in turn, facilitated the expansion of the social space of Jabal Nablus. The earliest reference we have as to the official readjustment of administrative boundaries in response to this expansion is a report by the deputy (*wakil*) *mutasallim* of Nablus, Umar *Agha* Nimr, on the amounts of taxes collected from its subdistricts and the amounts still owed for the year 1723. This report, submitted to the representative of Salih Pasha Tuqan—then governor of Gaza, Nablus, and Lajjun districts—shows that the number of subdistricts of Jabal Nablus had increased from four to seven, not counting the city itself.[84] Of these, the subdistrict of Bani Sa'b was the only one that retained its name—testimony to the continuity in leadership of the Jayyusi clan, whose preeminence in this area preceded the onset of Ottoman rule. The southern subdistrict, Jabal Qubla, had expanded south, east, and west to form three separate subdistricts: Jamma'in, Jorat Amra, and Shaykh Mansur.[85] The former subdistricts of Jabal Shami and Qaqun expanded north, east, and west to form three separate subdistricts: Wadi al-Sha'ir (valley of barley), Sha'rawiyya, and Jarrar. The fact that two of the subdistricts, Jarrar and Shaykh Mansur, were named after the ruling clans in them reflected how local power formations often determined Ottoman administrative divisions from above.

The expansion of Jabal Nablus's social space and administrative boundaries took place at the expense of the only new districts in Palestine that the Ottoman government established after it conquered the area in the sixteenth century: Ajlun and Lajjun. Unlike Palestine's other districts, each of which had an ancient city as its capital, Ajlun and Lajjun were carved out primarily for political and strategic reasons. Through Ajlun district passed the first crucial leg of the Damascus contingent of the pilgrimage caravans. Because this area was dominated by bedouin tribes, the Ottoman government needed a strong hand, provided by the Qansuh, then Furaykh, households to make sure that the caravans proceeded smoothly.[86] Through Lajjun passed the Damascus–Cairo land highway; and this district was set aside for the Turabay household, which was charged with the task of protecting it.[87]

Lajjun and Ajlun formed an arc that capped Jabal Nablus on three sides like a hat. In the mid-eighteenth century they were combined into a single administrative unit, with the town of Jenin as their administrative capital. Officially this continued to be the case until the turn of the nineteenth century, when the western part of this combined unit (Lajjun) became the district of Jenin.[88] As indicated in the above report, however, Jenin was firmly and fully integrated into the social space of Jabal Nablus under the control of the Jarrars in the late 1600s, and it remained so throughout the eighteenth and nineteenth centuries. For instance, the above report named the subdistricts of Sha'rawiyya and Jarrar as part of Jabal Nablus even though together they covered much of the territories that were officially part of Lajjun district.[89] In fact, Nablus had all along been the key urban center for the villages of both Ajlun and Lajjun.[90] The formal administrative arrangements, in other words, concealed an ongoing economic and, to a lesser extent, political absorption by Nablus of these two adjacent districts, especially Lajjun. As we shall soon see, part of Ajlun was appended to Jabal Nablus, albeit briefly, in the nineteenth century; and what was left of Lajjun in the early eighteenth century was severely diminished, between the hammer of Acre's political power and the anvil of Nablus's economic muscle.

The administrative arrangement sketched out in the 1723 document remained essentially unchanged until the end of Ottoman rule in 1917. Just as important was the stability of the ruling families mentioned by name in this document, including the Nimrs, Tuqans, and Jarrars. Over the course of the eighteenth century, the Nimrs and Tuqans traded positions of leadership in the city of Nablus and occasionally ruled other regions in Palestine, especially Jerusalem and Jaffa (including Lydda and Ramla).[91] Meanwhile, the Jarrars were the undisputed leading clan among subdistrict chiefs.[92] Despite their internal differences, this triumvirate managed to maintain a relatively strong grip on power until the Egyptian invasion of 1831 and, more often than not, was united in defending Jabal

Nablus against frontal attempts to conquer it by outside powers. The biggest challenge they faced came from the rulers of Acre.

The Rise of Acre

Officially, Jabal Nablus (that is, the districts of Nablus and Jenin) remained attached to the province of Damascus, albeit with brief interruptions, from 1516 until 1849/1850, after which it was attached to the province of Sidon, and then to the province of Beirut in 1887/1888.[93] In reality, the Damascus governors had only a tenuous hold over Jabal Nablus; during most of the eighteenth and early nineteenth centuries they exercised even less influence. Rather, it was the rulers of Acre—Zahir al-Umar (d. 1775), Ahmad Pasha al-Jazzar (d. 1804), Sulayman Pasha al-Adil (d. 1819), and Abdullah Pasha (who died shortly after the surrender of Acre and his exile to Egypt in 1831)—who wielded real power in much of southern Syria.[94]

Briefly put, the Damascus governors, with some important exceptions,[95] were rotated annually, could not project their limited military resources as far as Jabal Nablus, and, in any case, were too busy arranging for and accompanying annual pilgrimage caravans to impose their will. The rulers of Acre, in contrast, were in a much better position to influence events in Jabal Nablus: Acre was adjacent to Nablus, and its leaders possessed a well-trained and capable military force. They also effectively controlled the governorship of Acre for life and appointed their successors.[96] In fact, they were often called on by the governors of Damascus to render assistance in both fiscal and administrative matters relating to Palestine in general and to Jabal Nablus in particular.[97] In the late 1820s, for example, the governor of Acre, Abdullah Pasha, convinced the central government to reassign the district of Nablus to the province of Sidon, whose de facto capital was Acre. This was after the Damascus governor argued that it would cost him more to force the rebellious people of Jabal Nablus to pay their arrears than the amount of taxes they actually owed.[98]

The rise of Acre must be seen within the larger context of the emergence of power centers within the body of the empire but outside its direct control. This phenomenon swept all through the Ottoman domains, including Anatolia, during the eighteenth century, which was a period of largely weak central control. The stage was set during the late seventeenth century after a series of disastrous defeats in wars with Europe that resulted in the humiliating Treaty of Karlowitz in 1699. During the first half of the eighteenth century the Ottoman government had partial success in recouping some of its losses and in reasserting its power internally.[99] Beginning in 1768, however, the Ottoman government suffered major territorial losses in several wars with Russia over a period of three decades and watched Napoleon take over Egypt in 1798. Most demoralizing of all was their utter military defeat by the forces of one of their own subjects, Muhammad Ali Pasha of Egypt, when he occupied Greater Syria in 1831.

What was bad for the Ottoman government during this period, however, was often good for regional forces, which took advantage of weakness in the center to negotiate virtually autonomous political enclaves and to keep most of the surplus collected as taxes to themselves. Often they ruled these enclaves for life and even passed them on to their descendants or hand-picked successors.[100] The Jalilis in Mosul, the Mamluks in Egypt, and the Shihabs in Mount Lebanon are but a few examples of increased autonomy under the umbrella of Ottoman rule. These ruling households differed substantially from each other in terms of when they came to power, how they held on to it, and the nature of their relationship to the central government. Four features were common to most, however: political centralization on the district and provincial level, sometimes with the help and blessing of the central government, which needed these strong households to maintain its grip, if only indirectly; greater urban access to the rural surplus at the expense of both the central government and local forces at the subdistrict level; the imposition of virtual monopolies on the movement of key agricultural commodities; and growing trade with and sometimes political and military dependence on an industrializing Europe.

These features lay behind the rise of the fortified city of Acre as the political and military center of Palestine and as the de facto capital of the province of Sidon, which was created in the 1660s. Strategically located and easily defended, this ancient port and one-time Crusader stronghold became the headquarters for Zahir al-Umar. A native of the Galilee, Zahir al-Umar began his career as a minor tax collector and, over a forty-five-year period (1730–1775), emerged as the most powerful leader in Palestine. The key economic backdrop to his success was his ability to (partially) monopolize the trade in cotton, grain, and olive oil destined for export to Europe. From the profits of this trade, Zahir al-Umar built a military force that allowed him to expand the territories under his control and to withstand repeated attacks by the governors of Damascus.

Initially, the Jarrar clan bore the brunt of the military and political pressures from Acre because their territories lay between northern and central Palestine. The first major armed confrontation was over control of

Marj Ibn Amir and the market town of Nazareth. Through the fertile lands of the former passed one of the major routes of trade between Nablus and Damascus; and the latter was an important entrepôt for trade between Palestine and its northern regional markets. In 1735 the Jarrars were defeated by Zahir al-Umar, and their leader, Shaykh Ibrahim, was killed in the battle. Nazareth, which had previously paid taxes to the Jarrar clan, became part of Zahir al-Umar's domains.[101]

Over the next three decades Zahir al-Umar's stature became such that he found it possible to forge temporary alliances with the Russian government and to cooperate with the Mamluks in Egypt, who, with his help, invaded Greater Syria in 1771 and again in 1773. It was precisely in these two years that Zahir al-Umar twice laid siege to Nablus. The sieges threw into bold relief a century-long campaign (1730–1830) by the powerful rulers of Acre to contain and even partially reduce the social space of Jabal Nablus. From the military standpoint, these brief though bloody episodes ended in stalemates, but then Zahir al-Umar never intended to occupy the city and remove its local leadership. Rather, these sieges were meant as painful reminders to Nablus's population and its leaders that Acre, not the Ottoman government, was the source of political authority.

During Zahir al-Umar's long reign the leaders of Jabal Nablus learned to subtly maneuver between him and the Ottoman government (as represented by the governors of Damascus), with which he was constantly at odds. Struggles for power within Jabal Nablus, therefore, were often influenced and sometimes precipitated by the larger conflict between Zahir al-Umar and the Ottoman authorities. The former wielded real power in the region; the latter were key to securing political appointments and official legitimacy. Indeed, until the demise of Acre's political clout in 1831, its governors' primary mechanism for controlling Jabal Nablus was the time-honored strategy of divide and conquer, a task made easier by the Nabulsi leaders, who did not hesitate to enlist the help of the Acre rulers or of the governors of Damascus in order to gain advantage in their own internal struggles.[102]

In this respect, the sieges were also important in that they boosted the power of the Tuqan household which, just five years earlier, had embarked on a sustained campaign to centralize its control of Jabal Nablus as a whole. In 1766 Mustafa *Beik* Tuqan successfully maneuvered to have himself appointed as the subdistrict chief of Bani Sa'b in place of the Jayyusi clan.[103] This was the first time that an urban household attempted to directly control a section of the hinterland by forcing out a rural clan, thereby seriously challenging the balance of power between the city and the countryside. This fateful move put the Tuqans on a collision course with both Zahir al-Umar and the Jarrars.

That Bani Sa'b became the lightning rod of an escalating local and regional conflict was no accident. Its territories controlled a key section of the Damascus–Cairo highway as well the access of Nablus to its major sea outlet, the city of Jaffa. Bani Sa'b was also a cotton-producing district, and this was a time of vigorous expansion in cotton trade. This political dispute, therefore, reflected the twin processes of urban political domination over the hinterland and the integration of Palestine into the world economy. The Jarrars opposed the first process, while Zahir al-Umar attempted to impose a monopoly on the trade generated by the latter. Of course, these two processes preceded 1760 and only fully matured a century later, but this dispute was a clear signal of the new times ahead. As we shall see in subsequent chapters, the process of urban control over the countryside was eventually completed by the merchant community, whose primary mechanisms of control were not military power and tax collection but moneylending and local trade networks.

The danger posed by the Tuqan's bid for power was magnified in 1771, when the new governor of Damascus, Muhammad Pasha Azm, appointed Mustafa *Beik* Tuqan to the post of *mutasallim* of Nablus. The Jarrars' fears induced them to let the forces of Zahir al-Umar pass unimpeded through their territories on their way to lay siege to Nablus. Meanwhile, Mustafa *Beik* Tuqan, with the help of the Nimrs, prepared the city's defenses. This turn of events cast the Jarrars in the position of anti-Ottoman local forces, while the Tuqans represented themselves as the defenders of Jabal Nablus against Zahir al-Umar and his Mamluk allies, hence as loyal servants of the sultan.[104]

This political positioning proved to be crucial during the reign of Zahir al-Umar's even more powerful successor, Ahmad Pasha al-Jazzar (1775–1804). Unlike his predecessor, Ahmad Pasha al-Jazzar maintained good relations with the Ottoman central government by paying taxes on time and making sure that he remained indispensable for their hold over southern Syria. Simultaneously, he steadily maneuvered to increase his power, eventually becoming the governor of both Sidon and Damascus provinces.[105] By and large, the well-connected Tuqans received his support,[106] while the Jarrars, unwilling to bow to this centralization effort, suffered two (unsuccessful) military campaigns against their fortress in Sanur village in 1790 and 1795.[107]

Ahmad Pasha al-Jazzar's weak successor, Sulayman Pasha al-Adil, made little effort to directly intervene in the affairs of Jabal Nablus.

Rather, he parceled out his support to different factions at different times, alternating between the Jarrars, the Tuqans, and the Abd al-Hadis.[108] Meanwhile, the Tuqans, under the aggressive leadership of Musa *Beik* Tuqan (1801–1823), accelerated their drive for internal hegemony through violence and intimidation, eventually embroiling Jabal Nablus in a bloody civil war (1817–1823).[109] With the blessing of the Ottoman government, the Tuqans imported mercenary soldiers and stationed them in a hastily built fortress in the village of Junayd, on the outskirts of Nablus.[110] This move backfired, for it only served to increase local opposition. After a series of bloody clashes, some inside the city itself, the Tuqans were defeated and their leader poisoned on November 20, 1823.[111]

The anti-Tuqan coalition, led by the Jarrars and the Qasims (chiefs of the subdistrict of Jammaʿin) with occasional help from the Nimrs,[112] won the battles but lost the war. On one level, the entire struggle only served to enhance the growing importance of the city as the center of effective political power in Jabal Nablus. Henceforth, all struggles would revolve around securing the post of *mutasallim*, and all political contenders from the hinterland who managed to play a leading role in Jabal Nablus as a whole began by establishing residence in or near the city itself. On another level, the victorious Jarrars and Qasims were swimming against the tide of political centralization that was about to overwhelm Greater Syria. In 1825 the Jarrars' power in Jabal Nablus was irreparably damaged when their formidable fortress in Sanur village was destroyed, with the blessing of the Ottoman government, by the combined forces of Abdullah Pasha, Sulayman Pasha's successor in Acre, and of Amir Shihab, the powerful ruler of Mount Lebanon. Then, in 1831, all of Greater Syria fell under the rule of Muhammad Ali Pasha of Egypt, whose administration proved to be far more formidable and intrusive than that of the Ottoman government. Thus, when the Qasims led a revolt against the Egyptian forces in 1834, they were quickly defeated and their leaders beheaded.

Egyptian Rule, 1831–1840

The Egyptian military occupation of Greater Syria is the one dramatic moment in the nineteenth century that is most widely credited for causing a radical break with the past.[113] A more cautious assessment would view the brief period of Egyptian rule as having accelerated rather than precipitated ongoing trends, even though some important new dynamics were introduced, such as the establishment of city councils and the imposition of new controls on the peasantry through conscription and disarmament.

Undergirding Egypt's emergence as the most formidable regional power during the reign of Muhammad Ali Pasha (1805–1848) were the expansion in agricultural production and trade with Europe and the creation of a large modern army that, along the French model, turned peasants into foot soldiers. The military institutions were Muhammad Ali's primary vehicle for introducing wide-ranging administrative, fiscal, and economic structural changes in Egypt. The military also allowed him to project Egyptian power into the Sudan, into the Arabian Peninsula and, in 1831, into Greater Syria.

In a series of lightning battles beginning that year, the outnumbered Egyptian army, under the brilliant leadership of Muhammad Ali Pasha's son, Ibrahim Pasha, soundly defeated the Ottoman forces, causing the sultan to seek the help of the empire's nemesis, Russia. This move, in turn, brought the rest of the European states into the fray. Like the series of events triggered by Napoleon's invasion of Egypt in 1798, but on a much grander scale, the Egyptian invasion of Greater Syria firmly posed what became known as the Eastern Question; that is, how to integrate the Ottoman Empire and its far-flung domains into the European political and economic orbit without upsetting the balance of power in Europe and without igniting uncontrollable regional conflicts. The very question both assumed and reflected the existence of unprecedented opportunities for the European powers to increase their influence. In 1838 Great Britain negotiated the "free-trade" Anglo-Turkish Commercial Convention, which opened the Ottoman interior to European businesses. At the same time, indirect political incursions, under the cover of protecting religious minorities, were intensified.

The Egyptian authorities, for their part, heartily encouraged greater European involvement. Muhammad Ali Pasha, who had already oriented Egypt's economy firmly toward Europe, sought to preempt any hostile actions by the European powers by reassuring them that Egyptian policies would facilitate rather than hinder their economic interests in Greater Syria. For example, permission was given for the establishment of European consulates in cities, such as Damascus and Jerusalem, which were considered off limits before, and commercial agriculture and overseas trade were vigorously promoted and protected through the imposition of a centralized political and legal infrastructure. For the first time in memory, Greater Syria was brought under a single administration backed by a powerful army. To standardize the wide diversity of political configurations, the Egyptian authorities channeled administrative control through a new urban institution: the Advisory Council (*majlis al-shura*). Based in key cities and staffed by religious leaders, rich merchants, and political figures, these councils accelerated yet another ongoing process (aside from the integration of Greater Syria in the European orbit): urban political control and economic domination of the hinterland.

Initially, the rural leaders of hill regions in Greater Syria, including Jabal Nablus, were awed by the overwhelming Egyptian military forces and cautiously welcomed Ibrahim Pasha. Soon, however, they began to greatly resent their exclusion from the Advisory Councils, which were empowered by and answerable to the Egyptian authorities. This resentment turned to rebellion when they were ordered to implement the highly unpopular measures of disarming and conscripting the peasantry, as well as collecting a new head tax, the *ferde,* to be paid in cash by all adult males over the age of fifteen. All of these measures cut into their privileges and material base, and they undermined their hold over the peasantry.

Those rural leaders with the most to lose led revolts in Palestine, Mount Lebanon, and Jabal al-Druze (Hauran). The first of these revolts took place in Palestine in 1834.[114] Led by Qasim al-Ahmad, chief of the Jamma'in subdistrict in Jabal Nablus, this revolt was crushed, like the others that followed, by the overwhelming military force of the Egyptian army. Qasim al-Ahmad and his two oldest sons were executed. Other leaders either met the same fate, were exiled, and/or were relieved of their positions. Thus the political autonomy of Jabal Nablus, weakened by the interventions of the rulers of Acre and by internal struggles, was dealt a major blow by the Egyptian forces.

At the same time, the Egyptian occupation marked the rise of a new ruling household in Jabal Nablus: the Abd al-Hadis. Based in the village of Arraba, the Abd al-Hadis were already an important force at the time of Napoleon's siege of Acre, having been supported by the rulers of Acre (especially Ahmad Pasha al-Jazzar and Sulayman Pasha) as well as by the Tuqans as a counterweight to the Jarrars. Because the Abd al-Hadis represented a relatively new and fresh political force, Ibrahim Pasha picked their leader, Shaykh Husayn, to be his right-hand man for southern Syria. Because Husayn Abd al-Hadi proved to be a loyal and effective servant, he was promoted to the governorship of Sidon province, which, in the 1830s, included almost all of Palestine.

For a while it seemed as though Nablus might become both the political and economic capital of southern Syria, due to the demise of Acre and the meteoric rise of the Abd al-Hadis. Indicative was the expansion of the social space of Jabal Nablus into domains long controlled by the rulers of

Acre. In 1851, for instance, Mahmud *Beik* Abd al-Hadi, then the district-governor of Nablus, and his cousin, Salih *Beik* Abd al-Hadi, then the district-governor of Haifa, appointed the shaykhs of seven villages in Bilad al-Haritha located between the towns of Bisan and Nazareth.[115] Furthermore, that same year Yusuf Abd al-Hadi, a rich tax farmer, invested large amounts of money to rebuild the villages of Shifa'amr subdistrict (west of Haifa) as part of his *iltizam* (tax farm) holdings.[116]

Even the official administrative configuration of Jabal Nablus in the decade after the Egyptian occupation came closer than ever to reflecting its informal absorption of the former district of Lajjun. According to records of the Nablus Advisory Council, Jabal Nablus in the mid-nineteenth century formally consisted of the two districts (*sanjaqs*) of Nablus and Jenin (the former capital of the combined districts of Ajlun and Lajjun), plus nine subdistricts which contained a total of 213 villages, as shown in Table 1.

This expansion of Jabal Nablus, however, proved to be temporary. The European powers that forced Ibrahim Pasha's retreat in 1840 lavished their attention on Jerusalem instead. Because of its religious and symbolic significance, Jerusalem was the most suitable stepping-stone for increased European intervention through a process of redefining Palestine in Biblical terms as the Holy (as opposed to Ottoman or Arab) land. By the 1850s Jerusalem emerged as Palestine's political and administrative center—a role it has yet to relinquish. At the same time, the coastal towns of Jaffa and Haifa, like Beirut and Alexandria, were transformed into large, modern cities as they became the economic beachheads for the growing trade with Europe.

The rise of Jerusalem and the gradual shifting of the economic center of gravity to the coast led many Nabulsi merchants to focus on the east bank of the River Jordan as the new frontier for the investment of merchant capital. The economic integration of the former district of Ajlun into Jabal Nablus's sphere of influence had been going on since the early Ottoman period, but it proceeded apace with the extension of Ottoman central control into this bedouin-dominated environment during the second half of the nineteenth century. Many Nabulsi families, along with others from Jerusalem and Damascus, established households on the east bank, purchased lands, and extended credit to peasants.[117] Because Nabulsi merchants were historically the most active in this region, it was not surprising that in 1867 Jabal Nablus's administrative boundaries were redrawn again as the Ottoman authorities appended the middle portion of Ajlun district, al-Balqa (with Salt as its central town), to Jabal Nablus.

Table 1. Administrative Composition of Jabal Nablus, 1850:
Districts (*Sanjaqs*) and subdistricts (*Nahiyas*)*

Administrative Unit	Head	Number of Villages
Sanjaq Nablus	Mahmud *Beik* Abd al-Hadi	
Sanjaq Jenin	Yusuf Sulayman Abd al-Hadi	45
Mashariq al-Jarrar	Ahmad al-Yusuf, Muhammad al-Hajj and Qasim al-Dawud (Jarrar)	28
Bani Sa'b	Yusuf Jayyusi	27
Jamma'in (east)	Mahmud al-Qasim	21
Jamma'in (west)	Muhammad al-Sadiq (Rayyan)	25
Sha'rawiyya (east)	Salih *Beik* Abd al-Hadi	} 23
Sha'rawiyya (west)	Abd al-Rahman Husayn Abd al-Hadi	
Wadi al-Sha'ir (east)	*Abu* Bakr Burqawi (Sayf clan)	} 24
Wadi al-Sha'ir (west)	Musa al-Mir'i (al-Ahfa clan)	
Mashariq Nablus	Shaykhs of Bayta and Aqraba villages (Hajj Muhammad clan)	20

SOURCE: NMSR, pp. 76–77, 167.

*This table represents just one moment in time. One year earlier the subdistricts of Jamma'in and Wadi al-Sha'ir were not yet split into two parts, *sanjaq* Nablus was headed by Sulayman Tuqan, and *sanjaq* Jenin was headed by al-Qaddura Jarrar. Internal conflict between the two powerful branches of the Bani-Ghazi clan, Qasim and Rayyan, split the subdistrict of Jamma'in into two parts. In May 1859 Jamma'in (east) was headed by Sulayman *Agha* Rayyan; Jamma'in (west), by Mahmud *Afandi* al-Qasim. Both subdistricts were elevated to the status of *qada*, which means that a deputy judge was stationed in each one. The judge appointed to the latter subdistrict was Shaykh Muhammad *Afandi* Husayni, from Jerusalem (NICR, 12:249, 251, 254). Similarly, the subdistrict of Wadi al-Sha'ir was divided due to a struggle between the related clans of Sayf and Ahfa, largely over property and taxation questions involving the village of Burqa (NMSR, pp. 58, 60, 63–64, 67–68, 83; NIMR, 2:596–599). The former clan, under the leadership of the Burqawi family, eventually controlled the western section centered around Tulkarem village. In 1859 its chief was Muhammad Mustafa *Agha* Burqawi (NICR, 12:251). The eastern part centered around Burqa village (NMSR, p. 167). In May 1859 its chief was Shaykh Mas'ud al-Hamdan (NICR, 12:250).

Until this new part was detached in 1888, Jabal Nablus became officially known as the district (*mutasarrifiyya*) of Jabal Nablus and al-Balqa.

Ottoman Centralization and the Fall of Arraba

Beset by external pressures, a fiscal crisis, and separatist nationalist movements in its remaining European domains, the Ottoman authorities unveiled in 1839 an ambitious program of reforms known as the *Tanzimat*. This program aimed at modernizing the armed forces, centralizing political power, and increasing revenues from agricultural production, trade, and manufacturing. All of this required more knowledge about and greater control of the subjects of the empire: population counts, conscription, direct collection of taxes, and the establishment of political institutions which could facilitate direct central control.

Because many elements of this program were similar to ones already taken by Muhammad Ali Pasha during the Egyptian occupation of Greater Syria, the way was already paved for the implementation of the *Tanzimat*. The Ottoman government, for example, regulated and expanded the Advisory Councils, tried to keep the population disarmed, revived the policy of conscription, and maintained the head tax. They also conducted population-count campaigns in Greater Syria during the late 1840s and, in 1856, initiated the second wave of reforms, including a new land code (1858). All of these measures were backed by an increased military presence and an active policy of wooing the urban elites, primarily through the Advisory Councils.

Still, the large power vacuum created by the Egyptian retreat in 1840 could not be quickly filled by the Ottoman government. For the next two decades the reconfiguration of political relations in Jabal Nablus was punctuated by internal upheavals and violent clashes. The escalating civil strife largely emanated from below as peasant clans, no longer under the watchful gaze of the Egyptian forces, competed vigorously for land and water resources in the context of expanding agricultural production, population growth, and increasing demands on their surplus by the Ottoman government, local leaders, and urban merchants. Meanwhile, the members of the Nablus Advisory Council negotiated their relations with a much more aggressive and intrusive Ottoman state one crisis at a time.

For example, on December 26, 1849, the council members[118] met to draft a letter of defiance in response to a number of impatient missives from the governor of Jerusalem concerning the composition of the council. The last of these letters, addressed to the *qa'immaqam* of Nablus, Sulayman *Beik* Tuqan, had been received just eight days earlier:

> We have repeatedly requested that you quickly organize the drafting of a letter from the Nablus Advisory Council nominating ten Muslims and three for each of the remaining *millets* [non-Muslim religious communities], so that four . . . Muslims and one for each *millet* can be chosen in a lottery. [This is] aside from your person, the judge and the *mufti*—as was explained to you in a letter . . . from the Provincial Council [of Sidon]. Un-

til now, we have not received any such list from you, and it is necessary that you send it as soon as possible . . .[119]

The Jerusalem governor and his superiors, who had been trying to nurture this fledgling institution over the past few years, were unhappy about their lack of control over the composition of its members and about the fact that its current configuration deviated in two important respects from the guidelines proclaimed in a January 1840 imperial edict.[120] First, all the members were Muslims, even though representatives from the Samaritan and the Christian Greek Orthodox communities were supposed to have been included.[121] Second, the council members recruited an additional member, the *naqib al-ashraf* (steward of the descendants of the Prophet), Muhammad Murtada *Afandi* Hanbali, despite the fact that all four slots for Muslims were already filled.

At the same time, however, the governor and his superiors knew that any effort to unilaterally impose new members would lead to a political cul-de-sac. The cooperation of the current members of the Nablus council, therefore, was indispensable; and this is why they were asked to nominate their successors. The Nablus council members, in turn, were aware of the government's dilemma. In their reply they were neither humble nor shy about asserting their local will:

> We have received your order . . . but there is no one in these parts who is qualified to run this institution other than the ones who are members of it at the present. The *naqib* . . . [whom we] appointed as head of the council . . . has the qualifications and experience in these matters and in running the affairs of the people. . . . Likewise, all the other members have the experience and commitment [to do the same]. We petition you . . . to keep them in their posts.[122]

The council members referred to themselves in the third person ("the ones who are members") in order to highlight their claim, asserted in the title of their memo, that they had the full support of the city's notables, religious figures, and neighborhood leaders. Their reply, in effect, denied the central authorities the right to choose the members of the council, justified the inclusion of *naqib al-ashraf*, and declared his appointment as head of the council, even though the rules clearly stipulated that the *qa'immaqam* was to hold this post.

This confrontation, like many others that took place between the council and the Ottoman authorities in the mid-nineteenth century, eventually resulted in a negotiated compromise. A list was submitted four months after the above letter was sent, and some new members were chosen.[123]

Yet even though Muhammad Murtada *Afandi* Hanbali was specifically excluded, he continued to attend the council meetings and to sign his name along with the others on outgoing correspondence. The Ottoman authorities, for their part, turned a blind eye.[124]

The ability of the Nablus council to influence the composition of its own membership, and to do so in ways that contravened guidelines established at the highest levels, illustrates both the extent and the limits of Jabal Nablus's autonomy within Ottoman rule during the mid-nineteenth century. On the one hand, it was clear that the Ottoman reforms were filtered and reshaped by a local ruling elite, a religious leadership, and a merchant community composed entirely of native sons. On the other hand, detailed supervision of the kind indicated by the letters from the governor of Jerusalem would have been unthinkable just few decades earlier, as would the restructuring of local political authority that made the Advisory Council the locus of local political power.

In this context, it is significant that none of the letters sent by the council members ever questioned the legitimacy of the Advisory Council even though this rather new institution was clearly designed to reinforce central control at the expense of local autonomy. Indeed, their letters emphasized their desire to be active participants in the molding of a new political landscape, along with the central government, and enthusiastically insisted that they possessed the three classic qualifications for political office: merit, commitment, and popular support. This is because the cooperative posture of the Nablus council members was more than just a bow to superior authority driven by an instinct for self-preservation; it was also internally driven. Although the members came from a heterogeneous group of traditionally prominent families—religious, ruling, and mercantile—collectively they represented the emergence of a new social group and a new type of local notable. All were actively involved in trade and soap manufacturing, and all had a stake in the success of an institution that provided them with an effective forum through which they could project their power locally.

Control of the post of *mutasallim* (and by extension over the Advisory Council) during this transitional period (1840–1860) shifted between the Tuqans and the Abd al-Hadis, whose camps had become the lightning rods of the escalating civil strife. When the Ottoman Empire was distracted by the outbreak of the Crimean War (1854–1858), the factional conflicts turned into a bloody conflagration that swept all corners of Jabal Nablus, leaving behind numerous casualties and extensive property damage. Soon after the Crimean War ended, the Ottoman government launched a military campaign that led to the destruction of Arraba, the fortified home village of the Abd al-Hadi clan, and the permanent reassertion of central control. After this date, the highest political office (*mutasallim*) would no longer be held by native sons, and the struggle for power would be limited to competition for positions in the Advisory Council under the direct control and supervision of a non-Nabulsi official.

The fact that the rather small-scale and brief Ottoman military campaign in 1859 proved so decisive in permanently asserting central Ottoman control indicates that the political and economic realities in Nablus were ripe for such a change. The ruling households that emerged in the seventeenth century had already been seriously weakened by internal struggles and repeated blows by the rulers of Acre, the Egyptian occupation, and Ottoman centralization. As shall be seen, their material base, predicated on the control of the peasantry and their surplus, was also undermined by merchants who, during the eighteenth and nineteenth centuries, consolidated their rise from political obscurity and the confines of trade into the greener pastures of political office and control of the major means of production (land and soap factories).

CONCLUSION

When Shaykh Yusuf Jarrar wrote his poem in 1799, he assumed several meanings of autonomy: rule by native sons, most of whom had descended from the same families for generations; a common sense of identity, which ranked loyalty to Jabal Nablus far above that to the Ottoman Empire; and mutual defense against external and regional threats, whether against the French army or the rulers of Acre. The structure of the poem (praising the military prowess of leading families) also assumed a more specific meaning of autonomy: the division of Jabal Nablus itself into several territorially based autonomous enclaves headed by urban households or rural clans that built fortified compounds, controlled peasant militia, and established a diverse economic portfolio in order to secure basic needs without undue reliance on others.

These meanings were in turn layered on others. The city itself was fairly self-sufficient and remarkably stable. It was nestled within protective folding hills; its manufacturing sectors had access to cheap raw materials, plentiful water, and a large, secure market in the dozens of surrounding villages; and it was home to a strong merchant community and a stable group of ulama families. There was also the relative autonomy of the rural sphere. Until the 1830s the subdistrict chiefs were appointed by and—formally, at least—answerable to the governor of Damascus, not to the *mutasallim* of Nablus. The relative autonomy of the peasants also stemmed from the facts that they had access to leaders who lived among them; that they were armed and constituted the most effective military force in Jabal Nablus; that they were not chained to the land but were free agents who sometimes voted with their feet; that they belonged to closely knit village communities characterized by small landholdings; and that most lived in hill villages, whose meter-thick stone houses were packed together like the gnarled trunk of an olive tree, for self-defense and conservation of agricultural lands.

These layers of autonomy were not necessarily an obstacle to the political and economic development of Jabal Nablus as a social space. Quite the contrary, the population of Jabal Nablus grew significantly during the eighteenth and nineteenth centuries, its administrative borders expanded, and, most importantly, it became the leading economic center of Palestine despite severe containment pressures exerted by the rulers of Acre.

Ironically, Jabal Nablus's very success helped undermine its own autonomy. Long before the Egyptian invasion and Ottoman reforms reasserted central control, the commercialization of agriculture—spurred by expanding regional markets and growing trade with Europe, as well as deepened by the infiltration of merchant capital and spread of market relations into the farthest reaches of the hinterland—undermined the constituent elements of peasant autonomy. The city's growing political and economic control over its hinterland, in turn, precipitated a struggle for hegemony by the Tuqan household that threatened the political power of subdistrict chiefs, hence the rural-urban character of the conflict between the Tuqans and the Jarrars, even though each had allies from both the city and its hinterland.

The main beneficiary of these changes was the merchant community. In order to gain access to and control of the rural surplus, as well as to provide a secure atmosphere for trade during periods of political uncertainties, merchants built strong and deeply rooted local and regional networks that carved the hinterland into geographic spheres of influence and facilitated Nablus's economic ties to regional markets. Over time, these networks became the anchors of Jabal Nablus as a social space, for they undergirded the economic, social, and cultural stability of this region. In the process, these networks also knit the inhabitants of hinterlands with those of the city into a distinct and cohesive social formation. It is to these trade networks, and the ways in which they helped construct the meanings of family, community, and identity, that we turn next.

2   Family, Culture, and Trade

Send us the cloak immediately . . . for you are well aware that there
is a wedding coming up at *Abu* Muhammad's; and a new cloak is
important for a good image because strangers as well as relatives
will be present.

> From a peasant's letter to a textile merchant, circa 1890

You could say that Nablus, surrounded by villages on all sides, was
a port for the peasants, and every hinterland region had a merchant
it depended on.

> Najib Arafat (b. 1901), textile merchant, 1990

Shaykh Abd al-Razzaq Arafat, a wholesale textile merchant, died bankrupt in December 1810, leaving behind a wife, thirteen children, and a
large debt. To pay off the creditors, a carefully detailed inventory of his
belongings was drawn up and registered in the Nablus Islamic Court.[1] A
close look reveals some interesting items: 82 coffee cups in his home; 65
varieties of textile products in his warehouse (*hasil*); the names of 102
individuals who owed him small amounts of money, including 39 peasants
from at least 20 different villages; and a short list of individuals, mostly
soap producers, to whom he owed large amounts of money.

These items mark the contours of regional and local trade networks of
a typical textile merchant in Nablus during the eighteenth and nineteenth
centuries. For example, a significant proportion of the 65 types of textiles
was locally manufactured, but the bulk was imported from two places:
Egypt and, to a lesser extent, Damascus. These two places had long been
the primary destinations for Nabulsi soap, and it was not a coincidence
that Abd al-Razzaq Arafat died indebted to soap producers. He, like other
wholesale textile merchants, financed his imports partly by purchasing
soap in Nablus and selling it in Egypt or Damascus.

As to the 39 peasants, it is very likely that each, at one time or another,
had stayed a night or two at Abd al-Razzaq Arafat's house after spending
long hours in his shop choosing wedding wardrobes. Equally likely, they
sipped coffee from his 82 cups while they joyfully celebrated the evening
away—the payment postponed until harvest season. As shall be seen, the
provision of food and lodging were only a small part of a complex of

extraeconomic relations cultivated by merchants in order to construct and reproduce the local trade and clientele networks that literally carved the hinterland into geographic spheres of influence and that were passed from father to son.[2] The rootedness and resiliency of these networks allowed trading activities to flourish despite the decentralized and often unpredictable political environment in which merchants operated and were defining elements in the formation of the cultural identity of Jabal Nablus.

Palestinian merchants had no direct access to political office until they infiltrated the ranks of Advisory Councils in the 1840s. In the absence of direct political power, culturally constructed networks represented a viable strategy that could facilitate trade and agricultural production. Throughout the Ottoman period, therefore, trade was conducted through multilayered and, by today's Western standards, fairly intimate negotiations among a large number of actors whose consent was absolutely crucial for the movement of goods and people. This method of doing business was so rooted by the turn of the nineteenth century that the imposition of tighter central control by 1860 did not lead merchants to discontinue their true-and-tried method of reproducing trade networks based on personal ties and a wide range of services; it only brought them to the surface and reinforced them. Neither did the larger forces of a global economy seriously undermine the foundations of these networks by the end of the Ottoman period. Rather, they initially intensified them as merchants sought to protect their access to the rural surplus in the face of increased competition from coastal merchants and foreign trade.

A close look at how these local networks operated contradicts two assumptions still pervasive in the historical literature on the Ottoman period: that the city and the country were separate worlds, and that peasants were passive victims of the blind advance of merchant capital. We have already seen that there were no clear dividing lines between the urban and rural spheres of Jabal Nablus. True, the expansion of capitalist relations, centralization of Ottoman rule, and merchant domination of the city council—all phenomena that had matured by the mid-nineteenth century—did enhance the power of merchants over the peasantry and did exacerbate the already unequal relationship between the two. But these developments cannot be projected backward in time without qualification; nor can they be used to efface the fact that these negotiated networks survived well into the twentieth century, precisely because they met a variety of needs that went beyond simple economic intercourse.

Just as important, patronage networks were not a one-way exploitative relationship in which peasant were passive victims. True, patron-client relations often masked exploitative practices and undermined horizontal solidarity between peasant groups. But the ideological underpinning of these relations was the perception of a fair and just exchange that put a premium on honesty, trust, and honor and that was expressed through gift giving, visits, reciprocal favors, and kinship ties. The fluidity of a system that had to be constantly renegotiated left room for peasants to play a role in defining the parameters of each exchange as well as to resist through a variety of means.[3] These ranged from changing patrons or not paying debts to the more drastic measures of relocation or even violence.

The internal dynamics of these networks changed over time. But, in form if not in substance, their continuity provided Nabulsis with a shared sense of social norms. Although changing and not always followed, these norms served as a set of common reference points that helped define what it meant to be a Nabulsi. It is precisely the constant reproduction of these networks over time and space that imparted to Nablus its unique character as a conservative interior trade and manufacturing town in which family dynamics have long dominated social and political relations and in which merchants played, and continue to play, a leading role in economic and cultural life. Indeed, it can be argued that the remarkable continuity in habits and forms of social organization in Nablus was rooted in the daily rituals and practices which knit the participants of each network into a tightly woven and resilient social fabric. Like other trade and manufacturing towns with strong links to their hinterland—such as Hebron or Nazareth in Palestine, Zahleh or Tripoli in Lebanon, and Homs or Hama in Syria—Nablus loomed large in the eyes of its inhabitants, implanting in them a very strong sense of regional identification and perhaps an exaggerated pride in those social practices they believed unique to their city.

In short, local and regional networks, such as those fashioned by both the ancestors and the descendants of Abd al-Razzaq Arafat and his three brothers (also textile merchants), were the umbilical cords that connected Nablus to its hinterland and to the wider world. Unpacking these family-knit networks and the methods used to reproduce them is, therefore, largely an investigation of merchant life, urban-rural relations, and the connections between family, culture, and trade.

Informal by their very nature, these networks left few clues of the kind that would allow historians to draw a spatial grid on which to plot the number, size, and geographical location of merchant networks in Jabal Nablus. One can, however, investigate the inner workings of these networks and how they changed over time by digging deep into the history of a single family of textile merchants. Thus this chapter is largely a case study of the Arafat family which produced textile merchants for over a dozen generations. But, first, two questions: why textile merchants and not, say, oil or grain merchants? and why the Arafat family, instead of some other merchant family with equally deep mercantile roots in Nablus?

TEXTILE MERCHANTS

It is difficult to overestimate the importance of textiles to cultural and material life before and during the Ottoman period. In today's world, where mass-produced clothes have a very short life and where fleeting fashions ensure a high turnover, it is easy to forget that clothes were valuable property that was maintained with great care and passed from one generation to the next.[4] In the Islamic court's method of registering inheritance estates, the long list of personal and business properties always began with an itemization of the deceased's clothes: each garment was identified and priced, and its condition (old or worn out) was noted.[5] On average, clothes were more valuable, by far, than were furniture and other household goods in estates registered during the first two-thirds of the nineteenth century. Expensive articles of clothing were a form of savings, akin to precious metals and stones. This was especially true for women, in whose estates clothes represented a significant proportion of the total worth.[6]

An example is the protracted dispute that followed the sudden death, in 1860, of *Umm* Dawud,[7] wife of Abdullah, a middle-class Christian textile merchant in Nablus. *Umm* Dawud's mother accused her son-in-law of appropriating the best of his deceased wife's clothes, thus reducing the pool of property to be divided among the inheritors, of which she was one. Abdullah argued that most of his wife's clothes actually belonged to his own deceased mother and that he had merely lent them to his wife to wear, but not to possess, in the same manner that his deceased wife lent her clothes to her daughter-in-law. The dispute soon expanded beyond the confines of the immediate family and came to involve both the priest and the secular head of the small Christian community in Nablus. In the last negotiating session, a crowd of animated people ringed a pile of clothing, displaying and arguing the fate of each piece. Eventually the husband was awarded most of the items that his wife's family claimed to be hers, not his, private property.[8] Nevertheless, the cash value of the remaining clothes was 3,600 piasters—an amount equal at that time to the average purchase price of a *bayt* (pl. *buyut*), or single room in which a nuclear family lived.[9]

This example also shows that gifts of clothes could be used to establish a set of authoritative relations. Abdullah's mother established her authority over his wife, *Umm* Dawud, by giving her clothes. *Umm* Dawud, in turn, reproduced this set of relations by conferring clothing on her daughter-in-law. It is ironic that the manner by which hierarchical relations between the females of the household became established was used by a male (Abdullah) as an argument against his mother-in-law. In other words, he won partly because he cleverly packaged his argument in a gendered interpretation of local tradition and hierarchy, versus the mother-in-law's assertion of *Umm* Dawud's individual right to property.[10]

In addition to their monetary value and political uses, clothes were a signifier of multiple shades of social status, wealth, rank, and individual identity, as well as place of origin. The color, form, design, and type of materials used identified the wearer from a distance. More important for our purposes, textiles straddled the shared spaces between social organization, economic relations, and cultural life. Textiles and textile merchants, for instance, played a central role in major religious events—such as *id al-fitr* (Feast of Breaking the Ramadan Fast, or Lesser Bairam) or, especially, *id al-adha* (Feast of the Sacrifice, or Greater Bairam)—as well as in personal life events, such as birth, the first day in school, graduation, safe return from the pilgrimage to the Holy Cities of Mecca and Medina, or, most important, weddings.

All of these events were celebrated with the purchase and making of a new set of clothes, or wardrobes, called *kiswa*, at least for those who could afford them.[11] In his memoirs, Malik Masri, son of a textile merchant, recalled that in the early part of the twentieth century children did not go to sleep the night preceding *id al-adha* without first making sure that their holiday clothes were neatly folded and placed next to their beds so that they could quickly put them on the next morning.[12] Because the acquisition of a new set of clothes was an annual occasion for most people, especially for children, the holidays brought such a rush of orders that tailors and shoemakers in Nablus kept their shops open all night in order to meet the demand.[13]

The eager anticipation of family members for new holiday clothes also translated into many sleepless nights for the female members of the household who did the sewing. The desire to start the preparations early on is captured in the following letter, from a peasant to a textile merchant three weeks before *id al-adha*:

The Most Honorable Sir, Noble Brother, *Hajj* Isma'il Arafat . . .

After emphatic regards, we put before you our hope that your most noble person will send us one whole piece [*shaqqa*] of red-colored *dima* of good quality. Please let us know the price, and do not worry about the payment at all. With the grace of God, Most High, we will send you its price after the Holiday with the bearer [of this letter], Husayn son of Sulayman al-Muhammad. *We implore you not to delay its delivery to us at all, for you are well aware that the Holiday is upon us. . . .* God bless you.

> Ibrahim [not clear]
> Jaba [village]
> April 7, 1901 [14]

Textile wholesalers and retailers were also central to public life in Nablus in terms of cultural and physical space. Of all the various types of traders in this merchant city, they alone were referred to by the simple, generic term "merchant" (*tajir*), without qualification. All other merchants were identified by the particular commodity they dealt with, such as oil or grains. This predominance reflects the extent to which the meanings of "merchant" and "textiles" were intertwined, no doubt because textile merchants formed the largest subgroup within the merchant community and because Nablus contained a large textile-manufacturing sector.

The shops of textile merchants dominated Khan al-Tujjar (merchant caravansary), the most prestigious and expensive strip of commercial real estate in the city. In his memoirs Muhammad Izzat Darwaza (b. 1887), son of a textile merchant, noted, "From what I remember from my father and through my grandfather, the title merchant or merchants in Nablus mostly referred to owners of commercial textile and cloth shops. In Nablus, these shops were confined, or mostly confined, to a caravansary called Khan al-Tujjar, in the middle of Nablus." [15]

Mary Rogers, sister of the British consul in Haifa and a resident of Palestine during the second half of the 1850s, called this market "the finest arcade in Palestine." [16] Reverend John Mills, who spent three months in the city between 1855 and 1860 in order to study the Samaritan community, looked with great disdain on Nablus's Muslim population; but he had only glowing things to say about Khan al-Tujjar:

> The principal bazaar is arched, and is very large and fine for Nablus. It is the finest, by far, in Palestine, and equals any, as far as I observed, in the largest towns of the Turkish Empire. *This is the clothing Emporium,* and is well furnished with the bright silk productions of Damascus and Aleppo—the Abas of Bagdad—calicos and prints from Manchester, in vari-

eties too numerous to be named—as well as the production of the town it-self.[17]

The significance of Khan al-Tujjar also had a great deal to do with its central location, which divided the city in half, not just physically but also psychologically, between "easterners" and "westerners;" labels that are still used today.[18] For example, during the preparations for the Nabi Musa festival, held near Jericho every year for centuries until it was stopped by the British occupation in the late 1930s,[19] young men from the eastern and western parts of Nablus descended on Khan al-Tujjar, each shout-ing slogans praising their part of the city. In the middle of the market they played a game of "catch": they would face off and make forays into the other side, with the aim of catching the greater number of "prison-ers."[20]

Khan al-Tujjar was also where many key holidays and events were celebrated. On occasion of the Prophet's birthday, for example, the textile merchants worked collectively to decorate this market. They spread car-pets on the ground and covered the walls with a variety of textiles, includ-ing silks. Flowers and dishes of sweets were put on tables brought from their homes especially for the occasion.[21] After the evening prayers, peo-ple would saunter through Khan al-Tujjar, surrounded by merchants who displayed their brightly colored goods,and passed out free candy-covered almonds (*mlabbas*) and other sweets.[22]

The critical cultural importance of textile merchants is corroborated by statistical evidence, albeit tentative, which suggests that they constituted the largest group within the merchant community as a whole.[23] Between 1800 and 1860, 40 percent of the 51 inheritance cases that could be clearly identified as belonging to wholesale merchants were those of textile mer-chants.[24] (One must quickly add that most merchants did not specialize in one commodity. Rather, it was common to find at least three commodi-ties—textiles, oil, and grains—in the estates of most merchants.[25] As-signing an occupation to families on the basis of the major income of their leading members does not fully address this perennial problem in Middle East historiography.) In contrast, the richer and more powerful merchants who specialized in oil and soap came in second, at about 20 percent of the total. They, in turn, were followed by grain merchants at 10 percent; leather merchants at 7 percent; and 7 percent for those dealing with pre-cious metals and currencies. The remaining 16 percent included merchants who specialized in livestock, dried fruit, raw cotton, and a variety of other goods. Textile merchants, in other words, were twice as common as the next three ranking groups combined. Of these 51 cases, textiles were also the second most important commodity listed in the estates of merchants who dealt primarily in soap, oil, grains, or leather.[26]

Finally, textile merchants were also important because they dealt in a commodity that happened to be the spearhead of European industrialization and a key component of the growing trade between the Ottoman Empire and Europe, especially Great Britain. The changing patterns of regional trade, therefore, shed light on the process of the capitalist integration of Greater Syria, especially its interior towns, into the world economy. Just as important, local networks of textile merchants reveal the connections between merchants and peasants, as we shall see in the case study of the Arafat family.

THE ARAFAT FAMILY

"All or most of the Arafats are textile merchants; they have not transcended this fate."[27] Najib Arafat, who spoke these words, was no doubt taking pride in the continuity of tradition in both his family and his city, as well as in a line of work he has pursued since his early teens. Assertion of rootedness and affirmation of identity are two key elements of twentieth-century Palestinian nationalism, especially among members of established merchant families who were fairly successful and well-to-do during the Ottoman period—that is, before the tragic upheavals of the Mandate period and beyond.[28] In actual fact, the Arafat family is large, and during the nineteenth century some of its male members worked as soap manufacturers or artisans.[29] By the end of that century, some Arafat men were the first in Nablus to join the ranks of the emerging professional middle class in Greater Syria.[30] Nevertheless, and compared even with the families that produced textile merchants generation after generation—Sadder, Darwish-Ahmad, Zakar, Fityan, Zuʿaytar, Darwaza, Ghanim, Ghazzawi, Anabtawi, and Balbisi, among others—the Arafats can be said to have maintained a most remarkable continuity of engagement in this profession.[31]

Abd al-Razzaq Arafat (d. 1810), whom we met at the beginning of this chapter, was a textile merchant, as were his three brothers. This concentration almost surely means that their father was also a textile merchant, for one's line of work, as a general rule, passed from father to son. Most likely, the textile connection went farther back, because their father's paternal cousin, Shaykh Sulayman al-Shahid, traded in textiles and had a shop in Khan al-Tujjar.[32] Assuming that his similar line of work was not a coincidence, it would be safe to conclude that the Arafat's experience in this field extended at least as far back as Abd al-Razzaq's great-grandfather, Ahmad al-Shahid, whose life spanned the late seventeenth and early eighteenth centuries (see Plate 6).

The descendants of Abd al-Razzaq Arafat and his brothers have maintained the connection to this day. The inheritance estate of *Sayyid* Sa'id Arafat (d. 1847), Abd al-Razzaq's grandson, shows that he was a textile merchant in keeping with the family tradition.[33] During the late nineteenth and early twentieth centuries, Kamal al-Din Arafat, Abd al-Razzaq's great-great-grandson (also onetime member of the Nablus Municipal Council and twice mayor [1912, 1915]) also was a textile merchant.[34] A contemporary, Abdullah Arafat, the great-grandson of Abd al-Razzaq's brother, Shaykh Abd al-Ghani Arafat (d. 1823), had his textile shop in the east end of Khan al-Tujjar. He, in turn, was followed by his children, Shaykh Sadiq and Fawzi, as well as by his grandson, Adli Arafat.[35]

The descendants of Muhammad Arafat, another brother of Abd al-Razzaq, headed the strongest line of Arafat textile merchants. His great-grandson, *Hajj* Isma'il Arafat, was the recipient of the letter from Jaba village cited above. Six of *Hajj* Isma'il's seven sons became textile merchants, and they operated from two large stores located in the Wikala al-Farrukhiyya.[36] As late as 1960, the largest textile merchant in Nablus was Tawfiq Arafat, the great-great-great-grandson of Muhammad Arafat. According to Saba Arafat, the granddaughter of *Hajj* Isma'il, his descendants continue to be important proprietors in Khan al-Tujjar.[37]

One reason for choosing the Arafat family as a case study, therefore, is this remarkable continuity, which has left a trail of clues over a long period of time. This makes possible the task of tracing how business practices and modes of reproducing networks were affected by the Ottoman Empire's accelerated incorporation into the world economy during the nineteenth century.

Another reason for choosing this particular family is that the Arafats' business orientation was fairly typical of the overwhelming majority of textile merchants: over the past 250 years, if not longer, they catered primarily to the mass market, particularly peasants in the hinterland. The estate of Shaykh Abd al-Razzaq Arafat, for example, did not contain any of the expensive regional and/or tailored European items of clothing, such as the woolen coats and gold-embroidered jackets, that were produced for the urban upper classes. Rather, the 65 types of textile products in his warehouse consisted of such items as quilts, covers for pillows and mattresses, scarves, locally made handkerchiefs, silk belts, head kerchiefs, and large bolts of white and colored fabrics that were sold by the arm length (*dhira*). The same held true in the inheritance estates of his brother Abd-ullah and his grandson, Saʻid Arafat, as well as in those of the descendants of Shaykh Abd al-Razzaq's two other brothers, Shaykh Abd al-Ghani and Muhammad.[38] Their experiences, therefore, can serve as a convenient lens for viewing that most crucial sphere in the social, cultural, and economic life of an interior merchant town: urban-rural relations.

A case study of the Arafats can also shed light on the meanings of "merchant" and "family" in eighteenth- and nineteenth-century Nablus. Some aspects of their family history—ranging from how they acquired their family name to their social standing and marriage patterns—were characteristic of many other Nabulsi merchant families during this period.

The Making of a Family Name

One of the difficulties of tracing family histories through documentary evidence during this period is that family names were not used by the overwhelming majority of the population, especially peasants. Usually, a male was referred to as *x* son of *y*; his son, as *z* son of *x*; and so on.[39] Only the high-ranking political and religious families—such as Tuqan, Nimr, Jarrar, Jayyusi, Hanbali, Jawhari, Smadi, and Bustami, to mention a few— could boast of stable family names over the centuries. The middle and lower-middle classes, such as merchants and respected artisans, had a more complicated relationship with family names, because family names were, in a sense, a form of property whose value depended on the intimate connections between physical space, economic fortune, social standing, and cultural practices of the household.

The Arabic word for household, *dar*, refers both to an extended family and to an actual physical space. The latter was typically a building with high, thick walls facing the alleyways and streets. A narrow entrance led to an open courtyard ringed by several rooms (*bayt*, pl. *buyut*), each of which housed a nuclear family. Usually, income and resources were thrown together into one pot; and each nuclear family, headed by a son or younger brother of the patriarch, pitched in according to its capabilities and took out according to its needs. Each major life event, such as birth, marriage, or death, brought about a subtle shift in the internal balance among the family members; and the whole household would be restruc-tured to reflect the new realities.[40]

Households were under continuous pressure to reproduce a strong male line, in order to increase their wealth and social standing, maintain their unity, and concentrate their resources for business opportunities and other needs. This required discipline and loyalty to the collective, most often accomplished at the expense of the individual—especially female members, who were married off to cement new alliances and/or were sometimes deprived of their inheritance through various legal or illegal means in order to prevent the dispersal of the household's wealth. The property of children not in their majority at the time of their father's death, as well as of younger brothers in general, was sometimes appropriated by elders concerned with protecting the integrity of the household. The elders' actions could also be interpreted at times as part of an agenda for increasing their own personal standing within the family and outside it.[41]

As a rule, the coming and going of family names reflected the growing or fading fortunes of these households. Some family names disappeared, others were created by upstarts, and some were appropriated by poor folk who wished to attach themselves to a more powerful household.[42] More often than not, however, family names fell victim to the household members' very success in expanding their size and wealth; that is, the spawning of vigorous new branches which split off under a new family name.[43]

The Arafats are such a case. Abd al-Razzaq Arafat's grandfather, Shaykh *Hajj* Abd al-Majid, and his two paternal granduncles, Shaykh Salim and Salih (d. 1724), were referred to as "sons of al-Shahid" (*awlad al-shahid*) in the Islamic court records after their father, Ahmad al-Shahid.[44] The origin of this family name, al-Shahid, is not known, but the facts that the name means "witness" and that most men in the al-Shahid family were religious shaykhs and/or respected callers-to-prayers (*mu'adhdhinin*) suggest that the original patriarch and perhaps his sons were frequent witnesses in the daily cases brought before the Islamic court. In any case, a *waqf* endowment and a *hikr* (lease) document, both transacted in 1737, indicate that the al-Shahid sons—one of whom was a grandfather of Abd al-Razzaq Arafat—had earlier lived in a single household in the Qaryun quarter and that additional rooms were built as the family expanded.[45] To maintain the integrity of the household while it expanded outward, the three brothers endowed the entire property, identified in the court register as "the al-Shahid household" (*dar al-Shahid*), as a joint private family *waqf*, though they did not necessarily continue to live there. By the mid- to the latter part of the eighteenth century, Abd al-Razzaq's father, Arafat son of Abd al-Majid (who, in turn, was a son of Ahmad al-Shahid), had already established his own household in the Yasmina quarter and, before his death, had endowed it as a *waqf* for the benefit of his male and female children.[46]

The endowment of a household's physical space usually indicates a watershed in a household's restructuring as a result of a leap in family fortunes. There is no doubt that Arafat al-Shahid, Abd al-Razzaq's father and already a *hajj* by the 1720s, had made such a leap.[47] One need only mention that he fathered four very successful sons, who built on the family's tradition by combining wealth with high religious and social status.[48] All four came to be called in the Islamic court registers the "sons of Arafat." In adopting the family name Arafat, taken from their father's first name, Abd al-Razzaq and his brothers followed the normal practice of the times.

The key point here is that their sons and grandsons consciously decided not to follow normal practice of adopting the father's first name as a family name. Rather, they defined themselves as part of the Arafat family by adopting that word as their family name regardless of their father's first name. By so doing, they signaled the introduction into the larger community of a new family in the larger meaning of the word; that is, not just a kinship unit but also an economic, political, and social one. This was also an act of exclusion: by maintaining the family name Arafat, they signaled their successful branching off from the other descendants of "the sons of al-Shahid," although they were part of the same kinship unit.[49] In a sense, this was a declaration of intent on their part to draw boundaries within which family members were expected to cooperate and work in tandem on a range of social and economic issues through kin solidarity.

Social Status and Marriage Patterns

The Arafats' success or failure as textile merchants depended on their ability to reproduce and expand the networks that connected their family to peasants in the surrounding villages, as well as to artisans, small retailers, and powerful political, religious, and merchant families in the city. An honored position in society—or what might loosely be called cultural capital—was, in this context, as crucial as actual wealth, or material capital. Indeed, the two were organically linked, and to separate them would project current ideas about boundaries back in time. The linkage between cultural and material capital was essential to the continuity of merchant networks, because the reproduction of these networks depended on the construction of a history through shared memory of particular events, whether actually lived or invented. A peasant could, for example, ask for a loan from a particular merchant by recounting a story of an experience that their respective fathers had shared by way of affirming the tradition of mutual trust that had long bound their two families together. Connections based on tradition, whether real or not, were crucial to a business based on the extension of credit because most peasants, as shall be seen, paid their debts seasonally, at harvest time. Conversely, a merchant might recruit potential customers by highlighting his status as a pious, trustworthy, and dependable figure who enjoyed wide respect. This might ease a peasant's fears about the security of the arrangement ("This merchant would not risk his reputation by cheating me") and would provide him with essential contacts within the city ("This merchant can open doors for me.")

In other words, cultural capital was the glue that held these networks together. The surest way for merchants to accumulate this type of capital was through the cultivation of religious status, whether by means of education, marriage into a well-known family of religious scholars, service in a mosque, charity to religious institutions, or membership in a Sufi order. Combining a religious career with a business career was the norm rather than the exception and had the aura of a time-honored tradition. The religion-trade connection was so deeply ingrained, in fact, that the very language of merchants was, and still is, heavily coded with religious phrases. This does not mean that religion was used cynically as a tool of manipulation. Rather, it served as a medium of communication that reinforced actual or perceived attitudes and behavior. The aim was not to encourage popularity as much as to instill authority and respect, on the one hand, and to build a sound reputation for piety, honesty, trustworthiness, and moral uprightness, on the other. From the seventeenth to the twentieth centuries many of the Arafat men, like members of other established merchant families, were educated religious scholars, as indicated by their titles in the family tree, depicted in Plate 6.[50]

Charity (*zakat*) was also important: it was a religious duty incumbent upon any Muslim with means, and it fostered a reputation for caring and generosity. According to the (admittedly sympathetic) recollections of Saba Arafat, "My grandfather [*Hajj* Isma'il] made a habit of providing dinner for all mourners of a bereaved family and their friends in the neighborhood ... [and] my uncle Ahmad arranged for quantities of freshly baked bread to be given free to the poor every Friday. His son, Tawfiq, gave the poor in his neighborhood a banquet during [the Holy Month of] Ramadan. The latter custom was followed by a few other merchants in Nablus."[51]

Marriage alliances were key, as well. In the case of the Arafats, the dominant pattern was intrafamily marriage: as a general rule, Arafat men married Arafat women, or gave their daughters to other Arafat men. This protected the property and wealth of the family from fragmentation. This pattern was perhaps already in place in the eighteenth century, but it certainly was practiced in the nineteenth century, as the various court documents show in cases involving the sons and daughters of the four brothers.[52]

When the Arafat men and women did marry outside the family, the choices showed a clear preference for those individuals who combined high religious status with ownership of soap factories and, to a lesser extent, involvement in the textile trade. Abd al-Razzaq, for example, married into both the Hanbali and the Fityan families.[53] The Fityanis had a long tradition of involvement in the textile trade and were also known as a family of religious scholars. Some of its members, for example, served as superintendents of the Nasr Mosque's *waqf* properties from at least the eighteenth century until the latter part of the nineteenth century.[54] The Hashim branch of the Hanbali family, meanwhile, produced some of the top religious scholars in Nablus during the Ottoman period. At the same time, they maintained a long tradition of involvement in soap production (see Chapter 5). These two qualities, especially the latter, were shared by most of the other families with whom the Arafats established ties through marriage: Bashsha, Qadi-Shwayka, Shammut, Sadder, Tamimi, Tuffaha, and Bishtawi.[55]

The reasons for these choices are fairly clear. The Arafats come from a long tradition of educated religious figures; hence their wish to ally with families that enjoyed similar status. It is interesting to note, however, that the number of Arafat shaykhs declined markedly during the middle of the nineteenth century while the title *sayyid* began to be applied to almost all of them. The title of *sayyid* indicated descent from the Prophet Muhammad and, during this period, designated that the individual was exempt from certain taxes. A number of wealthy merchant families acquired the title of *sayyid* for the first time during this period, and it is highly likely that their claim of descent from the Prophet was an invented one. In this regard, the Arafats' connection to the Hanbali family, which dominated the post of *naqib al-ashraf*, probably proved helpful.[56] Indeed, the Hashims received the largest share of exogenous marriages.[57]

Alliances with soap merchants and manufacturers were also of great importance. There was a critical link between the export of soap and the import of textiles, and some members of the Arafat family belonged to this privileged elite of soap merchants and manufacturers. It is not a coincidence, therefore, that marriage patterns and business relations of the first two or three generations who adopted the family name Arafat, inasmuch as they married outside the family, favored those merchant households whose primary regional trade networks were concentrated in Egypt—such as the Balbisi (originally from the town of Bilbays, in Egypt), Kawkash, Ghazzawi, Jardani, Bishtawi, Jurri, Darwish-Ahmad, Hanbali, Tamimi, and Tuffaha, among others. Until the 1840s Egypt was still the primary source of imported textiles. It was also the largest market for Nabulsi soap—and had been so since Mamluk times, if not much earlier. Not surprisingly, therefore, these merchants constituted a network of their own: their members had joint business ventures, were co-owners of urban commercial real estate, and frequently served as each others' legal agents and witnesses.[58]

REGIONAL TRADE NETWORKS

The shops in Khan al-Tujjar carried a variety of cloth from all over the world, and textile merchants from India, Baghdad, Mosul, and Aleppo, among others, paid regular visits to Nablus.[59] But these direct contacts were marginal: Nablus had neither the size nor the location that would allow one to speak of patterns of international trade. Rather, it was regional trade within the Ottoman Empire—stretching from the Arabian Peninsula to Anatolia and from Iraq to Egypt—with which Nabulsi merchants were most familiar. Even then, the majority of regional trade connections were concentrated around the two cities whose spheres of influence overshadowed all of Palestine: Cairo and Damascus.[60]

Until the first half of the nineteenth century, Cairo and other Egyptian cities were the major source of textiles for Nabulsi merchants. By the latter part of this century, however, Beirut and Damascus took the lead. This spatial shift carried within it a number of other changes in the ways in which regional textile-trade networks were organized. These changes can be traced by examining the estates and business practices of two Arafat merchants who inhabited opposite ends of the nineteenth century: Shaykh Abd al-Razzaq (d. 1810) and *Hajj* Isma'il (d. 1903/1904).

Egypt

The estates of Shaykh Abd al-Razzaq, his brother Abdullah (registered in 1805), and the former's grandson, Sa'id (d. 1847), contained a wide variety of textiles: *dima, saya,* and a host of other goods from Damascus; locally manufactured products, such as *thiyab baladi;* the fez (*tarbush*) from North Africa; silk from Beirut; *alaja* from Damascus and Aleppo; *malti* (also called *mansuri* and *baft*) from England, cashmere from India; and various items from Hama, Anatolia, Mosul, Baghdad, and Istanbul.[61] But in terms of volume and value, their estates—like those of most other wholesale textile merchants who operated during the eighteenth century and first half of the nineteenth centuries—were dominated by the words *dimyati, ziftawi, wati, ashmuni, mahallawi, sirsawi* and *mawaldi*—all of which refer to specific regions in Egypt, such as Ashmun, Damietta (Dimyat), Mahalla, and Zifta.[62] These were imported in large bundles (*farda*), consisting of long bolts of cloth that were dyed and tailored in Nablus.

The general outlines of how the textile trade networks with Egypt were organized can be gleaned from a lawsuit dated August 7, 1812.[63] The beneficiaries of the inheritance estates of Shaykh Abd al-Razzaq Arafat and his brother, Shaykh *Hajj* Abdullah, were sued, along with five other textile merchants with operations in Egypt, by *Sayyid* Abdullah Qutub, a resident of Jaffa.[64] The plaintiff alleged that ten years earlier his father had received goods from Egypt for the above merchants via the port of Jaffa. At that time, the city was under siege by the late Ahmad Pasha al-Jazzar, and circumstances were such that the besieged strongman, Muhammad Pasha, forced the plaintiff's now-deceased father, *Sayyid* Muhammad Qutub, to pay him the customs and storage costs of the goods. The plaintiff demanded that each defendant pay back his share of the costs, which amounted to 730 piasters, a sum large enough to purchase two *buyut* at that time.

The defendants, all present in the Nablus Islamic Court, categorically denied the charges and claimed that a letter had previously arrived from Muhammad Pasha in which he testified to having received no moneys for customs and storage from the plaintiff's father. The judge asked the plaintiff to prove his allegations, but he could produce no witnesses. The lawsuit was dropped.

As this case illustrates, imported Egyptian textiles were usually transported by sea to Jaffa, where they were received by agents for Nabulsi merchants. These agents cleared the goods through the port authorities and arranged for overland transportation. This case also shows that Nabulsi merchants banded together into groups, ranging from full business partnerships to simple joint-shipping agreements. The chief reason for collective arrangements, aside from the need to pool capital, was to share risks, as demonstrated by this very case. Although these political uncertainties complicated regional trade, they were never a serious long-term obstacle to it. The primary reason is that the moneys generated by this trade were crucial to the political strongmen who competed, sometimes violently, for their share of the profits. This is why credit arrangements were both imperative and extensively used: it simply was not practical to move large amounts of cash back and forth across physically and politically dangerous terrain.

It is not a small matter that this lawsuit was initiated in the Nablus Islamic Court ten years after the event—and by the son of the aggrieved party, to boot. The Nablus Islamic Court, one of dozens of similar courts spread all over the vast Ottoman Empire, served as a commonly recognized arena for arbitration. That the plaintiff was able to find these merchants and pursue them after such a long time strongly suggests that his father's business relationship with them was not a casual one, free of personal connections. In fact, the Qutub family originated from the same Egyptian city, Bilbays, as did the Balbisi and Darwish-Ahmad families— two of whose members were among the defendants.[65] A branch of the Qutub family resided in Nablus, where they dealt in soap and had business relations with the Arafats and other textile merchants. The use of relatives and acquaintances as agents outside Nablus, in short, imparted resiliency and flexibility to regional networks and facilitated their smooth operation over long distances and under uncertain conditions. Finally, it is not surprising that the defendants did not break rank: they also shared something deeper than just a business relationship or even a common place of origin. As noted above, the defendants belonged to families that were interconnected in a complex web of mutual interests, ranging from co-ownership of shops and residential proximity to marriage ties.

Because long-distance trade with Egypt demanded large initial investments of capital, Nabulsi textile merchants usually pooled their money and sent one or more of the partners to Egypt to make arrangements for the purchase, storage, shipping, and payment.[66] In Cairo and Damietta, Nabulsi merchants, like their counterparts in Greater Syria as a whole, maintained offices, homes, and warehouses staffed by themselves, their relatives, or local agents.[67] According to Nimr, Nabulsi merchants preferred to send one of their own instead of depending on local agents,[68] and the available evidence shows that many Nabulsi merchants lived in Egypt.[69] Indeed, Nabulsi residents of Egypt sometimes went before the Islamic Court in Cairo or Damietta to transact the sale or purchase of real estate in Nablus or to appoint one of their partners as guardian for their children in case they did not come back alive.[70] Sudden death, especially while far from Nablus, was usually followed by a number of complicated lawsuits as both family members and business partners sought to protect, if not increase, their share of the deceased's business properties—often at the expense of vulnerable women and children.

An example is the lengthy dispute that followed the death of a very rich soap merchant, *Hajj* Hasan Safar. In August 1864 a guardian of one of *Hajj* Hasan's sons (who was still in his minority) demanded that the son's rightful share be paid out of the inheritance estate, which he claimed amounted to 630,000 piasters, according to documents prepared by the judge of Jerusalem.[71] The defendants tried to lower the actual worth of the estate by outlining a long chain of events that involved the partners and agents of the deceased in Cairo, Jeddah, and Damietta. Their detailed defense confirms that the major market for Nabulsi soap at that time was the city of Cairo, where the deceased had three agents—two from Nablus and one from Egypt. Jeddah and Damietta, in contrast, had only one agent each.

This court case also shows that the agents paid customs on soap received from Nablus and stored it in warehouses. Thereafter, they were free to decide on both the buyers and the timing of the sale, and they made arrangements for the transfer of money to Nablus, as needed. Terribly important—and this was the crux of testimony—was the timing of the sale, which usually meant the difference between a loss and a large profit margin. Hoarding, it seems, was a complicated and risky practice that tested the mettle of the agents, the strength of their knowledge of the market, and their connections to political figures and other merchants.

The Arafats, of course, were keenly aware of the importance of their agents' role in the sale of soap in Egypt. This was because most textile merchants, including the Arafats, arranged for the sale of soap in Egypt, the profits from which were used to purchase textiles that were then imported to Nablus. It is no surprise, therefore, that the inheritance estates of Abd al-Razzaq, Abdullah, and Sa'id Arafat all included significant amounts of soap.[72] Soap was the critical link in the textile trade with Egypt because this commodity provided Nabulsi textile merchants with a good opportunity to avoid depletion of their liquid capital: instead of transferring cash, they shipped soap that they bought at a low price in Nablus and sold at a high price in Egypt. Soap was the preferred item in this indirect exchange, partly because it fetched a good price, had a long shelf life (which gave flexibility to the crucial timing of sales), and was easy to transport. Most important, Nabulsi soap was much esteemed in Egypt and enjoyed a consistently high demand. The Egyptian market absorbed approximately three-fifths of Palestine's entire soap production in the

1830s,[73] and averaged roughly about three-quarters of Nablus's soap production throughout the Ottoman period.[74]

Beirut and Damascus

In the late nineteenth and early twentieth centuries *Hajj* Isma'il Arafat, great-grandson of Shaykh Abd al-Razzaq's brother, Muhammad, shared a number of similarities with his ancestors. Like them, he was a textile merchant who owned shops in Khan al-Tujjar and who catered primarily to the mass market. Unlike them, he bought and sold primarily Syrian and British textiles, as opposed to Egyptian ones; his regional network came to be organized differently, especially in terms of credit arrangements; and his capital-accumulation strategy was diversified when he bought a soap factory from Mahmud Hashim, thus sinking a significant proportion of the family's resources into the burgeoning soap industry.[75]

Hajj Isma'il first wife, Aysha Arafat, was said to be a very beautiful woman. She died young, but not before bearing her husband two sons: Ahmad and Amr. The older son, Ahmad, eventually established his own textile shop in the western end of Khan al-Tujjar, where he sold the same types of goods as did his father. The younger son, Shaykh Amr, married Wasfiyya Hashim, granddaughter of the above-mentioned Mahmud Hashim. Her father, Husayn Hashim, was a textile merchant and one-time *mufti* of Nablus. Shaykh Amr became a well-respected religious scholar, having studied at al-Azhar University in Cairo and in Istanbul. He worked as a judge in Nablus until 1912/1913, then built a soap factory and continued in the soap business until 1950, when he retired.

After the death of his first wife, *Hajj* Isma'il remarried, this time a woman from the Sadder family of soap and textile merchants. His second wife bore him five sons. Hammad, the oldest of the five, took over his father's textile shops and worked there along with his younger brothers. According to Najib Arafat, *Hajj* Isma'il's youngest son (b. 1901):

> I worked with textiles since I opened my eyes. We bought goods from Beirut, Aleppo, Damascus, Jaffa, and Jerusalem. Aside from Syrian manufactures, most goods came from England, though we had a variety. My father had two shops that faced each other east to west in the Wikala al-Farrukhiyya. Each shop was two stories high. The second story was reserved mostly for tailors who rented the space from us. A peasant would come to us, and if he wanted his piece tailored, we would send it upstairs and the tailor would get his fee from the peasant directly.[76]

Najib's recollections are supported by detailed information about the same period contained in the memoirs of Muhammad Izzat Darwaza, whose father, like *Hajj* Isma'il, owned a textile shop in Khan al-Tujjar and catered primarily to the mass peasant market. During his childhood, Darwaza recalled:

> The import of [textile] goods from the outside was, for the most part, through Beirut and Damascus. From Beirut came a variety of foreign clothes, whether cotton, wool, or silk. From Damascus came the domesti-cally made [*wataniyya*] textiles and manufactures. These were popular to the point that almost all the clothes of peasants and middle and lower ur-ban classes were made of it from head to toe. The exceptions were the white cotton cloth called *baft* and the off-white cloth that was called *malti* or *mansuri* or *kham*, from which shirts and baggy pants [*sarawil*] were made and with which Damascene textiles were lined. [*Mansuri* cloth] came mostly from British lands and was also used as quilts and bed covers. Some types of *baft* [cloth] were dyed with indigo blue in local factories and made into clothes by peasants and bedouin.[77]

In short, whereas Shaykh Abd al-Razzaq's regional trade network was oriented primarily south, toward Egypt, that of *Hajj* Isma'il and his sons pointed north, toward Damascus and Beirut. The causes and timing of this shift are familiar. By the early nineteenth century, European (primarily British) machine-produced textiles began to carve out a large market share in Greater Syria—a process enhanced by the lowering of tariffs and the abolition of monopolies after the free-trade Anglo-Ottoman Commercial Convention was signed in 1838. Most of these goods were imported through Beirut, which was fast becoming the principal port of entry for Greater Syria, or through the coastal cities of Jaffa and Haifa.

On the regional level, the direction of commercial flow was influenced by Ottoman centralization during the *Tanzimat* period, which tied Jabal Nablus ever closer, politically and economically, to the body politic of Greater Syria. In addition, infrastructural projects and services initiated during the second half of the nineteenth century—such as expanded ports, steamships, carriage roads, railroads, and telegraph lines—facilitated transportation and communication between Damascus, Beirut, and other cities and towns in this region. Regional and local factors also played a role. One such factor was the ability of the Damascene textile-manufac-turing sector to restructure in the face of European competition.[78] As the above two accounts suggest, the Damascene textile industry survived, al-beit much changed. This can be seen in the ways in which English, Dama-scene, and local textiles were literally woven together into a variety of finished products. Regional textile manufacturers not only were able to maintain a market share in the surrounding areas but also expanded that share as Damascene and Beiruti merchant capital extended more deeply into the Palestinian interior.

A second important difference was that whereas Shaykh Abd al-Razzaq and his brothers usually formed joint business ventures with a number of other textile merchant families and employed agents in Cairo, Damietta, and Jaffa, *Hajj* Isma'il and his sons, like most other textile merchants in Nablus, operated individually for the most part. One reason for this change, aside from better and safer communication, was the greater accumulation and concentration of merchant capital over the course of the nineteenth century (see Chapter 5).[79] This allowed well-to-do textile merchants in Nablus to raise the necessary initial capital without recourse to partners. A third difference was that textile merchants no longer invested as much capital in the finishing stages of production, such as dyeing and weaving. Imported fabrics were sold as is, and tailoring either was done by the merchant and his family or was contracted out.

The fourth difference was that the textile merchants of Nablus found it more and more difficult to compete with the few but much richer Beiruti and Damascene families who came to dominate regional trade in Greater Syria. Eventually they were subordinated to the position of middlemen between the large trade houses in Beirut and Damascus and the peasantry in Jabal Nablus. Thus, instead of employing agents, each merchant had his private account with these trade houses. Largely due to a more favorable legal and political climate and to more rapid and more efficient transportation by the late nineteenth century, both Beiruti and Damascene merchants acquired the confidence and ability to extend numerous credit lines to smaller merchants in the interior cities and towns. Over time, Beiruti merchants—as well as those of other port cities, such as Jaffa and Haifa—succeeded in establishing themselves as the indispensable go-betweens for the import/export trade with Europe. Large Damascene textile merchants, meanwhile, doubled as manufacturers of textiles geared for the mass regional market and developed their own trademarks.

The following account of what probably was a typical business trip by Nabulsi textile merchants to Beirut and Damascus, also culled from Darwaza's memoirs, best illustrates the general points made above.[80] At least once a year, Nabulsi merchants went personally to choose the types of goods they needed to stock their shops and to negotiate prices. The trip to Jaffa, Beirut, and Damascus, and back became easier and quicker with time. To Jaffa, the trip took only a few hours by carriage, compared to a day and a half on a mule before roads for wheeled transport were paved. From this ancient port city, Nabulsi merchants traveled on ships to Beirut.

The first morning in that bustling city—after eating breakfast, drinking coffee, and smoking water pipes at *Hajj* Dawud's cafe, one of their favorite haunts in al-Burj Square—they trekked to Suq al-Tawila, the heart of the textile commercial sector in Beirut, especially for foreign-manufactured goods. There, Nabulsi merchants visited one warehouse after another, chose fabrics, and bargained over prices.

Those who had sufficient capital paid on the spot and received a discount as a bonus. The majority, however, depended on loans from Beiruti merchants, who advanced the capital with interest. At the conclusion of each deal the materials were sent to one or another of the warehouses owned by these merchants who were called *jarrida* (from the verb *jarada:* to take stock or to make an inventory). In Beirut, Nabulsi merchants usually relied on people such as Musbah Qraytim and on others from the Zu'ni, Sharif, and Ghandur families.

In addition to advancing loans and providing storage facilities, the *jarrida* arranged for packaging and shipping—for a fee, of course. Specialized workers (*akkamin*) packed the cloth into bundles (*farda* or *hazma*), secured them with a thin rope (*massis*), and sent the goods via boat to Jaffa, where they were received by employees of the Beirut merchants, not agents of Nabulsi ones. From Jaffa, camel transporters—often the group called *harafisha*[81]—moved the goods to Nablus.

After finishing their business in Beirut, Nabulsi textile merchants traveled to Damascus, where they repeated the pattern, but with some important differences. First, there is no doubt that Nabulsi merchants felt much more at home in the conservative, traditional atmosphere of a sister interior city and that they established close personal relations with the merchants who supplied them with the goods. This was especially true for the Damascene Haffar family, who were friends with *Hajj* Isma'il Arafat and his children and grandchildren, as well as with the Darwaza and Masri families, among others.[82]

The *jarrida* of Damascus differed from their Beirut counterparts in that they doubled as manufacturers who operated their own production facilities, each with a distinct trademark that became well known in Nablus.[83] For example, in a letter to Isma'il Arafat, a villager named Uthman Abd al-Wahhab requested *dima* cloth of the "Haffari" kind, in reference to the Haffar family.[84] It was also in Damascus that Nabulsi merchants were most likely to find cloth made in Aleppo, Mosul, Baghdad, and India. The majority of Damascene textiles exported to Nablus consisted of a large variety of cotton and cotton/silk materials—especially *dima* cloth—all of which were used to make the most common male outergarment, the *qunbaz.* Otherwise, Damascene agents fulfilled the same basic economic function: they advanced credit with interest and arranged for storage, packaging, and shipping. From Damascus, textile goods were shipped overland by camel transporters, usually by residents of the Hauran region.

To collect their credit advances, the *jarrida* of Beirut and Damascus employed agents in Nablus who kept abreast of the retail market and collected on a weekly basis. The Haffars' office, for example, was conveniently located in Khan al-Tujjar. The length of the repayment period depended on how fast the Nablus textile merchants were able to sell their goods. Payment, according to Darwaza, was usually made in the form of gold coins, which were sent to Damascus and Beirut through the postal service. Occasionally there were disputes, and the *jarrida* had to visit Nablus personally and collect their debt through lawsuits.

For example, on December 27, 1862, the following lawsuit by a Damascene against two Nabulsi merchants was registered in the Nablus Islamic Court:

> On August 20, 1862, the honorable Rashid *Agha* Jabri the Damascene proved that he was owed the sum of 34,530 piasters by Ahmad Masri and his brother, Muhammad Masri. . . . Yet, since that date, they have stubbornly refused to pay the rest of the debt they owed. . . . Rashid *Agha* appeared before the court and testified that [the defendants] had commercial inventories and requested that the court order these inventories to be sold in order to pay back the debt. The aforementioned were brought to court and ordered to pay back the debt and to sell the inventories.[85]

Debt-collection cases of this kind began to appear in the Nablus Islamic Court registers only after the mid-nineteenth century. The same can be said about cases in which Nabulsi merchants brought peasants into the city to appear before the court on debt charges. Both developments stand in stark contrast to the period before Ottoman troops regained direct control of the region. Then, Nabulsi merchants in general and foreign merchants in particular would have found it extremely difficult to approach these matters directly, much less to enforce the collection of debts through the urban administrative and legal apparatus. Instead, they found it more convenient to rely on the leading political families of Nablus to for leverage. An example is a receipt, dated April 20, 1837, found among the private papers of the Nimr family. Signed by *Sayyid* Abd al-Ghani son of *Sayyid* Ali al-Sawwaf (wool dealer), this receipt was sent from Damascus to Ahmad *Agha* Nimr, scion of the Nimr family at the time and head of the local *sipahis:*

I . . . testify that in the month of February 1837 I turned over promissory notes, owed to me by debtors, to Ahmad *Agha* Nimr to cash the full amount [5,500 piasters] and to buy us soap with it. The above-mentioned . . . sent us the soap, and it arrived in . . . Damascus by way of his agent, Shaykh Sulayman al-Banna. . . . Ahmad *Agha* Nimr owes us nothing whatsoever [whether it be] in [business] account, safekeeping, or debt.[86]

Unlike the Haffar family, this Damascene merchant, who probably supplied woolens to Nablus textile traders, had neither agents to collect his money in gold nor even, perhaps, the expectation that he could collect his debt personally. Rather, he depended on the services of one of the locally powerful political families. The latter's payment was not in cash but in soap. Part of the reason for this arrangement was that soap was akin to liquid capital because of the high demand for it in Damascus and the opportunity it afforded the Damascene merchant to resell at a profit.[87] Payment in soap also benefited Ahmad *Agha* Nimr. First, he owned a soap factory, and this arrangement included a hidden profit in that it assured a sale for his own products. Second, he did not have to actually wait for the debtors to pay what they owed before shipping the soap. Instead, he could reschedule the debts and collect further interest or reach a variety of other arrangements with the debtors, most of whom were no doubt familiar to him.

Of course, it is very possible that the Masri brothers simply ignored the court order. Nevertheless, the very recourse of that merchant to the Nablus court implies that the contrary could also be expected. Thus, whereas earlier a local politically powerful person had been indispensable for the circulation of merchant capital, the new political climate allowed merchants to bypass these families, at least in the first stages of the debt-collection process. This development might not have been beneficial to all merchants, especially the smaller ones, because even though the previous debt-collection arrangements were informal and were precariously dependent on personal contacts, they had the advantage of being more flexible: money, as it were, was mediated through a number of cultural/political filters that refracted the cold and impersonal letter of the law. The establishment of an enforceable administrative/legal framework— such as the Advisory Council, commercial courts, and a more centralized Ottoman bureaucracy—significantly raised the power of large merchants over retailers and peasants. The power of money was now less fettered with personal ties, boding ill for the weak, the poor, and the unlucky, who could not avoid the debt traps or seek protection from their former patrons.

The changing patterns of regional trade in textiles and credit-collection arrangements are important indicators of how the integration of Jabal Nablus into the world and regional economies was actually experienced during the nineteenth century. True, the Arafats continued their work as textile merchants generation after generation, but the content of what it meant to be such a merchant changed perceptibly after the mid-nineteenth century. The environment of trade was slowly transformed, the bulk of connections shifted northward from Egypt to Syria, and even the products themselves became different as foreign manufactures established a foothold in the local markets. Nabulsi textile merchants, in general, became less important players in the regional trade in textiles, as indicated by the declining significance of soap to imports and by the growing domination of this market by merchant families from the port cities and from Damascus.

Urban-rural relations, not the wider world of regional networks, were the center of consciousness for most of the people in Jabal Nablus, though they were all affected to varying degrees by forces beyond their control. To dig more deeply into the culture of trade and the systems of meanings it helped create, therefore, we must examine the other side of the coin: how the Arafats and other textile merchants constructed and reproduced the local trade networks through which they marketed their goods among the peasantry in the surrounding hinterland. Here continuity, tradition, and personal connections were of even greater importance. Consequently, local networks were more deeply rooted than regional ones and less vulnerable to the winds of change.

LOCAL TRADE NETWORKS

In relation to its hinterland, the city of Nablus was the queen bee. It needed the peasants' surplus to survive, and it often depended on peasant militia to maintain its relative autonomy vis-à-vis regional powers and the Ottoman state. In return, it provided the peasants with the commodities they could not produce, the services they required, and a set of political and cultural departure points to the larger Ottoman world. The activities of local trade and manufacturing, therefore, absorbed the energies of the vast majority of Nabulsis, and much of what this city meant to its inhabitants in terms of daily life was informed by a primordial set of relations: those connecting it to the surrounding hinterland.

Because textile products were the most ubiquitous commodity of local trade and because the Arafats' primary customers, over many generations, have been the inhabitants of the hinterland—there is perhaps no better window on these multilayered connections than the local textile trade networks of this family. An examination of the inner workings of these networks and of how they have changed over time allows for a history from below of the dynamic roles that merchants and peasants together played in the constant reinvention of Jabal Nablus.

Space

The main arteries of local trade branched off the regional trade roads and wound through the hills and valleys to the larger villages. These, in turn, served as hubs for the surrounding clusters of smaller villages, two to three hundred in number, depending on the time period and the reach of Nabulsi merchants. Until the construction of carriage roads and railways in the late nineteenth century, movement was slow and difficult. The most prevalent means of local transport was the donkey, and two of the most familiar sights along the well-trodden paths were the pack animals of hired transporters (*makaris*) and the itinerant merchants (*haddars*). The *makaris*, often poor peasants with little or no land, moved goods and people back and forth for a fee. The *haddars*, usually from Nablus, Jenin, or one of the larger villages, hawked such things as textiles, cooking utensils, and shoes, especially during the harvest season, when they could exchange their goods for grains or olive oil.[88]

The physical network of paths etched on the limestone hills and brown valleys of Jabal Nablus also served as social, economic, and political boundaries for a multitude of local trade networks. The merchants of Nablus—especially the large textile wholesalers and the purchasers of the major agricultural products such as olive oil, cotton, and grains—literally carved the countryside into discrete spheres of influence, each merchant cultivating a thick web of relations with particular clans and villages. For example, Shaykh Abd al-Razzaq Arafat's peasant customers primarily came from the large but geographically dispersed villages of Kafr Qaddum, Jamma'in, Til, and Ya'bad.[89] Those of *Hajj* Isma'il Arafat a century later included Kafr Qaddum, Jaba, Tammun, and Dayr Istiya.[90] The most loyal customers of his son, Ahmad, and grandson, Tawfiq, came from Jaba, Silat al-Dhaher, Faqu'a, and Turmus Ayya. As for *Hajj* Isma'il's five youngest sons who were partners in the textile trade, their business was concentrated in Jaba, Silat al-Dhaher, Sanur, Maythalun, and Bayt Leed.[91] The largest concentration of these villages was in the Mashariq al-Jarrar subdistrict.

A merchant's access to these villages, as well as his ability to collect debts, depended on his relations not only with their residents but also with ruling families, both rural and urban, who dominated these villages politically and/or had substantial economic interests in them. In the case of the Arafats, this meant close relations with the once-powerful Jarrar clan that had ruled the northeastern part of Jabal Nablus for so long. Judging from letters sent by Ibrahim Khalil Jarrar to *Hajj* Isma'il Arafat, it seems that the former was a regular customer around the turn of the twentieth century.[92] On December 26, 1899, for example, Ibrahim Jarrar requested that he be sent, without delay, a caftan and a scarf. After specifying the colors, pattern, and sizes, he recounted moneys sent previously in order to correct any misunderstandings in his account. To this letter, in which he addressed *Hajj* Isma'il as "sir" and "our father," he appended a note that read: "Sir, beware and take care not to hand over anything to my sons unless they have a sealed letter from me"—implying that they sometimes abused this long-standing relationship and ran up their father's tab.[93]

The division of the hinterland into market shares, to use modern terminology, was not unique to merchants. Jabal Nablus was entangled by dozens of overlapping formal and informal networks: the political networks of urban ruling families and the rural subdistrict chiefs, the fiscal networks of *sipahi* officers and tax farmers, and the religious networks of Sufi leaders. These networks were not mutually exclusive, and the interaction in the shared spaces between them molded the overall political, cultural, and social landscape and determined the rhythms and dynamics of everyday life. Any major shift in the boundaries of these shared spaces reverberated through the entire social formation of Jabal Nablus, reconfiguring alliances and patterns of power and trade. Such, for example, was the effect of the Egyptian occupation in 1831.

Merchant networks were of the informal type: they neither required official sanction nor depended on the coercive power of the state. Rather, merchants and leading political families cooperated, and increasingly so during the course of the nineteenth century, in such matters as securing roads, enforcing contracts, and extracting debts. To maintain and reproduce their networks, therefore, Nabulsi merchants lent monies and made commercial opportunities available to political leaders. At the same time, they used a variety of economic and extraeconomic means to forge an intimate bond with their peasant clients.

These practices were not unique to Jabal Nablus. Merchant networks that relied on personal ties and patronage were the norm in societies characterized by a vigorous commercial life within the context of decentralized political structures. The most effective way to sustain movement and exchange across space and time in such an environment was through multiple layers of negotiation based on commonly held assumptions and on accountability between the actors. This meant that peasants were not passive actors and that their communities were not simply carved into spheres of influence, as the language above implies. On the contrary, peasants actively participated in the networking process, had choices and options as to what merchants to do business with, and possessed their own bargaining tools, such as nonpayment and relocation.

Economically, the primary link between merchants and peasants was the provision of credit services, given that payment was normally delayed until the harvest season. In addition, each merchant's shop served as a bank of sorts: peasants could open an account by depositing goods and money, and they could draw on that account and/or ask for credit during subsequent visits. Culturally, we have already discussed the importance of religion, trustworthiness, and a sound reputation to the very meaning of "merchant." Socially, merchants reinforced their trade networks by serving as the peasant's "key to the city." Textile merchants did much more than just sell goods on credit to loyal clients: they were brokers, who provided a wide range of services, as well as social acquaintances. They visited peasants in their villages, attended their weddings, and exchanged favors and gifts.[94] They also provided food and accommodations for their peasant customers visiting the city (that is why there were no boarding houses for peasants in Nablus), intervened on their behalf with other merchants, and offered their stores as a shopping headquarters for their rural clients.

In short, merchants linked culture with social practice and economic exchange to construct a resilient and flexible fiber that wove the various parts of Jabal Nablus into a single fabric and its inhabitants into a single social formation. The above generalizations are best illustrated through a discussion of weddings, because the purchase of textiles associated with this social ritual was the backbone of the textile merchant's business in the hinterland.

Weddings

Sometime around the end of the nineteenth century, *Hajj* Isma'il Arafat received the following letter from a peasant who was preparing to attend a wedding:

Our Respected Brother, *Abu* Ahmad . . .

After inquiring about that most dear to us, the health of your Noble Person, I put before you that since you will be receiving, through Mustafa Abd al-Latif, 2.5 French liras, 0.25 Majidi, 5 piasters, 1.5 bishlik, and 1 Majidi riyal, for a total of 336 [piasters], you might find it convenient to fill our order. We need a Haffari *dimaya* of pleasing form and fixed color; a dark-colored cloak [*abaya*] like the one you sent us earlier, with a head cover . . . and of a kind that you know to be of good quality. The [cloak's] length should be to below the knee. [Also send us] a fez and shoes. For the ladies, [send us] two and a half good-quality pieces of Haffari *dima* of fixed color, so that [the women] can tailor them at home. [Also], four arms' lengths of *mansuri* [cloth] and a large fez . . . and, very important, two undergarments, four pieces of good-quality *ibrim ansiri*, and four ladies' handkerchiefs. Make a bill of sale for the value of the goods, so that we could sign on to it verbally and in writing, as we did last year. Trustworthiness is yours; please do not worry [about the payment] and convey our regards to your children, and we wish you all the best.

> Yours,
> Uthman Abd al-Wahhab

[P.S.] We hope that you can send us the cloak immediately, before the other goods, because the one I have is no longer adequate. [For] *you are well aware that there is a wedding coming up at Abu Muhammad's, and a new cloak is important for a good image because strangers as well as relatives will be attending.* In any case, if you do not have [such a cloak], please get it from someone else. If no one has the kind I described to you earlier, send us a good-quality one made out of wool.[95]

The above is one of many such letters involving the purchase of textiles in preparation for a wedding. Religious holidays and major life events all were occasions for the purchase of clothes, but weddings were the most important by far. Like other rituals, weddings served many purposes: enhancing or affirming status, redistributing wealth among poor family members and neighbors, making allies, reconciling enemies, and sealing kinship bonds. Weddings, in short, were important exercises in power and influence and were central to the formation and cementing of ties within peasant clans and village communities.[96]

The purchase of clothes for weddings was a major social, economic, cultural, and political undertaking. The bride and groom were not the only ones who received clothes. Depending on the amount of resources available, the state of relations between families and clans, parents, paternal and maternal uncles, other relatives, neighbors, and even leaders of other clans in the village could also expect to receive gifts of clothes.[97] The aim was to reinforce clan solidarity, to recognize the importance of the village collective, and to secure the blessings of both.

In the estates of Shaykh Abd al-Razzaq Arafat and of his grandson, Sa'id, one can find all the varieties of textiles usually worn by peasants, especially items for weddings: silk belts (sing. *zinnar harir*), brightly colored silk headbands (sing. *asaba*), scarves (*manadil*), and plenty of *kamkh*, a type of velvet traditionally worn at weddings.[98] These and other basic items of formal outerwear for men and women, when put together, formed a *kiswa*.

According to Darwaza, "A few [Khan al-Tujjar] merchants sell textiles that only city people use. Most sell textiles used by both the city and village people, and most of those trade primarily in the *kiswa* needs of village people."[99] Although the word *kiswa* is popularly associated with the clothes bought for a bride before her wedding, it was also used in a much more general sense to refer to a set of clothes or wardrobe which might include nontextile items, such as shoes or jewelry.[100]

Each type of *kiswa* had specific components. These components differed according to local preferences and changed over time. Both Darwaza and Masri described the specific components of various *kiswas* and the ways in which they were prepared. Darwaza, for example, noted that at around the turn of the twentieth century many large textile merchants prepared the basic *kiswas* of daily wear in advance and sold them as ready packages to peasants:

> Some [merchants in Khan al-Tujjar] prepared *kiswas* for village people [consisting] of *qanabiz* [sing. *qunbaz*], *sadari* [waistcoats], *qumsan* [shirts], and *sarawil* [trousers]. Some were good at tailoring, so they cut [clothes], then put them out to home-based women who sewed them. Some sent the clothes to tailors. . . . My father and other colleagues were the kind who prepared *kiswas* and sold them ready-made. My father and grandfather used to cut the cloth with their own hands and then send them to our women and the women of our neighbors to sew them.[101]

Malik Masri, who learned the trade from his father and paternal uncles, wrote that wedding *kiswas* during the early twentieth century always included a silk *saya* (a type of *qunbaz*) and cloaks, the most expensive of which were made out of camel hair. He added that many textile merchants supplied headbands as complementary gifts to those peasants who came to the city and bought a *kiswa*.[102] He also made a distinction between *kiswas* for the bride and groom and those for relatives.[103] The former, for example, were formally divided into three parts—underwear, outerwear, and headwear—each of which had its specific components. Masri also claimed that the types and colors did not change over time, implying that the *kiswa* packages may have become rigidly formalized by the early twentieth century. Yet, judging from a series of textile orders included in the Arafat family papers, changes in fashion did take place, and there seems to have been a wide range of fabrics, colors, and styles from which to choose.[104] The final product reflected individual preferences because most peasant households, as the above letter illustrates, tailored their own everyday clothes. Masri, for example, noted that except for headgear and expensive silks, these textiles were sold by the *shaqqa* (piece), measuring around seven arms' lengths, or approximately 475 centimeters. These pieces were cut from a large bolt, and whatever could not be sewn by the peasants themselves was sent to tailors in the city. He added that peasants from the western part of Jabal Nablus normally wore brighter colors than did those from the easter part and that they preferred silk belts made in Lebanon.[105]

In order to purchase the *kiswa*, peasants walked or rode donkeys to Nablus (and later on Jenin[106]) in groups referred to as *mawkib al-kassaya* (procession of the wedding-wardrobe purchasers), so named because they usually entered the city with fanfare: singing, dancing, and carrying gifts in kind. James Finn, British consul in Jerusalem, stumbled on such a scene in the vicinity of Haifa in mid-September, 1855:

> Next day passing Tantoora and Athleet, and round the promontory of Carmel as the sun set, we arrived at Caifa, where we remained a few days, during which the ladies had the opportunity of seeing peasant holiday costumes different from those of the far south country; for a wedding being about to take place at Teereh [village], all or nearly all of the women repaired together in procession to Caifa, to purchase dresses and ornaments for the occasion, and they returned in similar line wearing the new dresses, very bright in colours, and singing a chorus as they swiftly shuffled along the road. Another similar body from another village did the same two or three days later, but returned with the music of drums and flutes.[107]

Because most villages were a day's travel away from Nablus, peasants remained one to three nights in the merchant's house, where they were provided with dinners, coffee, and sleeping accommodations. Masri recalled that females stayed in an extra room in their house, usually reserved for this purpose, while the men slept in the garden (*hakura*).[108] He added that the dinners were fairly substantial. Usually the meal consisted of big chunks of lamb over rice which, in turn, lay on a bed of bread soaked with cooked yogurt or tomato sauce.[109] According to Najib and Saba Arafat, sleeping accommodations at *Hajj* Isma'il's big house, located in the Qaryun quarter (demolished by the British during the 1936–1939 rebellion), were also segregated. Peasant women were housed in a room upstairs; accommodations for male peasant clients were set aside on the ground floor, which also contained a *diwan* (large reception room), stables, a water cistern, and a large fruit orchard.[110] Najib Arafat added that although food and lodging were made available to them, the same was not extended to their animals, which they had to leave somewhere else.

For the older members of merchant families, peasant guests were, more often than not, a burden. But for the younger members, especially females who did not venture far into public space, the evening festivities were one of the most pleasant memories of childhood. *Umm* Walid, Najib Arafat's wife, observed that "peasants added a beautiful atmosphere to the house, because the occasion was one of happiness. After dinner, they would take out the *dirbakka* [a conical, one-headed hand drum open at one end] and sing and dance all night long."[111]

Although some clients offered a small downpayment at the time of the purchase, most asked to have their payment postponed until the grain-or olive-harvest season. In letter after letter to *Hajj* Isma'il Arafat, peasants assured him that he should not worry about payment. Typical is the following letter from a well-to-do peasant dated April 24, 1900; that is, the beginning of the wedding season:

> Wanted:
> 1.5 [pieces] solid white *thawb* [light cotton cloth worn under the *qunbaz*]
> 1.5 [pieces] black *thawb*
> 5 blue *hatta* [head covers], of large size
> 5 *manadil* [head kerchiefs], red . . .
> 3 *manadil* . . . with black tassels
> 1/2 bundle of blue *shalayil* [long round columns made of cotton/silk strings].
> To the most eminent and high standing, our father, *Hajj* Isma'il *Afandi* Arafat, may he be preserved. Amen!
> After greetings and inquiry about your most distinguished person . . . our father, we need these goods from you. Please choose them from high-quality materials and do not delay at all in sending them to us with the bearer of this letter. He has with him one French lira, and the rest put on our account. We, God willing, will come to see you soon, and please do not worry. We plead with you emphatically that you choose good [pieces] and do not delay in sending them. . . . Our greetings to you

and your family and children and all those in your well-endowed
shop. . . .

> Your Son,
> Sa'id *Hajj* Zubayda

[P.S.] Let the bearer know the remaining cost.[112]

The writer's promise to travel soon to Nablus usually meant soon after
the harvest season, when payment was expected in cash, not kind.[113]
Sometimes, however, arrangements were made for payment in jars of
olive oil or measures of wheat.[114] Darwaza described the process as fol-
lows:

> Some [textile] merchants sold to whoever passed by, others had agents,
> and some combined both. My father and other colleagues were of the lat-
> ter kind. The agents were mostly peasants who bought their *kiswa* on
> credit until the grape, fig, oil, wheat, or barley seasons. Of course, the
> price was higher than cash sales [and varied] according to the length of the
> loan. They used to write IOUs on the peasants, specifying the payment
> date. When the harvest season . . . arrived, the agents came to sell their sea-
> sonal harvest and to pay their debts. The shop owners used to go to their
> agent's villages to check on their loans. My father and grandfather had
> agents in the villages of Hajja, Bayta, and Bayt Amrayn. . . . I went with
> them more than once.[115]

Upon arrival, textile merchants usually tied their horses next to the oil
press (*badd*) or the threshing floor (*baydar*), symbolically signaling their
intention to collect their due. Practically, they could keep an eye on the
economic health of both the overall harvest and the individual peasant
household. Sometimes they would remain steadfast in this prime location
until the entire debt was paid. Larger and richer merchants, such as the
Arafats, employed horsemen (*khayyala*), each referred to as *al-jabi* (collector), who would ride into these villages and demand payment. The collectors, often peasants themselves, were well suited for this task, for they
were keenly attuned to possible evasive tactics and tricks. Often the peasants could not or would not pay. But the collectors prolonged their stay,
thus taking advantage of the peasant tradition of hospitality (*diyafa*),
whereby the village collectively provided lodging, food, and other services
to visitors in a special room in the village square (*madafa*).[116]

To maximize their returns while maintaining some flexibility, the textile merchants—like tax collectors, politicians and subdistrict chiefs—
played the "good cop/bad cop" game.[117] According to Najib Arafat, his
half-brother Ahmad and Ahmad's sons, including Tawfiq, relied heavily

on horsemen to collect debts, whereas his other brothers were less strict with the peasants.

Because a peasant's ability to pay fluctuated widely, depending on a number of factors from weather conditions to tax burdens, bankruptcies were not uncommon in the ranks of textile merchants who operated on a system of credit. The estate of Abd al-Razzaq Arafat is a case in point. More than a century later, two of *Hajj* Isma'il Arafat's sons also went bankrupt, when they were unable to collect from peasants.[118]

In large villages, such as Jaba, the agents of textile merchants also doubled as middlemen who collected debts, placed orders on behalf of other peasants, and recommended potential customers from other villages. One such agent was Salih Yusuf, from the village of Kafr Qaddum. In 1897, he sent a letter of introduction to *Hajj* Isma'il: "Please note that you will soon be visited by Ahmad Abadi, from the village of Kafr Qari. He intends to purchase his *kiswa* from you. So please, and for my sake, take care of him with good-quality tailoring and *kamkh* [cloth]. My regards."[119]

In another letter, Mustafa Abu Asa, a long-time customer/agent, informed *Hajj* Isma'il that he was placing a large order on behalf of a relative. Apparently the relative thought that he would get a better price and special treatment if he went through the connection (*wasta*) of an agent. Mustafa requested that the bill be put on his account and stated that he would personally come to pay it off. Then he asked Isma'il Arafat to give his relative a discount as a gesture of their friendship.[120]

Some of these agents took advantage of their urban connection to venture into the retail trade in the countryside. As the following debt contract shows, they bought large quantities of textile goods on credit from wholesale urban merchants:

Price of a bundle (*farda*) of unprocessed [calico] foreign-made goods:	3210.10
Price of foreign-made yarn, 9.5 *ratl:*	487.10
	3739.20

Only 3,739 piasters and no more. Price of piaster: 5.75; price of *warzi:* 7 piasters.

Today, a man in his majority, Qasim son of Muhammad I'days al-Hammur from the village of Jaba, acknowledged and testified that he . . . owes . . . Isma'il Arafat the above-mentioned amount . . . for the [above-mentioned goods] which he legally purchased. . . . Payment is delayed for a period of three months, starting today, November 23, 1879. Mansur al-

Mas'ud al-Hammur and Amir al-Kaffan from the above-mentioned village have guaranteed the entire loan and assured complete payment, including penalty.[121]

Keys to the City

The manner in which local trade networks were constructed and reproduced assumed a set of mutual obligations that allowed both peasants and merchants to create space for themselves in the other's territory. Just as textile merchants used these networks to establish a foothold in the hinterland, peasants used merchants as their key to the city and its resources. A merchant's place of business was the headquarters for peasant clients who needed to store their surplus, purchase goods, send communications, receive credit, make connections with political figures, obtain legal council in the Islamic court, and so on.

Thus, even though poor peasants who bought on credit found themselves, more often than not, trapped by debts and enmeshed in patronage networks, they could still make a merchant's life very difficult by finding ways not to pay. Moreover, they were capable of taking their business to another merchant. An element of mutual trust and dependency, as illustrated by the merchants' provision of the above accommodations and services, was therefore crucial to the stability and continuity of local trade networks. Just as the sons of merchants "inherited" their father's customers, sons of peasants also claimed their parents' "key to the city."

For example, in the late nineteenth and early twentieth centuries, the peasants of Bayt Wazan, a village on the western edge of Nablus, usually sold their onion crops to the Asi merchant family, whose members visited the village annually during the onion-harvest season. In return, this family was the Wazanis' urban agent, and its stores became this village's urban nexus of operations.[122] It was members of the Asi family who accompanied the Wazanis when they bought their wedding and other *kiswas* from a well-established textile merchant, *Hajj* Abd al-Rahman Anabtawi, whose shop was conveniently located in Suq al-Basal (onion market). The Asi family provided a mediating influence in price negotiations and, just as important, an urban reference or a guarantee for purchase on credit. They also indirectly extended credit by purchasing and storing goods needed by the Wazanis, such as copper kitchenware. A few times every the year the Wazanis would visit the city to collect these goods and to arrange for future payment.

As the Bayt Wazan case illustrates, the peasants' key to the city was usually the merchant who purchased or helped market the most important agricultural cash crop they produced. Peasants who produced primarily olive oil in the village of Burqin, for example, usually sold this product to the Ashur family, who deposited it in wells beneath their soap factory.[123] Similarly, it was at the Ashur family's house that peasants from Burqin stayed for two or three nights every time they traveled to Nablus to take care of their needs and to sell their goods. The relationship of the Burqin villagers to the Ashur family differed among peasant families, depending on their financial situation. For example, those who borrowed and were in debt usually paid a 30 percent interest rate and were forced to sell their olive oil immediately after the harvest, when prices were low. Those who were not in debt could deposit the oil at the soap factory and usually chose to sell it at a later date, when prices were higher.[124]

Cheese merchants constructed similar networks. Khalid Qadri noted that during the cheese-making season from mid-February until June, his grandfather's shop received peasants primarily from four villages in the subdistrict of Mashariq al-Jarrar—Tubas, Tammun, Rujib, and Salim—as well as bedouins from the vicinity of Jabal al-Khalil. The peasants did not have to bring their cheese into the city, for many merchants sent agents out to the countryside. Yet they preferred to make the arduous trip, because these agents were often suspected of using inaccurate weighing scales with the intent of taking advantage of them. An established merchant in his city shop was assumed to be more trustworthy.[125]

Khalid's grandfather was neither a shaykh nor a *hajj*, but he was widely known as a straightforward and deeply religious man and as the person who officially opened the neighborhood mosque every morning for prayers. The villagers would leave the cheese at his shop and often receive neither cash nor receipts in return, only his word as to the amount and the price. He benefited from this arrangement, because this process increased his liquid capital and allowed him to extend loans to peasants as well as to expand his business. At the same time, however, peasants expected not only to receive their moneys upon demand but also to be granted loans when they experienced hard times.

Khalid Qadri's grandfather was called on to provide a wide range of other services, such as purchasing equipment and supplies for peasants, storing them, and charging the amount to that peasant family's account with him. He was frequently asked to intervene in his suppliers' behalf when they needed to purchase not only their *kiswa* but also gold, furniture, and other goods associated with wedding preparations. As with the Asi family, the Qadri family had prearranged deals with the textile and gold merchants to whom they would bring in customers for a commission, very much like today's tourist guides in Jerusalem and Bethlehem who bring buses to gift shops selling religious icons made out of olive wood and mother-of-pearl.

Of course, Nabulsi peasants, unlike foreign tourists, were familiar with local prices and business practices and did not blindly follow their key to the city. Still, peasants were the weaker party in this relationship, for urban merchants enjoyed higher status and commanded greater resources. Contracts, in any case, were usually verbal, because they were supposed to be based on mutual trust, word of honor, and commitment to a fair exchange. As mentioned earlier, peasants did not receive receipts for their goods, and many deposited money with merchants for safekeeping. In case of conflict, their word in court did not carry the same weight as did that of a respected merchant, nor could they easily find two credible witnesses in the city who would testify on their behalf. Most important, their disadvantage was structural: their needs were constant, but their meager resources fluctuated significantly in an economy based on rain-fed agriculture.

Less vulnerable were members of rural ruling families, as well as middle or well-to-do peasants who had significant land and financial resources and who were active in rural trade and moneylending.[126] True, both groups, especially the middle peasants, depended on urban connections but they were in a strong position to forge a more equal working relationship based on mutual advantage and services—as indicated in a number of letters from *Hajj* Ahmad Isma'il Abu Hijli (from the village of Dayr Istiya) to *Hajj* Isma'il Arafat around the turn of the century. Although the *Abu* Hijli clan was not part of the rural ruling families that had long monopolized administrative and tax-collecting positions, both the tone and content of these letters show *Hajj* Ahmad to be a wealthy man who perceived himself as an equal to his urban counterpart.[127] In these letters, he addressed *Hajj* Isma'il Arafat as "my brother," asked for the most expensive items in stock, requested that he locate certain coins for him, and made it very clear that money was not a problem:

> Wanted:
> —one *dimaya*, two *hindazas* and one-third long [163.5 cm] of the white *malti* kind with wide stripes, tailored for ladies . . . ;
> —one-half similar to the above, two *hindazas* and one-quarter long, for a quilt cover;
> —one chintz of the expensive kind with a blue background, two *hindaztayn* and one-third long, for a lining . . . ;

—one [silver]-lined head kerchief worth two Majidi riyals
—one-half . . . [word not clear] to our brother Yusuf . . . and a *dima* jacket
　　with a *malti* [cloth] lining. Ahmad al-Hijjawi knows the length;
—one large bed cover . . . of the expensive kind;
—one *dimaya* . . . to Hasan like that of his brother Ali, and what is left of
　　the cloth [to be made into] a jacket with *malti* [cloth] lining;
—nine *ratls* of cooked quince. Put it in six jugs.

Sir, my dear respected brother, *Hajj* Isma'il Arafat, may God preserve
you,

After inquiring about your Noble Person, I declare that the above-mentioned goods are for me. Please deliver them to Ahmad al-Hijjawi and
charge the price of the *dimaya* for my son Hassan in his [Hassan's] name.
Please order one of your protected ones to buy the cooked quince and deliver it to the bearer [of this letter]; and register its price in our name.
Charge my brother Yusuf's [account] for the rest of the *dima* and chintz
goods. Let me know the entire price, and I will send it with a bearer so he
can receive the goods deposited with Ahmad [al-Hijjawi]. Whatever you
do not deposit at Ahmad's, give to the bearer. If you receive any orders
from my brothers requesting anything at all, send them [goods] without
hesitation. If you have any . . . [word not clear] liras, keep them and let us
know how much they are worth and we will send you [money]. Previously, we asked you to tell us if any [such] liras fall in your hands. You
replied that *mukhkhamasat* are not be found anywhere, but I don't think
that . . . [word not clear] is empty. Also, if you find *majarrat* of the good
kind as we mentioned, send them. . . .

> Ahmad Isma'il *Abu* Hijli
> January 10, 1900 [128]

It was not unusual that cooked quince and rare coins were part of an
order for clothes from a textile merchant. In fact, *Hajj* Ahmad routinely
asked for a wide variety of items—special foods, coffee, tobacco, kitchenware, herbs, rope, a watch, and even onions—as well as favors, such as
forwarding mail. He also sent carpets and other goods to be sold on his
behalf and requested that the money made be subtracted from his account.[129] *Hajj* Ahmad and *Hajj* Isma'il Arafat, in other words, were agents
for each other's interests; and the relationship they developed was, judging from both the tone and content of the letters, a close and fairly equal
one. In one letter, for example, Ahmad *Abu* Hijli mentioned to *Hajj* Isma'il that he came upon a fine leopard skin and that he was sending it to
him as a gift on the occasion of the latter's purchase of a new horse. He
concluded: "As to your letter to us saying that you left our home satisfied
and grateful, . . . there is no need for this sort of talk. God willing, . . . we
will have a chance to be honored by seeing you at your place, and to kiss

you. It is our fate and yours that the Almighty, may he be willing, will preserve you for us. . . . Amen."[130]

CONCLUSION

The dispute over the clothes of *Umm* Dawud, the festive evenings in merchant houses by peasants flush from shopping for wedding wardrobes, the bright eyes of children waking up after *id al-adha* to put on a new set of garments, and the colorful celebrations of the Prophet's birthday in Khan al-Tujjar are just a few examples of the centrality of textiles to understanding the connections between culture and trade and the importance of merchant networks to both regional and urban-rural relations. As seen in the business practices of the Arafat textile merchants during the eighteenth and nineteenth centuries, local trade networks in Jabal Nablus were more than just economic mechanisms constructed for the purposes of exchange. They can be better characterized as dynamic social spaces created by a multitude of actors with competing interests. The interaction among these actors was governed by a common set of reference points that linked social practices with trade and personal family history—that is, by a system of meanings.

It is a testimony to the social weight of merchants and of their networks that Nabulsi society came to be characterized by many of the values and norms embedded in this system of meanings. The strong sense of regional identification, the importance of family in politics (broadly defined), the pervasive use of religiously coded language in everyday intercourse, the conservative social atmosphere, and the remarkable continuity of a wide range of cultural rituals—these were all partly products of the ways in which these trade networks were cultivated and reproduced.

This system of meanings, it is important to emphasize, did not emanate solely from the conservative nature of Arab/Muslim society, nor was it simply a thinly disguised cultural tool. For most merchants in eighteenth- and nineteenth-century Nablus the link between culture and trade was part and parcel not only of their livelihoods but also of their identities. Each merchant was heir to a constructed history that tied his family's material and social interests to those of specific rural villages, clans, and even individuals.

On the surface, this system of meanings seemed static—not surprising, given that its very existence was predicated on shared perceptions of tradition and personal connections that were passed down from father to son. Within this wider cultural envelope, however, local trade networks were in constant flux. We have seen, for example, that family was a dynamic construct constantly being reformulated in physical, social, and cultural space. Peasants were also far from being passive victims of these networks: they actively participated in their reproduction and took advantage of their keys to the city.

Local trade networks proved to be effective vehicles for merchants to organize and invest in the production of cash crops for both the regional and international markets. Personal connections based on notions of trust, honor, and a fair and just exchange anchored, protected, and facilitated the circulation of merchant capital in the rural sphere in the context of a decentralized and uncertain political environment. With the expansion of commercial agriculture and a money economy in the hinterland, merchants relied on these rooted yet flexible networks to compete with and eventually bypass the subdistrict chiefs and urban ruling families in the race for the control of the rural surplus. As shall be seen in the forthcoming chapters, these networks not only accounted for the resiliency of the merchant community in Nablus but also served as the economic, social, and political incubators for the emergence of a different breed of urban notables who took advantage of the new political atmosphere created by the Egyptian invasion and the Ottoman reforms.

Local networks embodied a great deal of tension. The sources play down these tensions and often ignore them altogether. But there can be little doubt that merchants competed with each other, with ruling political families, and even with their own agents, who served as a bridge between them and their clients in the surrounding villages. For these agents, most of whom belonged to a growing class of middle peasants, service in a large urban merchant's network was but the first step toward establishing their own network, often within the territory of their former employer. Most of all, there was tension between merchants and peasants over the fundamental issue of debt. Moneylending spearheaded the expansion of merchant capital, facilitated the appropriation of village lands, and eventually led to the integration of the rural areas into the urban legal and political spheres. By the second half of the nineteenth century, it seemed as if the hostility within the countryside over the spiraling problem of debt was matched by the patronizing and arrogant attitude of the urban population (see Chapter 4).

Instructive here is a satirical oration that Malik Masri learned from the peasants of Talluza village in the early twentieth century. Inspired by a song usually performed on the last Friday in the Holy Month of Ramadan (*al-jum'a al-yatima*, literally, "Orphan Friday"), the oration was structured in the *maqamat* genre of Arabic rhythmic prose. The following is a partial and somewhat loose translation of the more stylized version titled *al-Tarabish wa al-Barabish* (the fezzes [i.e., merchants] and the waterpipes, or, more accurately, the tubes of the waterpipe, or *nargila*):

> God is Great when the fezzes gather [on the village grounds], the waterpipe tubes are extended, and the voices of the [debt] collectors raised. The moneylenders listen for the sounds of the returning sheep; then they jump with their friend the police, looking for a victim to fleece. . . .
> God is Great when the people of the villages greet the coming of Blessed and Auspicious olive season. They go to the city markets to buy their provisions, clothes, and whatever else their heart desires. But there the debtor demands his due from the debtee, or else the loan is renewed for twice the fee. . . . The poor soul is forced to submit and God is Great, God is Great.[131]

Changes in regional trade networks also generated tensions, especially between Nabulsi merchants and their European and coastal competitors. Generally speaking, the locus of these networks shifted from Egypt to Damascus and Beirut; from multifamily to single-family enterprise; from politically mediated to legally enforced systems of credit extension and collection; from regional sources of textiles to increasingly European ones; and from a system of agents to individual accounts with regional trade houses. In other words, regional trade networks lost much of their autonomy as they were subordinated—or, more accurately, as Nabulsi merchants were integrated—into the larger regional and world economies.

In this context, the continuity and reinforcement of the system of meanings associated with local trade networks proved invaluable. Regional identification, religious and social status, and the cultivation of local connections through services and gift exchange were all indispensable to maintaining the access of Nabulsi merchants to the rural surplus in the face of the forces unleashed by Ottoman centralization policies and the process of integration into the world economy. Using the social life of cotton as an example, the next chapter investigates the changing politics of trade, especially the tensions generated by the competition among local, regional, and European merchants, as well as the Ottoman state, over the movement of commodities.

3   Cotton, Textiles, and the Politics of Trade

Collect the taxes-in-kind as soon as the harvest season begins,
because if you do not do so the . . . peasants will . . . sell it . . .
and the entire harvest will end up in the hands of the merchants.

Governor of Sidon province to the *qa'immaqam* of Nablus, 1850

The use to which the consumption of cotton is applied in Syria and
these countries is principally in the spinning of cotton-yarn of an
ordinary quality, with which coarse clothes are woven for under
garments, drawers, shirts, sheets, mattress coverings, stockings and a
variety of other articles of ordinary quality; but for the better kinds
the consumption has decreased by the introduction of our cotton-
yarn, and principally by the importation of the grey domestics, or
long clothes, which is one of the great articles of British
manufactured goods imported.

John Bowring, *Report on the Commercial Statistics of Syria*, 1840

Near the end of 1771 Zahir al-Umar, the ruler of Acre, laid siege to
Nablus. For years he had attempted to extend his authority over this rich
merchant city and its fertile hinterland, but to no avail. This year, however, was different. His Egyptian Mamluk allies had invaded Palestine on
their way to Damascus, and the Tuqan's greatest rivals, the Jarrar family,
had initiated an alliance with him.[1] His nemesis, Uthman Pasha, the governor of Damascus province since 1760, was replaced by Muhammad Pasha Azm, and the latter had already left for the Holy Cities of Mecca and
Medina in his capacity as leader of the pilgrimage caravan (*amir al-hajj*).
Shortly before the siege Zahir al-Umar succeeded in taking Jaffa and ex-
pelling its governor, Ahmad *Beik* Tuqan. He was also able to force Ahmad's brother, Mustafa *Beik* Tuqan, chief of the subdistrict of Bani-Sa'b,
to retreat to Nablus. With Nablus's key outlet to the sea and one of its
cotton-producing subdistricts under his control, he was poised for the final
blow.

According to Ibrahim Danafi al-Samiri (1712–1790)—the head scribe
(*katib*) and interpreter (*turjiman*) for the *mutasallim* of Nablus and an
eyewitness to the siege—the Tuqan and Nimr families divided the city in
half: the Nimrs defended all points east; the Tuqans, all points west.[2]

The dividing line between the two was Khan al-Tujjar, the textile market discussed in Chapter 2. By the time Zahir al-Umar had positioned his forces, he was faced (if we are to believe al-Samiri) with 12,000 riflemen, many of whom were peasants. After nine days of skirmishes and one heavy battle, Zahir al-Umar acknowledged the stalemate and withdrew his forces, but not before he laid waste a number of villages from which the peasant defenders had come.

The first trade caravan to leave Nablus after the siege consisted of one hundred camel-loads of "clothes, yarn and other things," heading for Damascus.[3] While resting at Uyun al-Tujjar (Merchant Springs) caravansary, located north of Jenin, the caravan was plundered by the forces of Zahir al-Umar and forced to turn around to Acre, his capital. To drive home the lesson that he controlled the arteries of trade connecting Nablus to its northern regional markets, Zahir al-Umar cut off the road to Damascus and harassed both trade caravans and travelers who sought to reach the defiant city.[4]

The 1771 siege of Nablus nicely illustrates the intersections of commercial agricultural production, urban manufacturing, and the politics of trade. First, this anecdote introduces many of the elements crucial to understanding the importance of cotton and textiles to the political economy of Palestine. It was not out of the ordinary that the first trade caravan to leave the city after the siege would carry primarily cotton clothes and yarn: the processing and trade in cotton goods constituted the core of the manufacturing sector in Nablus and consumed the energies of the majority of artisans, wage-earning women, and merchants. Nor was the destination of the caravan surprising: Damascus was one of Nablus's primary regional markets for cotton and textiles, and regional trade had always been central to the political economy of Jabal Nablus. Nor, finally, were the types of goods unusual: the Nablus textile sector has historically produced inexpensive clothes and yarn designed for the mass market of peasants and lower urban classes. How this particular type of textile manufacturing was affected by competition from European machine-made goods is addressed in the last section of this chapter.

Second, this anecdote sets the stage for the main focus of this chapter: the changing relationship between politics and trade. It is significant that we meet Zahir al-Umar (1690–1775) in this context, because he, more than any other Palestinian leader during the Ottoman period, was closely associated with the growing trade in cotton.[5] His imposition of a monopoly on the export of cotton changed the politics of trade in northern Palestine and put him on a collision course with the leaders of Jabal Nablus.

Zahir al-Umar's quarrels with the Tuqan ruling family, for instance, were precipitated, among other things, by the latter's takeover of an important cotton-growing area, the subdistrict of Bani Sa'b, and as well as of the port city of Jaffa, from which much of the cotton was exported. The siege, moreover, took place at a time when the commercial production and export of cotton became the primary link in a new phase of trade relations with Europe that would have far-reaching consequences by the second half of the nineteenth century. Hitherto, the role of Jabal Nablus in this trade has not been studied, even though this region became the largest cotton producer in Palestine, if not the Fertile Crescent as a whole, by the early nineteenth century. The first section of this chapter outlines the rise and fall of both cotton production and the politics of monopoly.

Nabulsi merchants posed the biggest challenge to Zahir al-Umar and his successors in Acre because they were able to successfully limit the expansion of the politics of monopoly: they used their networks to make Nablus the center of cotton processing in Palestine even though the cotton-producing villages were closer to the coastal cities from which cotton was shipped overseas. Yet precisely when they finally managed to dominate the cotton trade, they faced another, more serious, challenge: the rise of the politics of "free trade." The second section of this chapter investigates how Nabulsi merchants competed with each other, with coastal and foreign merchants, and with the Ottoman government for access to and control of the rural surplus. This competition took place within the context of a new political environment created by the Egyptian invasion and the Ottoman reforms that followed. Specifically, this section considers the process of integration into the world economy from the perspective of local merchants and details the ways in which they used their recent access to political office (the Advisory Council) in order to adjust the politics of "free trade" to their favor.

COTTON AND THE POLITICS OF MONOPOLY

The story of the commercial production of Palestinian cotton is not a new one, for this commodity has found its way to European shores since at least the tenth century, although the major market at that time, and until the eighteenth century, was Egypt. Whether most of the exported cotton was in a raw or processed form (such as yarn or clothes) depended on the health of the domestic economy and the nature of demand. Between the tenth and thirteenth centuries, for example, processed cotton constituted the bulk of exports. But by the early fifteenth century, Venice, which

Table 2. French Imports of Levant Cotton during the Eighteenth Century (Annual Averages) from All Ports, by Weight (in Quintals)*

	1700–1702	1717–1721	1736–1740	1750–1754	1785–1789
Raw	4,316	18,944	30,789	52,550	95,979
Spun	16,946	15,607	14,889	13,853	10,805

SOURCE: Reproduced from Owen, *Middle East*, p. 7.
*1 quintal = 100 kilograms.

dominated trade with the Greater Syria, imported mostly raw cotton and exported processed cotton goods.[6]

From the sixteenth to the early eighteenth centuries the chief commodity in Palestine's trade with Europe was processed cotton, mostly in its carded and spun forms.[7] During this period, France replaced Venice as the primary European trading partner with the Levant and practically monopolized the northern coast of Palestine.[8] In general, the French supplied woolen goods in exchange for primary products, especially raw cotton and cotton yarn, which were needed for their quickly expanding textile industry. French demand for Levant raw cotton increased more than fivefold over the eighteenth century, while its imports of processed cotton actually decreased (see Table 2).

This was part of a general trend of increasing European demand for raw cotton, for Europe's industrialization was spearheaded by textile production. Other parts of the Ottoman, Safavid, and Moghul empires witnessed a similar increase in the commercial production of cotton for export around the same time (see Table 3).[9]

Cotton and the Rulers of Acre

In order to secure their supply of raw cotton, French merchants took to investing in cotton production at the local level beginning in the 1720s. Following the example of local merchants (see Chapter 4), they paid village shaykhs for cotton harvests one year in advance.[10] The direct access of European merchants to Palestinian cotton, however, was severed two decades later, when Zahir al-Umar made Acre the seat of his rule in the mid-1740s and, with the help of Ibrahim Sabbagh, his long-time financial manager and political advisor, managed to implant himself as the middleman between French merchants and the cotton-growing villages under his domain.[11] The idea was to corner the surplus and control the prices at the point of sale to foreign merchants. Profits from this less-than-perfect

Table 3. British Cotton Imports from Turkey, 1725–1789

Year	Quantity (in Pounds)
1725	667,279
1755	738,412
1775	2,175,132
1785	2,190,027
1789	4,406,892

SOURCE: Adapted from Table 16.1 in Orhan Kurmus, "The Cotton Famine and Its Effects on the Ottoman Empire," in İslamoğlu-İnan, ed., *Ottoman Empire*, p. 161.

monopoly system helped Zahir al-Umar transform Acre from a little town into an imposing fortress city and the seat of an autonomous enclave within the Ottoman Empire.[12]

In 1784, nine years after Zahir al-Umar's death, his successor, Ahmad Pasha al-Jazzar (1775–1804), was able to enforce an even stricter monopoly over the buying and selling of cotton and cereals. By 1790 he had managed to break the French merchants' grip on the cotton trade and expelled them to Sidon.[13] By better controlling the supply end of the cotton market, Ahmad Pasha stood to make greater profits: he could increase his options among prospective buyers and put a stop to the French practice of bypassing his revenue-collecting apparatus through direct investment on the village level.

That same year Volney, an astute French observer who traveled widely in the region, wrote:

> The dependencies of Saida [Sidon province, whose de facto capital was Acre] are Sur [Tyre] and the towns of Palestine such as Ramleh, Jerusalem, Lydda, and Majdal. This area is one of the most important, importing 800–900 bales of woolen cloth for which it pays in raw cotton and cotton yarn. Here the French face no competition. In Saida they have one or two agents who buy cotton every Monday or Tuesday. They wished to do the same in Acre, but the pasha cornered all cotton stocks, forbade all sales, and became sole master of the market; since the merchants needed to buy goods in return for what they sold, he put a duty of 10 piasters on each quintal of cotton.[14]

The politics of monopoly were not unique to Palestine. The heavy-handed methods of Zahir al-Umar and Ahmad Pasha al-Jazzar were quite common at the time for strongmen who ruled semi-independent enclaves within the Ottoman, Safavid, and Moghul empires.[15] Indeed, a monopoly system over agricultural commodities destined for overseas exports reached its epitome under Muhammad Ali (1805–1848), the Ottoman viceroy of Egypt.[16] Ahmad Pasha al-Jazzar's efforts, however, took place in a context very different from that of Egypt. The expulsion of French merchants might not have helped him raise more revenues, because the areas of cotton cultivation, as shall be seen, had spread to regions beyond his control: that is, to Jabal Nablus. It is also likely that the trade in cotton might have become less profitable, due to transportation difficulties during the Napoleonic Wars as well as to increased competition from Anatolia and India (Egypt did not witness a substantial increase in cotton production until the early nineteenth century). Finally, there is reason to believe that the economic and demographic base of Acre began to decline during the last years of Jazzar's rule.[17]

In any case, Ahmad Pasha al-Jazzar's monopoly system did not survive his death intact. In addition to the growing weakness of Acre and the spread of cotton cultivation to areas beyond its control, his successor, Sulayman Pasha al-Adil (1805–1819), instituted a more decentralized political and fiscal set of policies. The difference in the approach of these two rulers is symbolized by the marked contrast in the appellations they acquired: Jazzar (butcher) versus Adil (just). Of course, just about anyone who succeeded al-Jazzar was bound to look good in comparison: his cruelty earned him this title long before he came to Palestine, and his death was greeted by celebrations as far away as Damascus. In fact, not a single contemporary chronicler had a kind remark to make about this Bosnian mercenary turned pasha.[18]

In order to reduce his expenses and to minimize the threat of rebellion, Sulayman Pasha gutted al-Jazzar's formidable military machine and relaxed his political control over Acre's dependencies. According to his sympathetic scribe, Sulayman Pasha preferred diplomacy over violence and rarely interfered in the affairs of his appointees.[19] Far from minutely supervising the affairs of his subjects, he turned the day-to-day operations of his regime in 1806/1807 to his three main advisors: Ali Pasha, his deputy; Haim Farhi, his financial manager; and Ibrahim Awra, his head scribe.[20] All had strong relations with the local merchant community. Ali Pasha's house was frequented by the local Muslim religious figures and merchants, and Haim Farhi and Ibrahim Awra—a Jew and a Christian, respectively—aggressively defended the interests of these two minority communities, many of whose members were well-to-do merchants.[21]

Political decentralization was accompanied by relaxation of control over the collection and sale of cotton, grains, and other commercial commodities. Merchants were no longer subject to extortion and confiscation on a routine basis, as was their fate under Ahmad Pasha al-Jazzar. On the contrary, Sulayman Pasha was so eager to reinvigorate the local economy that he gave the Acre merchants virtual ownership of the government-owned shops they had long rented, and many properties of Ahmad Pasha al-Jazzar were sold off to them as well.[22] Sulayman Pasha's more relaxed fiscal policy was based, or so we are told, on the following advice from his powerful financial manager, Haim Farhi:

> We must . . . reduce the taxation of our subjects and impose it on the foreigners. That is possible if the sale of grain, oil, and cotton to foreigners is limited exclusively to Acre; the people can get what they need directly from the peasants without imposts. Trustworthy agents should be appointed for this purpose, and at the end of every day the surplus of these three commodities taken in, over and above the needs of the [local] people, should be taken from the owners and they should be paid the price at which it was sold during that day. That which is obtained should be deposited in storehouses and sold by the government to the ships of foreigners at the highest possible price.[23]

Farhi—who served Ahmad Pasha al-Jazzar, Sulayman Pasha and, for a time, the latter's successor, Abdullah Pasha (1819–1831)—was proposing a limited monopoly that would not preempt local and regional consumption of, and trade in, cotton. In these two crucial spheres, peasants and merchants were to enjoy a relatively free cotton market. Farhi thus sought to maintain some political control over a profitable trade, but without endangering the peasant base of production that had suffered greatly under Ahmad Pasha al-Jazzar. Theoretically, artisans and merchants who needed to purchase cotton for local trade and manufacturing would not have to compete with foreign merchants who were willing to offer high prices in order not to return in empty ships.

This delicate balancing act seems to have been implemented in one form or another. During the reign of Sulayman Pasha there were five permanent employees dealing solely with buying, storing, and selling cotton, more than for any other agricultural product, including wheat. According to Awra, these employees included Rustum Kashif, who, along with two assistants, supervised the government's cotton storehouse in Acre, and the head of customs, who, along with an assistant, worked as an accountant for "the ginned cotton that comes from the storehouse, and which was bought from village peasants."[24]

The government, it seems, did not limit itself to purchasing the surplus left in the market at the end of each day. It also intervened directly at the

production level to ensure adequate supplies of cotton that it could resell
to French traders. It is not clear where Farhi drew the line in terms of how
much cotton was bought, what prices were offered to the peasants, and
how much foreign merchants were charged. Suffice it to say that he and
other high-ranking Acre officials amassed large fortunes through speculation in cash crops and stood to gain a great deal, personally, from loopholes in the monopoly.

Because these decisions directly affected the livelihoods of peasants,
merchants, and foreign traders, the balancing act was fraught with tension
and conducive to conflict and smuggling. Smuggling—essentially an attempt by merchants, peasants, and bedouins to bypass local and regional
monopolies—was spurred on by increasing European demand, making it
a common phenomenon all over the Middle East and North Africa.[25]
Smuggling not only undermined the politics of monopoly but also constituted a perennial problem for the Ottoman state in general, which was
concerned about losing control of the movement of commodities and the
customs revenues they generated.[26]

If the accession of Sulayman Pasha heralded the slow decline, from
above, of monopoly politics in northern Palestine, and if smuggling
eroded the politics of monopoly from below, the Egyptian invasion of
Greater Syria in 1831 dealt it a quick and fatal blow, for this invasion
spelled the end of Acre rulers' political and economic influence in Palestine in general. Surprisingly, the Egyptian authorities made no effort to
corner the cotton market in their newly acquired territories, even though
monopoly was Muhammad Ali's firm policy in Egypt at the time and even
though he was keenly aware that the profits from his control of the cotton
trade were essential to the war effort.[27] In a communiqué dated September
1833, Muhammad Ali instructed his son that the cotton harvest in the
districts of Acre, Nablus, Jaffa and Gaza need not be purchased because of
its small size (even though 1833 was a bad year for Egyptian cotton exports). Instead, the inhabitants (*ahali* was the word used in the communiqué) were to be allowed to dispose of it as they wished.[28] It is ironic (if
the reason given was indeed true) that although the monopoly of Acre
rulers was partly undermined by the expansion in cotton cultivation to
areas beyond their political control, this expansion was not impressive
enough for the Egyptians to impose their own monopoly.[29] A more likely
explanation for Muhammad Ali Pasha's decision is that he wanted to allay
the European powers' concern that Greater Syria would be subjected to
the same economic policies as Egypt, policies they considered to be obstacles to free trade.

Cotton Production in Jabal Nablus

The politics of monopoly never took hold in the rest of Palestine. As mentioned above, the large increase in lands devoted to the cultivation of cotton spilled over into areas not under the control of Acre's governors, primarily Jabal Nablus.[30] The strong position of the merchant community in Jabal Nablus, as well as the decentralized political structure of this region, meant that competition, not monopoly, characterized the politics of trade in cotton. Using their local trade networks—that is, the thick web of connections with specific villages, clans, or individuals—Nabulsi merchants were able to secure a regular supply of raw cotton, mostly as payments for debts.[31] By the 1830s, if not earlier, Jabal Nablus had become the largest producer of cotton not only in Palestine but in Greater Syria as a whole (see Table 4).

The figures in Table 4, of course, provide only a snapshot for one year.[32] But by that time, cotton grown in the Nablus region had already established a reputation as the best in the Fertile Crescent, and it commanded a ready market.[33] Fifteen years later, the quantity of cotton production in Jabal Nablus was still important enough for the central Ottoman government to initiate efforts to improve the quality of seeds in this region, as part of its general policy of promoting the export of cotton to Europe.[34] On April 28, 1851, the Nablus Advisory Council received a letter from the governor of Sidon province, informing them that they would soon receive four *uqqas* of cotton seeds courtesy of Ottoman officials in Istanbul. In return, they were to execute the following instructions:

> [The] cotton seeds are to be distributed to the *ahali* [inhabitants] under the supervision of the council and experts. [The *ahali*] are to plant [the seeds] this year in the good arable lands that accommodate the cultivation of this specie. [You are to] greatly motivate their willingness in this regard and do not allow them to ignore this order for cultivation. Send word upon arrival [of the seeds]. In addition, it is not permissible to charge the *ahali* a price for the above-mentioned seeds; [but] when the cotton matures you are to put two plants produced by them [along] with [the] soil in a box and seal it. [You are also] to put some of the cotton in a second box and seal it and send word to us. The entire crop [produced from these seeds] is to be put under safekeeping until orders are received from Istanbul.[35]

Five days later the council replied that they had delivered two *uqqas* of seeds to peasants in the Jenin area and one each to those in the subdistricts of Bani Saʿb and Shʿarawiyya al-Gharbiyya.[36] This reply provides the first concrete evidence as to the general areas in which cotton was grown in

Table 4. Cotton Production in the Levant, 1837
(in *Qintars*)

Aleppo	500–600
Edlib	700–800
Kilis, Beld, Azass	600–700
Antioch	100–150
Tripoli	30–50
Nablus	4,500–5,000
Latakia	?
Acre and Jaffa	?

SOURCE: Bowring, *Commercial Statistics*, pp. 13–14.

Jabal Nablus during the mid-nineteenth century. The names of the villages were not mentioned. Fortunately, however, a series of documents detailing human and material losses during factional fighting in 1850 provides additional clues in this regard. These documents listed, among other things, stolen properties supposed to be returned as part of a peace agreement between the peasant clans involved in the fighting. In many instances, raw and ginned cotton as well as cotton seeds and implements were the most important agricultural commodities listed.[37] Just one clan, for example, had 8,300 *waznas* of cotton-in-the-boll (*qashqutun*), 505 *waznas* of ginned cotton, 7 *qintars* of spun cotton, 145 *waznas* of cotton seeds, and a large amount of locally produced textiles, all to be returned by another clan that had plundered its village.[38] The villages of cotton-producing clans listed in this and other local sources include Attil, Dayr al-Ghusun, Zayta, Baqa, Shwayka, Qaqun, Talfit, Muqaybli, Arrana, Kafr Dan, Zaboya, and Dannaba.[39] Other villages not mentioned in the sources but still known for their cotton production include Zir'in, Jalama, Yamun and Silat al-Harithiyya.[40]

Never subjected to the politics of monopoly, the city of Nablus easily became Palestine's center for cotton processing and trade after the demise of the Acre rulers in 1831. Over time, Nablus became the place to which peasants from the cotton-growing areas sent their cotton to be ginned and sold, even though Acre and Jaffa, the ports from which much of this cotton found its way to Europe, were actually closer to many of these villages than was Nablus proper. Nabulsi merchants also organized the local production and sale of this cotton to European merchants. In 1837, for example, a full three-quarters of the entire harvest of Jabal Nablus was exported to the port of Marseilles, France.[41]

Decline of the Cotton Connection

Ironically, the production of cotton declined precisely when the integration of Palestine and the commercialization of its agriculture began to expand by leaps and bounds. Having helped pave the way for increased trade with Europe, it was overtaken during the mid-nineteenth century by the other commodities that became more important cash crops for export: wheat, barley, sesame seeds, olive oil, and, eventually, the famous Jaffa orange.

This decline was not a linear process. The decade of Egyptian rule most likely witnessed an overall increase in cotton cultivation, because the Egyptian authorities encouraged commercial agriculture and the trade with Europe. It is estimated, for instance, that Ibrahim Pasha's policy of "forced cultivation"[42] led to the doubling of the cotton-growing areas in Greater Syria by the end of the 1830s, but these figures are only guesses.[43] In short, cotton production seems to have declined by the mid-nineteenth century, peaked during the cotton famine in the early 1860s, then declined again (see Table 5).[44]

Regional competition, the changing nature of European demand, and the stagnation of textile-manufacturing sector were all important factors in the initial period of decline. First, both the quality of Egyptian cotton after the discovery of the Jumel (Mako) long-staple plant (1820) and the vast quantity produced in the Nile Valley greatly reduced the importance of Palestine as a source of cotton.[45] This small region's topography and climate simply did not allow for economy of scale or for the development of a monocrop economy, as Egypt's did, and the short staple of its cotton became less desirable.

Second, British demand for grains (wheat and barley), especially after the repeal of the Corn (wheat) Laws, caused a shift in the percentage of land allocated for this purpose.[46] Peasants welcomed this change, for they preferred to grow grains. Compared with cotton, grains were more hardy, easier to grow, needed less water, did not exhaust the soil as much, and involved far less labor. Grains were also a less risky proposition: there was always a local and regional market for wheat, whereas that for cotton was vulnerable to international price fluctuations and to the health of regional textile industries. Finally, increasing imports of machine-produced yarn from England undercut local and regional demand for Palestinian raw cotton and cotton yarn, because the English material was stronger and of better quality, though not necessarily always better suited for local manu-

Table 5. Cotton Exports from Acre, Haifa, and Jaffa, 1852–1875 (in *Uqqas*)

Year	Acre and Haifa	Jaffa
1852	446,545	?
1853	294,545	?
1854	37,091	?
1855	3,819	?
1856–1859	?	?
1859	5,273	?
1860	68,455	20,000
1861	58,909	?
1862	55,273	20,000
1863	?	190,678
1864–1872	?	?
1873	?	40,000
1874	?	10,000
1875	?	5,000

SOURCE: Adapted from Tables 1.3 and 1.7 in Schölch, "European Penetration," pp. 58, 61.

facture.[47] The impact of foreign competition, as shall be seen in the last section of this chapter, was less than devastating due to continued local and regional demand, and the role of Nablus as the cotton-processing center of Palestine survived well into the early twentieth century.[48]

THE POLITICS OF FREE TRADE

In the 1830s, precisely at the peak of Nablus's domination of the cotton trade, a new politics of trade threatened this city's position as the undisputed economic capital of Palestine. The centralization of political control in Greater Syria by the Egyptian authorities and their support of the activities of foreign merchants opened new vistas for trade and circulation of merchant capital. Sultan Mahmud II (1808–1839)—under duress from stinging military defeats by the Egyptian forces and dependent on help from the European powers to reassert his authority over Muhammad Ali Pasha—approved the free-trade 1838 Anglo-Turkish Commercial Convention that struck down monopolies, lowered tariffs on European goods, and opened up the interior markets of the empire.[49] He also laid the groundwork for a sweeping series of political, administrative, and fiscal reforms (*Tanzimat*), announced four months after his death in 1839, that were designed to facilitate greater control by the government over the empire's human and material resources. These reforms made it easier for European and regional merchants to gain access to interior markets at the expense of their entrenched local counterparts. Almost immediately, there was a sharp expansion in the size of foreign merchant communities in the Ottoman Empire, especially in Beirut and other coastal port cities.[50]

The gradual implementation of the *Tanzimat*, however, presented the Ottoman authorities with a contradiction: the administrative reforms, such as the establishment of the Advisory Councils, opened a window of opportunity for local merchants and other urban notables not only to participate in but also to resist and manipulate Ottoman fiscal and economic policies. For the first time in memory they gained public access to official political posts and institutions, which they could use to reinforce their position in the competition with outside merchants. This is why these reforms, although aggressively pursued by the Ottoman government, took more than two decades (1840–1860) to fully implement.

The new politics of trade, one must quickly add, were not due solely to external forces; they were also precipitated by an internal contradiction. The very success of Nabulsi merchants in organizing the local market for the export of agricultural products both regionally and overseas paved the way for the non-Nabulsi merchants to extend their networks into the interior.[51] Specifically, Nabulsi merchants faced increasingly stiffer competition for access to and control of the rural surplus from three external sources: European traders and their agents working out of the port cities; regional merchants, both in the coastal cities and in such interior urban centers as Damascus, Beirut, Acre, Jaffa, and Jerusalem; and a reinvigorated and intrusive Ottoman state bent on consolidating its control and increasing its revenues. The intense struggles for access and control among local and regional merchants, the Ottoman government, and foreign businessmen during these two transitional decades make this period a formative one in the history of Ottoman Palestine.

Each set of competitors had its own political and economic weapons. Foreign traders had the backing of their governments, which lobbied vigorously on behalf of their citizens, and successfully used their political influence to milk the Capitulations (agreements which in effect gave diplomatic immunity to all foreigners and their local agents) and favorable commercial treaties for all they were worth.[52] Just as important, foreign merchants were willing to offer fairly high prices for raw agricultural goods such as cotton and grains, thereby tempting peasants to redirect the flow of their products away from local markets.

Regional trading houses, headed by wealthy Beiruti or Damascene merchant families, did their best to secure the backing of the provincial government apparatus. This was no small advantage at a time when Ottoman centralization greatly expanded the prerogatives of the provinces over their districts in such matters as approving bids for tax farming and the purchase of agricultural commodities collected as taxes-in-kind (*zakhayir*). Nabulsi merchants, for their part, sought protection and commercial advantage through the Nablus Advisory Council and through their deeply rooted trade networks in the hinterlands. The Advisory Council also served as an arbitrator for commercial disputes, thus giving local merchants an important edge. In other words, what Nabulsi merchants lacked in overall economic and political influence on the regional and international levels they made up for through their connections to and superior knowledge of the local market and their control of the local government. By the early 1840s the stage was set for a series of complicated and tense maneuvers as each side pressed its advantages in order to secure their access to the rural surplus and to enlarge their share of profits in the lucrative trade of commercial agricultural products.

Merchants, the State, and the Movement of Commodities

The role of the Ottoman government was integral to the new politics of trade, for it controlled the collection of part of the surplus as taxes-in-kind and supervised the competition for its purchase by local, regional, and foreign merchants. One can analyze the new politics of trade, therefore, by investigating the pressures that were brought to bear on the physical movement of the *zakhayir* from point of production to point of sale.

During the mid-nineteenth century the types of agricultural commodities collected as taxes-in-kind varied from village to village. In general, however, they consisted of wheat, barley, meadow vetch, lentils, corn, olive oil, clarified butter, and cotton from the areas around the city of Nablus; and wheat, barley, corn, sesame, clarified butter, and cotton from the villages around the town of Jenin.[53] These crops were transported by peasants to central collection points, where they were measured and kept in storehouses rented from Nabulsi merchants.[54] The *zakhayir* were then put up for sale in auctions.

The first leg in this long trip of, say, grains or cotton was from the village to the storehouses. In order to minimize its expenses and maximize its revenue, the Ottoman government made every effort to ensure that the *zakhayir* were assessed, collected, and transported as cheaply and efficiently as possible. Their worry was that any delay would encourage peasants to sell these goods, leaving nothing for the state. Even before the harvest was in, therefore, local merchants and the state were involved in a race for access in a market that leaked like a sieve. In 1850, for example, Sulayman *Beik* Tuqan, the *qa'immaqam* of the districts of Nablus and Jenin, received a letter from the governor of Sidon province instructing him to begin collecting taxes as soon as the harvest season was at hand because "if you do not do so, the *ahali* and the peasants will take over the harvest and sell it. They will use the money to meet their personal needs and the entire harvest will end up in the hands of the merchants."[55]

Timing was critical for the state because merchants had a built-in advantage: they used their local trade networks to ensure future delivery of crops by extending loans to peasants, hence ensnaring them in debt obligations the previous season (see Chapter 4). This is why merchants were often willing to reschedule debts almost indefinitely: their patience encouraged heavily indebted peasants to continue working the land and assured a dependent relationship.[56]

The actual trip to the storehouses was also a bone of contention. Traditionally, peasants bore the responsibility and expense of delivering the *zakhayir* to the storehouses. In 1850, however, the governor of Jerusalem, Adham Pasha, abolished the use of corvée labor for the transportation of taxes-in-kind. Instead, peasants were to be paid according to distance traveled from their village to the storehouses.[57] The aim was to provide every incentive possible for peasants to deliver their surpluses to the government. The net effect was to reduce the taxation rate by eliminating the cost of labor involved in transportation and to shift the burden onto the shoulders of merchants, who would have to pay higher prices for these goods. The sources do not tell us whether this order was implemented or whether there was vocal opposition to it from the merchant community.

The struggle then moved to the storehouses themselves. The issues of inventory and control were important to the central government because, hitherto, all storage space had been rented from the rich merchants of Nablus: the same ones who bid on the purchase of the *zakhayir* and who were also represented in the ranks of the council that was authorized to oversee the bidding process. This cozy arrangement was further reinforced by another, even more nepotistic one: the employees of the storehouses were all recruited locally and were chosen by the council members.[58]

In order to regain control of this key stage in the movement of commodities, the provincial authorities in the mid-nineteenth century gladly approved a request by the Nablus Council to renovate and expand some of the storehouses. They also agreed to deduct the costs from Nablus's taxes to the central government.[59] In addition to greater control afforded by construction of independent government storehouses, the authorities introduced standardized weight and volume measures.[60] Just as important, in January 1851 they appointed an inspector general, who was dispatched to report on the administration of storehouses in Acre, Jaffa, and other regions.[61]

All of these actions indicated that the central government was concerned about embezzlement—not an unfounded worry, considering that the employees of the storehouses in Jabal Nablus, unlike their counterparts in other cities, were not salaried by the state. When challenged on this score, the Nablus Council members insisted that these employees—six in total (two supervisors, two accountants, and two measurers)—remain unsalaried, because, they argued, the "old way" of payment, which literally operated through sleight of hand, must be preserved. The council explained that incoming grains were measured differently from outgoing grains, though the same measuring container was used for both: the measurer allowed a dome to form on top of the container when scooping the former, but, in a quick movement of the hand, leveled the container off before pouring the latter. The difference—which accumulated every time a container scooped up grains—was used to pay salaries and rent, to buy furniture and stationery, and to meet other costs of operating the storehouses.[62] When the Ottoman authorities questioned this practice, the Nablus Council, in a long and convoluted reply, argued that it was important to preserve the traditional way, which they deemed both fair and equitable. The matter was then referred to the governor of Sidon who, after investigating whether the customary arrangement would cost the government more or less money, gave the Nablus Council permission to continue "as in the days of old."[63]

The importance of this seemingly small victory for Nabulsi merchants is that it cut to the heart of a larger political question: control of resources. The mid-nineteenth century was a transitional time in the political history of Palestine: the Ottoman administrative system was in the midst of reorganization as the *Tanzimat* were gradually implemented. In traditionally autonomous regions, including Jabal Nablus, the central government faced a dilemma: it established new institutions, such as the council, in order to centralize its rule at the expense of local notables, but it had to depend on these very notables to run these institutions. The ambiguity inherent in this situation made for fluid boundaries of power, and each side tested the waters through seemingly innocuous disputes over minor details. Thus Nabulsi merchants correctly perceived that both their fortunes and their political influence depended on how well they could use the council to bend the rules of the game to their advantage.

Aware of these difficulties, the Ottoman authorities concentrated their efforts on controlling the most important link in the movement of these commodities: the bidding process that determined which merchant would purchase what type of commodity at what price (and, indirectly, the ultimate destination). Judging from the correspondence on this issue, the provincial governors were far less flexible in entertaining exceptions and, more important, did all they could to maximize revenues by soliciting the highest bids possible, regardless of the source.

To achieve their goal, the authorities needed to be informed. One of the most striking aspects of the contested movement of commodities was struggle over knowledge. Repeatedly the provincial governors and their treasurers demanded that detailed reports be submitted on the types, amounts, and going prices of the *zakhayir* moved into and stored in the storehouses of Nablus and Jenin. An example of the detailed level of supervision that the central government attempted to implement (though not necessarily successfully) is this letter to the Nablus Council from Adham Pasha, dated September 18, 1849:

> You previously sent a memorandum concerning the taxes-in-kind presently in the storehouses of Nablus district, saying that if you had to sell the olive oil and clarified butter locally, you would not be able to find a buyer due to the good season and the presence of old stocks. . . . The provincial council . . . deems it absolutely necessary that the above-mentioned *zakhayir* be sold before they are ruined and cause a loss in the tax revenues. Considering the bad prices, you cannot sell them locally, and if you did, you would get only a very low price, and that also would be a loss to our tax revenues. A buyer in Beirut has not been found because a sample was not received in time. Therefore, you must consider: if you transport the above mentioned *zakhayir* to one of the nearby ports, would you or would you not get a higher net price after subtracting the transportation costs than you would if you sold them at the price levels available in your local market at this time? . . .
>
> We also received word from you that the *ahali* are satisfied [with your offer] that they can pay twenty piasters for each *irddab* of barley [they owe in taxes]. . . . As long as the *ahali* are satisfied [with this arrangement] . . . and if this price is profitable at this time, then you can collect [cash] in the place of barley and do the same for wheat and send all the proceeds to the Provincial Treasury. This is the order we received in this regards. [We have agreed to your request] because we do not know what the

current value of the *zakhayir* in Nablus is, nor what the quantity is. We also do not know the prices in the ports near Nablus, such as Haifa and Jaffa, nor the cost of transportation. . . .

Therefore, we are sending over . . . *Sayyid* Faydallah Alami . . . a member of the Jerusalem [Advisory] Council. Upon his arrival . . . the [Nablus] Council will investigate and report on: the prices currently available; the types and amounts of *zakhayir*; which port, Haifa or Jaffa, is closest and the easier for transport; the cost of transportation per *irddab* . . . the prices available in the ports; and whether the merchants there have a desire to buy [the *zakhayir*]. If necessary, also send samples [to the ports] and make sure the merchants there know about them. Once you compare the prices [in the ports] and the costs and possibility of transportation, then take note of the price levels at your end, the difference will become clear. As soon as it does, let us know quickly and in detail.[64]

There is no copy of the council's original memorandum that provoked this response, but, if it was an attempt to prepare the ground for an eventual sale to local merchants at low prices, it backfired. The governor's answer immediately ruled out the possibility of local sale and, in a patronizing manner, outlined the basic rules of trade to a council dominated by merchants. By pointing an obvious finger at the port cities as an alternative, he was making the subtle point that this thought would never have occurred to the Nablus Council independently of him. Moreover, he cleverly used the opening provided him as a justification to demand a whole range of information and to dispatch an outside (but friendly) observer in order keep the council in check.

It might seem puzzling that Adham Pasha would ask for information that he probably already had, such as prices in the port cities. After all, following market prices was, of necessity, an obsession of tax collectors and merchants because it directly affected their revenues and profits. It is more likely, therefore, that his pointed instructions were intended to remind the council of its obligations to keep the state informed about all phases of the taxation process, by putting them through an exercise he hoped they would repeat annually.

This speculation is not so far-fetched if one considers the context of the exchange. The Nablus Council had been established only a few years earlier, and the composition of its membership at the time of this memorandum was still a point of contention between the central government and the local ruling families (see Chapter 1). Also, at this time the council was supporting a tax strike against government-appointed customs collectors by soap merchants (all the members of the council traded in soap, as will be further discussed in Chapter 5). Just a few months later, the council would vigorously contest the results of a population count carried out in December 1849.[65] We have also seen how even the peripheral issues of measuring and storage became a testing ground for defining the boundaries of power and prerogative between local and central forces.

In short, Adham Pasha clearly distrusted the motives of council—and, by implication, the local merchant community—because he knew that when it came to the movement and prices of local agricultural production, they were busy pursuing an agenda contrary to that of the state. They cooperated with each other to choke competition from outside bidders in order to keep prices low, and they wanted to purchase as much of the agricultural surplus as possible. They were also keen on deciding the timing of the sales because the release of, say, grains could affect prices, especially during shortages.[66] The overall aims were to resell at high prices, especially to foreign merchants, and to ensure an adequate supply for local and regional needs on which the bulk of their business depended. These aims, one must quickly add, were not driven solely by the search for profits. Nabulsi merchants were also under a great deal of social and political pressure from below: namely, from retail merchants and artisanal groups whose livelihoods depended on the availability of cheap raw materials from the countryside.

Cotton was especially important in this regard, because the textile-manufacturing sector in the city was a large one. Indeed, so much cotton was ginned in Nablus that the newly appointed non-Nabulsi customs inspector, Uthman *Afandi*, wanted to tax the brisk trade in cotton seeds, which were separated from the white fibers and sold to peasants as fodder for their animals. This tax caused such an outrage that the Nablus Council, citing "a petition from the people," sent a letter to the customs inspector on September 9, 1852, insisting that it be abolished.[67] The primary argument that the council made in justifying its demand was the unfairness of taxing local trade. Cotton seeds, they argued, were a by-product of the trade between the city and its hinterlands. It was absolutely essential, they said, that this local circulation not be subject to any taxation. In the same vein, the council consistently supported petitions by peasants to pay cash in lieu of taxes-in-kind when prices were high. On September 13, 1850, the Nablus Council argued yet again in favor of such a request. The council members justified their position by claiming that the peasants of Nablus and Jenin could not meet their tax-in-kind obligations because heavy rains had severely reduced the grain harvest.[68] Judging from similar petitions, however, it could very well be that both merchants and peasants in Jabal Nablus wanted to hold on to the surplus in

kind in order to meet local demand as well as to take advantage of the rise
in prices caused by the grain shortage. In so doing, peasants effectively
lowered their taxes by selling their surplus at higher prices, while merchants, in turn, gained greater access to a precious commodity in a volatile
market.

Competition and Sabotage

The tight control of Nabulsi merchants over the surplus of Jabal Nablus
was a constant source of irritation for the Ottoman authorities. Indeed, in
a letter dated June 30, 1852, the non-Nabulsi customs inspectors, Haqqi
Afandi and *Khawaja* Casper, accused Nabulsi leaders of treating the hinterland as if it were their tax-farm for life (*malikane*).[69] In order to break
this stranglehold the central government actively recruited foreign and
regional merchants to take part in the bidding process for the *zakhayir*.[70]
This way, bidding prices would be invigorated while outside merchants
who loudly protested the difficulties they faced in penetrating this region
could be appeased. Much to the chagrin of Nabulsi merchants, the central
government occasionally rejected some local bids and, often at the last
minute, substituted bids from these outside merchants (see Chapter 5 for
a detailed example).

Unable to challenge the central government's insistence that it approve
all final bids, the Nablus Council occasionally resorted to delay and sabo-
tage tactics—that is, if we are to believe the angry accusations leveled
against the council by outside merchants. One example is the above letter
from Adham Pasha, in which he noted that he was unable to interest
Beiruti merchants in offering bids because samples from Nablus "were
not received in time." Another, more detailed, example of resistance to
outside competition and the volatility caused by European demand is the
following dispute. Sometime in early 1852, *Sayyid* Muhammad *Afandi*
Halawani, most likely a Beiruti merchant, successfully bid on 550 *kaylas*
of wheat from the storehouses of Nablus and Jenin. He was enraged, however, when the wheat he received turned out to be damaged by worm and
rot, or so he claimed in a lawsuit that asked for compensation for the
moneys he had lost in the process. *Sayyid* Halawani was obviously important enough to initiate an investigation of this matter by the highest-
ranking fiscal officer in the province. On May 29, 1852, the Nablus Council received a letter from the treasurer (*daftar dar*) of Sidon province, in
which he requested a sample of the wheat sold to *Sayyid* Halawani in
order to examine his allegations. The council replied that all of the wheat

in the storehouses had already been sold but that they would send the sample that was kept on the council's premises and on whose basis, they claimed, *Sayyid* Halawani had made his purchase. They also provided an alternative explanation for the wheat merchant's loss:

> When the bidding commenced, [wheat] prices reached a level much higher than their real worth. [This was] due to chance, because during that week there was a strong demand for [wheat] to be shipped to the ports. So the city (Nablus) was cut off from wheat for a number of days, causing prices to double. Buyers, hoping to take advantage of rising prices, paid 28 piasters per *kayla* . . . But, by the time *Sayyid* Halawani's bid was accepted and his agent Fayyad *Beik* Tuqan arrived to receive the [wheat], the price had already fallen steeply because a great deal of wheat came into the city [in response to the high prices]. So the agent was forced to sell the wheat quickly, and at a loss (before prices fell even further).[71]

If we are to believe the Nablus Council, *Sayyid* Halawani was a victim of circumstances. Working around the "export season" was imperative, for even an experienced merchant could be caught off guard and forced to bear a substantial loss. This held especially true for those merchants who risked investment in the products of a far-away city and its hinterland. Thus *Sayyid* Halawani paid dearly for being distant from the local scene by purchasing at the wrong time, even though he had hired a Nabulsi merchant precisely for the purpose of avoiding this mistake. The other possibility, of course, is that the Nablus Council used the phenomenon of European demand as an excuse to cover up what might have been a clever scheme to unload rotten grains on a faraway merchant who could not hold them accountable for their actions. But whether the council's explanation was truthful or not, the fact that it was used shows that the themes of outside competition from the port cities and the vagaries of European demand were already ingrained in the business discourse of Palestinian peasants and merchants, including those of an interior region like Jabal Nablus. There is little doubt that this discourse can be traced back at least as far as the eighteenth century.

What the council's letter also makes impressively clear is the dizzying speed with which peasants, merchants, and transporters responded to the lure of high prices offered by regional and foreign traders operating from the port cities: Nablus was emptied of its stocks within days. Thus the volatility of European demand and the ability of foreign merchants to pay high prices added another element of unpredictability into an increasingly contested and tense market. On more than one occasion the council's letters specifically stated that local merchants were aware that speculation in agricultural commodities must take into account the fact that prices for wheat, cotton, oil, and other crops rose sharply with the arrival of trade ships from overseas, then dropped off considerably after they left.[72]

Arab merchants from the regional metropolitan centers around Nablus, especially those from Beirut, faced numerous problems when dealing with their counterparts in Jabal Nablus.[73] For example, on April 4, 1850, the Nablus Council received a communiqué from the governor of Sidon province ordering the sale of wheat in the storehouses of Nablus and Jenin to *Khawaja* Ilyas Najjar, a Christian merchant from Beirut who also served as an employee of the U.S. consulate in that city.[74] If we are to believe the governor's accusations, the Nablus Council delayed the delivery for several weeks, and even then it remained incomplete.[75] Throughout, *Khawaja* Najjar bitterly complained that he was still waiting for the full amount and that the ship he had hired was sitting idly at the port.

Still another example of perceived delay tactics is the following commercial dispute, recorded on September 26, 1850, in which a foreign consul accused the Nablus customs inspector—then a Nabulsi who was replaced soon after by an outsider—of failing to deliver the ginned cotton he had successfully bid on:

> [Today], the Customs Inspector of Nablus, Mas'ud *Agha*, and the Customs Treasurer, *Khawaja* Arakil, appeared before the council. [They] testified that *Khawaja* "Escowage," consul at Acre, has accused them of delaying the shipment of ginned cotton that his Nablus agent, al-Abd Ikhrem, had purchased; and that due to their delay of the ginned cotton, he suffered a loss because the ship was forced to leave [empty]. He has demanded adjudication by the Acre Council to settle the account between him and the Nablus Customs Inspector. The aforementioned Mas'ud *Agha* and *Khawaja* Arakil testified that in no way did they delay any of . . . *Khawaja* Escowage's ginned cotton. [On the contrary], at the time of purchase, [it was sent with carriers] under the direction of *Hajj* Ahmad Najib Ashur, *Hajj* Yasin Qaraman, Ali [al-Ghlayyan?], and Salih Ikhrem, who signed out the ginned cotton in his name and in the name of his cousin, al-Abd Ikhrem, the agent of the aforementioned *Khawaja* Escowage. The above-mentioned individuals [were brought] before the council and asked about the testimony of Mas'ud *Agha* and the treasurer. They . . . testified that [the accused] in no way delayed or prevented the delivery of any of the ginned cotton purchased by the *Khawaja* [Escowage].[76]

The outcome of the case is not mentioned, but this is not our primary concern. More significant is the set of clues that this memorandum provides as to the tensions inherent in the relationship between local and foreign agents and, just as important, as to competition between Nabulsi merchants themselves, for it is clear that some sought to profit from this lucrative trade by acting as agents for the foreign merchants.

Consul "Escowage" resorted to the Acre Council, which raised the matter with its counterpart in Nablus. The Nablus Council naturally turned a sympathetic ear not to the foreign consul but to its fellow merchants, who simply denied the charges. Herein lies the crux of the new politics of trade: the "free" market in cotton was only free in the sense that it was no longer monopolized by a single ruling strongman, such as Ahmad Pasha al-Jazzar, and not in the sense that there were no political restrictions at all. On the contrary, local merchants "adjusted" the conditions of trade to work in their favor through their networks and through the Advisory Council. Foreign traders, in contrast, were strangers to the peasants and did not have the power, at least not in mid-nineteenth-century Nablus, to ensure the fulfillment of contracts. Also, there was not a single powerful ruler in Jabal Nablus to whom they could turn for redress, as there had been in the days of Zahir al-Umar in Acre or of Muhammad Ali Pasha in Egypt. That they wished for one was demonstrated by Alexander Schölch, who detailed the efforts of European powers to convince the Ottoman authorities that one single governor, based in Jerusalem, should be made responsible for all of the surrounding regions in Palestine.[77]

Still, foreign merchants had the ability to offer high prices, a factor that became increasingly important with the passage of time. The large profits to be made were recognized not only by the minority merchant communities in the coastal cities but also by Muslim merchants from the interior. As shown in the previous example, some Nabulsi merchants worked as agents for foreign traders. No doubt they were sought out because they were perceived to be more effective in managing commercial transactions in semiautonomous interior regions. Thus, Consul "Escowage" chose the Nabulsi merchant, al-Abd Ikhrem. The latter, in turn, employed both his cousin and three other locals to purchase cotton, and he signed out the consignment from the government storehouse in his name. It would not be accurate, therefore, to assume that all Nabulsi merchants were of one mind or presented a united front toward outsiders. Indeed, breaking ranks was one of the quickest ways for small merchants to gain access to credit from European traders, to assure themselves an outlet for their goods and, in general, to increase their fortunes and compete with the established merchants in their community.[78]

The integration of Palestine into a world economy, therefore, cannot be satisfactorily explained through the often-used dichotomies of internal/external, passive/active, or penetration/response. Rather, each link in the movement, measurement, storage, sale, and transport of commodities was a contested arena that involved competition among a wide variety of actors: peasants, village brokers, Nabulsi merchants, regional trading houses, and European traders, all within the fluid political context of an Ottoman state in the midst of reorganization and reform. This is not to say that all the participants enjoyed the same degree of power to make the new politics of trade work to their advantage. But, at least until the early 1850s, Nabulsi merchants had sufficient tools at their disposal to hold on to the lion's share of their hinterland's agricultural surplus. Documents detailing the results of auction bids on *zakhayir* over the five-year period (1848–1853) for which records are available, for example, show that the overwhelming majority of successful bids were made by Nabulsi merchants and that European and regional merchants were only occasionally able to successfully bid on wheat, cotton, and sesame, and then usually with the help of the central government.[79] Nevertheless, the trends were already in place for a shift in favor of those who controlled the largest reserves of capital and who had access to the corridors of power in Europe and Istanbul: foreign merchants and regional trading houses. Beginning in the 1850s, the power of local councils to affect the outcome of commercial disputes was steadily eroded, as commercial tribunals became dominated by Europeans and, more important, as European commercial laws were adopted and enforced by the Ottoman government.[80] Thus each delaying tactic only postponed the inevitable, as Jabal Nablus became irreversibly enmeshed in a world economic system dominated by Europe.

The other face of European competition was the export of machine-produced commodities that competed with local artisanal production. Textiles, usually made of cotton, were especially vulnerable to such a challenge, for they faced competition from the most advanced European industrial sector. The following analysis of how the textile sector in Nablus fared can shed light on the pace and rhythm of restructuring in the manufacturing sphere experienced by the market towns in the interior regions of Greater Syria.

TEXTILES: RESILIENCE AND RESTRUCTURING

In mid-August 1833 the Nablus Islamic Court inventoried the property of two textile weavers, *Hajj* Yasin Taha and Dali daughter of Bakur—a husband and wife who died around the same time.[81] They were an older couple, with only a daughter and two grandchildren surviving them. At one time *Hajj* Yasin had the resources and the opportunity to make the pilgrimage to the Holy Cities of Mecca and Medina. He must have fallen on hard times, however, because he and his wife died poor: the woman had no jewelry, and the man's clothes were cheap and worn out. In fact, their household goods at the time of death consisted of the absolute bare minimum for daily survival: a small stone hand mill for crushing wheat, a wooden board for preparing bread dough, a ceramic jug for water, two sieves for sorting grains, an oil lamp, an old rug, two mattresses, two blankets, two pillows, and some copper kitchenware. The only work-related items listed were two looms (*idatayn hiyaka*). Their life savings were six small gold pieces (*habbat dhahab*) worth only two piasters each. Half of the worth of their paltry estate went toward burial costs, court expenses, and a debt to a textile merchant.[82]

As weavers, *Hajj* Yasin and his wife were typical of a significant pro-portion of the population of Nablus, for the textile-production sector em-ployed the largest number of workers, and many of these were women and/or entire families who worked together as a single economic unit. Most, as in many other cities and towns in the Ottoman Empire, labored at home as part of a putting-out system and were paid by the piece.[83] Many, like the couple above, owned their means of production, but the looms were inexpensive, worth only 7.5 piasters each, or the price of two kilos of cotton yarn.[84]

It is tempting to view the saga of *Hajj* Yasin and Dali daughter of Bakur as a metaphor for the rise, decline, and death of the once-prosperous tex-tile-manufacturing sectors in the cities and market towns of Greater Syria due to competition from European machine-made textiles. Indeed, the "deindustrialization" argument is a common theme in both nationalist and colonialist discourses about the impact of the capitalist incorporation of the "non-Western" world. Such a metaphor, however, would not do justice to what actually was a much more complicated story of adaptation and restructuring. As will be seen below, the saga of these two individuals more accurately represents how this process of restructuring exacted a heavy toll from textile workers, especially women, who bore a dispropor-tionately large burden of declining living standards, low wages, and lim-ited opportunities.

The Textile Industry in Nablus

Evidence based on the amount of taxes levied on cloth, dye houses and cloth beaters—as listed in the Ottoman cadastral surveys (*defter-i mufas-sal*) for the years 1538/1539, 1548/1549, and 1596/1597—suggests that, next to Safad, Nablus was the most important center for the weaving and dyeing of textiles in sixteenth-century Palestine and that there was a steady expansion in the textile industry in Nablus in the last two-thirds of the century.[85] Much less is known about the size and importance of the textile sector during the seventeenth, eighteenth, and early nineteenth centuries. It is likely that it expanded in keeping with the economic and demographic growth of Jabal Nablus during most of this period. We do know that the textile industry of Safad collapsed in the seventeenth century, whereas that of Nablus remained the most important in Palestine well into the nineteenth century.[86] The major reason for this divergence, it seems, is that the Safad industry was based on the production of expensive woolen cloth for regional and overseas export, whereas that of Nablus was geared toward the local and regional mass market. The former was eventually suffocated by foreign competition, especially from France,[87] but the latter proved to be extremely resilient.

Invasion and Resistance

According to Halil İnalcik, the invasion of British and other European textile goods came in three stages.[88] First was the introduction, in the late eighteenth and early nineteenth centuries, of the highly competitive machine-manufactured cotton yarn, which was cheaper, stronger, and better made than locally spun yarn. This was followed by a conscious effort to imitate items of dress popular among the well-to-do urban elements. Third, by the 1850s a final push was made into the mass market of peasants and urban lower classes.

Great Britain became the dominant European trading partner of the Ottoman Empire in the first half of the nineteenth century, and the Ottoman Empire was England's third major trading partner. More than a third of the total British exports to the Ottoman Empire was in cotton cloth.[89] Table 6 shows a steady increase in Ottoman imports of British cotton goods, with an exponential jump occurring after 1850.

The numbers in Table 6, it must be emphasized, are not very accurate because record-keeping practices were irregular and differed from one region to the next. For example, Roger Owen noted that between 1831 and 1850, Ottoman imports of British twists and yarns rose from 1,700,000 pounds to nearly 6,350,000 pounds.[90] The latter figure is substantially higher than the one noted by İnalcik in Table 6, but there is no question of the trend: imports of yarn and, consequently, stiff competition for local spinners increased substantially beginning in the 1830s.

Table 6. English Exports of Cotton Goods to the Ottoman Empire, 1825–1860

Year	Cloth (in Thousands of Yards)	Yarn (in Thousands of Pounds)
1825	3,578	557
1830	15,940	1,528
1835	25,692	3,272
1840	?	?
1845	46,793	5,830
1850	31,124	2,384
1855	132,605	8,446
1860	229,201	22,824

SOURCES: Adapted from Table 17.2 in İnalcik, "When and How," p. 381.

Table 7. British Exports to Syria/Palestine, 1836–1850, Annual Averages (£—declared values)

Year	Total Exports	Cotton Goods	Percent
1836–1839	119,753	112,155	93.6
1840–1844	441,107	430,194	97.5
1845–1849	382,219	358,456	93.8
1850	303,254	271,457	89.5

SOURCES: Adapted from Tables 6 and 7 in Owen, *Middle East*, p. 85.

The centrality of textiles to British exports was even more pronounced in the case of Greater Syria. Table 7 shows a threefold increase in just five years between 1840–1844, then a slow decrease as the market leveled out.

This energetic expansion into Greater Syria—driven partly by technological improvements, such as the introduction of regular steamship service in the mid-nineteenth century, which lowered transportation costs, cut travel time, and made shipping safer and more predictable—led many contemporary Western observers to pronounce in their journals and reports the end of local handicrafts in general and of the textile industry in particular. These pronouncements, in turn, were often quoted by historians as accurate statements. Writing in 1975, Shmuel Avitsur noted that by the nineteenth century, "local textile centers like Bayt Jala, Nablus, and later also Hebron and other towns, were either completely ruined and disappeared or were reduced to the proportions of an ancillary trade furnishing an additional pittance to the hard-hit craftsman now struggling to make a living in other ways."[91]

Ihsan Nimr, a local historian, was of the same opinion. In a section entitled "The Undermining and Destruction of the [Jabal Nablus] Manufactures," he wrote:

> Local industry was undermined in inverse proportion to [the import of] Western manufactures. With the use of petrol lamps, gone were the oil lamps. . . . With the use of tin cans, leather pouches were put aside, as were the tanneries [which produced them]. With the use of foreign leather, the local leather industry started declining so that out of seven local leather factories, only one was left until it too closed down, and its remains were erased with the paving of Palestine Street.
>
> The death blow was the one that hit textile weaving. [Previously] the number of looms was so high in both city and countryside that a local saying—"Where is Fatima in the cotton market?"—became a common expression for a crowded place. The same blow was dealt to woolen textiles, and the *bisht* industry was wiped out during the last wool crisis [after World War II]. And with the destruction of the textile industry, the dyeing establishments were destroyed as well. [At one time] they used to be twenty in number, then they shrank to just a few simple cauldrons. Only a small dye establishment, that of the Abwa family, was left. . . .
>
> They [Nabulsis] used to use wooden spoons . . . but the arrival of metal ones put a stop to that. And with the use of Ottoman and foreign gold coins as necklaces, goldsmithing contracted to a very low level even though it was growing previously. With the introduction of oil-powered milling, the water, air, and animal-powered mills were gone. So were the stone olive and sesame presses, now replaced by machines imported from the outside. . . . And they [now] use caustic soda for soap, [thus] halting the production of *qilw*. Ironsmithing and carpentry have been greatly weakened, and with the use of foreign medicines, local drugs and prescriptions have fallen by the wayside.[92]

This detailed epitaph by a writer very much embittered by the decline of Nablus's traditional industries is a powerful reminder of the long-term impact of competition from the industrialized countries, but it must be taken with several grains of salt. Nimr painted this gloomy picture from the vantage point of the second half of the twentieth century; that is, he conflated developments of several periods, most of which took place after World War I.[93] Although there is no doubt about the overall trends, many of the old manufactures survived well into the twentieth century. In any case, the production of olive oil, soap, and other commodities did not cease; rather, it restructured with the adoption of new factors of production. After all, the large, round stones used for pressing oil or sesame were not exactly a major product of Nabulsi industry, and the *qilw* used in soapmaking was imported from bedouins on the east bank of the River Jordan.

One must also add that changing patterns of demand gave rise to new artisanal occupations and manufactures. Nimr himself, a few pages later, recounts the names of Nabulsis who learned to tailor Western suits and make Western shoes, as well as those of carpenters and ironsmiths who also learned how to use new tools and to produce new products, some of which were copied from advertisement catalogs! This is not to mention a whole range of services and industries connected with automobiles, printing, glassmaking, cement production, and so on.[94]

Manufacturing activities, therefore, were restructured and adapted to changing conditions. Dominique Chevalier's 1962 study of the resistance techniques of Syrian artisans was the first concrete rebuttal of the traditional view of unmitigated decline.[95] Later, Roger Owen and Donald Quataert raised more general objections. The former argued that the internal market of the Fertile Crescent was growing in the nineteenth century due to rising population. This increased local demand for textiles in general, because there were more and more people to be clothed. Owen also noted that European manufacturers failed to successfully imitate many local styles, patterns, and fabrics. Even when they were successful, they had to contend with the reverse process: local imitation of European products. Owen also cited a common example of restructuring concerning the contradictory effects of the importation of machine-made yarn. On the one hand, it was stronger and cheaper than locally woven yarn and quickly replaced it, undermining the spinners (and, by implication, weakening the household economy of the urban lower classes because spinners were usually females who worked at home). On the other hand, imported British yarn was used by the weavers (usually males) to produce a cheap, durable cloth composed of a mixture of local and imported yarn that proved to be highly competitive with British cloth in terms of cost.[96] Recall the example, in Chapter 2, of how Nabulsi weavers and tailors used both local and imported cloth in the production of basic textile items such as outergarments and mattress covers.

Quataert faulted historians for not taking into consideration the underlying assumptions of contemporary European observers or the contexts in which their reports about the destruction of handicrafts industries were made.[97] For example, one must be cautious of the ethnocentric assumption that lack of mechanized factories implied a lack of industry, of the narrow focus of observers on the large urban centers that were the most vulnerable to European competition, and of the scant attention paid to rural areas that were also important centers of production. Finally, he brought up the essential point that cheap labor, especially female labor, was very important in allowing locally produced goods to survive, restructure, and remain competitive with machine-made imports.

Most of the above caveats apply to the situation in Nablus during the period under study, and it is the combination of these factors that accounted for the resilience of the textile-manufacturing sector. Briefly summarized, Nablus was a relatively small, interior city blessed by a plentiful water supply (crucial for the fulling and dyeing stages of production). It was well provisioned with locally grown raw materials and a cheap labor force. It also had a textile-manufacturing sector geared toward meeting the less expensive needs of the mass market as well as the specific and varied tastes of the peasant communities in the hinterland (such as for wedding clothes). Both characteristics were reinforced by deeply rooted local merchant networks that assured supplies and markets as well as by the investments of textile merchants in this sector. Each textile merchant had loyal clients from specific villages and was well informed about his client's conditions, needs, and preferences. Large textile merchants also commissioned spinners, weavers, and tailors on an order-by-order basis, commissioned women for piecework in their homes and sank significant amounts of capital into the dyeing of clothes.[98]

The first set of issues has to do with Nablus's location, size, and basic economic orientation, all of which made it difficult to penetrate. The city of Nablus was less vulnerable to European competition because its interior location raised the costs of transportation. The elasticity of demand for luxury goods made this a relatively unimportant factor, but the same could not be said about the demand for low-cost textile goods. Nablus's small size compared with Damascus, Cairo, and Aleppo also made it a less important market for European merchants. None of them, for example, established a permanent trade mission in the city itself. The strong influence of the local merchant community, as well as Jabal Nablus's jealously guarded autonomy and conservative antiforeigner reputation, also limited outside access to its markets. Foreign merchants complained bitterly about the difficulties they encountered in establishing trading houses in the large interior cities, as well as in enforcing contracts, collecting debts, and receiving adequate support from local government for the practices of "free" trade.[99] These difficulties were multiplied manyfold in the case of the smaller and more autonomous urban areas in the interior. Haim Gerber argued, for example, that the textile-manufacturing towns of Palestine suffered much less than did Damascus, as evidenced by a comparison of the labor structures, and that locally produced textile goods remained popular among peasants and the urban lower classes.[100] As detailed in Chapter 2, the real competition for local production originated regionally rather than from overseas.

The second set of points has to do with the ready availability of relatively cheap raw materials for textile manufacturing, most of which were locally produced in commercial quantities. This was especially true for cotton. H. B. Tristram, who visited Nablus in the early 1860s, wrote: "The busy hum of the cotton gins greeted us on all sides, and heaps of cotton husks lay about the streets. . . . Though we had seen everywhere the signs of a nascent cotton-trade, yet in no place was it so developed as here."[101] Wool, the second most important raw material, was supplied by both peasants and bedouins. Most of the latter were based east of the River Jordan; the rest roamed the coastal region of Palestine and the flatlands of Marj Ibn Amir. The third most important raw material—natural dyestuffs such as gallnuts (*afas*), indigo (*nila*), or sumac (*summaq*)—were grown locally and/or in Bisan, Jericho, and other areas close to Nablus.[102] In 1824–1825, for example, Muhammad Ali Pasha, the viceroy of Egypt, sent a merchant to arrange for the importation of indigo seeds from the latter two areas.[103] All the above-mentioned dyestuffs were frequently encountered in the estates of merchants and artisans, but the most ubiquitous were gallnuts. These were used for dyeing both textiles and leather water pouches and were grown in sufficient quantities to allow for export to Egypt and Aleppo.[104]

The third set of issues has to do with the type of manufactures. Most textile articles produced in Nablus and some of the villages in its hinterland were geared toward the mass market of peasants and the lower classes in the urban areas. Bowring's list of locally produced textile products in the epigraph of this chapter summarizes well the orientation of the textile sector in Nablus, a city known for the eminently practical but hardly chic cotton *thawb* (pl. *thiyab*) and for the long-lasting woolen *bisht*, which kept many a peasant warm during cold winter days.

Thiyab were the most frequently mentioned type of locally manufactured clothes in the estates of textile merchants.[105] The trade caravan that left Nablus after the 1771 siege, recall, was carrying 100 camel loads of *thiyab*, yarn, and "other things" to Damascus. This particular product was also exported eastward, to points across the River Jordan. In the early nineteenth century, for example, James Silk Buckingham noted that a monthly caravan connected Nablus to Salt and that the stock of a textile merchant in the latter consisted of "cotton cloths from Nablous."[106] *Thiyab* were also present in the estate of a merchant from Mosul (in today's Iraq) who died in 1825 during the Holy Month of Ramadan, while on a business trip in Nablus.[107] Mass produced in three basic sizes—small, medium, or large—*thiyab* were not expensive, especially when compared with similar items imported regionally or from overseas. In the estate of Shaykh Abdullah Fityani (d. 1840), for example, a *thawb malti*—made from British cloth apparently imported through Malta—cost 44 piasters; a *thawb baladi wasat* (medium size, locally made) cost 13 piasters.[108]

"It was like wearing a carpet." This is how an older peasant from the village of Dayr Ghazzala, near Jenin, described the woolen *bisht*, the other textile item that Nablus was famous for producing.[109] Made of coarse, thick, tightly woven sheep wool thread, *bishts* were practically indestructible and very popular among peasants, shepherds, and poorer folk. Also mass produced in preset sizes, all *bishts* were white with wide red stripes, had short sleeves, and reached to just below the knees. They were worn almost continuously during the winter: "We used to sleep in it, inside and outside the house," said another peasant from the village of Bayt Wazan near Nablus.[110] The demand for this item was such that during the first half of the nineteenth century every quarter in the city had shops that made *bishts*.[111]

The fourth set of issues is the low cost of equipment and labor—two important elements of resistance to external competition. The prices of cotton gins ranged from 1.5 piasters in 1800 to 35 piasters in 1830; of looms, from 1.5 piasters in 1800 to 10 piasters in 1808 and 7.5 piasters in 1833.[112] These prices of used equipment found in the estates of deceased individuals suggest that those who wanted to purchase their own did not face serious obstacles in terms of costs.

The low cost of labor was a far more important factor. First, as shown by Sherry Vatter in the case of Damascus, it was not unusual for artisans who were worried about their employment prospects to grudgingly accept cuts in their standard of living, though not on an indefinite basis.[113] Second, women who worked for even lower wages were heavily employed in the spinning and weaving of textiles in the Fertile Crescent, Egypt, and Anatolia.[114]

In Nablus, Nimr claims that it was mostly women who spun the cotton and wool, either as paid workers or as individual producers for the market.[115] Nimr's claim is substantiated by a number of inheritance estates of merchants who dealt in wool and cotton. The court's inventory of the property and debts of these merchants often included a number of women who were owed money for labor rendered.[116] An example is the estate of Hasan son of Salah Zakar (d. 1806), who traded mostly with Damascus. Apart from family members, he owed small amounts of money to sixteen individuals, thirteen of whom were women.[117] The way the women were referred to is telling: only their first names were mentioned, which implies that they were hired labor with low social status. In contrast, other women mentioned in these estates, whether as inheritors or loaners, were identified as belonging to a particular family or male relative. Another example is the estate of *Sayyid* Muhammad Sadiq son of Muhammad *Afandi* Bustami, which listed ten looms in his shop.[118] He owed hundreds of piasters in wages to employees, many of whom were women. Judging from the inventory of textile products, the basic item his workers produced was the ubiquitous *thawb*. He exported his production to Damascus, and he even owned a shop there. This estate also shows that a substantial portion of his production was locally commissioned by textile merchants, many of whom owed him money at the time of his death. It is highly likely that rural women, especially those from the larger villages near Nablus, also worked as spinners, as was the case in other parts of the region, such as Egypt.[119]

Cheap labor, low cost of equipment, and a decentralized process of production all combined with the factors mentioned above to make the textile industry in Jabal Nablus a resilient one. Nevertheless, this sector was facing serious difficulties by the early nineteenth century. This is indicated by the following petition sent by the Nablus textile merchants to the city's Advisory Council on April 2, 1850:

> In 1254 [1838/1839], the Egyptians imposed on all those who sell cloth an offensive, illegal tax of 3,710 piasters, and this imposition has continued until today although [it] does not exist anywhere else in the Protected Dominions. [As a result] we have [suffered] decline and damage, especially during the tenure of the last *multazim* [tax farmer who collected taxes on textiles]. It is not hidden, your excellencies, that we pay import and export customs at the proper places according to the Noble Regulations on all the cloth and other goods that we bring. If this imposition continues we will be totally ruined, and since the [state] cannot allow its subjects to suffer treachery and decline we have found the courage to present this petition.[120]

The council forwarded the petition to the provincial headquarters in Sidon with the comment that, indeed, this was an illegal tax and should be looked into. The real issue, however, was almost certainly an effort to undermine the status of the previous *multazim*, because on the same day the petition bids for urban *iltizam* posts were posted, including that of textiles.[121] Yet, and even if we allow for the exaggeration implied in the phrase "total ruin," the underlying premise was that all had not been well with textile trade and manufacturing since the 1830s—that is, since before foreign competition had its greatest impact.

One must also look, therefore, for internal reasons for the slow contraction of the textile sector and the stagnation in cotton production, or, more accurately, its reduced weight in the political economy of Jabal Nablus as compared with the fate of other types of trade and manufacturing. The key factor in this regard is that merchant capital was increasingly diverted to other sectors of the economy. As the following chapters will show, the investment of merchant capital became concentrated in the lending of money to peasants, the purchase of agricultural lands and urban real estate, the trade in olive oil, and, most important, the production of soap. All of these areas took advantage of profit-making enterprises that were far less vulnerable to European competition than was textile manufacturing and which, especially in the case of soap, commanded a large and expanding regional market.

CONCLUSION

The stories of cotton and textiles shed light on the process of Palestine's integration into the world economy as well as on the role of local merchants in the changing relationship between politics and trade. The cotton connection shows that the qualitative leap in trade relations with Europe during the 1856–1882 period, which Schölch meticulously documented, was not a sudden development nor solely an outcome of European "penetration," as he phrased it. Palestinian society was more than ripe for accelerated trade relations with Europe, in large measure because Palestinian merchants and peasants, especially those in the interior, played an active role in preparing the basic social, economic, and political structures that made this leap possible in the first place. The question, therefore, is not one of the emergence of commercial agricultural production as a result of the encounter with Europe. These features were not new, and, in any case, regional trade remained paramount until the last decades of Ottoman rule, at least for interior regions such as Jabal Nablus. Rather, it is one of orientation and acceleration as the Ottoman Empire as a whole became slowly enmeshed in the European economic orbit.

During the eighteenth and early nineteenth centuries, control of cotton production and trade shifted from Acre to Nablus, but Jabal Nablus's integration into the world capitalist system was a slow process. Nablus's location in the interior, its influential merchant community, and its long tradition of jealously guarded autonomy all meant that external political and economic forces were incrementally absorbed and locally reproduced. Also, cotton production was geared to meet the demands of local and regional markets, not just those of French and British merchants. Jabal Nablus, therefore, was not totally vulnerable to shifting European demand. The process of integration was also uneven: cotton was only grown in the coastal areas and the plains. The villages in these areas were more involved in trade with Europe than were the primarily olive-producing villages of the central highlands and the eastern subdistricts.

The political ramifications of the process of integration were similarly uneven. In northern Palestine the cotton trade was subject to monopoly until the early nineteenth century, unlike Jabal Nablus, where merchants competed with each other. Indeed, Nabulsi merchants came to control the organization of production and trade, and they were able to make Nablus the center of cotton processing in Palestine even though the cotton-producing villages were closer to the coastal cities. Firmly anchored by the dense networks of a strong merchant community, Nablus did not experience the radical fluctuations in its economic and demographic structures that Acre did.

Starting in the 1830s, the Egyptian occupation and the Ottoman reforms that followed introduced new administrative and fiscal practices which greatly enhanced state control of the movement of people and commodities. This, combined with greater European economic involvement in the area, especially after the 1838 commercial convention, laid the groundwork for the politics of "free" trade which pitted the merchants of the interior against regional merchants in Beirut and Damascus, European businessmen and their local agents, and an increasingly intrusive Ottoman government that was eager to enhance its access and control of the rural surplus.

Within the context of this new political environment, the politics of "free" trade was analyzed from the perspective of Nabulsi merchants, especially the ways they acted on the new opportunities and constraints. What immediately became clear were the tensions and uncertainties created by the sometimes clashing and other times mutually reinforcing local, regional, and international dynamics. Through their deeply rooted local and regional networks and the Advisory Council, Nabulsi merchants struggled to adjust the new political environment to their favor. Judging from the correspondence of the Advisory Council, the prevailing goals of the merchant community during this period were preserving their control of the movement of commodities, meeting the needs of local manufacturing and regional trade, minimizing state interference while utilizing the legitimacy and protection it afforded them, and keeping out the prying hands of foreign and regional merchants who were willing to offer higher prices and resort to political pressures. In short, the council's actions sought to take advantage of changing political and economic realities while defending those aspects of the status quo that underpinned their material base.

Although the members of the Advisory Council, in their correspondence, consistently presented this institution as the representative, interpreter, and arbitrator of the larger population, there was, in fact, no clear internal consensus on the place and role of Jabal Nablus during this transitional yet formative period (1840–1860). Some resisted and others embraced the impersonal external forces that pushed and pulled Nablus into the wheel of international commerce. The main beneficiaries were Nabulsis who had capital to spare and who were not so concerned about maintaining the status quo; that is, those who sought quick profits from speculation on the availability and fluctuating prices of agricultural commodities, as well as from serving as agents for foreign and regional traders.

This process of adaptation and restructuring could also been seen clearly in the history of the textile industry, which, though the most vulnerable to foreign competition, showed great resilience and managed to survive well into the twentieth century, albeit much changed. The weaving together, so to speak, of local dynamics with regional and European ones could literally be seen in the ways in which artisans created new textile items using a combination of local and imported materials, as well as in their ability to successfully cater to changing consumer demands. This is not to say that all remained well with the textile industry, nor that the effects of its restructuring were spread evenly throughout Nabulsi society. The stagnation of the textile sector led some to change their investment options and others to encourage their children to seek other types of work. Over time, the accumulation of daily decisions made two commodities the primary focus of merchant capital: olive oil and soap, which, as will be seen in the next two chapters, have a great deal to tell us about the changing political economy and social history of Jabal Nablus.

PLATES

Plate 1. Nablus from the slopes of Mount Gerzim, late nineteenth century. Engraving on steel (Wilson, *Picturesque Palestine*, 1:248).

Plate 2. Nablus from the southwestern slopes of Mount Ebal, late nineteenth century. Engraving on steel (Wilson, *Picturesque Palestine*, 1:249).

Plate 3.   Nablus from the western approaches, 1855. Engraving on wood from a drawing by David Roberts (Croly, *The Holy Land,* 1:plate 42).

Plate 4.   Peasants threshing wheat near an olive tree, late nineteenth century.
Engraving on wood (Wilson, *Picturesque Palestine*, 1:227).

Plate 5.   Inverted cones of stacked soap cubes (*tananir*) stand watch like silent sentinels over two workers cutting soap in a Nablus factory. From Walid Khalidi, *Before Their Diaspora: A Photographic History of the Palestinians, 1876–1948*. Courtesy of the Institute for Palestine Studies.

Arafat Family Tree

Ahmad al-Shahid

- **Shaykh Hajj Abd al-Majid**
  - **Pride of Callers to Prayers Salih (d. 1724?)**
    - Zahra
    - Arifa
  - **Shaykh Hajj Abdullah (d. 1805?)**
    - *Sayyid* Ibrahim
      - *Sayyida* Ruqayya
    - Ahmad
    - Fatima
    - Khadija
    - Aysha
    - Mustafa
    - Khadraj
    - Asma
    - Aysha
  - **Hajj Arafat**
  - **Shaykh Abd al-Razzaq (d. 1810)**
    - *Sayyid* Hasan
      - Salih
      - Amina
      - *Sayyid* Sa'id
        - *Sayyid* Umar
          - Kamal al-Din
            - Taqi al-Din
              - Sa'id
    - Shaykh Mahmud
      - *Sayyid* Sa'id (d.1847)
        - Umar
        - Nafisa
        - Zahra
        - Umar
        - Uthman
    - As'ad
    - Ahmad
    - Abd al-Jalil
    - Aysha
    - Bihan
    - Sarah
    - Zaynab
    - Maryam
    - Khadija
    - Salha
    - Karbahan
  - **Shaykh Abd al-Ghani (d. 1823)**
    - *Sayyid* Muhyi al-Din
      - *Sayyid* Mustafa
      - Abd al-Manan
      - Aysha
      - Ibrahim
      - Abdullah
      - Shaykh Sadiq
        - Arif
        - Fawzi
      - Adli
      - Adnan
      - Muhammad
      - Abdullah
    - *Sayyid* Abd al-Manan
      - *Sayyida* Ammun
    - Fatima
    - Muhammad
    - Abd Al-Rahman

- **Shaykh Salim**
- **Shaykh Salah**
- **Shaykh Muhammad Asfour**
- **Pride of Callers to Prayer Shaykh Sulayman**
  - **Shaykh Muhammad**
    - **Shaykh Abd al-Rahim**
      - Muhammad
        - **Hajj Isma'il (d. 1903)**
          - Najib
          - Shaykh Amr
            - Ghaleb
            - Nasira
            - Afaf
            - Anuar
            - Saba
          - Ahmad
            - Wasif
            - Dawud
            - Tawfiq
              - Hani
          - Hammad
          - Hamid
          - Faris
          - Adib

Arafat Family Tree

4   The Political Economy
of Olive Oil

When the tax season opened, the peasants of Jaba village could not
pay the taxes they owed because the olive harvest was not yet at
hand. . . . Consequently, and as is the usual practice among people of
the villages, they were forced to sell their future crop of olive oil in
advance for reduced prices through a *salam* [advance-purchase]
contract with a merchant for the amount of taxes due from their
village.

> Mahmud *Beik* Abd al-Hadi, the *qa'immaqam* of Nablus,
> to Hafiz Pasha, the governor of Jerusalem, 1851

The upper classes [in Nablus] depend on agriculture, trade, and
industry. The agriculturalists work their lands through the peasants
and play a great role in tax farming. . . . As to merchants, most trade
in grains and textiles. . . . The richest people in Nablus are the merchants who manufacture and sell soap. Usually, the same people
work in all three spheres . . . and in moneylending as well. Moneylending is a very painful matter in Nablus, and most peasant
complaints are directed against these usurers.

> Muhammad Rafiq Tamimi and Muhammad Bahjat,
> *Wilayat Bayrut,* 1916–1917

In late February 1856 Mary Eliza Rogers, sister of the British vice-consul
in Haifa, entered the women's quarters of the Abd al-Hadis' residential
compound in their home village of Arraba. The females of the household,
eager to learn all about the first European woman they had ever met, plied
her with questions. They first inquired whether she was married. When
Mary Rogers replied that she was single, the topic immediately shifted to
her father. The first two questions she reported being asked about him
were: "How many camels does your father have?" and "Are your father's
olive trees new and fruitful?" [1]

With these two questions, the Abd al-Hadi women inquired about what
they assumed to be the two key indicators of the material base of any
important family. Camels were a measure of wealth, both as livestock and
as a means of transportation. The Abd al-Hadis, at that time, controlled

extensive tracts of land dedicated to the commercial production of agricultural commodities, and they used herds of camels to carry olive oil and grains to Nablus and the port cities. The second question revealed the centrality of olive trees to the economic and cultural life of the hill regions of Palestine in general and of Jabal Nablus in particular. The word "new" in reference to olive trees put the accent on the expansion in agricultural production taking place at the time, a process in which powerful families, such as the Abd al-Hadis, played a key role.

As discussed in Chapter 1, the importance of olive trees to most Palestinian peasants in Jabal Nablus was akin to that of camels to bedouins, and a peasant family's material worth was (and often still is) measured by the number of jars of olive oil their trees produced annually. Olive oil was Jabal Nablus's number one agricultural product and cash crop: it met local needs for food and fuel and was exported to regional and international markets. It was also used to make soap, Nablus's most important manufactured product. The social relations embedded in the production of and trade in olive oil and soap, therefore, can be seen as a microcosm for the social, economic, and political history of Jabal Nablus as a whole. What the economic organization, social basis, and political dynamics of soap production tell us about the urban sphere will be examined in the Chapter 5.

Because the key dynamic in Palestinian society until 1948 was urbanrural relations, there is perhaps no better departure point in investigating these relations than the following question: How did olive oil move from the hands of peasants to those of merchants? A lawsuit dated February 1862 points up some of the issues involved. That month, Hamad son of Mahmud Rummani, a peasant from Bayta, the seat village of the subdistrict of Mashariq Nablus (also known as Mashariq al-Baytawi), claimed that his relative, Khader Rummani, was his partner in an "[olive] oil *salam* contract in which they received a sum of money from *Sayyid* Mahmud Hashim [a rich urban soap manufacturer]. They then subcontracted the *salam* loan to others [with the understanding] that they would share the profits. The defendant has illegally appropriated the plaintiff's share of the profits, ten jars of oil, and the plaintiff wants this oil."[2]

Hamad could not prove that his relative was withholding the oil from him, so he lost the lawsuit. But what concerns us here is, first, that this case points to the primary mechanism used by merchants to gain access to the rural surplus: moneylending. Second, it refers to the most pervasive form of moneylending: *salam* contracts. Third, it suggests that Palestine's peasantry, far from being a homogeneous mass at the mercy of urban moneylenders, was a differentiated community in which a "rural middle class," for want of a better term, played a mediating role in the circulation of merchant capital and in urban-rural relations in general.

The terms "rural middle class" and "middle peasants" are used to refer to those villagers whose land and capital resources set them apart from both the majority of fellow peasants and from the ruling rural families—such as the Hajj Muhammad clan, also based in the village of Bayta (see Chapter 1). This is not to imply that differentiation in the rural sphere was a modern phenomenon or that this group was a homogeneous one. Like peasant society in Europe and Asia, if not the world, peasant society in Palestine had long been a dynamic and complex one that generated its own rhythms of change and appropriated and redefined the larger regional and global forces that made their presence felt.[3] What is unique about the eighteenth and nineteenth centuries is that the changing political economy of Palestine during this period led to further growth and consolidation of a group of well-to-do peasants who benefited from the accelerated spread of commercial relations in the hinterland. The entrepreneurial activities and expanded resources of this group allowed its members to concentrate landholdings, to purchase the labor of other peasants and/or to lease some of their lands in sharecropping arrangements, to engage in moneylending and trade in the rural sphere, to act as intermediaries for urban merchants, and to eventually establish residence in the city of Nablus in significant numbers.

Many members of the Rummani family—judging from their numerous appearances in the Nablus Islamic Court—belonged to this rural middle class, which was firmly entrenched by the mid-nineteenth century, if not earlier. For instance, at least six male members of the Rummani family—Hammad son of Mahmud, Khader and his two sons (Ahmad and Mustafa), and Ibrahim and his son (As'ad)—were all active moneylenders who operated a wide network of *salam* contracts for olive oil and, to a lesser extent, sesame seeds. They then sold these products to urban soap-factory owners and grain merchants. They also made non-interest-bearing loans (*qard*). These transactions were made with fellow peasants from either the same village (Bayta) or from nearby villages, such as Bayt Furik or Qabalan.[4]

The Rummanis' business operations and their preference for settling disputes in the urban Islamic court also illustrate the fruition of a coterminous process in the history of Palestine during the Ottoman period: the absorption of the countryside into the urban economic, political, cultural, and legal spheres. This lawsuit is but one example of how this process of urban-rural integration was driven from the countryside as well as from the city; that is, peasants were active participants in the transformation of Palestine during the modern period, especially middle peasants who played a key role in reproducing urban relations on the village level.

In exploring how merchants appropriated the olive oil surplus, this chapter charts the changing material circumstances, political notions, and cultural attitudes of Jabal Nablus's peasants, to the extent that the predominantly urban-generated sources allow. Specifically, three broad topics are addressed. The first section investigates the changing context for moneylending and taxation and their role in the spread of merchant capital into the rural areas. The second examines the impact of these developments on the peasants' relationships to city, to the land, and to each other. The third explores the connections between the state, class, and political authority as revealed in peasant petitions precipitated by moneylending practices.

In Chapter 3 my focus was primarily on the low-lying western and northwestern plains of Jabal Nablus, for the peasants in these areas were the first to be integrated into the world economy as producers of cotton and, later on, of grains. The focus on olive oil here is intended to shift attention to the central highlands and to gauge how the peasants in the primarily olive-producing villages of this area experienced the transformations of the modern period. This is not meant to suggest that the issues addressed below apply only to the central core of Jabal Nablus: there was not a single village in all of Jabal Nablus in which olive oil was not one of the top three commodities produced.

FROM THE HANDS OF THE PEASANTS

From the late eighteenth century and throughout the nineteenth century, moneylending occupied a quickly expanding social space and became the defining factor in urban-rural relations. Of course, moneylending had been an integral element of rural-urban networks since ancient times, but over the course of the nineteenth century a number of factors propelled it to unprecedented levels in terms of frequency of contracts, degree of infiltration into the rural areas, and level of enforcement of debt obligations.

As far as the social life of olive oil is concerned, the second half of the 1820s was an important turning point. The interruptions caused by a prolonged period of intermittent internal conflict in Jabal Nablus from the late 1790s until 1823—which happened to roughly coincide with the slackening of European demand during the Napoleonic Wars—were followed by a vigorous economic expansion. Most conspicuous was the beginning of large capital investment in the soap industry (see Chapter 5). Because this industry more than tripled in size during the nineteenth century and because its growth was predicated on the availability of olive oil, moneylending to olive-based villages, especially in the form of *salam* contracts, became far more pervasive. Later on in the century, increased exports of olive oil from the port cities also created incentives for urban merchants to redouble their efforts to secure this precious commodity from the peasants.

Reinforcing the greater reach of merchant capital was the political coming of age of the merchant community, which gave merchants the power to enforce the collection of debts and to facilitate the appropriation of land. Merchants were the main beneficiaries of the changes brought about by the Egyptian occupation and the implementation of Ottoman reforms (*Tanzimat*), especially their access to political office through the Advisory Council. By the late 1830s they had managed to infiltrate the exclusive club of soap-factory owners and, to a lesser extent, the ranks of tax farmers—in the latter case not only as financial backers but also as bidders in competition with ruling urban and rural families.[5] By the 1850s a new merchant-dominated elite—or, more accurately, a fluid alliance between influential members of the merchant community, key ruling families (both urban and rural), and the top religious leaders—had emerged (see Chapter 5). Although the various elements of this elite differed, often violently, on a number of issues, they all huddled in the same political corner when it came to relations with peasants. This is because almost all of them, regardless of their background, were heavily engaged in moneylending and the manufacture of soap made from pure olive oil.

Salam Moneylending Contracts

Of the many types of credit arrangements available, *salam* (advance-purchase) contracts were the most widely used, especially in olive-producing hill regions. The underlying principle of a *salam* contract is the immediate advance of money by the first party for the future delivery by the second party of movable collateral—usually foodstuffs—at a reduced price fixed at the time of agreement. The key provision is that the agreed-upon amount of, say, oil must be delivered to the first party in kind regardless of what the market price of this commodity happens to be at the time of harvest. Depending on the power relationship between the parties, the cash advance could contain a substantial (illegal) hidden rate of interest that insured a handsome profit for the moneylender even if market prices dipped below anticipated levels.

Salam contracts were not a modern innovation. The rules governing them had been laid out clearly in Islamic law many centuries before. The Hanafi school of jurisprudence,[6] for example, requires that the capital be advanced at the time the contract is drafted and that the type, quantity, and quality of the commodity be specified, along with the date and place of delivery and whether the commodity was grown on irrigated or rain-fed land.[7]

Moneylenders did not turn to state institutions to legitimize this type of transaction. Rather, *salam* contracts were drafted in what actual documents refer to as *majlis al-aqd* (contract assembly or meeting). *Majlis al-aqd* did not indicate a specific location or a public space. Rather, it was anywhere two people sat down together in order to draft a contract—usually at a merchant's shop or home. Consequently, there are, to my knowledge, no *salam* contracts recorded in the central Ottoman archives and certainly none in the records of the Islamic court or Advisory Council, though the latter two contain lawsuits that refer to the existence of such contracts.[8] Fortunately, the private papers of the Nimr family contain a sufficient number of *salam* contracts to allow for an in-depth look at how they worked and how their use changed over time.[9] These are supplemented by additional information in the lawsuits over *salam* arrangements, in some inheritance estates that listed outstanding loans, and in peasant petitions.

As the following example, dated early January 1828, shows, these contracts invariably conformed to guidelines set by the Hanafi school of jurisprudence:

> On the date [registered] below, Husayn Abd al-Qadir, Awad son of Shehada, Abd al-Hayy son of Jabir, and Musa son of Abid—all from the village of Salim—testified that they received from the Respected Right Honorable Ahmad *Agha* . . . al-Yusufi [Nimr] a sum of 1,025 piasters . . . as a legal *salam* for 100 jars of oil [measured by] the container of the [Yu-sufiyya] soap factory—each jar for 10.25 piasters—for a period of ten months. [They are to] deliver one-half [of the oil jars] now, and the other half in the middle of Rabi II, 1244 (late October 1828) to the Yusufiyya soap factory.[10]

Regardless of whether the price of olive oil multiplied many times during these ten months, the three peasants from Salim had to provide the amount of oil in kind that was agreed on and not ask for a single piaster over and above what they originally received. Of course, a bumper harvest might bring the price of oil to a point lower than the amount set earlier. Moneylending arrangements, however, usually worked in favor of the owner of capital: he could spread his risk around, had a far greater knowledge of the market, and, in the case of big merchants, was able to influence the market trends on certain commodities. Peasants were often in no position to bargain for favorable prices because they usually borrowed money out of dire necessity: to pay taxes, to recover from a bad harvest, to purchase goods for a wedding, or to meet a myriad of other needs.

Most important, *salam* contracts usually contained a calculated rate of interest disguised as an artificially low price for the commodity in question, hence guaranteeing a profitable return when the lender sold the goods on the open market after they were delivered by the borrower. Usury (*riba*), of course, was officially prohibited. In practice, however, moneylenders tied the amount of interest to the length of the waiting period: the farther away the delivery date, the lower the unit cost to the merchant (see below). Thus, Ahmad *Agha* Nimr advanced the paltry sum of 10.25 piasters for every jar of oil to be delivered ten months later, even though the price of each jar on the open market averaged 23 piasters.[11] The frequency with which moneylenders swore in writing at the end of many contracts that no usury was involved is in itself an indication of at least the perception that usury was an integral part of this arrangement.[12]

The ease with which a rate of interest could be hidden in *salam* contracts was one reason for their popularity. No matter how low the price, most peasants could not legally challenge these contracts in court as long as they technically fulfilled all the conditions of Islamic law.[13] Only one of the dozens of disputes over *salam* contracts registered in the Nablus Islamic Court between 1850–1870 mentioned usury as an issue.[14] In all of the rest, peasants insisted that no *salam* contract had been drawn up, that they were willing to reimburse the moneylender in cash, not in kind, or that the goods had already been delivered.[15]

The exception involved the case of two peasants from the village of Awarta, dated January 20, 1862.[16] The plaintiff, Odeh al-Qasim, testified that he had advanced the defendant, Sulayman al-Bashir, a sum of money in return for 68 jars of olive oil and claimed that he had only received 42.5 jars and 3 *uqiyyas*. He then demanded that the terms of the lawful *salam* contract be fulfilled. Sulayman al-Bashir freely admitted to the contract and the remaining debt, but he insisted that he was not obligated to provide the rest of the oil because usury was involved. The judge asked al-

Bashir to prove this charge, but he could not. The defendant's last hope lay in demanding that the first party swear under oath that no usury was involved. Odeh al-Qasim readily did so and won the case.

Another reason for the pervasiveness of this type of moneylending was the need of merchants and artisans to secure supplies of agricultural raw materials for the purposes of local production and regional trade. This was especially important with olive oil: urban soap merchants and manufacturers needed large quantities of olive oil every year, and they could not risk wide fluctuations in availability and price.[17] In the *salam* contract quoted above, Ahmad *Agha*—scion of the Nimr family at the time and *waqf* superintendent of the Yusufiyya soap factory (built by his ancestors more than two hundred years earlier)—clearly entered into an advance-purchase contract for precisely this reason. The contract was drawn at the end of the olive harvest season (early January 1828), and one-half of the olive oil was to be delivered ten months later, at the beginning of the next harvest season (late October 1828). In short, Ahmad *Agha* Nimr used this type of contract for the purposes of production, not for speculation, investment, or trade in agricultural commodities.

Salam contracts were also desirable because most other forms of moneylending required immovable property as collateral. Aside from their lands, peasants could offer little in return except the future delivery of their harvests. Finally, *salam* contracts negotiated directly with peasants allowed merchants to bypass market regulations and various revenue-collection measures imposed by the government and ruling families. *Salam* contracts, in short, were flexible and allowed for a wide range of urban-rural moneylending arrangements. As will be seen below, this flexibility also proved to be eminently suitable for speculation and for the local organization of commercial agricultural production for export overseas. Indeed, local moneylending arrangements cleared a path for the increasing involvement of foreign and coastal merchants who wanted to extend their operations to the interior.

The same factors that caused a steep rise in moneylending transactions, especially the much more conducive political environment, also led to a diversification in the social composition of moneylenders. Previously, the enforcement of debt obligations had been fraught with uncertainties despite the influence of the merchant community and the rootedness of its networks. By the 1840s, however, moneylending had become a much easier proposition for those who lacked political influence. Indeed, it seems that almost anyone with access to capital, no matter how small, found opportunities for moneylending and trade. Although this phenomenon was neither new nor unique to Jabal Nablus[18] or Greater Syria,[19] there is little doubt that during the nineteenth century moneylending came to involve far more people and to take on an even more central and defining role in the social formation of Jabal Nablus than it had during the previous Ottoman centuries. Illustrative in this regard is a comparison of two instances of moneylending to peasants in the same village, Salim.

The first case (1828), cited above, was typical of more traditional uses of the *salam* contracts. The male representatives of three peasant families who borrowed money from Ahmad *Agha* Nimr shared with him a common memory of frequent dealings over generations. Salim was located in an area east of Nablus to which the Nimr family had had privileged access for generations in the form of *timar* land grants and tax farms, as *sipahis* and *multazims*, respectively.[20] The brother of Ahmad *Agha* Nimr's great-grandfather, for example, collected taxes from Salim on a regular basis in the early 1700s.[21] Ahmad *Agha* Nimr, therefore, could rely on his family's historic ties and political influence over this region in order to secure supplies for his soap factory. The Nimrs also took advantage of long-standing political, economic, and social connections to subcontract *salam* loans on behalf of oil merchants and soap manufacturers.[22]

The second case (1861), shows that even a simple merchant was able to establish an impressive foothold in Salim village, primarily through moneylending—even though he was neither rich nor politically influential. This information can be gleaned from the inheritance estate of Abd al-Rahman Qan'ir, a retail grain merchant who dealt mostly in wheat, barley, corn, *burghul* (wheat that is cooked, parched, then crushed), and meadow vetch.[23] When his belongings were registered in late November 1861, he had eighteen outstanding loans, all of them owed by individual peasants from the village of Salim. Some of these loans were *salam* contracts for wheat and barley; others were non-interest-bearing loans (*qard*); and some were a combination of both. For instance, Jabir son of Yusuf al-Dabbagh owed Qan'ir 80 piasters' worth of wheat and barley, as specified in a *salam* contract. He also owed him 565.5 piasters for a non-interest-bearing loan for which he put up one-quarter of a *feddan* (one *feddan* being equal to one-quarter of an acre) as collateral (*rahn*).

Qan'ir also invested heavily in factors of production in order to better control the grain surplus of Salim village. For example, he helped the Salim peasants buy draft animals, and at the time of his death a number of them owed him shares of cows and bulls. He also had the right to shares of the proceeds of a number of *maris* lands,[24] put up as collateral by peasants who owed him money but were not able to pay on time. Over the years, therefore, Qan'ir managed to construct a network of dependency among eighteen peasant families. His business network illustrates how moneylending could be used not only to secure needed supplies but also to pave the way for urban investment in rural production and trade and for the commoditization of land and its appropriation by urban merchants.

In this supportive economic, political, and legal atmosphere, even poor artisans and small merchants could safely enter moneylending arrangements—though these were usually for minuscule amounts. For example, the estate of a poor artisan (1861), Abd al-Al al-Masri *al-munajjid* (upholsterer), showed that he had concluded a *salam* contract with a bedouin in order to secure his supply of wool.[25] Similarly, the estate of a small retailer (1863), Sa'id son of *Hajj* Salim al-Ra'i—who sold iron tools for peasants as well as grains and olive oil for city folk—included *salam* contracts for wheat, olive oil, and onions whose value amounted to almost half of the estate's total worth.[26] Around the same time (1864), the proprietor of a cotton-ginning shop, *Hajj* Rajab son of *Hajj* Salih Abi Suwwan, had a number of *salam* contracts with peasants from Baqa al-Gharbiyya and Attil villages for small amounts of cotton-in-the-boll and for cotton seeds.[27] These examples all illustrate the extent to which peasants had been individually recruited and integrated into a quickly expanding and increasingly depersonalized market of exchange.

This trend is further illustrated by two important developments in the use of *salam* contracts. First, *salam* contracts were frequently turned into a tool of speculation, trade, and investment in agricultural production for overseas markets. Second, *salam* contracts were resorted to on a routine basis not just by individual peasants but also by the populations of entire villages, primarily in order to meet their tax obligations. Both developments created dynamics that further facilitated the circulation of merchant capital in the hinterlands. These two developments will be addressed in turn.

Moneylending and Production for Overseas Markets

The increasing pervasiveness of moneylending and the deepening of market relations in Jabal Nablus helped pave the way for coastal and foreign merchants to invest in the interior regions of Palestine. The following *salam* contract, drafted in early May 1851 between a Christian merchant from Jaffa and a Nabulsi peasant from the village of Aqraba, provides some clues as to how this type of moneylending practice was used in the local organization of producing cash crops for European markets:

On the date [recorded] below, Khalil Mitri son of Yusuf *Khawaja* Mitri arrived and paid to the sane mature man, Abd al-Rahman al-Khalil, one of the people of Aqraba village, a sum of 2,997 piasters . . . as *salam* on the amount of 81 *kayla* of sesame—the good unirrigated sesame free of dirt and straw, and that is measured by the *kayla* of Nablus city in the usual *sa*. [It is to be] transported from this aforementioned town to Jaffa, where the *salam* was contracted. The [transportation] fee is to be paid by *Khawaja* Khalil . . . not by Abd al-Rahman. . . . [The grace period is] five months from this date. The aforementioned Abd al-Rahman has acknowledged receiving the *salam* capital [*ra'smal*] in full . . . after which, *Khawaja* Khalil promised that as soon as the sesame arrives and is sold, and no matter how much the Supreme God might bestow in profit, *he will pay a third of this profit* to the aforementioned Abd al-Rahman.[28]

Khawaja Mitri was apparently a well-informed merchant, for he invested in sesame production in 1851; and, according to Alexander Schölch, French imports of Palestinian sesame increased greatly beginning in 1852.[29] Because Schölch's conclusion is based on export statistics from Jaffa, the financing of this increase must have started the previous season, which is exactly when *Khawaja* Mitri signed the *salam* contract with Abd al-Rahman from Aqraba.

The stamp and list of witnesses on the contract tell us that Abd al-Rahman signed it in Jaffa. This might not sound striking, but considering the prevailing view of Palestinian peasants during the Ottoman period as living in isolated villages and engaged solely in subsistence agriculture, the initiative and entrepreneurial spirit of Abd al-Rahman are worthy of note. Indeed, Abd al-Rahman had come to Jaffa a few months earlier and negotiated a similar contract.[30] His actions indicate that he was free, willing, and capable of responding quickly to such offers and that he knew full well that his crops would be shipped to France. Abd al-Rahman should not be considered unique. As seen in the Chapter 3, and as Alexander Schölch and Marwan Buheiry both argued, on the basis of export statistics from the latter part of the nineteenth century, Palestinian peasants were sharply attuned to the fickle changes of international demand and acted accordingly.[31]

Abd al-Rahman, like most Palestinian peasants at that time, probably needed a quick infusion of cash in order to stay afloat in an increasingly monetarized agricultural sector. The availability of cash could make the difference between success or failure for many peasants, especially for those who were heavily dependent on rain-fed agriculture, where productivity fluctuated with the vagaries of the weather. His success in seeking out a faraway merchant at a time of high demand suggests that he had exerted considerable effort to negotiate the most favorable conditions for himself—in essence, bypassing the Nabulsi merchant community.

Apparently confident of the profit margin he was about to make on this deal and eager to insure the supply of sesame, *Khawaja* Mitri offered Abd al-Rahman two incentives not normally encountered in *salam* contracts. First, he agreed to cover the transportation costs, which were considerable given the distance involved. In effect, this increased the per-unit price in favor of the peasant. The second incentive was innovative and reflects the adaptability of *salam* contracts: a profit-sharing arrangement. Abd al-Rahman still had to provide the sesame regardless of weather conditions or price changes, but he could augment the moneys he received in advance with a percentage (one-third) of the profits made by the merchant.

It is not certain whether the incentives offered in this contract represented an isolated case or whether they were typical of the dealings between coastal merchants and the peasants of the interior. The latter was more likely, if only because non-Nabulsi merchants, as was seen in Chapter 3, had a difficult time bypassing local commercial networks and luring peasants, much less guaranteeing the enforcement of contracts.[32] In this regard, it is difficult to escape the conclusion that under certain conditions, like those that characterized this case, the use of the *salam* contract could encourage trade, help meet local needs for liquid capital, increase investment in agricultural production, promote economic growth, and even work to the benefit of both parties concerned.

Salam contracts took on a much more sinister character once the context was changed, however. Judging from the available evidence, the *salam* contracts drawn up by Nabulsi oil merchants reflected neither the urgency felt by *Khawaja* Mitri nor his need to sweeten loans with incentives. On the contrary, they were usually characterized by low prices, no profit sharing, and constant threat of enforcement by government officials and subdistrict chiefs. This is because most Nabulsi peasants suffered from a heavy imbalance in power relations with locally powerful moneylenders. At the same time, they were forced to turn to them in order to meet their tax obligations. The olive-based highland villages of Palestine became more vulnerable to this combination of taxes and debt over the course of the nineteenth century.

Moneylending, Taxation, and Olive-Based Villages

Elizabeth Anne Finn, wife of the British Consul of Jerusalem at midcentury, related the story of a woman from Bayt Jala—a village near Bethlehem—whose family turned to a soap merchant, Sulayman Asali, when it could not pay its taxes:

> He [the woman's father-in-law] pledged his olive trees for 500 piasters and wrote a bond upon himself to pay fifteen jars of oil to Sulaiman Assali; and if there is any deficient, he has to pay two jars of oil next year for every one. That year was also a bad one, and our olives were stolen, and we had only three jars of oil; so Sulaiman wrote a bond upon my father-in-law for twenty-four jars of oil for the next harvest, and if any were deficient, two were to be given for every one. . . . We now owe him eighty jars of oil.[33]

This story was probably exaggerated, both by an informant who hoped to elicit the sympathies and help of a European consular couple who earned a reputation for interference in local affairs and by the writer, who prided herself (and her husband) on being dedicated to giving "succour to the weak."[34] It does reveal, however, the vicious circle that can be created when the forces of taxation and moneylending intertwine.

The potentially devastating consequences of these combined forces have been a recurrent theme in peasant lore all over the world for centuries. But by the first half of the nineteenth century, a confluence of circumstances posed a serious dilemma for the olive-based villages in the central highlands of Palestine, even though, historically, they have been less vulnerable to the combined impact of moneylending and taxation than have the coastal villages, where the government's presence has always been stronger. First, a more aggressive and intrusive Ottoman state made tax collection more efficient and inflexible in the interior regions than it had been during most of the eighteenth century. Second, olive-based villages were especially hard hit because the timing of the increasingly predictable and rigorously enforced tax-collection season was based on the grain harvest, which fell months before olives matured in the late fall. To pay their taxes, peasants who depended primarily on the olive crop needed to have money saved from the previous season, or else they had to borrow money. Third, the peasants' patron-client relationship with once-powerful rural ruling families had become progressively frayed; hence their autonomy and ability to maneuver around the tax season were undermined. Fourth, Nabulsi olive oil merchants and soap-factory owners came to wield considerable political power in the nineteenth century, a development that only accelerated the already ongoing process of urban-rural integration. Fifth, as mentioned previously, these merchants became much more aggressive in ensuring future supplies of olive oil, due to the vigorous expansion of soap manufacturing at this time and due to the increased regional and international trade in this commodity.

Unlike foreign or coastal merchants, Nabulsi oil merchants and soap manufacturers did not need to lure peasants with high prices, profit sharing, and other incentives. Rather, they used their intimate knowledge of local conditions and their growing political clout to draw up highly unfavorable *salam* contracts not just with individuals but also with entire villages. An oil merchant, for example, would pay the taxes of a village and consider the sum a loan in the form of a *salam* contract. When the olives were harvested and pressed for oil, the village was then to deliver a formerly agreed upon number of olive oil jars to the soap factory specified by the merchant.[35] The following two documents from the Jerusalem Islamic Court records show that the story told by Elizabeth Finn would not have come as a surprise to the residents of Bayt Jala. In the 1830s and 1840s, this village was battered by the political, social, and economic tensions generated by the combined forces of taxes and moneylending.

The first is a somewhat unusual *salam* contract negotiated between the government and the elders of Bayt Jala. On September 6, 1833, an agent of the Nabulsi Shaykh Husayn Abd al-Hadi (then the Egyptian government's right-hand man in southern Syria) signed a contract in the Jerusalem Islamic Court with a number of peasants representing the entire population of Bayt Jala village.[36] The contract specified that in return for 30,000 piasters the peasants were to deliver four months hence (that is, at the end of the olive harvest season) a total of 1,000 jars of good-quality, unadulterated olive oil as measured by the jar of soap factories in Jerusalem.

What was unusual about the case, and probably the reason it was publicly registered in the Jerusalem Islamic Court in the first place, was that the capital advance was paid from the city's treasury. It was also specifically stipulated that the oil was to be delivered to the local government. Most likely, Bayt Jala was chosen because it had been behind in its tax payments for some time (see below) and because Shaykh Abd al-Hadi, no stranger to *salam* contracts, took the opportunity to gain access to its olive oil surplus. It is also probable that the olive oil was to be used to cook batches of soap for the Egyptian military forces then in Palestine; hence the use of public moneys. Shaykh Abd al-Hadi, who was soon to become the owner of a soap factory in Nablus, was probably commissioned to produce this soap, and he used his political position and Bayt Jala's vulnerability to secure his supplies. This arrangement brings to mind the early monopoly practices of Muhammad Ali Pasha in Egypt. Ken Cuno, for example, relates how government officials in the al-Mansura region in Egypt usurped the role of merchant-creditors by purchasing the harvest of entire villages beforehand and/or credited the future delivery of crops at fixed prices against taxes.[37]

The second case concerning Bayt Jala illustrates how this situation was further complicated by tensions arising from the growing social differentiation within the village itself. On March 15, 1835, Salama son of Issa Makhluf stood in front of the Jerusalem Islamic Court judge and testified that seven years earlier he had been imprisoned by the governor of Jerusalem because his village had not paid the 2,675 piasters it owed in taxes to the city's treasury.[38] He continued that when he was released shortly thereafter, he went to the leaders of Bayt Jala's clans and asked them to come up with the tax moneys (so he would not be imprisoned again). He then pointed his finger at three shaykhs from his village who had been summoned earlier to the court and accused them of having "ordered" him to write up a *salam* contract with the people of Bayt Jala so that the taxes could be paid. Salama went on to say that he had advanced his fellow villagers the sum of 1,500 piasters for the future delivery of 128 jars of oil, and he also paid the rest of the tax due (1,175 piasters) to the government in cash on their behalf. He further claimed that for the past seven years he had been asking the defendants to pay him back the oil in kind, according to the conditions of the *salam*, as well as the cash he had paid on their behalf, but to no avail.

The defendants denied that they had ordered the plaintiff to draw up a *salam* contract or to cover the rest of the taxes in cash. They argued, instead, that his imprisonment was a simple case of extortion. The governor, they said, "deprived him of this money as a matter of personal dispossession." When the presiding judge asked the plaintiff to prove his allegations, Salama Makhluf left the court for Bayt Jala and brought back two witnesses who corroborated his story. The judge accepted the witnesses' testimony as valid and ordered the shaykhs of Bayt Jala to pay back 128 jars of olive oil to the plaintiff, as well as 1,175 piasters in cash.

The fact that Salama Makhluf waited seven years to take his grievance to court provides a very important clue as to the complicated interactions among taxation, moneylending, and peasant differentiation. He was a well-to-do middle peasant whose wealth made him a target of both the government and fellow Bayt Jala villagers. No doubt the governor chose him because he had the money to pay Bayt Jala's taxes, and it was inconsequential to the governor whether Salama chose or was forced (depending on whose testimony one believed) to translate this payment into a moneylending arrangement whereby part of the village's olive harvest would be pledged to him in advance as reimbursement. The only difference was that the supplier of capital was not an outsider but, rather, a person who actually lived in the village itself. Salama probably waited this long because he was exposed to immense pressures from many of his fellow villagers to drop his claims, and it might have been very difficult for him to recruit two witnesses willing to testify on his behalf in the face of concerted opposition from the clan elders. Indeed, it must have taken some courage to pursue the enforcement of the *salam* contract in an urban court, because this involved crossing the boundaries of village solidarity and humiliating the village elders in public.

The vaunted collective ethos of this and other villages, if it ever existed in the manner described by nationalists who would romanticize the Palestinian peasantry, was certainly vulnerable to the triple blows of taxation, moneylending, and internal differentiation, all of which could not but be accompanied by painful and divisive political struggles. In this particular case, the conflict between a middle peasant and established village leaders, who based their authority on the twin pillars of kinship and seniority, can be seen as a symbol for the tensions that wracked the rural sphere during the nineteenth century.

The Bayt Jala cases were not unique. The following example from Jabal Nablus shows that by the mid-nineteenth century it became quite common for entire villages to enter into *salam* contracts with urban oil merchants in order to pay their taxes and that this situation combined with internal divisions to heighten tensions between villagers. Sometime during the olive harvest season in the fall of 1851, the inhabitants of Jaba village in Jabal Nablus sent a petition directly to the governor of Jerusalem, Hafiz Pasha, in which they complained bitterly against their own elders. The governor promptly passed it on to the Nablus Advisory Council, then headed by Mahmud *Beik* Abd al-Hadi, *qa'immaqam* of Nablus and son of Shaykh Husayn, who concluded the *salam* contract with the village of Bayt Jala mentioned earlier.

On December 28 of that year Mahmud *Beik* Abd al-Hadi wrote the following reply to the governor of Jerusalem:

> [I] have relayed to the council your Noble order containing the petition of the people of Jaba of Jabal Nablus in which they accuse the shaykhs of their own village of forcing them to sign promissory notes for this year worth 1,200 jars [of oil] and for next year, 1,400 jars. [The people of Jaba further claim] that this constitutes treachery against them because their shaykhs' motivation was no more than their own personal aggrandizement. In carrying out your . . . order that their complaint be relayed to the council and a report be written explaining the truth of the matter, and [in

order] to prevent the recurrence of such unlawful behavior, the respected and wise men of the village, who are relatives of the petitioners, were called in to the council [premises]. When . . . this case was examined, we found that the villagers' claim that this oil was only for the benefit of the shaykhs is untrue. Instead, what was ascertained from the report of the old and wise men of . . . Jaba, who were appointed by the people of the village to pursue their case, is that when the tax [*miri*] [season] opened, they could not pay the taxes owed by their village because the olive harvest was not yet at hand. *Consequently, and as is the usual practice among people of the villages, they were forced to sell their future crop of olive oil in advance for reduced prices through a* salam *[contract] for the amount of taxes due from their village.* It is well known that the oil season does not come until the middle or just after the middle of the [fiscal] year. They received from one of the merchants an advance sum of 34,966.3 piasters for 953 jars of oil [in order to pay] the 1266 [1849–1850] dues, and the oil was to be delivered to the aforementioned merchant from the oil harvest of 1267. Similarly, they received from the same merchant an advance sum of 30,511.3 piasters for 1,330 jars of oil. This money had already been used to pay the 1267 [1850–1851] taxes, and the aforementioned oil was to be delivered the aforementioned merchant during the 1268 [1851–1852] harvest. Yet 130 jars of oil are still owed by the villagers for the 1267 taxes, and they have yet to be paid. After clarifying this matter through receipts and vouchers presented in the council, and [after] persuading the people of the village of this, they made up and shook hands with each other. Accusations and counteraccusations were dropped, and each went his own way after they were warned not to cause such disturbance and to be loving and peaceful with each other. The shaykhs of the village were also warned that from now on they are not to draw up *salam* [contracts] without the knowledge of the entire village, so that such confusion and recrimination will be avoided.[39]

Before analyzing the implications of this document, it is important to point out that the same oil merchant paid the village's taxes two years in a row in return for a set number of olive oil jars to be delivered in two consecutive seasons. In a manner reminiscent of the predicament described by the woman of Bayt Jala to Elizabeth Anne Finn, the per-unit price given to the peasants went down by one-third, while the amounts owed went up. Thus the first *salam* contract specified 953 jars of oil at 36.7 piasters per jar, whereas the second involved 1,330 jars of oil at approximately 23 piasters per jar. There is no doubt here that a hidden interest was calculated into the price.

The council's statement that the village's collective resort to *salam* contracts in order to pay their taxes was the "usual practice" leaves no doubt as to the pervasiveness of this combined dynamic in mid-nineteenth-century Jabal Nablus. It is possible that entire villages entered into such contracts long before the first half of the nineteenth century, but the new elements here were the involvement of urban merchants, as opposed to ruling families, the more efficient tax-collection measures, and the clear political backing for the oil merchant by a new governing institution staffed by other merchants. Also new was the fact that these peasants challenged their elders and the entire Nabulsi political structure by petitioning the governor of Jerusalem directly.

The council's explanation that the timing of the tax season created the inexorable chain of circumstances must be qualified. As already argued, the collective resort to moneylending in order to pay taxes was not the outcome of an age-old technical problem but the result of the relatively recent political, social, and economic processes. In addition, the words "usual" and, more often, "customary" were frequently used in the council's correspondence with their superiors in order to justify practices that might actually be recent in origin—such as the "old way" of measuring of grains in storehouses discussed in Chapter 3. The argument of "tradition" was also often used as a weapon against those innovations of Ottoman reform policies that the council members deemed not to be in their favor (they did not complain about innovations they approved of, even those that did in fact challenge established practices). Indeed, the council consciously arrogated to itself a monopoly in the meanings of tradition—hence the position of interpreter of local realities—in order to strengthen its hand in dealings with the central authorities. This is because, as explained in Chapter 3, the fluid political boundaries between central and local forces during the era of reforms were negotiated one conflict at a time.

Another qualification to the meaning of "usual practice" was the complicated political background of this specific petition. Jaba was the seat village of the Jarrar clan, which split into two factions in 1848—that is, just before the first *salam* contract was signed.[40] Mahmud *Beik* Abd al-Hadi, who supported one of the Jarrar factions, was appointed *qa'immaqam* of Nablus in place of Sulayman *Beik* Tuqan, who supported the second faction, just six weeks before he received the peasants' petition from the governor of Jerusalem.[41] These events might well be related to the "misunderstanding" between the Jaba villagers and their elders—that is, the political balance was altered and the peasants seized the opportunity to go over the heads not only of their own shaykhs but also of the Nablus Council itself. By sending their petition directly to the governor of Jerusalem they, in effect, were asserting a more inclusive political identity for themselves that went beyond the borders of Jabal Nablus. The implications of this assertion for the issues of citizenship, sources of political authority, class tensions, and notions of justice will be addressed in more detail in the last section of this chapter.

The council's quick and paternalistic dismissal of this conflict was no doubt an attempt to close the door to further interference by the central government that the peasants' petition opened. Thus the council's report ignored political ramifications and presented the conflict in terms of a moneylending agreement gone awry. The manner in which the clearly unfavorable terms of the *salam* contract were negotiated was also left intentionally vague, and the council's letter raises many questions that cannot be easily answered: Was it possible that the Jaba shaykhs could have either forced their relatives into a *salam* contract or secretly negotiated this contract without the knowledge of members of their own clan and village? Who exactly were the "respected and wise men of the village" who allegedly represented the petitioners, if not the accused shaykhs themselves? Why was the oil merchant not named? Could he be one of the council members? And, finally, why were the villagers so easily persuaded, if they were at all, that this entire affair was only a simple misunderstanding?

The one person who escaped recrimination was the oil merchant/moneylender. The vagueness of the council members' letter, therefore, was the result not only of the strategy of selective feeding of information to their superiors but also of their unwillingness to question the modes of operations of moneylenders, much less the legitimacy of moneylending itself. All of them, it will be recalled, were engaged in soap manufacturing, and they relied on a steady supply of cheap olive oil in order to maintain their rates of profit. Any fundamental challenge to moneylending by the peasantry threatened to undermine the council members' economic interests no matter what their internal political differences were. The reasons for and consequences of the emergence of this new "notable" elite, dominated mostly by merchants, will be addressed in more detail in Chapter 5. For now, we turn to the impact of moneylending on the peasants' relationships to the land, to the city, and to each other during the nineteenth century.

A FORCED MARRIAGE?

During the nineteenth century, urban-rural relations in Jabal Nablus displayed all the symptoms of a forced marriage. On the one hand, countryside and city became more closely intertwined than ever before, as illustrated by the growth of a rural middle class that reproduced urban relations at the village level. On the other hand, the aggressive expansion of merchant capital, spearheaded by moneylending, sped up the commoditization of land and created an ever-widening rift between city and village and between peasants themselves, in terms of both socioeconomic disparities and mutual cultural hostility.

Polarization

In 1916 two young Ottoman officials, Muhammad Rafiq Tamimi and Muhammad Bahjat, were ordered to gather materials for a general "guide book" on the southern half of Beirut province.[42] Considering that the Ottoman Empire was in the middle of a war, it was more likely that they were asked to investigate the socioeconomic conditions and political attitudes of the population at large, for this is what their book is mostly about. In the first leg of their two-month-long trip they visited Jabal Nablus, beginning with Salfit, then one of the two largest olive-oil-producing villages in the district.[43]

As the first Ottoman officials to visit Salfit in some time, they were swamped with complaints, most of which were directed against the merchants of Nablus. The authors' words neatly frame the dilemma of a forced marriage: "The Salfitis are pained by the people of Nablus and complain about them. Previously, they used to respect the Nabulsis and tried to please them; but now that they are poor, they no longer care about them . . . nor bother to hide their animosity. Yet, and despite their recognition of this reality, they still find themselves dragged back to Nablus in order to settle their affairs and to borrow money with interest."[44]

The same set of complaints surfaced in every village they visited. In Dayr Istiya, for example, one peasant opined that "Nablus is the seat of corruption," and a second advised "wash after you shake hands with a Nabulsi." Being a Nabulsi himself, Tamimi rejoined that he saw no need to condemn all the city's inhabitants for the oppression of a few "moneyed people."[45] Nevertheless, the first issue the authors raised in their written report as to what the government should do to alleviate the widespread poverty, misery, and disease among the peasantry during this terrible year of war and famine was the need to eradicate the oppressive and usurious practices of Nabulsi notables over the countryside.[46] The rich of Nablus, they explained,

> lend money to a peasant at an interest rate of 15 percent for six months. . . . And after the rich man lends a bit of money to the peasant, he be-

comes his master and rules him because the poor villager, who has only a small despicable yearly income, cannot pay back the debt at the appointed time. [Therefore], the rich moneylender uses his influence among the government's men to threaten him, so the poor villager is in the end forced to renew his debt contract under even worse conditions than the first one. We have learned that most of the wealthy Nabulsis lend money at an annual interest rate ranging between 60 and 70 percent. Moneylending and borrowing have brought conditions of slavery to our constitutional lands . . . because [even though] the peasant keeps only despicably little of his summer and winter harvests to himself and gives the rest to the lender . . . he still cannot free himself from debt.[47]

To the Salfitis and to peasants from many other villages in Jabal Nablus the authors seem to be saying that Nabulsi moneylenders represented at one and the same time a lifeline they could not do without and an invisible rope that only tightened as they struggled against it. This bleak assessment was shared by most contemporary observers of Greater Syria in the early twentieth century. Muhammad Izzat Darwaza recalled in his autobiography that in the late nineteenth and early twentieth centuries all soap-factory owners lent widely to peasants and small traders and charged 15–35 percent interest. Impoverished peasants, he added, usually borrowed twice a year against the wheat and olive harvests and received low prices if they paid in kind for previous debt or sold in advance for credit.[48] Muhammad Kurd Ali, a well-informed Damascene intellectual, wrote in 1925 that "the trade in crops—which were secured through loans and *salam* [contracts]—was the ruin of the wretched Syrian peasant."[49]

Although they reflect a fundamental reality of peasant life, these observations are problematic in that they portray peasants in one-dimensional terms as passive victims of urban greed. They also imply that moneylending was somehow a new phenomenon. As we have seen, moneylending itself was not new; what was new were the political, economic, and social contexts in which it operated. All three writers, in addition, were modern nationalists who were bitterly critical of their traditional society. Typical of many other young supporters of the "modernist" Committee for Union and Progress in the early twentieth century, Tamimi and Bahjat's blanket condemnation of wealthy Nabulsis as a selfish, oppressive, conservative, shortsighted, and close-minded local elite had, as its counterpart, their description of peasants as primitive, ignorant, dirty, and superstitious. In other words, both groups were portrayed as reactionary elements out of touch with the realities of the modern world and incapable of comprehending nationalist visions of history.[50]

Integration

The process of rural-urban integration was far more ambiguous than the above black-and-white accounts suggest. For one thing, it was also driven from within the countryside. Alongside the tensions between city and country, for instance, were intense struggles among the peasants themselves over land, resources, and moneylending, as the example of the Rummani family and the cases of Bayt Jala and Jaba demonstrate. Urban and central authorities not only penetrated the countryside, they were also dragged in, sometimes against their will and better judgement. Many peasants, especially well-to-do ones like Salama Makhluf, were anxious to make the city's legal and political system work for them, even though it meant alienating the leaders of their own village clans.

One way of measuring the phases of urban-rural integration is to establish when peasants were absorbed into the city's legal culture—that is, when the locus of arbitration in the countryside shifted from customary law (*urf*) mediated by clan leaders and subdistrict chiefs to Islamic (*shari'a*) law and Ottoman decrees as interpreted by a city judge and enforced by the Ottoman government itself. Records of the Nablus Islamic Court—admittedly a biased urban perspective—shed some light on this issue.

When one reads all of the court cases from the 1798–1865 period in chronological order, the most striking impression in terms of the social composition of the participants is the virtual absence of peasants until the second half of the 1830s. Then one encounters a small wave of cases involving peasants, albeit one that quickly slowed down to a trickle over the next two decades. Commencing in the late 1850s, peasant participation turned into a flood that showed no signs of abating, hence signaling the culmination of the hinterland's integration into the urban legal and cultural spheres.

The second wave also marked a change in the types of cases that were brought before the court. In the late 1830s almost all of the cases involving peasants traversed a narrow range and had a clear ranking. The most frequent were land disputes. The rest—far fewer in number—were criminal cases or moneylending lawsuits.[51] There was also a smattering of cases involving land purchases, but these were limited almost exclusively to the Abd al-Hadi family. Starting in the 1850s the Nablus court became the theater for a much broader range of cases involving peasants; and the ranking changed as well. The most frequent type of cases was now civil lawsuits involving moneylending, especially *salam* contracts. Land disputes ranked a close second, followed by land purchases and, a distant fourth, criminal and personal-status cases.[52] A much higher percentage of cases were ones in which peasants brought other peasants to court.

These observations are not meant to suggest that archival phenomena closely reflected actual historical realities, especially because most disputes involving peasants never came before the court in the first place. But these two waves do coincide with the ebb and flow of the extension of central authority and with the marked increase in moneylending and transactions in land. For instance, the first wave followed on the heels of the Egyptian occupation and reflected the political and economic dislocations it caused, especially its violent repression of most rural subdistrict chiefs for their role in leading the 1834 revolt. The Egyptians also reinforced the power of cities over their hinterlands by establishing local councils with jurisdiction over the countryside. Many peasants seized this opportunity and took their grievances directly to Nablus. Similarly, the second wave came directly after the end of the last cycle of violent internal struggle in Jabal Nablus (the 1850s) and the permanent assertion of central Ottoman authority (1860). The latter was symbolized by the government's successful attack on the village of Arraba in 1859 and the imposition, for the first time, of a non-Nabulsi *qa'immaqam* who was more than just a temporary figurehead (see the Conclusion).

Three other factors distinguished the second wave from the first. First was the promulgation of the 1858 land law, which constituted an important step in the Ottoman government's campaign to increase its revenues by streamlining land-tenure relations in its domains. The law's most significant innovation—the legalization and registration of private ownership (*milk*) of what had long been considered inalienable state (*miri*) lands—proved to be a boon for local urban elites and greatly reinforced their already substantial economic and political power over the hinterlands. The Ottoman government, it must be remembered, depended on these elites to implement its centralizing fiscal, military, and administrative reforms. Second was the coming of age of Palestine's rural middle class, which turned to the city's legal apparatus in order to assert its growing power and to protect the properties and resources it was in the process of accumulating. Third were the increased pressures on land due to the expansion of cultivation and the growth of population.

The combination of these factors accelerated the already irreversible process of urban domination over the hinterland and accounted for the expanding social base of litigants appearing before the Islamic court. An example of the new type of cases encountered beginning in the 1850s concerned the issue of access of peasant women to land. Usually, village lands were passed down the generations through the male offspring even though Islamic law clearly defined the right of females to inherit, albeit one-half the share of a male heir. The only exception to this practice was if the male head of a household died without leaving an adult male heir to take his place. In this case, it was not unusual for daughters or wives to inherit the land. The same general practice held true in Egypt.[53]

By the mid-nineteenth century, however, this situation had become more complicated. On the one hand, the concentration of holdings, the rise of a rural middle class, and the spread of market relations encouraged neighbors as well as agnates to disinherit females who were the sole heirs after the death of the male head of a household. On the other hand, the same forces that precipitated these changes also pushed the countryside into the urban legal sphere and made the enforcement of Islamic rules of inheritance more likely. Peasant women were not unaware of this contradiction, and they increasingly resorted to the Nablus Islamic Court in the hope that the judge was predisposed to enforce Islamic laws concerning the right of women to inherit and control property.[54]

This is not to say that women were automatically cheated of property. Recent research has shown that Nabulsi women often voluntarily did not press or even retracted property claims if to do otherwise would mean that they would lose the protection and support of certain male relatives without whom the claim could not be made to yield a profit.[55] Much depended, therefore, on the family context, which is why most cases never reached the court in the first place. Still, for those peasant women who wanted to resist pressures to strip them of their properties, the growing availability of the urban legal system created a means for them to do so, albeit with certain risks and no guarantee of success.

For instance, the wife, daughter, and mother of Salman al-Dabbak from the village of Jammaʿin—the sole legal inheritors following his death in September 1860—claimed that Salman's property had been appropriated by Ahmad son of Abdullah al-Akhras from the same village. They had traveled all the way to Nablus to state their case in person, for the deceased had been a rich peasant: under dispute were four cows and 23 separate pieces of land, such as olive groves, fig orchards, and flatlands used for growing grains and tobacco, as well as a house. The description of the borders of the agricultural properties reveals that twelve of the disputed pieces of land were located next to the defendant's own lands. The defendant, for his part, did not deny that these properties belonged to the deceased or that the plaintiffs were the sole inheritors. He did not even argue that he bought these lands from them. Instead, he claimed that just the day before the case was brought to court, they testified in front of witnesses that they had no rights to these lands and that they now belonged to him as "private property." The women vigorously denied this version of events, but they lost because the defendant was able to provide two witnesses who corroborated his story.[56]

In other cases a variety of arguments was used to disinherit women: the land had already been sold, the property had not been their male relative's in the first place, their parents or husbands had given it away before they died, or a will in their favor had never been made.[57] In one case, three men claimed that they were related to a recently deceased peasant, whose sole survivors were a wife and a sister. This was a very unusual argument, because Palestinians at that time paid special attention to kinship connections, and one could easily determine who was related to whom. In this instance, the three men failed to prove any blood relation to the deceased.[58]

Regardless of the various arguments brought forth, a single pattern prevailed: all of the cases were precipitated by the death of a male head of household who left no adult male children, and all were brought before the court by peasant women against (mostly) male relatives. This, in itself, was probably not new. The difference is that these cases reached the Islamic Court in Nablus instead of being settled on the village level through the mediation of clan elders or subdistrict chiefs. This change, which reflected the process of urban-rural integration, was actively precipitated by village women. Judging from the available evidence, many were not disappointed in the results: the court's final decision was as likely to favor the women as the men.

If the sociocultural and legal spaces of the rural sphere had ever been isolated, they were no longer so by the mid-nineteenth century. Fortunately for the historian, the rush of cases involving peasants also provides direct evidence of the impact of moneylending on the land regime and on the relationship of peasants to each other as peasant society became more differentiated.

Commoditization of Land

Private and state ownership of land had coexisted in the Middle East since ancient times, but their legal boundaries and the rights of the peasants as opposed to those of the state have long been contentious issues. As far as the Ottoman government and a majority of Ottoman jurists were concerned, most agricultural lands belonged to the state.[59] Fully owned private (*milk*) lands were, generally speaking, limited to those spaces located within the physical boundaries of population settlements—that is, inside cities, towns, or villages—plus a narrow perimeter around them that consisted mostly of terraced land.[60] The city of Nablus, for example, was surrounded by a belt of terraced olive groves, fruit orchards, vineyards, and irrigated gardens, all of which were divided into hundreds of plots, each called by a name. These plots, in turn, were subdivided into shares that were bought and sold as fully private property with the same legal status as residences, shops, and factories inside the city walls.

The wide stretches of land lying beyond the perimeters of cities, towns, and villages—that is, the "dry belt" on which mostly grains and cotton were grown—technically belonged to the state and could not be bought and sold as fully private property. Peasants did not have a legal right to full private ownership of state agricultural lands. Rather, they had usufruct rights as long as they did not allow these lands to lie fallow for more than three years.[61] This right of use had no time limit: the land could be and was passed down through inheritance for generations. In return for its use, peasants paid taxes (such as *ushr*, or tithe, also called *miri*) that were levied both in cash and kind, plus a whole range of other (sometimes illegal) exactions.

The power of the Ottoman government to enforce this legal framework ebbed and flowed, but generally speaking it managed to exercise real power over state lands. Large areas of state lands, for example, were designated as part of the private holdings of the sultan and his family, endowed as a revenue-producing charitable *waqfs*, parceled out as fiefs (*timars*) for cavalry officers (*sipahis*), auctioned off as tax-farms (*iltizam*) to the highest bidder, or granted as lifelong tax-farms to individuals (*malikane*).

As far as the peasants who actually farmed these lands were concerned, however, none of these arrangements touched the essential character of their relationship to the land: they considered it their own. Perhaps unbeknown to many peasants, their conception of land as their own private property was also supported by a minority of Muslim jurists in the Fertile Crescent. The minority school—represented by such influential figures as Khayr al-Din Ramli (1585–1671) and Ibn Abidin (1784–1836)—argued away most if not all of the legal obstacles to private ownership of such lands.[62] In any case, peasant attitudes in this regard were reinforced over the centuries as each clan and village became identified with particular lands, which they treated as their private property regardless of the changing faces of the tax collectors. At least, this was the case in the highlands of Palestine, where small landholdings prevailed and where the average male peasant could expect to inherit a piece of land, the proceeds of which could provide a living for himself and his family. Consequently, village communities were characterized by a strong bond with their place of origin, as well as by a spirit of autonomy that was impatient with interference by the state. These qualities were especially apparent in the olive-based hill villages, where horticulture was a way of life.

Court cases registered in the eighteenth and early nineteenth centuries show that the peasants of Jabal Nablus, like those of Egypt, did indeed dispose of nominally state lands as if they were their private property by mortgaging, renting, or selling their usufruct rights.[63] The most common practice was for peasants to mortgage their land. For example, in a lawsuit dated mid-January 1724 we learn that an urban moneylender gained control of the two pieces of *timar* land in the village of Askar after the peasant who had previously worked that land defaulted on a debt amounting to 25 piasters and a basket of rice worth 0.25 piaster. For the next seven years the moneylender had another peasant family plant this land. He also kept the proceeds, from which he paid the *timar* dues to a *sipahi* from the Nimr family. When the peasant attempted to take his land back, the moneylender took him to court and proved that the land was his to control because it had been put up as collateral for the loan and because the peasant had previously agreed in their private contract that the moneylender was to enjoy the right of use as long as that loan remained unpaid.[64] In theory, the peasant's right of use was merely postponed, not negated, but in practice he lost access to his land.

One step further was selling usufruct rights outright. Peasants who sold their usufruct rights to other peasants or to urban dwellers were left with no legal recourse to regain control of their land. This is because secular Ottoman law (*qanun*) (also justified by Islamic law) stipulated that usufruct rights belonged to those who tilled the land for three consecutive years and that challenges to these rights would not be allowed after a period of fifteen years.[65] An example is a case recorded on May 29, 1837:

> Today, Yusuf al-Asmar son of Abdullah al-Jabali from the village of Bayta appeared before the noble council. Being of sound mind and body he voluntarily testified . . . that he ceded, evacuated, and lifted his hand from the piece of land located in Khirbat Balata . . . to the pride of honorable

princes, Sulayman *Afandi* son of . . . Husayn *Afandi* Abd al-Hadi. [The lat-
ter] compensated him 700 piasters . . . and the aforementioned Yusuf al-
Asmar gave permission to Sulayman *Afandi* to take over the piece of
land.[66]

The document carefully avoided words which that imply full private
ownership and clearly stated that Yusuf al-Asmar sold his right to this
land, not the land itself. But, as all the parties to the transaction no doubt
understood, this was a sale of state-owned land in all but name. At first
glance, it seems that the sale of usufruct rights was not a widespread practice: only a small number of such transactions were recorded in the Nablus
Islamic Court before 1850, and this particular transaction was first concluded in the chambers of the Advisory Council, headed by none other
than the buyer himself, then sent to the Islamic court to be registered.
Yet there is evidence from Greater Syria and Egypt that land sales among
peasants were not unusual long before the mid-nineteenth century, and
the dearth of recorded cases has more to do with the nature of the sources
than with actual practice.[67] As shown above, the peasants of Jabal Nablus
rarely appeared in court before the 1850s, for a variety of reasons. In
addition, court fees and exposure to taxes made registration of purchases
an expensive and undesirable proposition.[68] Perhaps more important,
peasants were aware that the judges of the Nablus Islamic Court were
staunch defenders of the government's views on land-tenure relations.
Indeed, and in case after case, these judges ruled accordingly.[69]

This tension between informal practice and state law caused legal quan-
daries for the judges on those rare occasions when private arrangements
surfaced in court. The following lawsuit is a typical example of the difficulties encountered. In April/May 1860 a peasant, also from Bayta,
brought a suit against another peasant from the same village. He claimed
that twelve years earlier, the defendant had "sold" four pieces of land
located in the valley between Askar and Balata villages—that is, state
land—and since he "owned" lands adjacent to the properties sold, he
claimed the right of *shufʿa* (preemption) to these lands. The judge ruled
that these were *sipahi* lands and that the right of *shufʿa* did not extend to
such lands.[70] In effect, the judge vindicated the earlier sale of this land as
private property even though it had taken place before the 1858 land code,
yet denied the plaintiff's request on the basis that this was state-owned
land. This must have caused understandable confusion on part of the peasants, because the judge let stand the assumptions about the earlier sale
but ignored its consequences.[71] In fairness to the judge, it must be noted
that scribes in the court had to register testimony as it was given by the

litigants. The characterization of land as "owned" and "sold" in the documents, therefore, does not imply that the judge accepted the terminology. Nor could he shift the focus of the case in order to challenge the validity of the earlier sale. All he could do was rule on whether state-owned lands could be preempted by *shufʿa*, and his decision in this matter followed the correct procedure: that is, usufruct rights to state lands were not subject to preemption.

The 1858 law, which required the registration of lands, must have seemed to the peasants like yet another initiative by the Ottoman government to improve its tax-collection efforts and to acquire knowledge about individual peasants for conscription purposes. This perception was not far from the truth, and it helps explain the peasants' lack of cooperation in implementing the law. Unfortunately for the peasants, their unwillingness to vigorously pursue the registration of their lands in their own names made it easier for urban notables to lay claim to these lands and to expand their holdings.

The Ottoman government, one must quickly add, did not design the law to encourage the formation of large private estates or to lay the foundation for a class of absentee urban landholders. On the contrary, the intent, in addition to streamlining tax collection, was to protect the peasant base of production by preserving small landownership and, in the process, give small landholding peasants the incentive to increase production.[72] The reasons why the consequences of the 1858 land law turned out so differently from the intentions are threefold. First, the material infrastructure for a commercial market in land was in place long before the 1858 land law. Second, the same conditions allowed urban notables to achieve economic dominance over the hinterland. Third, the Egyptian occupation and Ottoman reforms helped to reconfigure local politics by channeling power through a new, merchant-dominated urban elite. Without this power, this elite would not have been able to manipulate the land law to their advantage as quickly and as efficiently as they did, hence creating the impression—which, until two decades ago, was widely accepted—that private property and large landownership developed in Greater Syria as a direct result of the 1858 land law.[73]

In the case of Jabal Nablus, we have evidence that state lands had actually been converted into full private property—that is, involved more than just the sale of usufruct rights—since at least the late 1830s, or roughly two decades before the 1858 land code was promulgated, much less enforced. Most of these conversions were privately concluded and were not registered in the Islamic court. Some, however, were registered in the

Islamic court, proving that the exercise of political power, given the right conditions, could bend the will of presiding judges. The latter type of cases came in two waves, both initiated by the Abd al-Hadi family and registered in the latter half of the 1830s. During this period the Abd al-Hadis were the peak of their power in Jabal Nablus and set up residences in the city itself.

The first wave of these purchases, dating from 1836–1838, was concentrated in the lands of Arraba and Yaʿbad and to a lesser extent, in Ajja and Kafr Qaddum.[74] The much larger second wave, amounting to twenty-one land purchases, took place over the following two years: that is, when it became clear to the Abd al-Hadis that the days of the Egyptian occupation were numbered and that the time was ripe to cash in on the power and wealth they had accumulated while serving as the Egyptian government's primary political bulwark in southern Syria.[75] Simultaneously, for instance, the Abd al-Hadis endowed as *waqf* the most important of the urban properties they had acquired so far, such as their primary residence, soap factories, mills, warehouses in the commercial districts, and so on.[76]

The second wave of purchases involved far more extensive tracts of state lands. On May 27, 1838, for example, dozens of people gathered in the Nablus Islamic Court to participate in and witness the sale of several large properties to Muhammad Abd al-Hadi for 29,500 piasters—roughly the price of a fully equipped soap factory, the most expensive and coveted form of real estate in Nablus (see Appendix 3).[77] These were fertile flatlands, located in valleys and plains, where mostly grains and cotton were grown. In fact, the properties lay in areas so remote that their location was defined by the crossroads leading to various destinations, such as the city of Jaffa and the villages of Qaqun, Anabta, and Attil. The closest that any of the pieces of land came to a population settlement was one described as "near the lands of Tulkarem."

Another clue to the remoteness of the lands and the immensity of the sale was the number and identities of the sellers involved: more than fifty individuals from four villages—Shwayka, Arraba, Yaʿbad, and Kafr Raʿi—were listed. Most of them were adult men, each representing an extended family household. But there were also more than a dozen adult women, a smaller number of military recruits then absent and represented by agents, and (apparently orphaned) children represented by court-appointed guardians. The presiding judge—addressing the large crowd in a loud voice—expounded for the record that these sellers came of their own free will and that he viewed the sale of properties owned by minor children as justified, for the sale was meant to provide for their needs.

The organizational effort invested in this sale—mapping out the extensive lands, determining which pieces belonged to whom, convincing all the parties to sell, including representatives of absent individuals and orphans, negotiating prices, and then gathering them all in one large sitting—must have been enormous. Only a politically powerful family deeply involved in commercial agriculture could and would invest the time and money in this and other similar purchases registered during this period.[78]

The available evidence from court records shows that merchants did not become heavily involved in such purchases before the 1850s. Unlike the Abd al-Hadis, it would have been difficult for them to directly supervise and enforce sharecropping agreements in areas that neither they nor the central Ottoman government sufficiently controlled, despite their deeply rooted trade networks. Thus, until the Ottoman government asserted direct control of the interior regions in the 1860s, most merchants were not interested in many of the lands they could have appropriated as a result of defaults on loans. Rather, their primary concern was with maintaining a village or an individual peasant perpetually in debt so that they could secure a steady and cheap supply of agricultural commodities. Besides, merchants found sufficient outlets for their investment in lands much closer to the city. Between 1830 and 1850 the overwhelming majority of agricultural properties purchased by urban merchants and registered in the court were located on the slopes of the two steep mountains that sandwiched Nablus between them or in the valley lands that widened westward. Beginning in the early 1850s the circle of purchases expanded to include villages within walking distance of Nablus, such as Rafidya, Junayd, Bayt Wazan, and Asira al-Shamaliyya.[79] Soap manufacturers and oil merchants were particularly active in this regard, and each came to own dozens of olive groves in these areas.

Aside from a jump in the number of land purchases beginning in the early 1850s, these transactions were not unusual: most of these properties, including those located inside the villages mentioned above, were considered *milk* to begin with. This was not to remain the case for long, however. In the late 1850s the circle of land purchases by merchants widened again, spurred by the concentration of capital and by the extension of state authority. More and more of these purchases involved former state lands in the "dry belt" far from Nablus, including flatlands used for grain and cotton production.

Many of these lands were often appropriated directly as a result of defaults on olive oil *salam* contracts with urban moneylenders. In early April 1864, for example, Abd al-Rahman al-Shaykh Husayn from the village of Aqraba initiated a lawsuit against two powerful soap merchants, *Sayyid* Sulayman Hashim Hanbali and *Sayyid Hajj* Yusuf Hashim Hanbali. Standing before the judge, he admitted to owing 3,333 piasters to the former and 30 jars of oil to the latter. But, he continued, "I have spent four months in prison, and I have nothing to pay them [the defendants] back with except for some lands in Aqraba village." He then asked the judge to allow him to sell a portion of these properties to the defendants so that he could pay off his debts and be set free.[80]

The alienation of land as a result of unpaid debts accelerated as the enforcement of debt obligations came to involve the entire urban political and legal apparatus: the Islamic court judge, the *mufti*, the Advisory Council, the governor, and the subdistrict tax collectors, all of whom were mobilized and worked together to protect the interests of moneylenders. For example, one debtor, Abdullah son of *Hajj* Isma'il from the village of Asira al-Qibliyya disappeared without paying his allotted amount of olive oil jars to a rich soap merchant, *Sayyid Hajj* Yusuf son of *Sayyid* As'ad Bishtawi. Sometime afterward, *Hajj* Yusuf Bishtawi obtained a *fatwa* (a religious ruling, akin to a legal opinion) from the Nablus *mufti* allowing him to expropriate the sheep of the debtor, which were being held by a fellow peasant from the same village.

The matter did not end there. On October 16, 1862, *Hajj* Yusuf Bishtawi enrolled the Islamic court judge in the effort. The judge sent a letter to the Nablus governor informing him of the situation and asked that he order the chief of the subdistrict in which that village was located to collect all the debtor's movable properties and send them to Nablus so they could be auctioned off and the proceeds could be applied to the debt.[81] This was done, but the amount raised was not sufficient. Then, in 1865, *Hajj* Yusuf Bishtawi initiated another lawsuit, this time against Khalil son of Khalaf from the same village, who had the misfortune of guaranteeing the runaway's debt.[82] The defendant lost the case, but he did not have the means to pay back the 20 jars of olive oil stipulated in the *salam* contract or the 600 piasters originally borrowed. The judge responded by putting his seal on a sales deed that transferred the defendant's vine-orchard to the plaintiff.[83]

The appropriation of lands by merchants as a result of defaults on loans was more frequent, penetrated deeper into the hinterland, and began earlier than the cases registered in court would suggest. An example of a private contract, culled from the Nimr family papers, involved *Khawaja* Mitri, the Christian merchant from Jaffa whom we met earlier. On August 1, 1852, *Khawaja* Mitri bought as fully private property what technically were state agricultural lands in Jabal Nablus from peasants indebted both to him and to other merchants. One of these peasants was none other than the same Abd al-Rahman with whom he had concluded the sesame *salam* contract in 1851 quoted above:

> *Khawaja* Khalil Mitri son of the Christian Yusuf Mitri from the people of Jaffa Port bought . . . from Abd al-Rahman and his brother Mustafa, sons of the deceased al-Saʿada from the Saʿada branch of the *Hajj* Muhammad clan of [the subdistrict of] Mashariq Nablus . . . one half . . . of the cleared land, empty of trees, called al-Wasiyya that is part of the lands of Kafr Bayta in Mashariq Nablus—bordered on the south by the line separating the plain from the rough lands; on the east by the lands of the Abi Awad family *(dar)*; on the north by the main road; and on the west by the land of Ismaʿil al-Asʿad. [Also] one half of *maris* land called Maris al-Arqadat, bordered on the south by the land of the Abi Abbas family; on the east by the lands of Salim [village]; on the north by the land of the Uthman family; and on the west by the line separating the plain from the rough lands. [Also] the lands called Miʿani al-Najma, bordered on the south by the land of the Uthman family; on the east by the line; on the north by the lands of Abi Awad; and on the west by the line separating the plain from the rough lands. All of that, along with its roads, terraces and walls . . . located in the lands of Kafr Bayta . . . for 10,000 piasters. [*Khawaja* Mitri] deducted from this price 4,420 piasters that they owed him according to vouchers in his hand, in addition to 1,420 piasters that Abd al-Rahman owed to Qasim son of Yusuf al-Nabulsi.[84]

This case clearly shows, first, that as early as 1852 a coastal merchant like *Khawaja* Mitri faced no insurmountable difficulties in appropriating prime agricultural lands from a peasant in Nablus—even one who belonged to a powerful rural clan that controlled the subdistrict of Mashariq Nablus. Second, *Khawaja* Mitri's access to this land was a direct result of a default on a *salam* contract he had extended just a few months earlier. There is little doubt that these lands were sold in distress, for the two brothers owed more than half of the value of the land to two merchants— one from Nablus and the other from Jaffa—who apparently were business partners. Third, this purchase involved sizable pieces of land (judging by the price paid) and included at least some state lands (judging by the description of the borders).[85] No wonder, therefore, that this purchase, made six years prior to the 1858 land code, was not registered in the Nablus Islamic Court. Undeterred by the absence of a legitimizing legal framework, the parties involved simply ignored the court altogether. *Khawaja* Mitri ignored it again when he sold the same land, three years later, to Abd al-Fattah *Agha* Nimr.[86]

The widespread traffic in transactions of this kind deeply worried the central government: it undermined its legitimacy and control of land and threatened its fiscal basis. The same, by the way, could be said of ruling families. The expansion of cultivation put pressure on land, leading many peasants to plow new territories considered by these families to be their private property. Afraid that peasants would lay claims to these lands by right of *ihya al-mawat* (cultivation of virgin lands), they sought to have their claims recognized by the Nablus Advisory Council. For example, on July 30, 1852, a tribal chief, *amir* (prince) Faris al-Harithy, requested that the council notarize his *"haq al-milkiyya"* (right of ownership) over large tracts of unplowed valley lands, because peasants from nearby villages were putting these lands under cultivation and claiming them as their own.[87]

Indicative of these concerns about uncontrolled developments in land-holding patterns and challenges to state authority was an 1855 decree—communicated by the Advisory Council of Sidon and relayed by the governor of Jerusalem on March 15 of that year to the *qa'immaqam* and council members of Nablus—warning all concerned that property transactions must be legally registered in the Islamic court:

> [I]t is a practice and a requirement that the selling of shops and houses [*mahallat*] and lands by their owners . . . be done under the supervision of Islamic law and according to legal and correct procedures. . . . [Yet], in some places, these principles are not respected, and houses and lands are being [traded] by brokers and speculators, and registered in documents and deeds that might cause trouble in the future. . . . Henceforth, if such documents are drawn up by brokers and speculators without informing the court, the appropriate punishment will be meted out to the sellers and buyers, and the documents [which were not approved by the court] shall be considered null and void. If they [the documents] reappear and become cause for quarrels, the local council shall carry out an investigation . . . and new correct and legal deeds shall be drawn up by the Islamic court, copied into its records, and given to its owners. Those who dare disobey this order shall not be allowed any excuse . . . [and] are to be reported to us.[88]

This warning was not heeded, and the pressures from below generated by the commercial traffic in land could not be contained by the Islamic court—or by any institution, for that matter. In this context, it could be argued that the 1858 land law was not an initiator of new land-tenure relations but, rather, a recognition by the Ottoman government of the need to contain and streamline already ongoing processes that threatened to undermine the fiscal basis and, by extension, the political effectiveness of its rule.

REDEFINING IDENTITY AND POLITICAL AUTHORITY

Long before the 1830s the commercialization of agriculture and the atten-
dant expansion of merchant capital into the countryside through moneylending (especially olive-oil *salam* contracts) had begun to undermine
the old patronage networks between long-time ruling clans and the peasants in their subdistricts. Meanwhile, the peasants of Jabal Nablus, like
their counterparts elsewhere in Greater Syria, were increasingly linked to
urban trade networks, attuned to shifting European demand, and no doubt
informed about the new political and administrative changes introduced
by the Egyptian occupation and the *Tanzimat*. Slowly, the leveling effect
of a cash nexus in the hinterlands facilitated the spread of horizontal connections at the expense of vertical loyalties. It was only a matter of time
before the peasants' cultural, economic, and political horizons stretched
beyond their own village or region. Not surprisingly, their perceptions of
their own identity and place in society, as well as their notions of legitimacy, political authority, and justice, were incrementally redefined.

Islam, the Rural Middle Class, and the Subdistrict Chiefs

Hitherto, the decline of subdistrict chiefs has been attributed solely to
state intervention from above; that is, to the Egyptian occupation (1831–
1840), which crushed centrifugal forces, disarmed the peasantry, and imposed a centralized administrative apparatus. These actions, the argument
continues, paved the way for the implementation of the *Tanzimat* (reforms) and the extension of centralized Ottoman rule.[89] Although the
centralizing tendencies of Egyptian and Ottoman rule were indeed important, they only accelerated a number of ongoing processes on the economic, cultural, and political levels.

On the economic level, moneylending, in addition to laying some of
the groundwork for the commoditization of land, helped deepen the cleav-
ages among peasants by, among other things, widening the social space of
the rural middle class. The spread of market relations encouraged many
well-to-do peasants to reproduce the business practices and institutions
developed by urban merchants on the village level. This, in turn, helped
clear a path for urban, coastal, and foreign merchant activities in the interior of Palestine. One indication of increasing differentiation is that by
the mid-nineteenth century it had become common for peasants to sue
each other in court over disputed olive oil *salam* contracts, over the purchase of rural lands, and even over business partnerships.[90] Recall the

examples in Chapter 2 of how some rural agents for textile merchants established their own commercial networks and ventured into retail trade in the countryside, as well as examples in this chapter of the moneylend-ing activities by the Rummani family in Bayta and by Salama Makhluf in Bayt Jala.

The social space between the majority of peasants and the few rural-based ruling families first expanded in the large villages of each subdis-trict: Tubas, Bayta, Burqa, Umm al-Fahm, Jaba, Dayr al-Ghusun, Arraba, Qabatya, Ya'bad, and Salfit, to name a few. These and similar villages have long been centers of commercial activities that mediated relations between the city of Nablus (as well the town of Jenin) and the more re-mote and smaller villages. It is not clear when the expansion of this rural middle class began in earnest, but this process in the central highlands of Palestine probably reflected a larger, regionwide process beginning around the mid-eighteenth century. In her study of Zahleh, a village in Mount Lebanon that grew into an important market town, Alixa Naff argues that "a nebulous middle stratum" before the nineteenth century had become "an unmistakable class of entrepreneurs" by 1840.[91] Dina Khoury also shows how internal and regional dynamics in the hinterlands of Mosul (in today's Iraq) during the 1750–1850 period precipitated the expansion of commercial agriculture and the de facto privatization of land. Both de-velopments, she continues, led to an increase in social differentiation on the village level, including the rise of "middle" and "rich" peasants who were able to "exploit the labor power of other peasants."[92]

In any event, not until the mid-nineteenth century did the cases regis-tered in the Islamic Court of Nablus begin to reveal the pervasiveness and sophistication of entrepreneurial activities of this class. An example is a document, dated May 19, 1849, dividing the profits of a company set up by five villagers:

> Before this date, the Pride of Honorable Scholars, Shaykh Uthman al-Labadi from the village of Kafr al-Labad and Hasan Khattab, Muhammad al-Bab, Khalil Abd al-Rahim, and the Master Yusuf Elias the Christian, all from the village of Burqa, formed a silent partnership company (*sharikat mudaraba*) with a capital of 4,000 piasters. All of the money belonged to Shaykh Uthman al-Labadi. Hasan Khattab received the money in order to buy and sell, take and give, loan and collect on oil, wheat, barley, and other [crops]. . . . Whatever profit God bestowed on them, Shaykh Uth-man would receive one-half because he provided the capital and the rest would equally share the other half. The aforementioned Hasan Khattab in-vested the . . . money in oil and other [crops] through *salam* [contracts] and, needing more money, he borrowed 243 piasters . . . to put more

money into the oil *salam* that belonged to this company. On this date, they appeared [in court] . . . and settled the company's accounts. . . . The profit was 743 piasters, from which the 243 piasters that Hasan Khattab had borrowed . . . were deducted.[93]

The owner of capital was a religious leader from a medium-sized village; the other partners were residents of Burqa, one of the largest villages in Jabal Nablus and the administrative headquarters for the subdistrict of Wadi al-Sh'ir.[94] Burqa had an artisanal sector, and some of its families worked in textile production. The partners from Burqa were ideally suited for negotiating *salam* contracts because their village acted as a hub for smaller ones around it and therefore enjoyed a built-in network of relations. Again, the preferred business mechanism was the *salam* system of moneylending, and the commodities that were the object of speculation—oil, wheat, and barley—were the main cash crops of Jabal Nablus.

None of the partners belonged to ruling clans or to the majority of poor peasants. Their partnership also cut across geographical, kinship, and religious boundaries: Burqa was far from Kafr al-Labad, and the partners were not of the same clan or even the same religion. The combination of these factors—the pooling of capital for investment in commercial agriculture through moneylending and the social diversity of the moneylenders—constitutes a classic characteristic of a rural middle class united by the search for profit and capital accumulation.

Peasant involvement in trade and moneylending created new opportunities for upward mobility, as attested to by the inheritance estates of rich villagers (who were not members of ruling clans) registered in the Nablus Islamic Court.[95] Over time, the expansion of commercial activities generated from within the hinterlands crossed not only geographic and religious boundaries but also social, cultural, and political ones. Urban-rural intermarriage, adoption of city habits, alliances with urban merchants, resort to the Islamic court for settling disputes, and eventually moving into the city, were all becoming common phenomena (see below).

On the cultural level, the undercutting of patronage networks based on customary law was accomplished primarily by the reproduction in the rural sphere of urban legal, social, and business practices based on Islamic law.[96] In order to facilitate their profitable commercial activities and to consolidate their social position, members of the rural middle class turned their backs on the folk religious practices common among peasants and began to appropriate the system of meanings articulated in what one might call orthodox or urban Islam. As will be seen in greater detail below, they used Islamic law not only to construct and legally protect moneylending networks and investment companies but also to weave a new tapestry of relations with both poorer peasants and their long-time ruling clans; that is, to expand their own social space at the expense of both. This process was hastened in the second half of the nineteenth century, when mosques were built in many villages and when Islamic courts were introduced into the seat villages of the subdistricts during the 1850s.[97]

Islamic law proved ideologically and practically well suited for the capitalist transformation of the countryside. As a universal ideology it cut across social boundaries, such as those of kinship, regional identity, and other particularistic customs typical of vertical loyalties. Trade and investment, moreover, are not considered in Islamic law as undesirable activities or somehow inferior to, say, landholding. On the contrary, Islam celebrates honest profits from commercial activities and provides legitimacy to those who convey themselves as God-fearing and righteous businessmen. On a practical level, Islamic law—especially the Hanafi school of jurisprudence, which, as mentioned earlier, was officially adopted by the Ottoman government—makes available a detailed body of rules and regulations well suited for structuring moneylending contracts, business partnerships, and so on. It also provides a clear set of guidelines for the resolution of disputes. In short, Islamic law offers a common denominator or, more precisely, a set of shared reference points that made it an appealing framework at a time when market relations were carving an ever-larger space in the hinterlands of the interior.

An example that combines all the above issues is a business dispute dated April 29, 1864.[98] The plaintiff, Abdullah son of Muhammad al-Hammud, was a rich villager from Jaba village who was then temporarily living in Damascus while serving as a recruit in the Ottoman military. The defendant, Shaykh Ibrahim son of Shaykh Abdullah Jarrar, was the head of the most powerful rural-based clan in that subdistrict (Mashariq al-Jarrar) and had recently relocated to the city of Nablus. The plaintiff's agent in the Nablus court, *Hajj* Abdullah *Abu* Ali al-Zaybaq, came from the village of Zamalka, near Damascus.

The agent testified that the plaintiff had advanced Shaykh Ibrahim the sum of 5,000 piasters a year and a half earlier in a lawful silent partnership (*sharikat mudaraba*) for the purpose of speculation. Their understanding was that no matter what the profits might be, they would split them evenly. The purpose of the plaintiff's lawsuit was to make sure that Shaykh Ibrahim Jarrar would pay back the original investment of 5,000 piasters plus half of the profits. Shaykh Ibrahim admitted to the business arrangement and testified that the profit he had made over the past eighteen months (2,600 piasters) exceeded half the principal. What he contested was the status of *Hajj* Abdullah as a lawful agent for the plaintiff. *Hajj* Abdullah proved to the satisfaction of the judge that he did indeed represent the plaintiff, and Shaykh Ibrahim Jarrar had to hand over 6,300 piasters.

The most striking aspects of this lawsuit were, first, the reversal of historic roles between peasant and ruling subdistrict chief. A rich villager enrolled his subdistrict chief as an agent in a contract calculated to take advantage of the latter's connections. In the process he subverted the chief's traditional patronage network by turning it into a business instrument within his own modern network.[99] Second, this lawsuit also shows how the new networks of the rural middle class cut across not only social and political boundaries but also geographic ones. The plaintiff initiated this lawsuit in Damascus using a peasant from the Syrian village of Zamalka as an agent. The defendant came from the same village as the plaintiff but was now a resident of Nablus. The supporting witnesses on behalf of the plaintiff, meanwhile, came from the village of Silat al-Dhaher, in the Sha'rawiyya al-Sharqiyya subdistrict of Jabal Nablus. In short, this villager from Jaba was, at one and the same time, a soldier who traveled widely and an investor who made business connections that integrated people from a number of areas.[100]

Third, the rich villager, by initiating this partnership while absent from his home base, assumed that his investment—which took the form of a business partnership recognized as legitimate by Islamic law—would be protected even against the possible extortion of a clan that had ruled generations of his ancestors. This case confirmed that his assumption was well founded: lawsuits that hinge on the status of an agent to one of the parties were widely used as legal mechanisms to prevent future disputes. In other words, there was no real disagreement. Rather, Shaykh Ibrahim wanted to protect himself from the possibility that the plaintiff, upon his return from Damascus, would demand the same moneys again by claiming that *Hajj* Abdullah was not his lawful agent.

On a political level, villagers also resorted to urban legal institutions, specifically the Islamic court, in order to challenge the authority and sometimes arbitrary practices of subdistrict chiefs. For example, on March 18, 1861, Odeh al-Bab, a well-to-do villager from Burqa, accused Shaykh Isma'il son of Shaykh Khader al-Burqawi—a member of one of the two clans, Sayf and al-Ahfa, that ruled the subdistrict of Wadi al-Sha'ir—of unlawfully usurping six pieces of land and an olive oil press through "force, compulsion, imprisonment, and threats."[101] Shaykh Isma'il al-

Burqawi claimed that he had bought these lands in 1856–1857 for 7,000 piasters, but he lost the case when the plaintiff produced two credible witnesses from both of the ruling clans mentioned above. It is not known whether the court's order that these properties be returned was ever carried out, but the fact remains that the subdistrict chief was forced to appear and defend himself in the Islamic court against a peasant from his own seat village.

As this and other cases cited throughout this chapter suggest, therefore, the internal transformation of peasant society was an important dynamic in the declining influence and status of subdistrict chiefs. This does not mean that rural shaykhs were completely marginalized: the post of subdistrict chief remained under the control, by and large, of the same families that had dominated the hinterland for generation. Many also continued to wield real power, at least as far as most peasants in their subdistricts were concerned. But during the 1700–1900 period these individuals were transformed from a virtually independent and powerful group of rural leaders into appendages of the urban merchant and political elite, as well as into servants of the state. Their networks and political autonomy were undermined to the point that the real meaning of "subdistrict chief" came to approximate more and more the official (but long unrealized) Ottoman vision of their role: tax collectors and rural administrators whose powers stemmed solely from the fountainhead of the central bureaucracy.

Gone were the days when the subdistrict chiefs were personally visited by the governor of Damascus in their seat village and dressed in a cloak that symbolized their status as equal to the *mutasallim* of Nablus. By the 1850s they were sent a brief letter of appointment that they had to register in the Nablus Islamic Court, and then they had to be sworn in by the Nablus Advisory Council.[102] Even their official title had changed, from the broad and respectful *shaykh al-nahiya* to the more narrowly defined and bureaucratic *muhassil* (tax collector).[103]

The subdistrict chiefs did not forgo their traditional privileges easily. The contested nature of this transformation can be seen in the following letter from the governor of Sidon province to the Nablus Advisory Council and its head, Sulayman *Beik* Tuqan, dated December 20, 1850:

> Under the excuse that they are unsalaried, the supervisors and shaykhs
> of the subdistricts of Jabal Nablus are taking moneys from the people and
> villages under their administration above and beyond the assessed
> [amount] of state taxes and using these moneys for their own purposes.
> As a result, the people and residents are in a disturbed and weakened state.
> These aforementioned supervisors and shaykhs do not have salaries set

aside for them, but they do enjoy the respect and admiration of their peers as a result of our utilizing them in these positions, and this is an act of great generosity and providence [on our part]. Therefore, their aggression toward the people under their care with the excuse that they have no salaries contravenes the Supreme Wishes. [This behavior] is absolutely forbidden, and it is imperative that it be stopped quickly.[104]

Just a century before, the central government would not have even considered holding subdistrict chiefs responsible for illegal taxation, much less attempted to interfere. In response to the new realties, some of the subdistrict chiefs, such as the Abd al-Hadis, quickly assimilated to the changing political economy of Palestine and used it to their advantage. Others, such as the Jarrars, became internally divided over which course the extended family should pursue in the context of an eroding economic, political, and social base. Most took the middle road. In this regard, the justification used by these chiefs for their actions is revealing. By emphasizing the lack of salary they were, at one and the same time, protesting the onerous duties and limitations imposed on them and opening the door to further integration into the government bureaucracy.[105]

The process of differentiation was also accompanied by serious dislocations and internal power struggles within each village. Tensions heightened as villagers manipulated their fellow villagers and became embroiled in disputes with their neighbors, clan members, and even their own families. By the turn of the twentieth century, the divisive impact of moneylending and the dominant role of merchant capital was a festering sore, apparent to all. During their tour through the villages of Jabal Nablus in 1916–1917, Tamimi and Bahjat quoted one peasant from Dayr Istiya as saying that "the Nabulsis have set brother against brother"[106]—clearly implying that many well-to-do villagers and merchants were allied in a single system that tore at the social fabric of each village. Some peasants from Salfit articulated the situation to Tamimi and Bahjat in these terms: "Nabulsis, for their own personal gain, have sown the seeds of discord, and *now we have become like them:* hurting others so we can get ahead. ... The Nabulsis have profited from these conflicts: they appropriated all that we have, with the excuse that they are saving us from the pitfalls we put ourselves in. Now we are poor, powerless prisoners in the hands of the Nabulsis."[107]

Resistance and Notions of Justice

The shifting boundaries of political and economic power in the rural sphere generated intense conflicts that threatened the stability of Jabal

Nablus as a whole. In the above letter the Sidon governor's claim that the peasants of Jabal Nablus were in a "disturbed and weakened state" contained more than a grain of truth. Most peasants did not reap the benefit of Palestine's economic growth during this period, for this growth was predicated largely on the enhanced ability of urban merchants to gain access to and control their surplus.

The slow dissolution of patronage ties between peasants and their long-time ruling subdistrict chiefs, as well as the transformation of the latter into agents of urban interests (and eventually into urban merchants and landholders), no doubt exacerbated the peasants' feelings of alienation, isolation, and lack of control over their lives. Peasant notions of identity, political authority, and justice, therefore, were bound to be challenged and redefined, especially as their various means of resistance were often repressed by force.[108]

Peasant petitions provide important clues as to these notions and show that peasant complaints were usually precipitated by attempts of the local government to enforce moneylending contracts, especially olive oil *salam* contracts. For example, in early February 1852 the peasants of Asira al-Shamiyya[109] submitted a petition to the governor of Jerusalem, Hafiz Pasha, in which they said:

> [We] the destitute . . . of Asira village from the district (*sanjaq*) of Nablus have paid all the taxes (*miri*) required from us in cash and kind to the last penny (*para*) . . . and the account books of the treasury are cleared of all that was or could be [required of us]. A few days ago, Ahmad al-Yusuf [Jarrar]—[on the basis] of his power, influence, and lack of fear of the rule of law—demanded from us, in a criminal and corrupt manner, a sum [of money and crops] for no legitimate reason. *He has crossed the line and broken the rules of [decent behavior] and just regulations.* [As part of his illegal behavior] he sent cavalrymen [who] picked ten persons from among us and imprisoned them in Nablus. They have been imprisoned for more than eight days and remain there for no satisfactory reason. *Because this overstepping of bounds is a matter contradictory to your [sense of] justice,* we have found the courage to petition your Munificent Highness and beg that you issue an order to Mahmud *Beik* Abd al-Hadi, the *qaʾimmaqam* of Nablus, [instructing him] to go over the tax books. If a single penny or the smallest measure of crops is found to be owed by us, we will bring it over. If nothing [owed by us] is found, then our people should be released, for the disposition of your justice does not condone or allow . . . a person, such as the above mentioned, to imprison our people [just to satisfy] his aim for bribery. Our just government has the power to remove the above mentioned.

> The Poor of Asira, Nablus District[110]

It must have been disconcerting for the governor of Jerusalem to receive this petition, because it laid the matter squarely on his shoulders and boldly challenged him to dismiss a government official. Also, by addressing the petition to him instead of going through normal hierarchy of political authority in Jabal Nablus, the peasants of Asira al-Shamiyya implicitly accused the council in general, and Mahmud *Beik* Abd al-Hadi in particular, of complicity in what they deemed to be an unjust act. After all, it was the urban ruling elite of Nablus who controlled the cavalry that made the arrests and ran the prisons in which the men were incarcerated.

A few days later, on February 12, 1852, the assistant governor of Jerusalem sent a copy of the petition to Mahmud *Beik* Abd al-Hadi, along with this terse and hardly impartial note: "Provide in a memorandum a detailed explanation of the reasons for imprisoning the aforementioned individuals and the foul misdeeds that necessitated their imprisonment."[111] The council's answer is worth quoting in full:

> The reason for the imprisonment of some individuals from Asira village is that one of the oil merchants, Shaykh Muhammad Abu Hijli, is owed through a *salam* contract by the peasants of the aforementioned village an amount of oil for which they received money in advance in order to pay the taxes due from their village. When he demanded his right, the people of the village gave excuses . . . so he complained very persistently. Shaykh Ahmad al-Yusuf, chief of the al-Jarrar subdistrict, requested cavalrymen . . . and sent them with a representative of his in order to collect the merchant's due. When his representative arrived in the village, some of its people gathered around him and pelted him with stones. His sword was broken, and the metal piece fitted on the sword sheath below the handle fell. [Also] one of the pistols tucked in his belt was broken, and his cloak [*mashlah*] fell, as did the tassel on his fez and his money pouch. He arrived back to these parts in this state. *Your Excellency knows that such disrespect for the state's cavalry is considered insolence toward the government.* The punishment of these individuals could not be overlooked. So an investigation was made about those persons who headed this movement, and four were found. They were brought [here] and put into prison so that they can be taught a lesson [*min ajl al-tarbiya*] . . . and made an example to others. They can be released only after they promise not to display such insolence again. But now the cavalryman has been brought in [to the council's premises] and the missing items noted. He deserves [the payment of] 120 piasters from the aforementioned imprisoned men in order to fix his sword and gun and to replace his coat, the missing money from his money pouch, the fez's tassel, and the metal piece of his sword. . . . He received all . . . and the prisoners were released.[112]

The major elements of this story should be familiar by now. The inhabitants of an entire village had entered into a *salam* moneylending contract with an olive oil merchant so that they could pay their taxes. The oil merchant, Muhammad *Abu* Hijli, was himself a member of the rural middle class, for he had only recently relocated to the city. This illustrates once again the differentiation within the rural sphere and the reproduction, by this class, of urban commercial networks. In fact, the Abu Hijli clan—most of whose members were still in Dayr Istya, their home village—was already well-to-do in the 1830s. During that time, they were involved in moneylending to other peasants and controlled a fair amount of *timar* lands.[113] By the Mandate period they were large landlords. In Chapter 2, recall, we met a wealthy villager by the name of *Hajj* Ahmad Ismaʿil *Abu* Hijli who, in the year 1900, still lived in Dayr Istiya. This also fits the development pattern of rural middle-class families: they usually relocated only some of their members to the city, leaving others behind to supervise agricultural workers on their lands.

Allied with the olive oil merchant was Ahmad Yusuf al-Jarrar, head of the Mashariq al-Jarrar subdistrict. As shown in Chapter 1, the Jarrars were famous as key protectors of Jabal Nablus by virtue of their military resources and control of the formidable Sanur fortress. By the mid-nineteenth century, however, their influence was much reduced, and, as far as the peasants of Asira al-Shamiyya were concerned, they had become repressive local shaykhs whose actions—extortion of peasants in their subdistrict and use of force and intimidation in the collection of debts, even those owed to an oil merchant who came from another subdistrict (Jammaʿin)—placed them outside the rule of law.

Shaykh Ahmad al-Yusuf Jarrar, in turn, was supported by the *qaʾimmaqam* of Nablus as well as by the Advisory Council. They legitimated his actions by granting his request for cavalry and by branding the peasants' resistance to his demands as "insolence toward the government." At least, this is the impression they sought to convey to the governor of Jerusalem in order to represent themselves as the forces of law and order in Jabal Nablus.[114] The peasants of Asira, like those in Mount Lebanon during this period, were openly challenging the authority and privileges of their long-time ruling subdistrict chiefs.[115] However, unlike the situation in Mount Lebanon, where there was a spatial division of political authority (Dayr al-Qamar) and economic life (Beirut)—the location of Nablus at the very heart of the core hill region meant that this city combined both. Hence the welding of rural shaykhs, rich merchants, and urban ruling families into a united political bloc that weighed heavily on the majority of peasants.

Both this petition and the one from the village of Jaba cited earlier show that the peasants of Jabal Nablus were very much aware of this alliance, as well as of its internal hierarchy. By communicating their grievances to the governor of Jerusalem, they made it clear that they expected no justice from the council and the *qa'immaqam* of Nablus, much less from the traditional rural leaders of their subdistrict. Indeed, the wording of the Asira al-Shamiyya petition clearly implied that the urban political elite was a coconspirator, if not the main culprit, in this affair.

This accusation was based on bitter experience, not posturing. During the same year, for example, the Nablus Council made excuses for not sending a member of the Jarrar family who had been accused of murdering villagers to Beirut, where he was to stand trial.[116] In yet another case, the council lamely justified the reason why witnesses against another member of the Jarrar family, also accused of murder, could not be sent to Beirut to testify.[117]

Under the suffocating weight of both the rural and the urban elites of Jabal Nablus, the peasants' best hope of carving out a political space for themselves lay in involving the state and appealing to its sense of justice. The Asira peasants' concepts of state justice and the rule of law are not entirely clear, because they were only expressed in exclusionary terms in the petition—that is, the unlawful behavior of their subdistrict chiefs and the Advisory Council of Nablus. What is clear is that their appeal was calculated to take advantage of the state's own propaganda, which harped on the need to protect the peasant base of production. In written orders during the 1840s and 1850s, the government passionately called for justice and the rule of law, specifically warned city councils and subdistrict chiefs against the abuse of peasants, and tacitly recognized the social differentiation within villages, as well as the concentration of landholdings. These issues were ideologically framed as an appeal both to Islam and to the common citizenship of all Ottoman subjects and were driven by the need to reinforce the legitimacy of the state in the eyes of all of its subjects, including peasants.[118]

On June 24, 1841, for example, the central authorities warned that the flight of peasants from the land due to extortion, corvée labor, or unfair practices leading to undercultivation or loss of land would not be tolerated. In this letter to the Nablus Advisory Council, the governor of Damascus ordered, among other things, the cancellation of all illegal taxes and a stop to the practices that forced peasants to sell their crops for less than half of their worth.[119] He also forbade the confiscation of animals for free transportation and, most important, the eviction of those who were unable to pay their debts.[120] On December 2, 1850, the *mutasarrif* of Jerusalem reminded the Nablus Council that the harvest season was at hand, yet in every subdistrict and village there were "poor and old persons who do not possess the means to plow and plant . . . [and] who need either lands or threshing floors or animals or . . . all of these things combined."[121] He went on to urge all Muslims to help those poor villagers because "the equitable and just will of our Sultan will not allow the existence of a single person who is deprived of earnings and enjoyment." Significant here is that non-Muslims of means were encouraged to do the same, because "those who are not coreligionists are [still] brothers in the fatherland [*ikhwan fi al-watan*]."[122] He then called on people of means to help through loans, through permission to use threshing floors, and through sharing "some of the surplus lands that are in their hands." Finally, he commanded that copies of this order be sent to all subdistrict chiefs and that a list of poor people in every village be compiled. Next to each name the council was to describe the manner in which that person had been put back in a position that would allow him to pursue his vocation as a productive peasant.

Only eighteen days later, as mentioned above, the governor of Sidon province warned the tax collectors (*muhassils*) of the subdistricts of Nablus and Jenin that they would be severely punished if they continued their practice of extorting moneys and crops from peasants under the pretext of being unsalaried government employees who were merely covering their expenses.[123] We know from the council's own records that they sent copies of this order to all 13 *muhassils*, as well as to 213 villages in Jabal Nablus. The order was read aloud in each village square, and the inhabitants were specifically instructed that any complaints about extortion should be addressed to the Nablus Advisory Council.[124]

Within this context, it is significant that the authors of both the Asira al-Shamiyya and Jaba petitions decided to deliberately bypass the Advisory Council. More important, their arguments echoed the main thrust of *Tanzimat* ideology: equality before the law. In the words of the peasants of Asira, Ahmad al-Yusuf Jarrar "crossed the line and broke the rules of [decent behavior] and just regulations." The peasants were saying, in effect, that all of the inhabitants of Jabal Nablus were members of a much larger polity (the Ottoman Empire), whose boundaries of legitimacy and rules of behavior were clearly delineated, and that all members of this polity were subject to those rules regardless of their official position, historical privileges, or personal power. The long-time rulers of Jabal Nablus, even though they were native sons, were portrayed in the petitions as public servants with a clear (and limited) mandate. The ultimate source of political authority, the peasants insisted, was the Ottoman state or, more accurately, an abstract notion of what state meant.

A key constituent element of the meanings ascribed to this abstract notion, as suggested by the wording of the petition, was the peasants' right as tax-paying citizens to protection by the central authorities from arbitrary extortion. It was not a coincidence that the peasants of Asira al-Shamiyya began their argument with the premise that they had paid all their taxes in full. As long as they met this responsibility, the state had an obligation to protect them. Local authorities, they insisted, had no right to impose other demands on them, no right to interfere in their affairs.

The political essence of the Asira petition, therefore, was an attempt to reduce the political space of the ruling elite of Jabal Nablus and to draw the state's protective boundaries around themselves. This is why the underlying and primary cause of the conflict, a debt incurred to an oil merchant through a *salam* contract, was not mentioned by the peasants. Hoping to deal with the oil merchant on their own terms, the peasants were asking, "Why should Shaykh Ahmad al-Yusuf Jarrar and the entire ruling elite of Nablus get involved in this matter? Our taxes are paid and that is all they should be concerned with!"

It must have been an embarrassing and humiliating experience, as well as politically inconvenient, for the Nablus Council and Mahmud *Beik* Abd al-Hadi to have the governor of Jerusalem dragged into a local matter by the peasants of Asira. Not only did they receive the petition via Jerusalem, but it suggested that they be "ordered" to check the tax books when they knew full well, as did the petitioners, that these taxes had indeed been paid. This is why the memorandum from the council, like the previous one concerning the Jaba petition, first presented the issue of debt as the root of the dispute then relegated it to the background and did not indicate whether and how it was resolved. Rather, the council focused the governor's attention on the organic link between their common interests and those of the state, by portraying peasant resistance to them as a challenge to state authority. Unhappy about the prospect of further outside interference, especially in such vital issues as collection of debt and enforcement of *salam* contracts, the council's aim was to short-circuit these petitions and neutralize their negative effects while maintaining a free hand in dealing with the peasantry. Consequently, the council moved quickly to defuse the situation by setting the prisoners free, with the excuse that they had been taught a lesson and that damages to the injured cavalryman—that is, a small fine of 120 piasters—had been paid.[125]

The Asira and Jaba petitions also demonstrate that local disputes between merchants and peasants, in both instances over *salam* contracts for olive oil, escalated to the point that the Ottoman state, through the office of the governor of Jerusalem, was dragged in and entangled. In other words, internal contradictions and pressures from below, as much as re- forms from above, served to increase the role of the state in local affairs. This is key to a fuller understanding of the driving forces behind the Ottoman state's policies of centralization and administrative and fiscal re- structuring during the nineteenth century. Just as the promulgation and implementation of the 1858 land code were precipitated and guided, re- spectively, by concrete long-term changes in the land regime, Ottoman reforms and policies in general during the last two-thirds of the nine- teenth century were just as much responses to as initiators of changes in the political economy of the regions under their control.

The changes that overtook peasant society during the *Tanzimat* period allowed for more than one political trajectory. Judging from the two peti- tions, the peasants of Jabal Nablus extended their hand to the Ottoman authorities and expressed a willingness to become active participants in a new political order—under certain conditions, of course. But the latter's responses to the brewing crisis in urban-rural relations were often deter- mined by pragmatic political concerns rather than by their publicly stated policy of protecting the peasant base of production. In this and similar cases in Jabal Nablus during the mid-nineteenth century the response was a conservative one, more concerned with shoring up urban notables in order to maintain the status quo than with effecting any real change.

Not surprisingly, therefore, Tamimi and Bahjat had this to say upon concluding their visit to Salfit: "Of course, the Salfitis are ignorant of the sacred patriotic [symbols] such as the flag, the nation, and sacrifice. The government in their eyes is nothing but subdistrict administrators and a number of police . . . and a door that does not answer the complaints of the people."[126]

CONCLUSION

"The Olive is the physical document of history," wrote David Urquhart during his stay in Mount Lebanon (1849–1850).[127] This assessment of the importance of the olive tree in the material and cultural life of Mount Lebanon since ancient times was even more true at that time for Palestine in general and for Jabal Nablus in particular, because of their inhabitants' greater dependence on it.

Today the olive tree is a national icon among Palestinians. Its ubiquitous presence in the contoured hills and valleys and its stubborn longevity sym-bolize rootedness, belonging, and survival against all odds. Eulogized in po-etry and with its image crafted into silver pendants, the olive tree evokes an idealized past, a time when most Palestinians were not refugees or an oppressed minority under colonial rule but free peasants who lived off the fruits of the land. Ironically, the significance of the olive tree in the political consciousness of Palestinians has increased in inverse proportion to its im-portance to material life. At the present, only a minority of Palestinians sustain themselves through agriculture, and a smaller proportion still de-pend solely on the olive for their livelihood. Even the famous Nablus soap is now made out of imported olive oil (mostly from Spain).

The question posed at the outset of this chapter—How did olive oil move from the hands of peasants to those of merchants?—opens for Pal-estinians a painful and long-closed chapter of their history during the Ottoman period. It brings to the surface the tensions, contradictions, and internal fissures that characterized their society before it was subject to European colonization. The evidence introduced in response to this ques-tion indicates that the Ottoman government's political centralization and its administrative reforms, such as the promulgation of the 1858 land code, were both precipitated by and shaped by many of the very changes they were later credited with introducing. By the early nineteenth cen-tury, the processes of peasant differentiation, urban-rural integration, commoditization of land, and monetization of the rural economy—all in-creasingly driven by pervasive moneylending practices—came to domi-nate everyday life even in the olive-based villages of the central highlands, whose assimilation into the world economy proceeded at a slower pace than did that of the grain and cotton-based villages on the western slopes and in coastal areas.

These processes were, in part, driven from within by urban merchants and manufacturers and by peasants. The rural middle class, in particular, played a defining role in this regard. Members of this class were heavily involved in moneylending, in the purchase and concentration of landhold-ings, and in the formation of business partnerships for speculation and trade in agricultural products. The power of subdistrict chiefs was there-fore being eroded by the expansion of this class long before these chiefs were militarily defeated by the Egyptian forces and marginalized by Otto-man reforms. It is also clear that the economic and cultural urbanization of the hinterland was partly the result of the reproduction of urban insti-tutions on the local level by the peasants themselves, not simply an in-stance of hegemonic absorption by an urban merchant elite.

This question also put the focus squarely on the role of moneylending practices in general and of *salam* contracts in particular in the integration and subordination of the hinterland. Although moneylending had been a well-established component of urban-rural relations since ancient times, the nineteenth century witnessed a qualitative change in the pervasiveness, uses, and social bases of *salam* contracts. These contracts helped secure large amounts of olive oil in advance for Nabulsi merchants and manufacturers, who financed the rapidly expanding soap industry. Also, both coastal and Nabulsi merchants involved in overseas trade put these flexible contracts to use in the local organization of commercial agricultural production in the interior. Finally, moneylending combined with taxation to accelerate the expansion of merchant capital and a market economy into the farthest reaches of the countryside.

The qualitative changes in moneylending practices cannot be seen apart from the changing political and economic contexts in which they took place: the slow and uneven integration of Palestine into the European-dominated world capitalist economy, population and economic growth, the Egyptian occupation, and the gradual extension of central Ottoman control. The latter two helped provide crucial institutional support and a conducive political atmosphere. By the mid-nineteenth century the profound impact of these developments on the social fabric of Jabal Nablus could be clearly seen in the consolidation of a rural middle class and in the commoditization of land, the two most important developments on the social and economic levels. On the cultural level, the assimilation of the countryside into the urban legal sphere was also clearly expressed in the increasing resort by many peasants to the organizing concepts and practical guidelines of Islamic law. These guidelines provided a framework for the introduction of urban business practices, the resolution of social conflicts (such as the access of women to land), and for legitimating and consolidating the painful process of social differentiation.[128]

Politically, the heightened tensions acquired, dare one say, some characteristics of class struggle. A nascent class consciousness could be detected in peasant petitions and lawsuits against their own traditional leaders, not to mention against the urban merchants. Peasants clearly perceived themselves as being oppressed by a socially diverse elite of moneyed individuals, as represented by the Nablus Advisory Council. Their petitions suggest that their world view, as well as their notions of justice and of the sources of political authority, contained many modern elements—such as their representation of themselves as tax-paying citizens who had the right to equal protection under the law. They also openly adopted the government's public interpretation of the *Tanzimat* and used it as a weapon against the authority and privileges of their traditional leaders. In the process, they helped precipitate greater involvement by the state on the local level, and their resistance contributed to the reconfiguration of the entire political grid of Jabal Nablus.

For a more detailed and balanced understanding of these internally generated developments in Jabal Nablus, we need to consider the transformations in the urban sphere. We have already discussed the political economy of cotton, textiles, and merchant networks, but the narrative cannot be completed without telling the story of the social life of the most important commodity produced in the city of Nablus: soap.

5   Soap, Class, and State

If Hebron could boast of its glass bracelets, its big he-goat skins, and
its fine grapes; if Gaza was still the granary of Palestine; if Lydda
was reputed for its oil markets and mat industry; Nablus could point
with pride to its soap manufactories, one of the most important
factors of the wealth of that prosperous inland town.

> Hassan Yaseen *Abu* Razek, a native of Hebron, as quoted by
> Philip Baldensperger in *The Immovable East*, 1913

[You claim] that Nablus is the only district in which soap merchants
have refused to pay their taxes, and that they are withholding the
money so that they could invest it and enjoy its profits. . . . As we
explained previously, . . . until they are reimbursed taxes on oil that
you illegally collected, they will not hand over the taxes on soap, for
that is the essence of fairness and justice.

> Nablus Advisory Council to customs officials, 1852

In December 1829, Muhyi al-Din Arafat—nephew of Abd al-Razzaq Arafat, the textile merchant we met in Chapter 2—bought the Hallaqiyya
soap factory for 6,000 piasters.[1] The factory was sold to him by Asaʿd *Beik*
Tuqan, the former *mutasallim* of Nablus, on behalf of himself and his
two brothers.[2] Painfully conscious of the authoritarian rule of the Tuqan
family during the reign of the seller's uncle, Musa *Beik* Tuqan (1801–
1823) and nervous that this prized possession might be forced out of his
hand in the future, Muhyi al-Din requested that "a copy of this purchase
and sale document be registered for fear of dispute and argument, and [in
order] to protect the price."[3] He also arranged for an impressive group of
witnesses to acknowledge the sale. Among the nineteen witnesses were
the *mufti* of Nablus at the time and members of the Burqawi family,
leaders of the subdistrict of Wadi al-Shaʿir.

A few months later, in March 1830, Muhyi al-Din consolidated his
investment by buying from a family of artisans a number of houses (*buyut*), located on top of the soap factory, for 4,500 piasters.[4] The total investment amounted to a hefty 10,500 piasters. Then, on September 14,
1835, Muhyi al-Din contracted a loan from his wife Ruqayya for 27,431
piasters and put up his soap factory, along with two-thirds of the houses

plus an adjacent storage area (*bayka*), as collateral in the form of a temporary sale; that is, she would hand over the property after he paid his debts
to her.[5] Ruqayya, daughter of *Sayyid* Ibrahim Arafat, was Muhyi al-Din's
cousin and heir to a substantial portion of her parents' estate. On two
previous occasions she had advanced large sums of money to her husband,
and, apparently, he was not able to pay her back.[6]

Ruqayya was serious about protecting her property and investments.
In early January 1847 she sued Shaykh Yusuf *Afandi* son of Shaykh Abd
al-Ghani Zayd Qadri—a leading member of the Qadriyya Sufi order, a
close ally and business partner of the ruling Abd al-Hadi family and one of
the most powerful and wealthy men in Nablus—over the same property.[7]
Ruqayya claimed through her agent in court that exactly seven years earlier, on January 7, 1840, her husband Muhyi al-Din had sold the Hallaqiyya soap factory, along with the houses and the *bayka*, to Shaykh Yusuf
Qadri for 50,000 piasters without her knowledge or consent, even though
she was the legal owner. She produced her purchase deed of September
14, 1835, and demanded that this sale be invalidated and her property
returned. Shaykh Yusuf confirmed that he did buy this property from her
husband in 1840 but argued that Ruqayya knew about the sale, sanctioned
it, and even signed the sales deed. He failed to produce this deed, but he
did win the case by securing two male witnesses who corroborated his
testimony.

The saga of the Hallaqiyya soap factory contains within it many of the
elements crucial to understanding the key role of the soap industry in
the transformation of Jabal Nablus during the late eighteenth and the
nineteenth centuries. To begin with, Muhyi al-Din seems to have been a
shrewd businessman. Although heir to a long tradition of involvement in
the textile trade, he shifted his resources to soap manufacturing in the
latter half of the 1820s: precisely the time when the soap industry witnessed a vigorous expansion that only gathered steam over the next few
decades. Consequently, the value of soap factories appreciated steeply. Regardless of whether Ruqayya's story was true, there is no doubt that the
price of the Hallaqiyya soap factory increased almost 500 percent over an
eleven-year period!

At a time when European competition caused other manufacturing sectors to stagnate, soap manufacturing became Nablus's dominant and most
dynamic economic sector: the number of fully operational soap factories
in Nablus tripled, the volume of production increased roughly fourfold,
and the prices of soap factories soared (see Appendix 3). This was not part

of a general revival of the soap industry in Greater Syria. In fact, soap production declined precipitously in all the other cities and towns of this region, with the possible exception of Tripoli.[8]

It is difficult to overestimate the significance of these developments to our understanding the political economy of Nablus and the changing role of the merchant community. Nablus, like most interior regions in Greater Syria during the nineteenth century, may have been overshadowed by the growing coastal cities and undermined by the importation of European manufactured goods, but as long as there was a market to be found and a profit to be made, Nabulsi merchants and manufacturers showed no hesitation or timidity about investing capital in local industries.

A multitude of factors converged to propel this industry forward. Nabulsi soap was made out of olive oil, the primary agricultural product of Jabal Nablus. This made soap production potentially the most efficient way to exploit the rural surplus, the main source of wealth in Jabal Nablus. Nablus is also located conveniently close to the east bank of the River Jordan, where the second most important raw material, the barilla plant, the burned ashes of which made a natural alkaline soda called *qilw*, grew most abundantly.

Soap production was also a capital-intensive industry with high margins of profit. As a field of investment, it was eminently suitable for the concentration of wealth taking place in Jabal Nablus and a tempting alternative to other manufacturing activities, such as textile production, that were beginning to feel the brunt of European and regional competition. The concentration of wealth took place not only within the merchant community but also within each merchant family. Assuming the accuracy of her story, Ruqayya's unfortunate experience with the Hallaqiyya soap factory was only one of many instances in which females and children still in their legal minority had their resources absorbed into the "family firm," which was invariably headed by one or two dominant male members.

Soap factories were also prized because they were the largest and most important credit institutions in Jabal Nablus and thus functioned as banks. A significant portion of the region's olive oil was deposited in the numerous large wells dug beneath each factory. These wells were used not only for storing the olive oil destined to become soap but also for the safekeeping of deposits and withdrawals by peasants, merchants, and even local government tax collectors, who were often paid in oil. Because soap-factory owners lent money to peasants for future harvests through *salam* contracts, soap factories also extended high-interest credit (see Chapter 4).

Just as textile merchants carved out geographical enclaves of clients in the hinterland of Nablus, each soap factory had a clientele from specific villages, as the discussion of the Bishtawi brothers below will demonstrate.

For those with large amounts of capital at their disposal and a modicum of political influence, investment in soap production was a low-risk affair, because the quality of Nablus's soap assured a high and steady demand in regional markets, especially Egypt. In fact, Nablus was well known for its soap production since at least as far back as the fourteenth century, and the reputation of its soap was well established long before Ottoman rule.[9] In the words of Shaykh Shams al-Din al-Ansari al-Dimashqi (d. A.H.727/ A.D.1326–1327), "The city of Nablus . . . was bestowed by God Almighty with the blessed olive tree. Its olive oil is carried by bedouins to the Egyptian and Damascene lands, to the Hijaz, and the steppes. . . . In it a superior soap is produced and sent to the above-mentioned destinations and to the islands of the Mediterranean Sea."[10]

Throughout the Ottoman period and beyond, Nabulsi soap maintained its reputation as the best of its kind in Greater Syria and Egypt, if not further afield. John Bowring, writing in the late 1830s, noted that "Nablous soap is highly esteemed in the Levant";[11] and the Syrian historian Muhammad Kurd Ali wrote a century later that "Nablus soap is the best and most famous soap today for it has, it seems, a quality not found in others and the secret is that it is unadulterated and well produced."[12] It enjoyed such a high reputation that all similarly made soap, whether manufactured in Syria or Egypt, came to be labeled "Nabulsi Soap." Even into the twentieth century, a modern oil factory established by Jewish settlers in Palestine during the British Mandate, Shemen Ltd., advertised that its premium brand of soap was "of Nablus quality."[13]

Investments in soap production accelerated as merchant capital came to dominate ever-widening swaths of Nablus's hinterland and as administrative reorganizations during the *Tanzimat* period increased the political weight of the merchant community. The first section of this chapter investigates the capital-intensive nature of this industry and its profitability, the timing and reasons for its expansion, the concentration of wealth in family firms of soap manufacturers, the changing division of labor between oil merchants and soap-factory owners, and the vertical integration of the various stages of production.

The saga of the Hallaqiyya soap factory also reveals three important trends in the changing social composition of soap-factory owners and the emergence of a new ruling elite in Jabal Nablus by the mid-nineteenth century—the topics addressed in the second section of this chapter. First was the growing power and self-confidence of the merchant community. By purchasing a soap factory in 1829 from the Tuqans, Muhyi al-Din Arafat, a merchant, joined a powerful and exclusive club of soap-factory owners that had long been dominated by members of the old ruling elite families, such as the Nimrs and Tuqans.

The second trend was the decline of this old elite. It was no coincidence that Muhyi al-Din purchased the Hallaqiyya from the Tuqans, for the latter's fortunes had just suffered a serious setback. Musa *Beik* Tuqan, the most powerful and longest-reigning *mutasallim* of Nablus since at least the late seventeenth century, was assassinated by his rivals on December 20, 1823, putting an end to a prolonged period of conflict during which the Tuqan family's material base had been seriously eroded.[14] Many of the family's key properties, including those that were endowed as family *waqfs*, were confiscated after Musa *Beik* Tuqan's death and still had not been returned at the time of the purchase.[15] Muhyi al-Din's nervousness, therefore, was due to his recognition that the sale was precipitated largely by the Tuqan family's present weakness and immediate need for money. Consequently, it was impossible for him to know whether this was a temporary situation or a permanent reality. In fact, only one year after the purchase the governor of Acre, Abdullah Pasha, ordered the release of confiscated properties that had been part of the Tuqan family *waqfs*.[16] Fortunately for Muhyi al-Din, this reprieve proved temporary. Soon after their occupation of Syria in 1831, the Egyptians deported the leading figures of the Tuqan family to Egypt and promoted the Abd al-Hadi family instead.

The third trend was the entry into this exclusive club of the Abd al-Hadi family and its allies. The most prominent of the latter was none other than the person who bought the Hallaqiyya soap factory from Muhyi al-Din: Shaykh Yusuf Zayd Qadri.[17] The date of purchase, 1840, was the pinnacle of the Abd al-Hadi's rise to power. Indeed, the Abd al-Hadis, as the key local allies of the Egyptian government, had been busy expanding and consolidating their material base since the early 1830s, and this included establishing a base in the city of Nablus itself. By the mid-nineteenth century, a new composite elite anchored by the merchant community had crystallized in Jabal Nablus.

As implied by these transactions, political power was important to soap production because factory owners needed great influence in order to bring together the various factors and forces of production. In order to secure supplies and labor, they had to construct a complex network that involved a wide range of geographically dispersed social groups: peasants in Jabal Nablus and Ajlun who produced and transported the olive oil and lime (*shid*, the third major ingredient); bedouins on the east bank of the River Jordan who gathered the barilla plant in huge quantities, burned it, and transported the ashes to Nablus in large caravans; teams of artisans and workers who cooked, cut, and packaged the soap; and merchants who acquired oil, commissioned cooked batches (*tabkhas*) of soap, and operated regional trade networks. Without a modicum of political power or, at least, access to such power, the merchant community could not invest heavily in soap production, and the city's natural advantages in comparison to some other soap-producing centers would have amounted to little.

The intimate connection between politics and soap production took on additional significance during the era of Ottoman reforms, when the merchant community gained access to political office. Because all the Muslim members of the newly established Nablus Advisory Council were soap merchants and factory owners, the exchanges between the council and the Ottoman authorities over matters dealing directly with this industry can tell us a great deal about relations with the Ottoman government. The third section of this chapter analyzes the material bases of the politics of notables and the contradictions of Ottoman reform through two examples: a tax strike by soap manufacturers and the bitter conflicts between the council and the governor of Sidon over the allocation of bids for the purchase of olive oil collected as taxes-in-kind.

SOAP AND THE ECONOMY

Three elements made soap production in Nablus a capital-intensive industry. First, the fixed assets—the huge building, the wells where the oil was stored, and the large copper vat in which the soap was cooked—were expensive to purchase, construct, and maintain. Second, soap was cooked in large amounts, necessitating a substantial initial investment in raw materials. Third, anywhere from two to three years could pass before soap merchants received returns on their investment: raw materials had to be secured one year in advance in order to ensure adequate supplies, and cooking, drying, packing, shipping, and selling the soap took at least another year.[18]

Consequently, capital had to be accumulated and pooled on a number of levels in order to raise the amounts necessary for all of the stages of production. With rare exceptions, the basic division of labor in terms of capital input until the early nineteenth century was between merchants who commissioned soap and made available the most expensive raw material, oil, and soap-factory owners who provided the premises, labor, and other raw materials. Within each camp, partnerships also prevailed. Soap factories were, more often than not, jointly owned, and outside investors were recruited to cover the costs of production. Similarly, oil merchants usually combined their resources in order to contract a single batch of soap (each batch consumed more than five tons of olive oil).

No later than the mid-nineteenth century, as shall be seen in a case study of two soap factories, a process of concentration of wealth in Nablus led to the vertical integration of this industry, whereby single individuals came to finance all of the stages of production. This development did not lead to qualitative changes in the process of production, which remained remarkably the same throughout the entire Ottoman era and, to a large extent, until today (see Appendix 3). More indicative were the increases in the number and prices of soap factories, as well as in the volume of production. What needs to be addressed at this juncture are the phases of expansion and their effect on the organization of production in terms of capital input, ownership, and profits.

Expansion

The Yusufiyya is one of the oldest extant soap factories in Nablus, and it was still being operated in 1994. Located in the Habala quarter next to the Nimr family compound, it was named after Yusuf son of Abdullah Pasha Nimr (d. A.H.1097/A.D.1685–1686), the founding member of the Nimr clan in Nablus. Yusuf was a *sipahi* officer, a government official, and, later on, an active trader and soap manufacturer.[19] In January 18, 1729, his grandson, *Hajj* Umar *Agha* (d. A.H.1182/A.D.1768–1769), endowed one-fourth of the factory as a *waqf ahli* (family endowment). He also endowed one-half of another factory, the Sawwariyya,[20] as well as the Yusufiyya's copper vat (due to their expense, the large copper vats merited mention as items distinct from each soap factory).[21] As mentioned in Chapter 2, endowing the family's major residential and revenue-producing properties in perpetuity for the future descendants usually signaled the consolidation of a substantial leap in that family's fortunes. It also helped protect these properties from arbitrary confiscation, sudden economic downturn in the family's fortunes, and fragmentation due to inheritance and marriage.

In endowing his share of this property as *waqf, Hajj* Umar made a choice typical of both previous and future soap-factory owners during the Ottoman period: all, without exception, used this legal mechanism to protect this important form of property from the vicissitudes of political and

economic upheavals. Among *Hajj* Umar's conditions in the *waqf* endowment was one which stated that only his sons and their male offspring
could benefit from the *waqf*. His clear intention was to prevent the fragmentation of this property due to inheritance laws and to make sure that
other families would not be able to gain shares through marriage to his
female descendants. The immediate timing, however, was triggered by an
attempt to assassinate him shortly before he endowed the *waqf*. No doubt
he felt an urgent need to protect the Yusufiyya from possible confiscation
or internal bickering after his death.[22]

Hajj Umar was the *mutasallim* of Nablus at the time. He also served
as the *mutasallim* of Jerusalem and Ramla.[23] The other partners in the
Yusufiyya were his father, who owned one-half, and his brother Muhammad, who owned the remaining quarter.[24] The copper vat he owned outright. Most soap-factory owners during the seventeenth, eighteenth, and
early nineteenth centuries were like the Nimrs: ruling families that could
afford the substantial capital investment and that could forge the necessary political and social connections to bring together the various forces
and factors of production.

Over the next century the Yusufiyya was consolidated in a single *waqf*,
but we are told that it had fallen into disrepair. In August 1825 *Hajj*
Umar's grandson, Ahmad *Agha*, now the superintendent (*mutawwali*) of
the *waqf*, went to court to ask for permission to renovate the soap factory.
He testified that due to lack of maintenance and the ravages of time, the
roof of the *al-mafrash* (the second floor, where the liquid soap was spread
to dry) had collapsed, the copper vat was useless, and the building was so
full of dirt that it had become "a refuge for dogs."[25] As standard legal
procedure for *waqfs* dictated, this account was verified through a field
visit by the judge, head of the builder's guild, and other experts. Then,
after a formal court hearing, permission was granted for renovation and
for the conversion of the expenses into a right-of-use deposit (*khuluw
mursad*), from which the usual rent payment of 15 piasters to the *waqf*
was to be deducted annually.

The application for permission to renovate as well as the inspection
were, in reality, only formalities. A detailed work-expense report in the
Nimr family papers shows that the repair work actually began two months
before the request was put before the court,[26] and the "repairs" included
the costly construction of two new storage wells for olive oil.[27] The application, therefore, was a technical step designed to facilitate the legal deduc-
tion of the renovation costs from future rent and a political move designed
to reaffirm Ahmad *Agha*'s status as superintendent of the *waqf*. The pri-

mary motivation behind the renovations, however, was an economic one: the desire to expand production through a capital investment.

The investment was substantial. According to the expense report, renovation costs reached approximately 20,000 piasters, many times the average price of an entire soap factory just two decades earlier. The investment was also efficient and profitable: renovations were finished by late January 1825, just in time for the end of the olive-harvest season.[28] By April of 1826 the factory had already made 10,000 piasters in profit from the commission of 21 cooked *tabkhas* of soap.[29] To put the Yusufiyya's production during these three short months into perspective, 21 *tabkhas* amounted to 20 percent more than what had been produced in all of Damascus, a city many times the size of Nablus, ten years later (see Appendix 3, Table 12).

How did Ahmad *Agha* finance this expansion? Where did he raise the capital to pay for the labor and raw materials necessary to cook so many batches of soap, and why did he decide to expand his production facilities at this time, not before or after? In part the expansion took advantage of a changed political environment. Just two years before Ahmad *Agha* made his investment, Musa *Beik* Tuqan had been poisoned, and his long reign finally came to an end.[30] The Nimrs had opposed Musa Tuqan's centralizing efforts for most of this period and suffered greatly as a result (they were evicted from the city in the early 1820s, though not for very long). Only after Musa Tuqan's death in 1823, therefore, could the Nimrs (and others) divert their capital to more productive projects. Also, Ahmad *Agha*'s political position was strengthened in 1825, when he was appointed deputy (*wakil*) to the *mutasallim* of Nablus and elected by the local *sipahis* and *za'ims* as their chief (*mir'alay*).[31]

Economic factors were also at work. Ahmad *Agha* was neither alone nor a visionary: roughly half of Nablus's soap factories were renovated by leading families during the 1820s. Their endeavors suggest that in addition to the improved political atmosphere, the market for Nablus soap was expanding and large profits were to be made. In most cases the capital for this investment drive was raised through multiple partnerships. For example, three soap manufacturers from the Akhrami, Amr, and Qaddumi families applied for permission to renovate the Bashawiyya factory (Habala quarter) in exactly the same month and year (August 1825) as Ahmad *Agha* Nimr's application.[32] Not as rich or as powerful as the Nimr ruling family, they shared the costs equally, as is apparent from an expense report they submitted five months later (February 1826).[33]

The system of multiple ownerships and partnerships in most soap factories was reproduced here in one of its many forms. On the one hand, the Bashawiyya factory was, as per the usual pattern, completely endowed as *waqf*. Half of this *waqf* was part of a larger charitable endowment (*waqf khayri*), which supported the Prophet Abraham (*nabi Ibrahim*) mosque in Hebron. Two of the partners, Shaykh Amr son of Ahmad Amr and Shaykh Hamid son of *Hajj* Ahmad Qaddumi, had rented this half in 1820–1821.[34] The other half of the Bashawiyya was part of a family *waqf* controlled by *Sayyid* Ahmad Fakhr al-Din Akhrami, a member of the old elite of Nablus. *Sayyid* Ahmad Fakhr al-Din had also applied for permission to renovate his share of this factory. In fact, three months before this application, in May 1825, he had bought out his brother's share in the Bashawiyya—that is, the entire matter was planned beforehand to coincide with the efforts of his partners.[35] In addition, he controlled shares in the Uthmaniyya factory (Qaryun quarter), in which he was partners with the Tuqan family.[36] Half of this factory was part of his family's *waqf*, and in January 1826 he submitted another application for renovation in his capacity as superintendent.[37]

Another example of expansion at this time, and of how it was financed by multilayered ownership and access rights, is the case of the Sawwari-yya factory. In December 1825 Isma'il son of Muhammad *Beik* Sawwar, the superintendent of the family's *waqf* properties, received permission from the judge to exchange part of these properties (one-third of a garden and a water pool) for 600 piasters in cash for the express purpose of renovating this factory.[38] His partners included *Sayyid* Ahmad Fakhr al-Din, whose family's *waqf* encompassed a share of this factory, and members of the Nimr family who also had a share in their *waqf* portfolio.[39] Each one of these activities, it remains to be mentioned, was timed to coincide with the olive harvest of that year.

From this first vigorous revival beginning in the latter half of the 1820s, investment in soap factories gathered steam at a steady pace until the early twentieth century. Above-average growth could be detected during the late 1830s/early 1840s and during the 1860s. The first witnessed a strong push by the Abd al-Hadi family and its allies into soap production as they gained control of some factories and rebuilt others. The second period was notable for the building of new factories and the expansion of existing ones by merchants (see below).

Organization and Profits

In addition to joint ownerships of single soap factories, each shareholder often formed partnerships with wealthy individuals (akin to venture capitalists) who, in return for a percentage of the profit, financed the cost of labor, equipment, and all the raw materials except olive oil. This pattern of organization is illustrated by the 1826 expense and income account sheet of the Yusufiyya soap factory found among the Nimr Family Papers.[40]

This document shows that Ahmad *Agha* Nimr formed a partnership with *Sayyid* Hasan Fakhr al-Din Akhrami, almost certainly the brother of *Sayyid* Ahmad Fakhr al-Din Akhrami, whom we met before. *Sayyid* Hasan advanced 21,500 piasters for the purchase of *qilw*, lime, and *jift* (crushed olive pits used as fuel to cook the soap), as well as labor and other miscellaneous expenses, for 21 batches (*tabkhas*) of soap. Oil is not listed among the expenses, which means that it was supplied by the merchants who commissioned the *tabkhas*. This amount corresponds roughly to the total sum (20,000 piasters) paid by Ahmad *Agha* Nimr to renovate and expand the factory that year. No doubt, therefore, this partnership was concluded before the renovations began.

Of the 21,500 piasters invested by *Sayyid* Hasan, approximately 70 percent were spent on *qilw*. By comparison, the cost of lime amounted to 4.5 percent; *jift*, 4 percent; taxes, 5 percent; labor, 4 percent; and equipment and miscellaneous expenses, 12.5 percent. These figures generally agree with those calculated from a much briefer account sheet for the Yusufiyya factory for the year 1855–1856. Of the total capital invested in that year, 64 percent went toward the purchase of *qilw*; *jift* cost 6.6 percent; lime, 4.3 percent; labor, 10.6 percent; rent, 3 percent; and miscellaneous expenses, 11.5 percent.[41]

In 1826 Ahmad *Agha* and Hasan Fakhr al-Din charged oil merchants 1500 piasters for each cooked batch, making a profit of roughly 476 piasters per *tabkha* after the costs of labor and raw materials were deducted. The profits were then split evenly: half to Ahmad *Agha* for renovating the *waqf* property of which he was the superintendent and half to *Sayyid* Hasan for supplying the additional capital. Their return on their initial investment (over and above the renovations), after only three months' work, was a respectable 30 percent.

This partnership was political as well as economic, in the sense that Ahmad *Agha*'s connections were important for securing the needed supplies; that is, some merchants during this period still found it easier to back a large venture by an established ruling family than to bear the entire risk themselves. One needs to consider, for example, the sources of the raw materials purchased by *Sayyid* Hasan for the Yusufiyya factory. First, 147 out of the 166 *qintars* of *qilw* purchased came from the Salt region:

consistent supplies of this raw material depended primarily on the relationship between Nablus and the bedouins of the eastern bank of the River
Jordan, especially members of the Bani-Sakhr tribe. Second, the lime came
from three villages east of Nablus: Awarta, Salim, and Bayt Furik.[42] As
discussed in Chapter 4, these villages had been closely connected to the
Nimr family since the seventeenth century as part of their *timar* and,
later on, their tax-farming holdings.

The fact that patronage, official position, and political power defined
the relationship between the Nimr family and the peasants of these villages throughout the last three centuries of Ottoman rule does not mean,
however, that this relationship did not change dramatically over time. The
Nimrs shifted from being *sipahis*, or military officers with rights to a
percentage of the surplus, to becoming tax collectors (*multazims*) and,
finally, entrepreneurs who simply took advantage of previous connections
but no longer had the political influence to enforce them. It was only in
the last phase of this changing relationship that merchants could begin to
make major inroads into the hinterland, successfully compete with old
ruling families, and eventually be able to directly decide what was produced, to whom it was sold, and for how much.

The 1855–1856 account sheet of expenses and income for the Yusufiyya factory shows that the division of labor in financing the production
of soap was somewhat similar. Ahmad *Agha*'s son, Abd al-Fattah, put
up one-quarter of the capital, and three partners put up the rest.[43] They
contracted an unspecified number of *tabkhas*, making a profit of 20.1 percent, or a third less than in 1825–1826. Because costs averaged roughly
the same percentages as in the previous account sheet, it is not clear what
the reasons for the decline in profit were. Perhaps greater competition
from a rising number of soap factories encouraged merchants to offer a
lower fee for each *tabkha*. In any case, profit margins of 20–30 percent
for just the short-term production stage of the soap industry are not only
impressive but also similar to the figures given by Tamimi and Bahjat
more than six decades later, suggesting that a steady high profit was one
of the factors behind the expansion of the soap industry during the second
half of the nineteenth century.[44]

As for the soap merchants, it is not known how much profit they made
on the soap, but it must have been considerable. After all, it was the soap
merchants who bore the brunt of capital investment in soap production.
The cost of oil alone for the 21 *tabkhas* in 1825–1826 was more than
120,000 piasters, or more than three times the joint investment by the
soap-factory owner and his partner.[45] This is not to mention the rent for

storing the oil, the 1,500 piasters' fee for each batch, the export taxes and transportation,[46] and the long waiting period while the soap was dried, packaged, and shipped. Not surprisingly, therefore, soap merchants also formed partnerships in order to defray the high costs of production.

Concentration and Integration

Closely connected to the expansion of soap production was the concentration of wealth within the merchant community, a process that led to the vertical integration of production by the mid-nineteenth century. The inheritance estate of two merchants—*Sayyid* As'ad son of Yusuf Bishtawi and his brother *Sayyid* Sa'id—dated July 2, 1857, provides a rare look into the organization of soap production. As it happened, *Sayyid* As'ad died while the *al-mafrash* was still full of recently cooked soap that had not yet been distributed to the various merchants.[47] Consequently, the court's inventory had to take account of business arrangements that were left suspended.

The income and expense columns in the inheritance estate show that the Bishtawi brothers headed what can only be described as a highly centralized family firm or, put more precisely, a corporate three-generational patrilocal household the resources of which were monopolized and concentrated by two brothers. Thus, even though only one died, the court had to take into account the estates of both because they jointly owned both commercial and personal property. For instance, they jointly financed the construction of the soap factory and evenly split all business expenses and profits. They also held equal shares in the family's residence, shops, warehouses, agricultural lands, olive groves, fruit orchards, miscellaneous goods, cash reserves, and outstanding loans. They even jointly owned furniture, copper kitchen utensils, and the clothes they wore.[48] Putting into and eating out of the same pot, so to speak, lent itself to capital accumulation and concentration in ways far better suited to large-scale investments than if each adult family member managed his or her separate income and expenses.

The forces behind this concentration did not dissipate as a result of *Sayyid* As'ad's death, for the deceased's oldest son, *Hajj* Yusuf, quickly moved to take his father's place. In fact, *Hajj* Yusuf secured his appointment as the legal guardian (*wasi*) over his male siblings—all in their legal minority—before his father died. He also became the legal agent for his two sisters, who were in their legal majority, and represented them in court. With the competition out of the way and his father's half of the family firm's resources intact and centralized in his own hands, the fast-paced accumulation of property and wealth interrupted by his father's death continued without delay. Only a few days after the estate was settled in court, *Hajj* Yusuf and his uncle resumed in earnest the purchase of dozens of olive groves, shops, oil presses, and houses, each paying half the cost.[49]

This reconstitution of the family firm was consolidated through an orchestrated set of appearances before the court by *Hajj* Yusuf's relatives. Only four days after the settlement was recorded, his mother went to court and testified that she was entitled to nothing from the property of her husband, other than what she had received when the estate was divided.[50] That same day *Hajj* Yusuf bought all of her shares in twenty parcels of agricultural land—mostly olive groves and fruit orchards located just outside the city—in addition to her shares in three shops inside the city.[51] None of these shares included property in the soap factory, residence, warehouses, olive presses, or other such real estate. Because none of these properties was mentioned in the inheritance estate, one can safely assume that she (in)voluntarily excluded herself from the bulk of the revenue-producing immovable properties that the Bishtawi brothers had accumulated. This, in itself, was not an unusual situation. Women in corporate households, as Deniz Kandiyoti has persuasively argued, consider sons their most critical resource, and "ensuring their life-long loyalty is an enduring preoccupation."[52] If a woman was to enjoy protection as well as exercise control and authority, especially over other women and certainly over her daughters-in-law, the support of her sons was absolutely essential. Handing over inherited commercial properties to her sons, therefore, could enhance both their status in the household and their loyalty to her.

A few months later *Hajj* Yusuf also bought one of his sister's shares in exactly the same properties that their mother had sold. Two days after that, his other sister went to court and testified that she had no claims against her brother. Even the extended family was not spared this quest for centralization: *Hajj* Yusuf and his uncle put up equal capital to buy parcels of agricultural land, mostly olive groves on the outskirts of Nablus, from less wealthy relatives.[53]

The concentration of wealth was paralleled by the vertical integration of soap production. *Sayyids* As'ad and Sa'id financed the construction of their own soap factory by converting a building of warehouses and shops in the Wikala Asaliyya.[54] They also purchased shares in another soap factory.[55] Not content to cook soap for merchants in return for a fee, profitable as that arrangement was, they also cooked soap for their own account—that is, they combined the role of soap merchants with that of factory owners.

At the time of *Sayyid* As'ad's death 80 percent of the soap left on the floor of their factory's *al-mafrash* was commissioned by other merchants. As illustrated in Table 8, the amount of soap commissioned varied from merchant to merchant and was measured in terms of the oil provided.

Each of these items was recorded as "To [name of merchant], oil cooked into soap [*zayt matbukh sabun*]," which shows that the merchant's share of soap was measured by the amount of oil he provided. Except for the Sadder brothers, there were no joint commissions for soap production, but some merchants only commissioned parts of one *tabkha*.

The key point here is that the Bishtawi brothers cooked for their own account 20 percent of the factory's entire output for that cycle (each cycle filled the *al-mafrash* and, as soon as the soap was dry enough to be cut and stacked, another cycle was started). This meant an investment of 40,000 piasters in this particular cycle (there were 180,000 piasters' worth of uncut soap still lying on the *mafrash* floor). This was a sizable investment, but only part of the whole: still left in the storage rooms inside their factory were 297 *qintars* of *qilw*, 375 *qintars* of lime, and 644 piasters' worth of *jift*. These amounts of raw materials were adequate for at least 28 to 30 more *tabkhas* of soap, or three and a half times as much as had already been cooked.

In order to secure the large amounts of olive oil they needed every year, the Bishtawi brothers pursued a two-track strategy: landownership and moneylending. They acquired numerous olive groves outside the city, along with olive-oil presses, and they established a network of *salam* moneylending contracts with individual peasants to cover the shortfall. At the time of *Sayyid* As'ad's death, a number of *salam* loans were left outstanding with peasants from eight villages: Asira, Rafidya, Aqraba, Bayta, Adhmut, Salim, Ajansinya, and Bayt Dajan. All but one are located in a single subdistrict. The geographic concentration of moneylending patterns fits with the usual practice of urban merchant networks that sought to carve out spheres of influence in the hinterland.

In short, the Bishtawi brothers had the capital and political influence to finance and organize the production of soap from the ground up. They were at one and the same time moneylenders, oil merchants, soap manufacturers, and large landowners. Their estate also showed that they traded in rice, coffee, grain, and other goods. As mentioned in Chapter 2, labels such as "merchant," "manufacturer," and "landowner" should not be

Table 8. Commissions for Soap in the Bishtawi Estate, 1857

Name	Oil Jars	Value of Cooked Soap (in Piasters)
Hajj Ahmad Abi Odeh	187.5	16,875
Ahmad and Abdullah Qumhiyya	250.0	22,500
Hajj Salman Sadder	400.0	36,000
Hajj Umar Tamimi	437.5	38,765
Qasim Nabulsi	62.5	5,625
Khawaja Salim Zarifa	250.0	22,500
Khalil Mustafa Masri	5.0	450
Wife of Sa'id Bishtawi	2.5	220
Total	1595.0	142,940

SOURCE: NICR, 12:205–206.

thought of as separate categories or as denoting discrete classes. Most wealthy Nabulsi households engaged in all of these activities simultaneously, though they rarely divided their resources equally among them. Patterns of investment strategies, therefore, are important indicators of larger political and economic developments. In this particular case, the Bishtawi brothers' heavy emphasis on soap production illustrates the shifting investment strategies that laid the material basis for the entry of merchants into the formerly exclusive club of soap-factory owners and, indirectly, the crystallization of a new ruling elite by the mid-nineteenth century.

SOAP AND SOCIETY

In relation to each other, the social groups involved in the process of soap production were shaped exactly like the *tananir* (inverted cones of stacked soap cubes left to dry) that stood like silent sentinels in the *al-mafrash*. At the bottom, supporting the entire structure, were the peasants who produced the olive oil, the bedouins who provided the *qilw*, and unskilled workers. Above them were the various groups of middlemen and small merchants who operated like the numerous suction cups of a giant octopus: small-time buyers and sellers, creditors, agents, and supervisors.

Interspersed among the second layer was a relatively small group of skilled and semiskilled soap-factory workers who held the core jobs in soap manufacturing. Their position depended on an internal hierarchy based on the type of job performed, family background, and patronage ties with the factory owners. Their ability to carve out a privileged space for themselves over time is illustrated by the fact that most of these workers belonged to families that monopolized various stages of the production process, from long before the nineteenth century up to the Mandate period in the twentieth century.

Near the very top were the soap merchants who, either individually or in groups, provided the oil, commissioned *tabkhas*, and marketed the soap. Many of these merchants dealt primarily in other goods. Their ranks, for example, included most of the wholesale textile merchants. At the apex were the proprietors of the soap factories who, along with their partners, provided the facilities, the equipment, and all of the raw materials except oil and who supervised the organization of production. The inner core of their ranks up to the early nineteenth century included the ruling political families and the ranking members of the religious hierarchy.

Of all the social groups involved in soap production in Jabal Nablus from the late eighteenth to the late nineteenth centuries, we know the most about the soap-factory owners and, to a lesser extent, the soap merchants. These two groups left a substantial trail for historians to follow, for they generated documents every time they purchased, sold, endowed, or exchanged immovable properties. They were also involved in lawsuits and petitions and/or had their inheritance estates registered in court. Through such documents, one can trace changes in their social composition and, consequently, changes in the ruling elite of Jabal Nablus as a whole. Before embarking on a detailed look at this documentary trail, however, a few words must be said about the role of workers and bedouins in the soap industry.

Soap-Factory Workers

Soap production was not a labor-intensive process, did not require a wide range of skilled workers, and generated little by way of related industries. Aside from the fixed assets, the equipment—shovels, pails, jars, stirring oar, mortars, and pestles—was simple and required no special design or quality. Some artisans, usually from the Fatayir or Shami families, specialized in making stiff sacks designed to minimize friction between the soap cubes so that they would maintain their weight and shape over the long trip to Egypt and other regional markets. As for the copper vat, it lasted for many years, and there is no evidence that it was made locally in specialized shops.

Inside the factory itself, labor was organized in two general groups: those who worked "downstairs" in the cooking process and those who worked "upstairs" with the cooked soap. Fewer than fifteen workers were involved in the cooking process on the ground floor. The first person a peasant or merchant was likely to meet when he brought oil for sale or storage was the oil-measurer (*shayyal*). The *shayyal* placed the leather oil pouch on a slanted table and checked to see whether water collected on the bottom. His examination of the oil determined its purity, quality, and price. It was not unusual for those who were desperate to sell their oil to pass on a little extra to the measurer, for their fate was in his hands.[56]

Deeper inside the huge building, the most prominent person—usually standing with a long, wooden, oarlike stirring stick (*dukshab*) in his hands—was the "chief" or "boss" (*ra'is*). Most of the workers around him were "his" men; that is, they were part of a team (*joqa*) that went from factory to factory as work slowed down in one place and picked up in another. The members of the team operated within a strict hierarchy in which the chief was the uncontested leader. For them, job security and their ability to pass the line of work down from father to son were key advantages that balanced the difficult work conditions, the unexceptional pay, the sometimes arbitrary rule of the chief, and the seasonal nature of the job. In short, it was to their advantage (considering the unskilled nature of most of the work) to be part of a patronage relationship based on long-standing ties that expressed themselves through social and kinship networks.

For the chief, acceptance of the social limitations of such an arrangement in terms of his power over who was or was not included in the team was balanced by the consequent privileges he gained as the sole mediator between proprietors and workers: status, authority, and much higher wages. The proprietors' acceptance of this semicollective labor arrangement deprived them of total control of the workers and increased the cost of labor. At the same time, however, this arrangement reduced the surface area for friction between employer and employee, because it allowed the chief to play a strong mediating role.

The chief's job required skills that could only be acquired through long experience, and his decisions directly affected the quality of the soap produced. His main duty, aside from supervising workers, was to closely follow the minute transformations in the coagulated liquid as it brewed in the copper vat over a number of days. He alone was allowed to stir the liquid, and he alone determined when the soap was ready. This was done by dipping a 60-centimeter-long wooden stick (*shammama*) into the vat and smelling the hot soap that coated it. If the proprietor did not agree with the chief's assessment, a local expert would be called in to arbitrate.[57]

The lowest paying, least prestigious, and most difficult jobs—stoking the furnace with crushed olive pits, lifting oil from the wells, and carrying barrels of hot liquid soap up the steep and narrow stone stairs—were done by the same group of all-around menial workers. This work was physically demanding and dangerous: flying sparks and embers sometimes blinded the stokers (*rashshash*, pl. *rashshashin*), and it was not always possible for carriers to maintain their footing over the soap-caked stone surface. The rest of the workers pounded the *qilw*, mixed it with lime, put the mixture into fermentation pits, and channeled hot water from the bottom of the copper vat to the pits. This mixture was poured back into the copper vat, and the process was repeated dozens of times, until the alkaline content reached the desired levels. The downstairs workers were usually recruited from the Fatayir, Hudhud, Asi, Takruri, M'ani, Marmash, or Ghalayini families. Usually the chief came from one of the first three.[58]

Upstairs the primary job was laying out, cutting, stamping, stacking, and packaging the soap (see Plate 5). Here the work was also monopolized for generations by a small number of families, such as the Hijazi, Annab, and Kukhun. But the most famous by far were members of the Tbeila family. Indeed, the name of this family became so closely identified with upstairs work that the word "tbeila" became a generic one. Until now, and even though members of this family no longer pursue this type of work as a primary occupation, it is not unusual for a soap-factory owner to ask another the question, "Who is your tbeila?"—that is, who is working upstairs for you? Ironically, the Tbeila family in the early eighteenth century produced some of Nablus's leading merchants and religious leaders, as indicated by their titles of *fakhr al-tujjar* (pride of merchants), *khawaja*, and *shaykh*. They also owned a soap factory and were intermarried with the Khammash and other leading families. Apparently they were reduced to artisan status by the late eighteenth century.[59]

Soap-factory workers were paid in cash and kind after each cooked batch. There is no information on the range of wages for each type of job during the nineteenth century, but no doubt the rate differed substantially within the hierarchy of work and that there were ample opportunities to embezzle oil and other raw material. Payment in kind was in olive oil and in the finely ground, charcoallike remains of the crushed olive pits after they had been burned. The latter, called (*duqq*) are still used today by many as fuel for braziers.

There is also no information on the tensions between workers and proprietors or between the workers themselves and no record of lawsuits over the conditions of work or of strikes until the Mandate period. No doubt, and as suggested by anecdotal evidence in interviews, these tensions did exist; but the patronage-type arrangements typical of mobile teams of laborers meant that problems were resolved without recourse to the Islamic court for arbitration. Indeed, the impressive continuity of control over the limited number of soap-factory jobs by a few families made it imperative that disputes be handled within the informal arena of custom, precedent, and solidarity, not the abstract rules of Islamic law. Nevertheless, and as the soap-manufacturing sector expanded, family control over these jobs diminished, and by the early Mandate period the major factory owners preferred to import skilled soap workers from Egypt rather than to accede to local strikes and demands for better wages.[60]

Bedouins

Of all the social groups in Palestinian society during the Ottoman period, bedouins have been the most stereotyped. Advocates of modernization theory who contrast the so-called traditional period with the modern era place a heavy explanatory burden on bedouins by portraying them as the agents of backwardness, stagnation, and anarchy. For example, in setting the stage for the beginnings of modernization in Greater Syria, Moshe Maʿoz described the period before the Egyptian invasion in unambiguously negative terms, giving bedouins the lion's share of the blame: "[Bedouins were] the chief cause of the destruction of the countryside and the subsequent ruin of agriculture and commerce. These powerful nomads *infested* the Syrian provinces, *pillaged* caravans and travellers along the roads, *ravaged* large pieces of cultivated land, and even *dared* to raid villages that were situated on the outskirts of big towns."[61]

In support of his view that the Egyptian occupation "put an end to a long period of confusion and backwardness, and opened a new era in Syrian history," Maʿoz casts the bedouin in a role similar to that of the ancient barbarians at the gates of Rome.[62] The inevitable results, we are told, were anarchy, depopulation, and a drastic decline in economic productivity.[63]

Although sometimes nomads could be very destructive, the view of bedouins as essentially predatory and a threat to civilization is no longer widely shared. The emphasis has shifted from antagonism to linkages, gray areas, and complementary roles between the settled and nomadic populations as they interacted in a larger socioeconomic system.[64] In the words of Talal Asad:

> The basic opposition, therefore, is not between nomads and sedentaries,
> but between those who engage in the production of surplus and those who

have control of such surplus. . . . This is especially important in the historic Middle East where pastoral, agricultural, and trade activities are interdependent parts of a single economic system, where different elements of
the exploitable population are mobilized at different levels to support the
power structure, and where—in consequence—popular rebellions have often involved the temporary alliance of peasants and pastoralists.[65]

There is much in the history of Jabal Nablus to support Asad's con-
tentions. To begin with, the lines between nomads and peasants in Palestine were blurred. M. Volney, whose work is often cited to support the
view of bedouins as predators, had this to say about the interpenetration
of bedouin and peasant life:

> [A]s often as the different hordes and wandering tribes find peace and
> security, and a possibility of procuring sufficient provisions, in any dis-
> trict, they take up their residence in it and adopt, insensibly, a settled life,
> and the arts of cultivation. But when, on the contrary, the tyranny of gov-
> ernments drives the inhabitants of a village to extremity, the peasants de-
> sert their houses, withdraw with their families into the mountains or wan-
> der in the plains, taking care frequently to change their place of habitation,
> to avoid being surprised.[66]

A few pages later Volney offered a second significant observation: not
all bedouins are the same. Those of the Beka valley, Jordan, and Palestine,
he noted, "approach nearer to the conditions of the peasants; but these
[tribes] are despised by the others who look upon them as bastard arabs."[67] John Lewis Burckhardt, another contemporary observer, described
how the nomads of the Jordan Valley cultivated wheat, barley, and *dhura*
(a variety of sorghum). He also noted that some tribes "belonged" to Nazareth and Jabal Nablus—meaning that they were linked to the urban centers in a subordinate manner.[68]

There is little doubt that bedouin tribes were indeed within the sphere
of mobilization of urban power centers. During the 1854–1858 internal
conflict in Nablus, for example, both urban-led factions boasted bedouin
allies and referred to them as junior—though fierce and valuable—partners.[69] The same held true during factional struggles in the Jerusalem,
Hebron, and Gaza regions.[70] Nimr's view of relations between bedouin
tribes and the leaders of Jabal Nablus uncannily supports Asad's argument: "The princes of Jabal Nablus did not subordinate themselves to
the bedouin but exploited them instead. They disciplined the bedouin of
neighboring regions and forced them to abide by an alliance system in
order to secure the means of transportation, so that the caravans of Nablus

were able to reach all neighboring regions and from there to the various parts of the Ottoman Empire."[71]

As Nimr's comments explain and, more important, as the prosperity of Jabal Nablus in the eighteenth century clearly demonstrates, economic life could and did thrive through continually reproduced and negotiated alliance systems.[72] The occasional breakdowns were merely the exceptions that proved the rule. If one puts aside spectacular accounts of a few bedouin raids and focuses on the routines of everyday life, mutual dependency and cooperation become clear. For instance, the area east of the River Jordan where most of the bedouins dwelled was economically integrated by Nabulsi merchants as a source of, among other things, olive oil, livestock (sheep, goats, horses, camels), clarified butter (samn), and, most of all, qilw. This district also constituted an important market for Nabulsi manufactures and trade goods, such as textiles, weapons, and metal products. This is not to mention the fact that many of the clans that made Jabal Nablus their home could trace their origins to the eastern desert. As shown in Chapter 1, this economic integration was expressed politically through the creation of a combined district in 1867 called Jabal Nablus and al-Balqa.

The social history of soap fits well with Talal Asad's contention that interdependency of economic activities was the organizing framework. There was not a single relationship of an everyday nature that tied bedouins with Jabal Nablus in a subordinate but mutually dependent manner more thoroughly than the supply of qilw for soap production. Until the introduction of caustic soda in the 1860s, large numbers of bedouins from the Bani-Sakhr, Huwaytat, and Adwan tribes gathered barilla in the valleys of M'an, especially around Salt and Tadmur (Palmyra).[73] In the summertime they piled these plants in towering stacks, burned them, gathered the ashes and coals into sacks, and carried them to Nablus in large caravans.[74]

Burckhardt witnessed this process in 1812, and had this to say about the complex reciprocal obligations built around the qilw trade and other economic contacts with bedouins:

> The Arabs of the Belka [Balqa], especially the Beni Szakher [Bani Sakhr], bring here Kelly or soap-ashes, which they burn during the summer in large quantities: these are bought up by a merchant of Nablous, who has for many years monopolized the trade in this article. The soap-ashes obtained from the herb Shiman, of the Belka, are esteemed the best in the country . . . They are sold by the Arabs . . . but the purchaser is obliged to pay heavy duties upon them. The chief of the Arabs of El Ad-

ouan . . . exacts for himself five piasters from every camel load, two piasters for his writer, and two piasters for his slave. The town of Szalt [Salt]
takes one piaster for every load, the produce of which duty is divided
among the public taverns of the town. The quantity of soap-ashes brought
to the Osha market amounts, one year with another, to about three thousand camel loads. The Nablous merchant is obliged to come in person to
Szalt in autumn. According to old customs, he alights at a private house,
all the expenses of which he pays during his stay; he is bound also to feed
all strangers who arrive during the same period at Szalt; in consequence of
which the Menzels [public taverns] remain shut; and he makes considerable presents on quitting the place. In order that all the inhabitants may
share the advantages arising from his visits, he alights at a different house
every year.[75]

Burckhardt's observation that three thousand camel loads were sent to
Nablus annually in the early nineteenth century seems to be fairly accurate. Each *tabkha* of soap required at least 7 camel loads, or *qintars* of
qilw. Because Nablus soap production ranged, at the very least, from 100
to 400 *tabkhas* a year, a minimum of 700 to 2,800 camel loads arrived in
Nablus annually. Merchants from Nablus and the town of Salt also exported *qilw* to nearby soap-producing centers, such as Gaza, Jaffa, Lydda,
Jerusalem, and Acre.[76]

Nablus merchants put conditions on the type and quality of *qilw* as
well as on the time of delivery. According to Nimr, caravan shaykhs expected, in return, a certain percentage of the overall price as commission
upon delivery, as well as some "gifts" in kind. For instance, Nimr claims
that for every 100 camel loads, the caravan leader received money plus
one large basket (*quffa*) of rice, as well as one *ratel* each of tobacco, sugar,
soap, and coffee. He also received a cloak, a pair of boots, and a fur saddle
blanket.[77]

This system did not materialize overnight, nor was the web of relations
connecting Jabal Nablus with Salt and the bedouin tribes so fragile that it
could not overcome the bedouins' alleged natural urge to pillage. On the
contrary, the key elements of this network of mutual dependency, rights,
and obligations—sometimes contested, sometimes jealously guarded—
were reproduced over time and space by the conscious participation of all
of its members.

This network was also flexible enough to adjust to changing conditions,
such as the tripling of demand for *qilw* supplies to Nablus over the course
of the nineteenth century. In addition, when the Ottoman state established a permanent military presence on the east bank of the River Jordan
beginning in the last quarter of the nineteenth century, these relations

became channels for the large flow of capital into this area. Wealthy Nabulsi families quickly established a permanent presence and soon became the region's leading moneylenders, landowners, merchants, and, later on, public officials.[78] Not surprisingly, many of these families came to occupy important positions in the Jordanian government during the twentieth century.

Factory Owners

In a small city the size of Nablus, soap-factory owners constituted an exclusive club of powerful individuals who combined political power with wealth and high social status. Points of entry into this exclusive club were determined by two coexisting dynamics: long-term structural transformation in Nabulsi society, on the one hand, and relatively sudden shifts in the balance of political power within the ruling elite, on the other. Perhaps the words that best describe each dynamic would be infiltration and accession, respectively. Thus one would speak, for example, of the slow but steady infiltration of merchants and, at the same time, of the dramatic accession of new ruling families, such as the Abd al-Hadis.

These two dynamics were related, and they reinforced each other over time. During the eighteenth and nineteenth centuries their interaction had an integrative effect: they both led inexorably to the emergence of a single elite with a common material base. This integrative effect can be clearly seen in the case of old ruling families, such as the Tuqans and Nimrs, that managed to maintain a foothold in this exclusive club throughout the Ottoman period. Their continued membership was due primarily to the transformation of their material base. In all but name and reputation, these old ruling families that successfully adapted to the changing political economy of Jabal Nablus came more and more to resemble merchants or, more accurately, what it meant to be a merchant in the mid-nineteenth century.

Despite the intertwined nature of old and new, changes in the social composition of soap-factory owners can easily be detected when one compares cross-sections of the membership at different points in time. A telling (and dramatic) moment in this regard took place one day in February 1807, when the most prominent soap merchants and factory owners of Nablus gathered in the Islamic court. They had come to participate in the disposal of the estate of *Sayyid* Abd al-Qadir *Afandi* Hanbali, the *naqib al-ashraf* (steward of the descendants of the Prophet) of Nablus, owner of the Ya'ishiyya soap factory, and a man deeply in debt when he died.[79]

Also present in the court was *Sayyid* Muhammad *Afandi* Daqqaq, a special envoy of Muhammad Ali Khalidi, the judge of Jerusalem at the time. The deceased's family had used its close ties to the religious leaders of Jerusalem to make sure that a respectable outsider would oversee the disposal of the properties.[80] The family needed outside protection because *Sayyid* Abd al-Qadir's death came at a very inopportune moment: his only male heir was still a child in his legal minority. This situation, combined with the inevitability of having to sell the deceased's considerable immovable properties in order to satisfy debtors, left the family at the mercy of the wealthy and powerful of Nablus who were attracted to the court like bears to honey.

Sayyid Muhammad Daqqaq came armed with an official letter of appointment that contained clear instructions for protecting the family's interests, especially those of the child. Facing him in the court were the *mutasallim*, Musa *Beik* Tuqan; the chief of *sipahis* of Nablus, Hasan *Agha* Nimr; the new *naqib al-ashraf*, *Sayyid* Muhammad Salih *Afandi* Hanbali;[81] Yusuf son of Shaykh Sulayman *Afandi* Bishtawi; and the latter's brother, Salih.[82] Also present were a number of merchants, including *Sayyid* Hasan Tuffaha Husayni; Shaykh Mustafa Ashur; Shaykh Mahmud Arafat son of Abd al-Razzaq Arafat; and Shaykh Abd al-Ghani Zayd Qadri. Members of the former group were soap-factory owners;[83] members of the latter were oil, soap, and textile merchants who commissioned *tabkhas* from the deceased.[84]

First picks went to Tuqan family. Musa *Beik* Tuqan purchased the right of use (*khuluw*) of the deceased's soap factory. He also purchased the all-important copper vat, the *qilw* and the lime left in the factory, and the grand new residence that the deceased had recently built. Shortly thereafter, Shaykh Ashur bought a number of properties, including half of a very large oil-storage well (*bahra*, lit. lake) in an abandoned soap factory owned by the deceased, plus another, smaller, oil well. Leading members of the Bishtawi, Shammut, and Arafat families, all of which had business dealings with the deceased, also bought commercial properties, mostly shops and warehouses.[85]

The events unleashed by *Sayyid* Abd al-Qadir Hanbali's death neatly anticipated future trends in the social composition of soap-factory owners. First, with the exception of the Khammashs,[86] all of the soap-factory-owning families (that we know of from the sources) that did not make an appearance in court—Akhrami, Sawwar, Shafi'i, Bustami, and Tbeila—were to lose all or most of their shares in soap factories by 1840.[87] The first three were old ruling families with *timar* and *za'ama* holdings dating to the late seventeenth century. The Bustamis were part of the established ulama elite, and the Tbeilas, as discussed above, were both merchants and ulama who later became artisans. In contrast, the factory owners who did show up in court—Nimr, Tuqan, Hanbali, and Bishtawi—were the only members of the old Nablus elite to retain a foothold in this exclusive club.

Second, and without exception, all of the merchant families listed in the estate as having commissioned soap from the deceased were destined to become soap-factory owners (see below for details).[88] Third, it so happens that the one person who accounted for more than half of the deceased's total debt was Mustafa al-Ahmad, a resident of Arraba village. There are no clues as to who this person was or why he was owed the then considerable sum of 13,000 piasters, but Arraba was the home village of the Abd al-Hadi family, which came to dominate the politics of Jabal Nablus in the 1830s as well as to own and operate three soap factories.

Encapsulated within this inheritance case, therefore, were the three trends in the changing composition of soap-factory owners: the decline of the old urban elite during the first two decades of the nineteenth century; the rise of a recently urbanized elite during the next two decades; and, finally, the eventual domination by the merchant community in the 1850s and 1860s. Before we consider the next three cross-sections of the social composition of factory owners—dated 1839, 1842–1843, and 1853—the timing of and dynamics behind these three trends need to be detailed.

The turn of the nineteenth century was an important watershed. The slowly eroding material base of the old ruling *sipahi* families over the course of the eighteenth century was suddenly subjected to intense pressures during the reign of Musa *Beik* Tuqan in the first two decades of the nineteenth century. Musa *Beik* Tuqan's drive for political centralization was mirrored by an equally aggressive drive to dominate soap production by acquiring soap factories. To appreciate the importance of this development to the changing composition of soap-factory owners, one need only follow the paper trail in the Islamic court records, as well as note the heavy-handed exercise of power involved. For example, Muhammad son of Ali Tuqan forced a *waqf* exchange of the entire Shafi'iyya soap factory from Qasim Shafi'i for the ridiculously low sum of 150 piasters in 1801.[89] Three years earlier, in September 1798, the Tuqan family had arranged the purchase of part of the Rukabiyya soap factory by one of its followers, who then turned it over to them.[90] A few months later, in early January 1799, they consolidated their hold over the Uthmaniyya factory through a *waqf* exchange with a less wealthy branch of their family.[91] In February 1807 Musa *Beik* Tuqan gained control of the Ya'ishiyya from the Hanbalis after the leading member of that family died indebted.[92] In mid-December 1811 the Tuqans endowed two-thirds of the Shaytaniyya as a private family *waqf*, the implication being that this share was newly acquired.[93] In another instance, Musa *Beik* Tuqan "persuaded" Muhammad son of Isma'il Qadi-Shwayka to invalidate a previous sale of his right of use of one-quarter of the Bashawiyya soap factory to Muhammad Sa'id Bustami in December 1815/January 1816 and to sell it to him instead.[94] Finally, in April 1817 he purchased the allegedly damaged Gharzaniyya after another *waqf* exchange within his own extended family.[95]

This process of concentration in the context of prolonged conflict and civil strife set the stage for fundamental changes in the social composition of soap-factory owners over the next two generations. Musa *Beik* Tuqan's sudden death, coming soon after he had managed to undermine the hold of other members of the old ruling elite on Nablus's soap factories, created a vacuum. His death also unleashed a flurry of investments that were held in reserve pending the outcome of the drawn-out political struggle. As seen in the first section, those members of the old elite who managed to hold on to some shares of soap factories during his reign—Nimr, Sawwar, Akhrami, and Hanbali—now surged forward with renewed vigor. More important, new faces emerged, both through infiltration and through accession. Muhyi al-Din Arafat's nervous purchase of the Hallaqiyya factory from the Tuqans signaled the beginning of a sustained campaign of infiltration by merchants into the exclusive club of soap-factory owners. As to accession, the first order of business for the two subdistrict chiefs who led the fight against Musa *Beik* Tuqan—Ahmad Qasim Jarrar and Qasim al-Ahmad—was to acquire soap factories.[96]

These two chiefs' accession to membership in the soap-factory-owner's circles had more than just economic significance. Soap factories were icons of power, and the transformation of peasant-produced oil into urban-manufactured soap symbolized their own metamorphosis from subdistrict chiefs based in seat villages to *mutasallims* based in Nablus. Unfortunately for them, however, the Egyptian invasion of 1831 caused yet another shift in political power: that is, it precipitated another wave of accession, directly at their expense. Qasim al-Ahmad led an unsuccessful uprising against Ibrahim Pasha and lost both his soap factory and his head as a result. Ahmad Qasim Jarrar, meanwhile, plotted to assassinate Ibrahim Pasha by inviting him to see his soap factory, then throwing him into a copper vat full of boiling soap.[97] He also failed and lost his soap factory.

The plot was allegedly uncovered by Ibrahim Pasha's right-hand man in southern Syria, the Nabulsi subdistrict chief, Husayn Abd al-Hadi, who came from the village of Arraba. Like Qasim al-Ahmad, he relocated to the city, and like all the *mutasallims* before him, he immediately proceeded to buy a soap factory. His first acquisition was almost literally registered in blood: he bought, for only 8,000 piasters, one-half of both the house and the soap factory of Qasim al-Ahmad on October 16, 1834, not long after the latter was executed by Ibrahim Pasha.[98]

The Abd al-Hadi's other purchases were not so convenient: all of the prime urban properties in Nablus at that time—whether they be large residential compounds, soap factories, or shops and warehouses in the commercial districts—were already endowed as family *waqfs* and could not be legally sold. The only way around this obstacle was to arrange for *waqf* exchanges (*istibdal*). For this type of transaction the judge's permission was needed, because a number of conditions had to be satisfied in order for the exchange to be valid. For example, the *waqf* superintendent had to prove that the property concerned was no longer revenue producing or was in a deteriorating condition due to lack of repair, lack of money, or natural disaster, among other things. He also had to show that the property he was to receive in return was equal or greater in value.

Because of their fairly sudden move into the city, the Abd al-Hadis could not wait indefinitely for the *waqf* superintendents of the properties they coveted to step forward and exchange these properties for cash—which was all the Abd al-Hadis had to offer in return, because they did not own any real estate in Nablus. Even if the *waqf* superintendents were willing to come forward, the transactions would not meet the necessary legal conditions, because most of the key commercial and residential properties were either well kept or had been renovated during the economic expansion of the 1820s. The Abd al-Hadis therefore used their power and wealth to persuade the superintendents to offer these properties, then left it to the judge and other religious scholars to supply the necessary legal cover. It was through these means, for example, that the Abd al-Hadis exchanged for cash the Sawwariyya soap factory from the Sawwar, Akhrami, and Nimr families and the very large residential complex of the Sultan family, both concluded during 1832–1833.[99]

Representing the Abd al-Hadis in court were usually members of the Jawhari and Bustami families, which had held important positions in the religious hierarchy during the eighteenth and early nineteenth centuries. The key figure, however, was the judge himself, Abd al-Wahid al-Khammash, who served longer in this position than any other judge in Nablus during the nineteenth century.[100] Early on, he formed an alliance with the Abd al-Hadis, approved all of their exchange bids, and organized a petition against the pro-Ottoman sympathies of Ahmad *Agha* Nimr, which led to the latter's deportation.[101] Abd al-Wahid's political instincts served him well: he was annually reconfirmed as judge during the entire Egyptian period, and he accumulated enough capital to become one of the few individuals at the time who could afford to build a new soap factory from scratch. Constructed sometime in the mid-1840s, the *masbanant al-qadi* (judge's soap factory), as it has been called since, was still operational at the time of this writing, albeit on a much-reduced scale.[102]

Politically powerful, wealthy, and on the ascendent, the Abd al-Hadis and their allies acquired ownership of a number of soap factories during the 1830s, usually at the expense of the old elite. For example, Ahmad *Agha* Nimr was forced to exchange his *waqf* share in the Sawwariyya with Husayn Abd al-Hadi for 1,250 piasters in November 1836, at the height of the olive-harvest season.[103] The real blow for the Nimrs came thirteen months later, in January 1838, when they were forced to exchange half of the Yusufiyya, their family's prized soap factory, which they had operated continuously for more than 250 years, with *Hajj* Ibrahim Muhammad Anabtawi, an ally and business partner of Husayn Abd al-Hadi, for 18,000 piasters.[104] Ironically, this *waqf* exchange took place exactly when the soap-making season was about to start.

The Nimrs, up to that point, had not openly protested the Egyptian occupation, despite their pro-Ottoman sympathies. Ahmad *Agha* had even enrolled his son in the Egyptian military.[105] Moreover, he wisely chose *Sayyid* Mahmud Tuffaha Husayni as a partner in the Yusufiyya soap factory. In addition to being family allies and wealthy merchants, the Tuffahas were also one of the most respected *ashraf* families in Nablus. Their status provided some protection for an enterprise which, only a few years earlier, had been renovated at the cost of 20,000 piasters.[106] This partnership lasted for most of the Egyptian period (1245/1829–1830 to 1253/1837–1838) but ended abruptly with the forced *waqf* exchange mentioned above.[107] It is not surprising, therefore, that when the end of the Egyptian occupation seemed imminent in 1840, Ahmad *Agha* Nimr publicly declared his loyalty to the Ottomans. Unfortunately for him, his timing was premature. He was promptly exiled to Egypt (then Sudan) just months before the final withdrawal of the Egyptian forces.[108] By the time he was allowed to return to Nablus (1841–1842), he was blind and sickly.[109]

The Nimr family did not easily forget this series of events. Abd al-Fattah Nimr, resentful over the loss of half of the Yusufiyya in 1838 and angered by the exile of his father, waited until the judge Abd al-Wahid Khammash was removed from his office in 1865, then took over the half of the Yusufiyya that his father had been forced to exchange with the Anabtawis. In a lawsuit recorded in late March of that year, Abd al-Fattah was accused by *Sayyid* Hasan son of *Hajj* Ibrahim Muhammad Anabtawi of "putting his hands" on the entire Yusufiyya factory even though half of it had been legally exchanged in 1838 and then had been endowed in 1849 as a *waqf* by his father, Ibrahim Anabtawi.[110] Abd al-Fattah, however, easily won the case by proving what was obvious all along: namely, that the exchange was illegal because the soap factory was operational and profitable and not without benefit, as had been claimed at the time of exchange. The exchange was invalidated, as was *Hajj* Anabtawi's *waqf*. In return, Abd al-Fattah agreed to reimburse the 18,000 piasters to the Anabtawi family and gained full control, once again, of the Yusufiyya.

The Egyptian occupation accelerated ongoing trends and led to permanent changes in the social composition of soap-factory owners. As the second cross-section shows, the major soap-factory owners in the late 1830s were a mixed bag of old and new faces representing the various components of an emerging composite ruling elite: old ruling families, merchants, the Abd al-Hadis themselves, and their recently urbanized wealthy peasant allies.

Leaders of the Soap-Manufacturer's Guild
(*jama'at al-masabiniyya*), 1839

1. *Sayyid* Muhammad *Afandi* Murtada Hanbali
2. *Sayyid* Abd al-Qadir Hashim Hanbali
3. *Sayyid* Mahmud Tuffaha Husayni
4. Shaykh Abdullah Hamid Qaddumi
5. *Hajj* As'ad Shammut
6. *Hajj* Isma'il Kamal
7. *Sayyid* Muhyi al-Din Arafat
8. Shaykh Yusuf Zayd Qadri
9. As'ad al-Tahir Salih
10. Yusuf son of *Khawaja* Ahmad Tuqan[111]

This cross-section is based on a document, drawn up on the eve of the Egyptian departure, that reported an agreement by representatives of the soap-manufacturer's guild on a formula for payment of taxes for the fiscal year 1838–1839. It must be emphasized that this was not an exhaustive list, but rather one of representatives. The composition of the representatives was skewed in favor of the largest proprietors and/or of those who adjusted well to the political climate of the Egyptian occupation. Missing from this list, for example, was Ahmad *Agha* Nimr. Instead, his partner, Mahmud Tuffaha Husayni, was included, even though he did not own a soap factory at the time. In addition, the Abd al-Hadis were not mentioned as part of the guild leadership, although the whole point of the document was to exempt them from having to pay taxes on the two soap factories they owned.

Still, the key soap manufacturers are mentioned, and there is no doubt that this exclusive club was now dominated by merchants, many of whom were religious leaders as well. The first three (Hanbali, Tuffaha, Qaddumi), for example, combined a religious career with soap production. The latter activity was one they had pursued for decades. The next three (Shammut, Kamal, and Arafat) came from merchant families that also produced religious scholars. Unlike the first three, however, they were infiltrators who finally acquired factories after many years of involvement in the soap trade. The next two (Qadri and Tahir) were allies of the Abd al-Hadis, on their way to becoming two of the largest soap manufacturers in Nablus. The latter was a member of the recently urbanized rural middle class. Both became soap-factory owners after the Egyptian occupation.[112] The last person, Yusuf Tuqan, was the only representative of old ruling elite that once dominated this industry, but even he was from the merchant (*khawaja*), not political (*beik*), branch of the family.[113]

The third cross-section (Table 9) shows that, only a few years later, the ranks of the old Nablus elite had thinned further and that the newly urbanized allies of the Abd al-Hadis had reinforced their position. The number of merchants, meanwhile, remained the same, though they probably accounted for a greater share of the output.

The aim of this document—which detailed the amount of soap cooked by proprietors of soap factories ten years earlier and the amount of taxes due from them—was to exclude the Abd al-Hadis from taxation, even though this family had expanded its ownership of soap factories even further.[114] Although the list is partial, it shows that the most important change was the expansion in the number of the recently urbanized elite allied with the Abd al-Hadis. Most of the property they acquired changed hands between 1838 and 1840—that is, just before their Egyptian backers had left. One of their new members was *Hajj* Ibrahim Muhammad Anabtawi, who exchanged cash for half of the Yusufiyya from Ahmad *Agha* Nimr in January 1838.[115] Meanwhile, As'ad al-Tahir, who was married to the daughter of *Hajj* Ibrahim Anabtawi, began a seventeen-year-long

Table 9. Account of the Soap Cooked in Nablus's Soap Factories and of the Amount of Taxes Assessed for Each Individual, 1842–1843

Name	Tabkhas	Taxes (in Piasters)
As'ad al-Tahir	7	5,852
Mahmud Ya'ish	17	14,212
Abdullah Hamid Qaddumi	8	6,688
Ibrahim Qutub	16	13,794
Yusuf Shammut	9	7,542
Ibrahim Muhammad Anabtawi	7	5,852
Hassan Tuffaha Husayni	3	2,508
Abd al-Qadir Hashim Hanbali	5	4,180
Abd al-Wahid Khammash	5.5	4,598
Yusuf Zayd Qadri	12	10,032
TOTAL	90	75,240

SOURCE: Abd al-Hadi Family Papers, 1.1.4; dated 1268/1851–1852.

piecemeal purchase and renovation of the Rukabiyya soap factory in the fall of 1839.[116] At the same time, he purchased part of the Uthmaniyya factory from the Tuqan family (mid-September 1839).[117] Yet another close ally and business partner, Shaykh Yusuf Zayd Qadri, bought the Hallaqiyya factory from Muhyi al-Din Arafat in January 7, 1840, then sold half of it to Husayn Abd al-Hadi's son, Mahmud, in late June 1841.[118]

Of the remaining three new members, one was Abd al-Wahid Khammash, the Nablus judge and an ally of the Abd al-Hadis, who built his own soap factory sometime between 1839 and 1842.[119] The other two were merchants. Mahmud Ya'ish was a member of an old merchant family that has maintained its strong position since at least the eighteenth century. Nothing is known about Ibrahim Qutub, the last new member, except that he was part of the Qutub family in Jerusalem and that a relative of his, Ahmad Qutub, served as the judge of Nablus in the early 1860s.[120] The last two individuals most likely entered this exclusive club largely on the basis of their wealth, which must have been considerable, because their factories accounted for over 36 percent of the total taxable production of soap outlined in Table 9.

If the 1830s and early 1840s were the best years for the Abd al-Hadis and their allies, it was wealthy merchant families that made the greatest inroads into the ranks of soap manufacturers during the rest of the century. As a rule, all of the new soap-factory owners were already oil merchants who had commissioned soap from the old political and religious elite of Nablus. They included, for example, the descendants of the soap merchants mentioned above who commissioned soap from *Sayyid* Abd al-Qadir Hanbali (Ashur, Shammut, and Arafat). The same held true for those merchants listed in Table 8, who commissioned soap from the Bishtawi brothers in 1857 (Tamimi, Sadder, Nabulsi, Masri, and Qumhiyya).

To these families we can add names from a list of the major soap merchants of Nablus in 1853 who signed a petition protesting the imposition of new export taxes on soap:

Soap Merchants (*tujjar al-sabun*) of Nablus, circa 1853

1. Khalil Qamhawi
2. As'ad Khayyat
3. Isma'il Ati
4. Abdullah Kan'an
5. Abd al-Rahman Nabulsi
6. Ibrahim Qutub
7. As'ad Bishtawi
8. Mahmud Ya'ish
9. Muhammad Ashur
10. Yusuf Zayd Qadri
11. Abd al-Qadir Hashim Hanbali.[121]

All of these merchants who did not already own soap factories at that time would do so within a few decades. The most important of them (Nabulsi, Khayyat, Ashur, and Kan'an[122]) had become owners by the early 1860s.

Symbolic of this trend was the Bishtawi brothers' transformation of their shops and warehouses in the Wikala al-Asaliyya into a new soap factory.[123] Their decision illustrated the ongoing shift in the investment of merchant capital from some manufacturing and trading activities, such as in textiles, into soap. The highly centralized family firm of the Bishtawis was also symbolic of the process of concentration that was taking place in the soap industry. By the early twentieth century 75 percent of Nablus's entire soap production was controlled by just ten families, even though 29 factories were in operation.[124] The most important was the Nabulsi family, which came to own three of the largest factories. They alone accounted for more than 40 percent of the city's entire soap production during World War I.[125]

Some of these soap-factory owners were very wealthy. Tamimi and Bahjat estimated the average worth of a rich soap manufacturer during the early twentieth century to be about 10–15 million piasters.[126] Not surprisingly, the same individuals were also the major moneylenders, landowners, and merchants of Jabal Nablus. Moreover, they dominated the political positions in the city, especially the Municipal Council (formerly the Advisory Council). In short, these merchant families replaced the old elite of Nablus as the repositories of power, wealth, and social status.

On the surface, these three criteria for membership in the exclusive club of soap-factory owners had remained the same. In reality, the meanings of these criteria had changed along with the changing social composition of the membership. Wealth was now far more important than the other two criteria, and power no longer rested on military capability or domination of the top religious positions in the city. Indeed, the entire political atmosphere had been transformed: the rise of the merchant community and the imposition of direct Ottoman control combined to redefine the parameters of the discourse between local and central forces.

The changing social composition of soap-factory owners, therefore, reflects more than just the emergence of the merchant community into a position of leadership. The more fundamental change was the crystallization of a new elite, composed of a coalition of previously disparate elements: old ruling families and religious functionaries, tax-farmers, leading merchants, and the newly urbanized rural elite. These discrete elements maintained their social and cultural identities for a long time, in the sense that intermarriage between some of them was rare. Nevertheless, they developed common economic interests: all now were manufacturers, traders, landowners, and moneylenders.

The crystallization of this elite in the mid-nineteenth century was most evident in the united stand these groups took when it came to relations with the peasantry and with the Ottoman government, the two major sources of pressure from below and from above. On the one hand, it was imperative that they maintain their access to and control of the rural surplus in the face of increased peasant resistance. On the other hand, they wished to take advantage of the state's protection and the opportunities offered by Ottoman reforms. At the same time, they greatly resented the central government's efforts to undermine some of their political and economic privileges, and they were incensed by the arrival of non-Nabulsi government representatives eager to interfere in their daily business affairs.

It was these sets of circumstances that made the mid-nineteenth century a watershed period in the politics of notables of Jabal Nablus. Because soap manufacturers were the richest and most powerful members of the Nablus social elite and because the entire membership of the Advisory

Council at midcentury—except for Dawud Tannus, representing the Christian community, and Salama al-Kahin, representing the Samaritan community—was composed of soap-factory owners, there is no better window on the material basis of the politics of notables and their relationship to the Ottoman state than the points of conflicts between them over issues related to soap production and trade.[127]

SOAP AND THE STATE

The longevity of Ottoman rule, impressive by any standard, was based on maintaining flexible, permeable, and porous boundaries of power and privilege between center and periphery. This pragmatic approach to the exercise of authority was essential to an empire that did not have the capability or even the intention of micromanaging the vast territories under its control. From the beginning, existing local forces were coopted— by force or by persuasion—into a political arena that could potentially serve their interests, as well as those of their superiors.

This approach expressed itself most clearly in regions which, by the very nature of their location or character of their social formation, were difficult and costly to control. Palestine, especially the central hill areas, was such a region. Not until the late 1840s did the Ottoman authorities begin to effectively reassert or, more accurately, assert for the first time, direct central administrative and fiscal control over this historically autonomous enclave. At precisely the same time European political and economic influence, on the rise for decades, increased dramatically following the blazing trail of the short-lived Egyptian occupation. It was the combination of these two circumstances—Ottoman centralization and integration into the world economy—that provided the larger context for relations between the Nablus ruling elite and the Ottoman state.

Meanwhile, the changing internal grid of Nabulsi economic and political life allowed merchants to position themselves in an advantageous position vis-à-vis the ruling urban and rural families and, eventually, to anchor a new composite local elite. This elite was eager to make the most of the economic opportunities that the Egyptian occupation and Ottoman reforms offered and was quite content to participate in the molding of a new political landscape through the Advisory Council. The story of relations between the central Ottoman government and this local Nabulsi elite during the *Tanzimat* era, therefore, is not about the imposition of Western-inspired modernization from above and knee-jerk resistance by old-fashioned traditional elements from below. Rather, it is a story about the clashing interests of two forces that spoke the same language and that were heavily, though unequally, dependent on each other. In their discourse, both forces seized on the long history of flexible and permeable boundaries between center and periphery as well as on the exigencies of rapidly changing political and economic realities in order to expand their respective space for maneuvering and, in the process, to reinvent their mutual relationship.

Instructive in this regard are two areas of conflict between soap manufacturers in Nablus and the central Ottoman authorities that stand out in the pages of the Nablus Advisory Council records: the bidding process on and the disposal of olive oil collected as taxes-in-kind (*zakhayir*); and the interpretation and application of new customs regulations specifying the types and amounts of taxes soap merchants had to pay. The latter was more important because it involved the greatest amounts of money, directly affected the pocketbooks of these merchants, and led to a tax strike that remained largely unresolved after two years of continual correspondence, arguments, and veiled threats. The disputes over these and similar issues helped define the new politics of Ottoman Palestine during this formative period and, it could be argued, laid the essential groundwork for the emergence of various forms of Palestinian nationalism in the early twentieth century.

The Bidding Battle

As explained in Chapter 3, one of the main duties of the Nablus Council was to oversee the bidding process on and disposal of taxes collected in kind that were stored in government-operated storehouses in Nablus and Jenin. Merchants from outside Nablus were free to participate in the bidding process, and, theoretically, these commodities were to be sold to the highest bidder. From the point of view of the council, the participation of regional and foreign merchants—based mostly in the coastal cities of Beirut, Acre, or Jaffa—had two negative effects: it raised the prices of these commodities, and it lowered the quantities available for local trade and manufacturing. This, in turn, encouraged peasants to hold out for higher prices and forced merchants, manufacturers, and artisans to compete more intensely with each other for supplies.

The soap producers and merchants of Nablus, therefore, were threatened with losing first rights to oil and other commodities collected as taxes-in-kind and, potentially, of having their access and control of the surplus of Jabal Nablus seriously undermined. These concerns, not principled opposition to Ottoman rule, spurred them to challenge some, but not all, of the new administrative rules and regulations. Because the council members were also soap merchants and manufacturers, they resorted to various means in order to restrict the bidding process over olive oil and tried to keep prices low. They waged a polite and indirect but stubborn campaign against repeated efforts by the central government to maintain an open and effective bidding process. The Ottoman government, in contrast, was keen to promote free bidding. High prices meant more money for its coffers, a stronger hold over the networks of trade, expanded access to the agricultural surplus in the various regions, and, not least, a window of opportunity for provincial governors and administrators to build patronage networks and make money by favoring certain bidders against others.

The opening salvo of the major battle over olive oil was fired in late March 1852, when the council members responded to an inquiry by Hafiz Pasha, the governor of Jerusalem, about the amount of oil collected in kind, when it would be sold, and to whom:

> Of the 1267 [1851–1852] dues, 2,745 *uqqas* of oil have been collected thus far. . . . Your Noble Command was issued that it be put up for auction and the bids sent to you . . . [but] *as is known and famous in the city of Nablus*, the local government (*miri*) does not have its own wells to store the oil collected. Rather, it is an *old tradition* that [the oil] be put in one of the merchants' soap-factory wells. Because the oil is collected both at the beginning and the end of the year, it is well known that it precipitates and cannot be taken out in the same pure state that it entered in. So if it is put on auction now and someone bids on it, he would want it in the same pure state as the merchants who ship it overseas are accustomed to taking it. Therefore the cloudy part that filtered down will stay as the property of the oil-well owner and the amount of oil [sold] will be less [than what was brought in]. Either way, both the soap-factory owner and the *miri* will be cheated. Because the oil has already been deposited with Sayyid Mahmud Fakhr al-Din, it should be sold to him. This way, it does not have to change hands and it will not be necessary to sell only the clear oil, leaving behind the cloudy [part]. Because the aforementioned cooks soap in his soap factory, it is immaterial to him whether the cloudy [part] mixes in with the clear [part], for that does not hurt the production of soap. . . . [Furthermore,] this way we would not have to pay a fee for storing the oil, nor the expenses of measurers and lifters or any other costs. . . . We asked about the price of oil in these parts . . . and found that each *uqqa* is worth 3.5 piasters. . . . If the Noble Order sanctions this sale, we will collect the price from the aforementioned buyer and enter it into the treasury account books.[128]

It is of crucial significance that the council cited both traditional practices and new economic circumstances to explain why open bidding, from
their point of view, was impossible. They could easily have rented space
for storing the oil or built, at the central government's expense, public
well(s) over the years—but this would not have been in their own interests. Rather, they seized on tradition as a defense in order to reinforce
their role as the interpreters of local realities—a point that was discussed
in Chapter 4. They were well aware that the Ottoman government had
long recognized previous customs as a legitimate precedent in a variety of
circumstances (such as in land-tenure cases). Indeed, the central government's respect for the precedent of custom was synonymous with the
autonomy that had been enjoyed by Jabal Nablus over the preceding centuries.

In addition to the argument of tradition, they cited the exigencies of
international trade in oil to justify why it was not cost effective to export
oil already deposited in private wells. In essence, therefore, the council
members asserted their control over the bidding process by the very act
of depositing oil in one of the soap-factory wells and then presenting the
provincial governor with a fait accompli: no matter who was chosen, it
would always have to be one of the Nablus soap-factory owners because
tradition dictated that their wells be used to store the oil.

The Jerusalem governor, unhappy about the lack of choice in the matter, insisted that the oil be put on auction anyway. He also ordered that
the council provide full information on the bids and send him the money
as soon as taxes-in-kind were sold to the highest bidder. The council members, however, still had some tricks up their sleeves. On April 30, 1852,
they wrote a letter offering three other bids.[129] All three, however, came
from soap-factory owners in Nablus, and all three offered a lower price
than the original bid. In other words, more bids amounted to less choice,
unless Hafiz Pasha was willing to accept an even lower price.

The explanations the council members gave are very instructive, in
that they took refuge in a newly invented tradition: fluctuations in prices
caused by international trade. They noted that most Nablus soap-factory
owners refused to bid because 3.5 piasters per *uqqa* was too high now.
This amount reflected the price of oil two months earlier, when international demand for oil through Haifa and Jaffa ports was at its peak. International oil merchants had since loaded the ships, and local soap merchants had secured their supplies. With the slackening of demand, the
price of oil dropped to its normal level.

The council members reinforced their arguments by displaying the

greater freedom for maneuver afforded by their knowledge of the specific-
ities of local customs and conditions. They noted that the oil merchants
were no longer as interested in bidding because, after selling the clear oil,
they had enough of the cloudy part left over to cook soap with—hence
they no longer needed more oil for this season's soap production. The
important point, whether the statement was true or not, was that the local
soap-factory owners alone knew the actual situation.

To reinforce their subtle threats they announced that whoever bought
the oil must buy it complete and pay the rent and other expenses. They
reduced the governor's room for maneuvering even further by concluding
that *Sayyid* Mahmud Fakhr al-Din had decided to withdraw his bid and
that he no longer cared who bought the oil as long as his storage costs
were reimbursed. The best they could come up with, therefore, was yet
another Nablus soap-factory owner, *Sayyid* Ahmad son of *Hajj* As'ad al-
Tahir, who was willing to pay 3.25 piasters per *uqqa* as well as all of the
other expenses. Most likely, this new offer—which was one-quarter of a
piaster per *uqqa* lower than the previous one—was not a serious one.
Rather, it was a bargaining chip to push through the original candidate
without conceding anything.

The governor of Jerusalem must have construed their purpose in this
light, for he fired back an angry missive in record time, lecturing the
council that his intent in ordering that the oil be put on auction was "not
to reduce the price, but to increase it" and stating that the second offer was
"unacceptable."[130] He further insisted that the council give the greatest
consideration to having a real auction and report on the results as soon as
possible.

Somewhat akin to a chess game, the council members returned to their
old position, but only after securing another concession. On May 11,
1852, they sent a note assuring the governor that he should not doubt
their sincerity.[131] Far from attempting to manipulate the price of oil or to
keep it artificially low, they reiterated, it was forces larger than themselves, namely supply and demand for oil on the international market,
that drove the price down. Second, if they were to have a real auction
now, its price might slide downward even further. Therefore, and in order
to dispel any misgivings about their motivations, they announced the
happy news that they had managed to convince *Sayyid* Mahmud Fakhr
al-Din to resubmit his original offer, but they had to promise him in
return that he could postpone payment for four months instead of paying
immediately, as the governor had requested.

It must have become obvious to Hafiz Pasha that securing a higher price for the oil through the council was hopeless. Nablus was not only ruled by native sons, but all of the council members happened to be soap-factory owners to boot. In this particular situation, they were in a very strong position to control the bidding process on olive oil collected as taxes-in-kind. Therefore, he personally searched for outside bidders, settling on a Beiruti merchant who was willing to pay a mere 5 fiddas, or one-eighth of a piaster, more per *uqqa* than the candidate picked by the council. Immediately afterward he sent a letter demanding that the oil be surrendered to this merchant forthwith.[132] To rub salt into the wound, he even retracted his previous demand for immediate payment and ordered that the Beiruti merchant be given the same four months' grace period as *Sayyid* Mahmud Fakhr al-Din demanded. He specifically commanded, moreover, that the Beiruti merchant not be made to pay any of the storage and other costs. The last order sought sweet revenge, for it aimed at embarrassing the council members, on the one hand, and at forcing *Sayyid* Mahmud Fakhr al-Din to bear these expenses, on the other.

It was the council's turn to become angry and bare its teeth for the first time. In a pointed response dated June 24, 1852, it gave a number of reasons why it flatly refused to sell the oil to the Beiruti merchant.[133] First, it noted that the governor had not answered its last letter within twenty days, as he had promised, so it had assumed agreement on his part. Second, the oil had already been sold and used to cook soap. The reason was that part of the oil-well wall had collapsed, so the sale to *Sayyid* Mahmud Fakhr al-Din had to be finalized immediately or else the cost of moving the oil to another well would have had to be borne by the treasury. Third, it would be unacceptable in any case that the service charges on storage and other expenses not be reimbursed, and the council could not sell oil under such conditions.

To make sure that all of the possible avenues for counterattack by Hafiz Pasha were closed, the council members went on to accuse the Beiruti merchant of attempted bribery. They claimed this merchant, during a visit to Nablus, noted the empty well and threatened to outbid *Sayyid* Mahmud Fakhr al-Din unless he received a bribe. In other words, even if the oil were still available, they could not possibly approve its sale to such an unethical merchant. Finally, slamming the door shut, they complained that too many letters had been written and too much time had been spent on this matter. They threatened that if such methods were employed in the future, Nablus soap-factory owners would simply refuse to store the olive oil collected as taxes-in-kind in their wells. To sweeten this blatant refusal and threat, they announced that they had managed to force their candidate to add the 5 fiddas to the original price and declared the matter closed.

This stubborn and united opposition by the council members, it must be emphasized, was not motivated by the amount of olive oil at stake. That was worth approximately 10,000 piasters—a large but relatively insignificant sum compared with the millions of piasters sunk into soap production every year. Neither was this battle motivated principally by the possibility of personal gain: council members did not stand to make an immediate and direct profit on these bids, because the entire amount would be transferred to the central treasury. Rather, they cared deeply about the outcome of the bidding process because it was, in essence, a political struggle between the central government and the local council over control of the price and movement of the rural surplus, the major source of income for both sides.

Members of the council, it must be emphasized, were not simply government representatives. They were also soap-factory owners, local businessmen, and regional traders who had a direct financial stake in who bought what and for how much, as well as a political stake in maintaining their primacy over a hinterland they considered to be theirs, not the government's or the foreign merchants'. A crucial factor in this regard was keeping the central government in the dark about how much of each commodity was produced, where, and through what channels it was moved to its final destination. If the central government were allowed to dominate the bidding process, it would eventually be privy to the full range of information about the productive capacity of Jabal Nablus and the business connections of its merchants. Eventually, the hundreds of leaks feeding local middlemen at the expense of government revenue would be plugged up, and the material base of the merchant community would be narrowed considerably.

These were not theoretical concerns. For example, the above scenario was precisely the trap that council members found themselves in when they tried to convince the governor of Jerusalem to allow the peasants of Jenin district to pay cash for that part of their taxes that was normally collected in kind. Instead of flatly agreeing or refusing, the governor cleverly pursued the matter by demanding to know why the request was made, what villages were affected, the kind and amount of commodities they produced over the years, the range of prices offered, and so on. After a long series of evasive letters, the council members finally backtracked on their original request and practically begged that the case be closed.[134]

The Tax Strike

The most serious conflict between soap merchants and the central government revolved around the imposition of new and increased taxes on the manufacture and export of soap. The root causes of the conflict were threefold: structural changes in the Ottoman system of customs regulations after the free-trade Anglo-Turkish Commercial Convention was signed in 1838; the systematic campaign by the Ottoman government to centralize its control over historically semiautonomous regions such as Jabal Nablus after the Egyptian occupation; and the simultaneous consolidation of a cohesive ruling elite in Jabal Nablus led by the Advisory Council members.

The new customs regulations reflected the weak position of the Ottoman government as it was further integrated into the world capitalist economy and revealed the serious dilemma it faced. These regulations opened internal markets by lowering taxes on foreign imports and by exacting a higher tax on exports. At the same time, they aimed at increasing revenue through tighter control of the circulation of locally produced raw and manufactured goods. Ironically, this policy—allowing freer trade opportunities for Europeans while taxing local production and trade more efficiently—only served to undermine the government's fiscal basis. Worse, the high profits to be made from the smuggling of locally produced commodities to overseas destinations encouraged many merchants to circumvent the government's attempts to control the flow of commodities.[135] In short, the new regulations reduced the government's access to the very surplus it badly needed as a source of revenue, and they were certainly a factor in the eventual bankruptcy of the Ottoman Empire in 1876.

But this puts us ahead of the story. Over the next two decades after the signing of the treaty, the government faced considerable difficulties in its attempts to enforce these new regulations, especially in semiautonomous regions of Greater Syria. Smuggling and resistance by local merchants were not the only problems. The government also suffered from lack of an adequate infrastructure in terms of port facilities and efficiently staffed customs bureaus that could track and streamline the large variety of local conditions, tax arrangements, and networks of trade.

Throughout the 1840s, therefore, all the government could do was to continuously reaffirm these new regulations and to take concrete and incremental steps to slowly enforce them by appointing nonlocal customs officials.[136] For example, on February 27, 1846, copies of a *firman* were sent to the all of the high officials of Damascus and Sidon provinces.[137] This *firman* reiterated the key elements of the trade regulations issued in 1838 and indicated the government's main concern: namely, that the agricultural commodities collected as taxes-in-kind must start flowing back into the government storehouses instead of finding their way overseas. Specifically, the movement of basic grains needed by the mass of consumers within the empire, such as wheat, barley, and corn, were not to be taxed unless they were to be shipped overseas. Then they would be subject to a total of 12 percent in taxes (9 percent entry [*amed*] and export [*kharaj*] tax upon arriving at the ports, plus a 3 percent exit [*reft*] tax upon being loaded on ships and exiting the port).

Other *firmans* further detailed the customs regulations for other goods. For example, semiprocessed commodities, such as clarified butter (*samn*), cheese, molasses (*dibs*), honey, rice, and sesame oil, were also exempt from taxes on local movement, but not when they were traded between one province and another, such as between Egypt and Damascus. Finally, processed goods, such as textiles made from cotton or soap made from olive oil, that were imported into or exported from a locality must pay the three basic customs taxes: *amed, reft,* and *kharaj*.[138] Key to all of these goals was greater central government control of the movement of goods overland from the interior regions to the port cities and the interception of smuggling networks that took advantage of inadequate customs facilities between the provinces.

These guidelines or, more accurately, the enforcement of these guidelines, signaled a major erosion in local control of the movement of commodities. Yet, and despite repeated clarifications and explanations by the central authorities over the years, this new system was still meeting resistance from merchants in Jabal Nablus in the early 1850s.[139] The spotlight fell on soap merchants and manufacturers for a number of reasons. Soap manufacturing and trade generated, relative to other economic activities in Nablus, a substantial portion of the overall revenues—that is, this sector was a tempting target for Ottoman customs officials. Soap manufacturers and merchants, moreover, were the wealthiest elements in Nabulsi society, as well as the most prominent socially and politically. Because they also dominated the Advisory Council and were outspoken about defending their interests, their actions reverberated in the political atmosphere of Jabal Nablus as a whole.

Soap merchants and manufacturers keenly felt the burden of the new regulations. If enforced, they would mean a large increase in taxation over the trade of soap, especially the export trade with Egypt which, until recently, had been virtually exempt from taxation. These new regulations also meant a significant increase in the cost of production. Not surprisingly, the council searched for loopholes in the new regulations, and it arrived at an interpretation of their meaning that was significantly different from what the central government intended. The conflicting interpretations sparked a tax strike by soap manufacturers and merchants that remained partially unresolved when the available records ended in 1853.[140]

During this time the soap merchants and the governors of Sidon and Jerusalem exchanged a number of letters and petitions through the offices of the Nablus Advisory Council. Usually the council presented itself as a neutral vehicle that simply passed communications back and forth. But at the critical junctures it showed its true colors by openly supporting the tax strike and labeling the merchants' position as fair and just.[141] Tensions reached such a point that the newly appointed non-Nabulsi head of the customs bureau retaliated against the strike by closing the gates and forbidding the exit of manufactured soap from the city.[142]

Two sets of economic issues were of grave concern to the soap merchants and manufacturers. The first set revolved around the most important raw material: oil. Prior to enforcement of the new customs regulations at the beginning of the 1851/1852 fiscal year,[143] all oil entering the city paid an entry (amed) tax, and all of the soap leaving the city paid only the exit (reft) tax. Now merchants had to pay both the entry and the exit taxes on soap exported from the city. In other words, oil produced in the hinterland of Jabal Nablus was not to be taxed upon entering the city, but that portion of the oil which was consumed in the soap-manufacturing process was now to be subject to taxation when it left the city in the form of soap. This tax would be collected in addition to the normal exit taxes on soap.[144]

There were three connected problems in this first set of issues. Because most of the oil that entered the city was stored in the wells of soap-factory owners, a method had to be found to calculate how much oil to tax.[145] More important, because much of the soap in the 1852/1853 fiscal year was made from oil that had already paid the entry tax the year before, soap merchants wanted those taxes reimbursed before going along with the new arrangement.[146] Furthermore, not all of the oil for soap production came from the hinterland of Nablus. Soap merchants also imported oil from Jabal Ajlun on the east bank of the River Jordan.[147] Because Jabal Ajlun was not officially part of Jabal Nablus and because oil was no longer considered one of the basic commodities exempt from interregional taxation, merchants who imported it had to pay the entry tax when it passed through the city gates. Therefore, soap made with Ajluni oil had only to pay the normal exit tax when leaving the city because the entry tax on the oil used to make this soap had already been assessed and collected.

This created further complications. Apparently, some soap merchants and manufacturers attempted to avoid paying the entry and exit taxes on oil altogether by secretly smuggling it into the city and then claiming that all their soap was made from Ajluni oil.[148] At least that was the charge made by Haqqi *Afandi* and *Khawaja* Qasbar, the newly appointed non-Nabulsi customs officials. Both the soap merchants and the Nablus Council, on the other hand, complained that the customs officials were disobeying the Sultan's *firman* by continuing to charge entry taxes on all oil entering the city and, at the same time, also charging both the entry and the exit taxes on all soap leaving the city.[149] The council members complained repeatedly that the customs officials were not cooperating with them or providing information on the amount of entry taxes collected in the 1850–1851 fiscal year. They threatened that unless they received such cooperation, they could not be expected to pay both entry and exit taxes on outgoing soap.[150]

The second major set of issues concerned the export (*kharaj*) tax on soap destined for Egypt, Damascus, the Hijaz, Anatolia, and other regions. The Nablus soap merchants insisted that the new regulations did not necessitate their paying the *kharaj* tax unless the soap was to be shipped out by sea from port cities such as Jaffa and Haifa. They based this position on a literal interpretation of the third article of the new customs regulations, which specified sea transport but did not mention ground transport. They argued that if the sultan meant all exports he would not have specified port cities. Furthermore, they continued, ground transport was not mentioned in any of the fourteen articles of the new regulations.[151]

The customs officials, of course, insisted that the *kharaj* tax be applied to all exports regardless of the form of transportation. They knew, as did the merchants, that the major markets for Nabulsi soap—Egypt, Damascus, and Jerusalem—were accessible by land. They also knew that Nabulsi merchants paid only half of the *kharaj* tax when soap was shipped through the ports (export merchants in Jaffa and Acre paid the other half), whereas they would have to pay the entire amount for soap exported by land. In other words, they knew that the soap merchants wanted to avoid export taxes, especially those on land routes, at any cost.

The willingness of soap merchants and producers to challenge directly the most important of government priorities—the collection of taxes—as well as their ability to form and sustain a united front for a long period of time, underline the seriousness with which they treated this matter. In part their actions reflect their resentment over the loss of past privileges. In a *firman* regulating customs fees on commodities entering and leaving Nablus registered in the Islamic court records in late May 1820, for example, soap exported to Jaffa, Egypt, and Gaza was the only one out of 40 commodities listed not subject to customs fees.[152] The newly proposed taxes, in short, would cut into the profit margin of soap manufacturers and merchants, complicate their business, and slow down the expansion of this industry.

The strength and determination of soap merchants can be gauged from the fact that twelve years after the signing of the 1838 commercial convention, the customs bureau in Nablus, manned by local officials, was still, for the most part, operating according to the old system. Even those new taxes that were being assessed on oil and soap were unusually light: 4 piasters and 20 paras entry tax on each jar of oil, and only 9.5 piasters exit tax on each *qintar* of soap. In fact, the council members felt obligated to explain to the provincial governor why these fees were not higher.[153]

There is little doubt that it was the blatant incongruity and uniqueness of customs collection in Nablus that precipitated the appointment of new non-Nabulsi officials and, in the final analysis, sustained an equal, if not greater, show of stubbornness and determination on part of the governors in Sidon and Jerusalem. Soon after their arrival, these customs officials began to log a myriad of complaints against the soap merchants in memorandums to their superiors and to the Nablus Advisory Council. In one such letter they claimed that Nablus was the only city in which soap merchants did not pay the taxes due from them.[154]

Another economic factor that sustained the strike was the amount of money involved. In a document detailing the tax structure of Nablus, dated June 24, 1841, revenues from soap production far surpassed any other source—such as taxes on shops, olive and sesame presses, weaving establishments, tanneries, and the import of cheese and tobacco into the city—with the exception of the head tax.[155] Taxes on meat brought into the city was the only revenue source that came close. Just five months' worth of entry and exit fees on soap leaving Nablus in 1852, for example, amounted to more than 184,000 piasters.[156]

Ironically, the council cited the large sums involved as one reason why the merchants would not pay their taxes to the head customs official. This person, they said, simply could not be trusted with so much money. Rather, they suggested that the 500–600 purses of money (250,000–300,000 piasters) be deposited in the Nablus treasury or sent directly to Jerusalem.[157] Meanwhile, Haqqi *Afandi* and *Khawaja* Qasbar accused the soap merchants of fomenting a tax strike so that they could invest the large sums of extra capital remaining in their hands and "enjoy its profits."[158]

Finally, one must point out again that the battle over the interpretation of new customs taxes on soap and oil was only one of many similar battles which pitted a centralizing government against a new merchant-dominated elite struggling to consolidate its control over the rural surplus. For example, customs officials wrote angry letters accusing the council members of undermining the bidding process on tax-farming (*iltizam*) to such an extent that, in their words, "tax farms had become akin to individual *malikanes* [life-time grants]." They also accused the council members of, among other things, embezzlement and interference.[159] The council members, on the other hand, made no secret of their opinion that it was the customs officials who were out of line and that most of the problems would be solved if it were not for the obstinacy of these officials. On more than one occasion they accused them of extortion and lack of cooperation.[160]

The running argument between the council members and the customs officials underscored the political dimension of the conflict. Essentially, their arguments were a microcosm of the larger battle over the boundaries of power, privilege, and jurisdiction between the Ottoman government and the council members who, technically, were that government's employees. Thus the battle over customs taxes expanded to include the role of the new non-Nabulsi customs employees appointed by the central government and the extent of their jurisdiction. For example, arguments broke out as to who had the right to control the local employees of the customs bureau, whether they be gatekeepers, inspectors, or accountants. On this and other matters, each side repeatedly accused the other of imposing its will.[161]

Although the final outcome of these disagreements is not known, indications are that it was the soap merchants and the council members who had to give in. Sensing this disturbing trend, the council members, on more than one occasion, appealed to the governor of Sidon province, urging him, in effect, to decide whose cooperation he valued more: theirs or the customs officials'. To their dismay, the governor consistently came down on the side of the customs officials. Even then, the soap merchants still withheld payment. When they were finally and directly ordered to pay up, they resisted yet again.

On May 1, 1853, the soap merchants handed a petition to the council in which they feigned obedience while actually raising the stakes by challenging the authority of the governor and casting doubt on his intentions:

> Today we were called in to the council [premises] . . . and the Noble Order . . . was read to us concerning the decision of the Provincial Council that we are obligated to pay for what was and will be due in the *kharaj* [tax] on the soap exported from our city to all areas. . . . Your wish is our command . . . and we are ready to obey the orders of the . . . government at any time. But, what we know is that the government . . . made the new customs laws, procedures, and regulations and organized them into articles and sections that no one can transcend or change. We appeal to you once again that the [new regulations] do not mention, in any one of the articles, that the *kharaj* is to be paid except on goods sent to seaports. This is shown clearly in the third article. . . . So by what proof or argument can we be convinced that we have to pay the *kharaj* on all shipments to all destinations? If this is to be so just because you [arbitrarily] order it, then, in any case, we, our money, and all that our hands own are . . . ready to obey our superiors. But, if this is to be so because that is what the new law . . . [intends] then we beg clarification of the phrase in this article that says that we have to pay, and where we can find it so we can obey it. . . . As long as our superiors are not forcing us to behave except as outlined in the customs regulations, then please convince us [of your interpretation] of this law so we can begin to comply.[162]

This petition was turned down. The last recorded attempt of council members to hold off the final showdown was yet another petition, in which they requested that demands for payment be postponed until August 8, 1853, so that they could send a representative to Beirut to argue their case one last time. They added that they would abide by the decision regardless of the outcome.[163]

Nevertheless, there were limits to the maneuvering power of the council and the soap merchants. Gone were the days when control of the movement of oil and soap was left largely in the hands of local forces and when their immediate predecessors paid little or no taxes. Already, in April 1850, the council agreed that all oil entering the city would have to be inspected, then accompanied by an official to the soap factories.[164] They also agreed that oil destined for soap production was to be put into special wells that were closed with a wooden door and locked by the customs official, who kept the key. The door, in addition, was to be sealed by that same official and could be opened again only when he was present.

Only two days before the last petition mentioned above—that is, July 30, 1853—they also agreed that special wells were to be set aside for Ajluni oil and that these wells would be sealed according to the same procedures. Finally, the tax strike lost much of its punch once the first of the two major areas of conflict—taxes over oil processed into soap—was settled when soap merchants agreed to pay entry and exit taxes on soap leaving the city gates.[165] True, they still did not pay the *kharaj* taxes, but these accounted for a small portion of the total amount that had been long withheld.

The fact that the Nablus soap merchants were not able to gain any concessions from the central government in return for their partial compliance signaled the turning of the tide in favor of the latter. By the early 1860s, and after a successful military campaign to end the factional conflict that gripped Jabal Nablus during the Crimean War, the Ottoman authorities were able, for the first time, to impose a non-Nabulsi as the effective *qa'immaqam* of Jabal Nablus.

This does not mean that an unbridgeable gap was created between the leading Nabulsi families and the Ottoman government. In fact, the government all along viewed the local notables, including the leaders of the merchant community, as their natural local allies in the region. By the same token, these same leading families reinforced their power and political legitimacy by joining the ranks of the Ottoman government's bureaucracy, particularly the newly established Advisory Council. The battles of will between the council members and the provincial governors, therefore, were not informed by black-and-white dichotomies that pitted, as nationalists would have it, independence versus colonial occupation, or, as modernization theorists would have it, traditional feudal leaders versus a modernizing state. On the contrary, the most striking dimension of the bidding and customs battles was the fact that both sides spoke the same language. Their discourse, in other words, was built on a shared set of assumptions, such as the primacy of market forces, and the sources of political legitimacy, though not necessarily the boundaries of political power. In their last challenge to the governor about the interpretation of the third article of the new customs regulations, for example, soap merchants did not explicitly question the government's position on international trade or its right to collect taxes on that trade. Rather, they cited the sultan as the supreme authority on customs regulations but considered the provincial governor's view of the meanings of these regulations as just an opinion that was no more and nor less valid than their own. In other words, they claimed equal rights before the law, like all other servants of the sultan, regardless of rank.

By the same token, these conflicts were not mere tempests in teapots. On the contrary, they went to the heart of the material interests of the local merchant community and directly affected what they considered to be their legitimate efforts to mold the ways in which state power affected the particulars of their daily existence. Being part of the state, in other words, conferred on them both advantages and drawbacks. Their discourse with the provincial governor constantly aimed at maximizing the former and minimizing the latter. The soap merchants and manufacturers in Nablus consistently underscored their obedience to higher authorities as a general principle, but, just as consistently, they also tried to exploit the permeable and porous boundaries that long characterized the relations between the Ottoman state and the leaders of semiautonomous regions by emphasizing their superior knowledge of local conditions and citing the precedent of customary practices. They used this argument, it is important to emphasize, not as objective observers or as loyal bureaucrats but as creators of meanings—that is, they chose to emphasize only those aspects of tradition that suited their purposes, then recast or reinvented them in the context of the new economic and political realities of which they themselves were a product.

What these merchants objected to the most was the Ottoman government's attempt to harden these boundaries in a manner that cut into their material base without providing any real protection against growing European hegemony or arbitrary exactions by their superiors. True, some aspects of the government's reforms offered merchants a place at the political table in return (the Advisory Council), and this did increase their ability to manipulate local economic forces in their favor. But other aspects of the reforms—such as the encouragement of bids by foreign merchants, the imposition of nonlocal governors and customs officials bent on squeezing the merchant's margin of profit, and minute control over the movement of commodities—all undermined the basic pillars of this interdependent relationship between the government and its local allies. As the century progressed and new technological innovations such as railroads and telegraph lines greatly increased central government control, many in the merchant community must have felt a growing need to reconsider the advantages of Ottoman rule and to search for alternatives.

CONCLUSION

Nabulsi soap factories have been transforming oil into soap for hundreds of years, but the nineteenth century stands out as an exceptional period of dynamic growth and expansion. Precisely at a time when the interior regions of the Ottoman domains were falling prey to a new pattern of trade that used coastal cities to suck out raw materials and to heave back imported goods, an ancient manufacturing sector in a small interior city managed to grow and prosper without the introduction of new technology, the development of new techniques, the opening of new markets, or dependence on foreign investment capital. This expansion was organized by interior merchants who secured enormous and ever-increasing amounts of olive oil, who operated far-flung networks, especially with Egypt, Anatolia, and the Arabian Peninsula, and who managed relations with bedouin tribes, peasants, and townsmen on the east bank of the River Jordan, an area the Ottoman government itself did not even minimally control until the last quarter of the nineteenth century.

Just as the expansion of the soap industry was paralleled by a concentration of wealth and by integration of the various factors of production, the boundaries between political power, wealth, and social status were also melting away, turning these once-discrete roads to social mobility into a single avenue in which wealth came to predominate. The infiltration of merchants into the exclusive club of soap-factory owners began before the Egyptian occupation, as did the first sustained phase in the expansion of soap production. The new political atmosphere created in the 1830s and then sustained by a centralizing Ottoman government and its program of reforms helped to crystallize a new composite elite in Jabal Nablus anchored by the merchant community and to shape its world view.

From this perspective, perhaps the most important aspect of the tax strike and the battle over bids for oil collected as taxes-in-kind is that the soap merchants and factory owners of Nablus, despite the heterogeneity of their social backgrounds and their numerous political grudges, put up a united and stubborn political front over an extended period of time. In so doing, they acted remarkably, to borrow Marx's famous phrase, like a class in itself and for itself.

The exclusive club of soap-factory owners constituted the social core of this composite elite, and the Advisory Council served as its primary political vehicle. Drawing both on Nablus's long tradition of autonomy and on the exigencies of new economic and political realities, the council members engaged the Ottoman authorities in a discourse which actively sought to contest, filter, and direct the impact of Ottoman reforms in ways that best suited their interests. Both they and the Ottoman government displayed an enviable degree of patience and determination, at least on paper. In many ways this give-and-take process was to continue until 1917, when the British Empire replaced the Ottoman Empire as the ruler of Jabal Nablus.

Conclusion

On Sunday afternoon, April 17, 1859, a tall black slave accompanied by six young boys burst into the residence of the British vice-consul in Haifa. They had traveled in great haste and secrecy from the fortified village of Arraba, and as soon as they were all safely inside they closed the door behind them with a sigh of relief. Mary Eliza Rogers, sister of the vice-consul, described the startling scene:

> They looked frightened, fatigued and excited, as if they were seeking escape from some great danger. The boys caught hold of us, kissed our hands and our garments vehemently, and cried out: "Ya dakhaliek! Ya dakhaliek!" *i.e.* " *Oh, saviour!*" or "*Oh, protector!*" I immediately perceived that the boys were the sons and nephews of Saleh Bek Abdul Hady. The slave who was with them explained, in a few hurried words, that Arrabeh was being besieged by Turkish troops, assisted by the Jerrar and Tokan factions, and that the Abdul Hady family had no hope of being able to defend the town, so Saleh Bek sent his young sons away, to seek an asylum in Haifa. . . . The slave concluded by saying: "Thank God, I have seen these children in safety under the roof of my lord, their protector!" Then he hastened away before we could answer him.[1]

Salih Abd al-Hadi's decision to stretch the boundaries of bedouin customary law of protection into the domestic sphere of British subjects was neither arbitrary nor based on political sympathies for a foreign government.[2] As the former governor of Haifa he had, with great foresight, cultivated close relations with the Rogerses at a time when Jabal Nablus was caught in the grip of violent internal conflict that pitted his family against the Tuqans and their allies. He was a frequent chess partner of Mary Rogers, and she had visited his family both in Haifa and in Arraba on a number of occasions. In an intimate yet public diplomatic gesture, he even named his youngest daughter after her.³ In the desperate heat of the moment, he took advantage of this long-standing personal connection and assumed, correctly as it turned out, that the Ottoman authorities would not harm his sons once they were safely inside the vice-consulate.

Meanwhile, hundreds of Ottoman soldiers, supported by two field cannons and armed peasants mobilized by the Tuqan and Jarrar families, broke through the defenses of Arraba after a short but bloody battle. The village was plundered, its ramparts destroyed, and the large, fortified residences of the Abd al-Hadi family were dismantled, one stone at a time, by masons brought in specifically for that purpose.⁴

With the fall of Arraba, the centuries-long period of autonomy enjoyed by Jabal Nablus under Ottoman rule came to a formal end, as the Ottoman government had finally achieved a monopoly of the means of coercion and was able to impose direct political control. The Tuqan-Jarrar faction might have been on the winning side, but their victory was pyrrhic. After that day, native sons could no longer aspire to hold the position of *mutasallim*, Jabal Nablus would no longer be an arena for violent power struggles, and competition between leading families would be limited to maneuvering among merchant-led factions within the city council.⁵

It is ironic that the Ottoman government singled out the Abd al-Hadis for an object lesson for the people of Jabal Nablus on the true source of political authority and power while the family's distant relatives, the Jarrars, stood cheering outside the walls of Arraba. Of all the leading political families, both urban and rural, the Abd al-Hadis were the most aggressive in taking advantage of the winds of change and the Jarrars were the most stubborn in resisting them.

The Jarrar's once-formidable fortress at Sanur had long symbolized their leadership role in limiting direct Ottoman control by keeping the governors of Damascus at bay, thwarting the centralizing ambitions of the rulers of Acre, and defeating Musa *Beik* Tuqan's persistent attempts to singlehandedly rule all of Jabal Nablus. Yet, despite the opportunities that their military power and occasional victories created, they never made a concerted effort to establish a permanent base in the city, even though that was where the political and economic levers of power were located. Rather, they stuck to their rural roots until the last decades of Ottoman rule.

The Abd al-Hadis, in contrast, used Arraba as a springboard to penetrate the urban sphere. Immediately after they cemented their alliance with the new Egyptian rulers in the early 1830s, they purchased large residential compounds and a soap factory in the city. Over the next decade they consolidated their political and economic base by purchasing more soap factories as well as warehouses, shops, grain mills, oil presses, and orchards. At the same time, they invested heavily in the commercialization of agriculture, especially the export of grains to Europe, pioneered the concentration of landholding, and established wide-ranging moneylending networks. Throughout, they worked diligently to expand their business interests by cultivating close relations with the urban merchant community, the European consuls, and, of course, the Ottoman officials. It was precisely their economic success and growing political power that precipitated their violent bid for control of Jabal Nablus and consequently made them vulnerable to a crackdown by the central government.[6]

The divergent careers of these two families hint at who benefited and who lost during Jabal Nablus's long and labyrinthine journey from a politically fragmented and semiautonomous region to one that became more integrated and centralized on a number of levels: locally, as the hinterland was subordinated and absorbed into the city's political, economic, and legal orbits; regionally, as administrators and businessmen based in Beirut and Damascus began to wield real influence on the economic and political life of the Palestinian interior and as a centralizing Ottoman government consolidated its control by dispatching armed forces into the region and by coopting its leaders into new political and information-gathering institutions, such as the Advisory Council; and internationally, as Palestine as a whole was integrated into the European-dominated world economic system. These developments made Jabal Nablus ripe for the imposition of direct Ottoman rule in 1860: how else can we explain the ease of the Ottoman victory and the stability of the new political arrangement it augured?

The divergent careers of the Abd al-Hadi and Jarrar families also reveal the range of choices that the inhabitants of Jabal Nablus had in determining which paths they could choose along this journey. Options, of course, were limited, for both the pace and the trajectory of change were strongly influenced by the opportunities (or lack thereof) created by forces beyond local control. These forces, however, were sometimes taken advantage of, were at others times resisted, and were, in all cases, translated into the language of everyday life.

The socioeconomic transformation of Jabal Nablus, like that of many other interior regions in the Ottoman Empire during the eighteenth and nineteenth centuries was, therefore, neither a linear march into the modern period nor predicated on a sharp break with the past, the two points of departure for prevalent scholarship on Ottoman Palestine. Rather, many of the features associated with capitalist transformation had indigenous roots that were clearly evident before they were supposedly initiated by outside forces, and ingrained modes of social organization and cultural life, far from being shattered, proved highly resilient and adaptable. The meanings of modernity were redefined here, as they were everywhere, in uneven, contradictory, and internally differentiated ways, depending on the region, social group, period, and sectors of the economy in question.

THE LABYRINTHINE JOURNEY

During the seventeenth, eighteenth, and early nineteenth centuries the social space of Jabal Nablus grew geographically, demographically, and economically. In fits and starts its merchants and artisans benefited from the opportunities created by the imposition of Ottoman rule in terms of expanded regional trade and from the government's consistent efforts to safeguard and finance the annual pilgrimage caravans from Damascus to the Hijaz. The local political and religious leadership that emerged in the late seventeenth century proved to be stable, strong, and durable: Jabal Nablus was not caught in an unbreakable cycle of violent internal conflict, it shook off all attempts by the rulers of Acre and other regional powers to dominate it, and many of the leading political and religious families continued to exercise a significant degree of influence until virtually the end of the Ottoman period.

Over the course of the eighteenth century Nablus emerged as the trading and manufacturing center of Palestine, and its hinterland became the largest producer in all of Greater Syria of the single most important commodity exported to Europe: cotton. The expansion of commercial agriculture empowered Nablus's already strong merchant community by providing ample opportunities for investment in the production, trade, and processing of agricultural commodities. Neither the decentralized political structure in Jabal Nablus nor the weakness of the Ottoman government during this period proved to be serious obstacles to the accumulation of capital. On the contrary, merchants adapted to these circumstances by constructing resilient, flexible, and culturally rooted trade networks, which they successfully used to control the movement of commodities and to undermine the attempts by the rulers of Acre to monopolize the trade in cotton. These networks, for example, made Nablus the center of cotton processing and trade in Palestine, even though many of the cotton-producing villages were located closer to the port cities.

It was this set of circumstances that allowed Nablus to play a leading role in the capitalist transformation of Palestine during the eighteenth century and that set the stage for the accelerated pace of centralization during the nineteenth century. The spread of a money economy, greater urban control of peasant production, and the growing influence of a middle peasantry all eroded the material underpinnings of the vertical patronage networks that provided the hinterland with a critical degree of autonomy from the city for generations. Merchant networks, in other words, seriously undermined the power of subdistrict chiefs in the hinterland long before these chiefs were dealt severe political blows by the Egyptian invasion and the implementation of Ottoman reforms. By the mid-nineteenth century, both individual peasants and entire villages were inextricably enmeshed in commercial networks emanating both from the city and from the large central villages: moneylending became far more pervasive, taxes were more efficiently collected, and debt contracts were more strictly enforced. Well-to-do peasants began to enter into business partnerships with long-time ruling clans and learned how to take advantage of the latter's social and political connections for the purposes of speculation and investment. Eventually, the reproduction of urban business practices and legal norms on the village level fully exposed most peasants to the volatility of market forces, exacerbated social tensions within and between villages, increased disparities in landholdings, and undermined traditional loyalties.

These social and economic developments both precipitated and were driven by escalating political upheaval, as symbolized by the power struggles over the post of *mutasallim*. The Tuqan family's bid for control of the subdistrict of Bani Sa'ab in the 1760s marked the opening round of a process of political centralization in much the same pattern as seen elsewhere in the Ottoman domains. The pace of socioeconomic change, however, was slow and uneven enough to preclude resolution of these power struggles. This can be seen by contrasting the political economy of silk in Mount Lebanon with that of cotton in Jabal Nablus. In the former, silk production for French merchants transformed the mountain villages of the interior, because that was where mulberry trees flourished. In contrast, cotton production in the latter, also for French merchants, skirted the core concentration of highland villages, which remained olive based. This is one reason why *Amir* Bashir succeeded in subordinating the other ruling families of Mount Lebanon, whereas Musa *Beik* Tuqan, after two decades of aggressive and bloody maneuvers, failed to militarily overcome the subdistrict chiefs in Jabal Nablus.

The political vacuum created by the sudden demise of Musa *Beik* Tuqan in 1823 only quickened the process of urban domination of the hinterland as the merchant community, the only cohesive internal force, again took advantage of the stalemated political situation. The capital that accumulated during the prosperous eighteenth century (but that had been held in reserve during the upheavals of the preceding two decades) was now released. The 1820s, in effect, signaled the beginning of a vigorous investment campaign in agricultural production, urban real estate, regional trade, and, most important, the soap industry. The Egyptian occupation energized these trends. The primacy of the city, for example, was assured after Ibrahim Pasha, the Egyptian military commander, crushed the 1834 rebellion led largely by the subdistrict chiefs of Jabal Nablus. His economic and administrative policies—central control, encouragement of commercial agriculture, and establishment of advisory councils, to name but a few—also opened additional vistas for leading members of the merchant community and helped thrust them into positions of political authority.

The importance of local investment strategies in precipitating changes in the political economy of Jabal Nablus during the nineteenth century can be seen by contrasting the careers of two commodities: textiles and soap. Both had long been central to the urban economy of Nablus; both relied on home-grown cash crops (cotton and olive oil); and both were integrated into the same circuits of local and regional trade, with Cairo and Damascus as the nodal points. Yet by the early nineteenth century the textile sector had begun to stagnate, while the soap-manufacturing industry underwent a rapid and steady expansion. Why did the careers of these two commodities bifurcate?

The easy answer is that textiles had to compete with European machine-made goods, whereas soap did not. But European competition with locally manufactured textiles was not of great significance until the mid-nineteenth century, because the textile industry in Nablus was specialized in low- to medium-grade goods designed for the mass market. Also, European competition was offset by the availability of both raw materials and plentiful labor at low cost. In addition, the local market was difficult to penetrate: textile-merchant families had built, over generations, a resilient network of social and economic relations with villagers, making it very difficult for outside merchants to compete. In short, the textile sector in Nablus was strongest in precisely those areas in which the European competitors were weakest.

At the same time, however, the historical dependence on and popularity of Egyptian and Damascene textiles, as well as the increased importation of machine-made textiles from overseas, put limits on the expansion of local manufacturing, making it a poor choice for large capital investments. The textile trade also represented a piecemeal pattern of capital accumulation that was becoming less popular: capital was dispersed in countless small loans to peasants who purchased their clothes on credit and who, all too often, did not or could not pay their bills.

But the above arguments only tell half the story. They cannot explain the growth of the soap industry. One must, therefore, search for additional answers, and these can be found in the dynamics of capitalist transformation as defined by the Nabulsi merchants themselves. The merchants' focus on soap was partly due, first, to the fact that the commercialization of agriculture and the growing pervasiveness of moneylending had paved the way for greater merchant access to the surplus of the olive-based villages in the central highlands and, second, to their growing political power, which helped them acquire the means of production, soap factories, from the old ruling families.

The soap industry was tailor-made for the new circumstances: it was capital intensive and rewarded the concentration of wealth; it efficiently exploited the number one cash commodity of Jabal Nablus, olive oil; it consistently turned high profits and enjoyed a secure and expanding market share; it encouraged the accumulation of agricultural lands, especially olive groves; and its factories were akin to banks that anchored large moneylending networks. In addition, it endowed the owner with great prestige, for soap factories had long been symbols of power, wealth, and social status. In short, soap production combined manufacturing with the more popular strategies of capital accumulation in the Ottoman domains at that time: moneylending, landownership, urban real estate, and trade.

Unless investigated from below, the transformations in the political economy of Jabal Nablus would not be readily apparent. If one were to gaze at Nablus through the eyes of Western observers or the central Ottoman authorities, the most striking image, judging from their writings and reports, would be that of a city frozen in time, or at the very least of a population that stubbornly resisted any changes in its modes of economic, social, or cultural organization. Nor would this image be necessarily contradicted by the inhabitants themselves. Even today most Nabulsis, like their counterparts in other socially conservative regions of the interior, take great pride in clinging to customs and practices that reinforce their sense of local identification. But, as we have seen in any number of cases discussed in previous chapters, the meanings of tradition were being constantly redefined, and the apparent continuity masked very important transformations in the material foundations of daily life.

For example, the methods and technologies used in the production of soap have remained the same for centuries, albeit with minor changes such as the substitution of industrially produced caustic soda for *qilw*. Yet a process of capital accumulation during the nineteenth century changed the financial organization of soap production from one characterized by multiple partnerships and a division of labor between oil merchants and soap-factory owners to one characterized by concentration and vertical integration. Since World War II, one might also add, the olive oil used in soap production no longer comes from Palestinian villages: it is imported, mostly from Spain. This last fact alone has fundamentally changed the relationship between soap-factory owners and the peasants of Jabal Nablus. Similarly, the meanings of power and status were redefined along with the transformation in the social composition of soap-factory owners from old ruling political families to rich merchants.

Another example is the partial transformation of the *salam* moneylending contract from a time-honored mechanism for guaranteeing future supplies of raw materials to urban manufacturers and traders into one also used for the local organization of agricultural production for overseas exports. Similarly, regional textile-trade networks were reproduced, seemingly unchanged, for generations. Yet Nabulsi merchants shifted from being direct managers who pooled capital and opened offices abroad to middlemen for powerful trade houses in Beirut and Damascus, which used them as agents for infiltrating the interior. Finally, we have the example of the urban ruling families themselves. The Nimrs, for instance, played a leading role for most of the Ottoman period. But the defining core of their material base metamorphosed from *timar* land grants to tax-farms and, by the 1830s, to trade and urban real estate.

THE DISCOURSES OF MODERNITY

Over the course of the eighteenth and nineteenth centuries a new ruling elite and a new type of notable emerged in Jabal Nablus, as did a new political discourse. This elite was composed of the beneficiaries of the changing political economy of Jabal Nablus: those who had access to capital and who were willing to invest, primarily through moneylending, in the production, trade, and processing of agricultural commodities for regional and international markets. Merchants were in the best position to take advantage of the new opportunities, as were those families and individuals of the old political and religious elite who were willing to subordinate their pride and devote most of their energies to playing an aggressive role in business matters. Over time, the boundaries separating these formerly disparate groups collapsed as survivors within each, despite political differences and varying perceptions of their identity, came to share a material base characterized by a diverse portfolio: moneylending, land ownership, urban real estate, trade, and soap manufacturing.

The Nablus Advisory Council became the forum of this new composite elite of urban notables. These notables used the council to bargain with the Ottoman government over the boundaries of political authority and tried to promote their own interpretations of the meanings of citizenship, identity, custom, and tradition. The central government had little choice but to cooperate. It could not even replace the tax-farmers with a salaried expatriate bureaucratic cadre of its own, much less abolish the tax-farms as the reforms publicly intended to do. As late as the mid-nineteenth century, the only resident non-Nabulsi official with any authority was the head of customs. Newly appointed along with an assistant, his correspondence was full of bitter complaints against the council, which, in his opinion, worked diligently to undermine his authority.

The central government's attempt to play a much more direct and intrusive role in the affairs of Jabal Nablus through a local council that it did not fully control was bound to falter frequently. To complicate matters further, this new political discourse was conducted in the context of the fluid and transitional political atmosphere of the *Tanzimat* era, not to mention the dislocations caused by the Egyptian occupation. Thus the emergence of a new configuration of political reference points took place one crisis at a time: that is, through the accumulation of dozens of separate negotiated deals concerning specific issues, the outcomes of which spilled over into an ever-widening political and cultural space.

Most of these specific issues revolved around the struggle over access to and control of the rural surplus and its disposition and, consequently, over knowledge about the political economy of Jabal Nablus. Patiently and with remarkable persistence, the Ottoman government tried to gather information about a range of matters, from population figures to the bidding procedures for commodities collected as taxes-in-kind. Just as patiently and with great stubbornness, the Advisory Council members spoon-fed their insatiable superiors a constructed reality and often invoked a whole range of alleged traditions and customary practices (whether real or invented), which they insisted had to be respected. In each bargaining session, their responses to requests and admonitions from the central authorities were designed to facilitate their own objectives and, at the same time, to secure the state's recognition of their legitimacy.

The Nablus Advisory Council records provide many fascinating accounts of these encounters and of the tense and complicated give-and-take that ensued: the disputes over the composition of the council's membership, the monitoring of the movement of *zakhayir* (taxes collected in kind) into and out of storehouses, the bidding procedures for these taxes, the methods of storing olive oil, and the implementation of new customs regulations affecting the production and export of soap. In all of these disputes, two primary contradictions stood out. The first, faced by the central authorities, concerned the double role of new bureaucratic institutions such as the Advisory Council. On the one hand, these institutions were formed in order to implement the state's reform policies, especially those concerning tax collection and conscription. On the other hand, they were manned by the very social elements that stood to lose from an uncensored implementation of these policies. Instead of faithfully carrying out government instructions, these local elements used their official positions to resist, alter, and only selectively execute those measures that best suited their own interests.

For example, the council admitted into its ranks certain individuals who were specifically excluded by the state and excluded others who were supposed to hold a position. In one instance they not only included the *naqib al-ashraf* despite repeated warnings to the contrary, they also made him head of the council.[7] They also tried to reduce the number of people registered as inhabitants of Jabal Nablus, even though they, along with the shaykhs of the city's quarters and the subdistrict chiefs, put their signatures on the document containing the results of the population count immediately upon its completion.[8] The council members also politely but vigorously challenged the central government's efforts to free the bidding process on taxes collected in kind by sabotaging bids made by outsiders and, in one case, by refusing to sell olive oil to merchants not from their city. Most important, they waged a protracted tax strike, involving hundreds of thousands of piasters, that lasted for more than two years.

The second contradiction was faced by the council members. On the one hand, they needed the political legitimacy, administrative power, and control over the local militia, all of which were offered by the state, in order to protect their privileges and to enforce the expropriation of the rural surplus from a disgruntled peasantry. On the other hand, they could not prevent the state from using its leverage to make inroads on their share of the rural surplus or to stop it from slowly chipping away at their long-standing tradition of self-rule. The unequal relationship was illustrated by the fact that they were forced, albeit after long delays, to submit to the central government's selection procedures for membership in the council and to pay most of the taxes on soap exports that they had withheld.

Caught between the two were the peasants of Jabal Nablus. Disarmed, conscripted, indebted, and largely abandoned by their long-time subdistrict chiefs, peasants tried to capitalize on the ambiguous political boundaries and contradictions between the central government and the local elite. Through violent resistance and petitions, they tried to drag the state into arbitrating their disputes with the subdistrict chiefs and the notables of Jabal Nablus. Both of the petitions discussed in Chapter 4 called on the state to live up to two publicly held principles that, in their eyes, legitimated the state's right to tax its subjects: protection of the peasant base of production and accountability of all citizens before the law. Both principles posed a challenge to the exploitative practices of the local ruling elite, and both put limits on this elite's room for maneuvering.

In so doing, the peasants were signaling their openness to the possibility of transforming their loyalties or, more accurately, of extending their self-definition to include not only their village, clan, and district but also the state, in the sense of becoming citizens, not simply subjects. The Ottoman government constantly vacillated in its response to this open invitation, caught, as it were, between the need to centralize its control by co-opting local notables and the need to maintain its political legitimacy in the eyes of the peasants. Judging from its actions in Jabal Nablus up to the last quarter of the nineteenth century, the Ottoman government, when forced to choose sides, usually backed the urban notables, albeit with occasional admonishments and slaps on the wrist. Nevertheless, the peasants often succeeded in effectively dragging in the state. From this perspective, one can see how the processes of Ottoman centralization and political recategorization of the population could be driven from below as much as from above.

Peasants, in short, were not simply the goose that laid the golden egg—that is, passive objects of competition for access and control between local merchant communities, ruling families, the Ottoman government, and foreign businessmen. Rather, they were an internally differentiated community whose members were fully capable of adjusting to new circumstances. The accelerated commercialization of agriculture, the further spread of a money economy, and the decline of the power of rural chiefs created numerous opportunities, not just difficulties. Speculation in rural production and trade in agricultural commodities, for example, were activities in which almost anyone with capital, no matter how small, engaged in because they offered the most promising avenues for upward mobility. The nineteenth century, in particular, witnessed the growing influence of a middle peasantry that occupied a crucial mediating position between urban merchants and the mass of poorer peasants. By reproducing urban business, legal, and social practices at the village level, they amassed lands, constructed their own moneylending and trade networks, and eventually established shops and residences in the city. Their movement in increasing numbers to Nablus and other urban centers, especially those along the coast, can be considered one of the central social and cultural dynamics of the modern period. Indeed, if the role of this group in Egypt and Syria during the same period is any indication, their story needs to be told in detail if we are to have a clear understanding of the history of Palestine during the late Ottoman and Mandate periods.

Writing the middle peasantry into history is only one of a myriad of research projects needed to excavate the wide-open field of the social, cultural, and economic history of Ottoman Palestine. The period from the late sixteenth to the early eighteenth centuries remains largely unexcavated, even though it was during this time that the institutional and cultural practices of Ottoman rule became rooted, with all the consequences that entailed for the next two centuries. Similarly, Hebron, Nazareth, Gaza, and their hinterlands, to mention but a few places, still await systematic study for almost the entire Ottoman period, as do artisans, ulama, women, bedouin, and other social groups.

Detailed knowledge about these places and groups can have significant implications for our conceptualization of the dynamics of Palestinian society during the British Mandate, as well for understanding the context in which the Zionist movement laid the foundations for a future state. For example, one could argue that the pattern of Jewish settlements and land purchases was determined largely by ongoing political, demographic, and economic changes, such as the process of commoditization of land, which began prior to the 1858 land code. By the same token, the pronounced social dimensions of the 1936–1939 revolt against British rule revolved around the issues of debt, loss of land, vulnerability to the machinations of urban elites, and internal power struggles, all of which also had their origins in the Ottoman period. Similarly, if we were to draw a line around the areas where the small landholding peasantry was rooted and where population settlements were the most stable historically, we would get the Galilee and what is known today as the West Bank. It is not surprising, therefore, that the Galilee remains the heartland of the Palestinian-Arab community in Israel, nor was it simply a coincidence of war that the West Bank has become the geographical center of a future Palestinian state.

Similar arguments could be made on the political and cultural levels. A cursory look at the surnames of leading members of the Palestinian national movement, as well as at those of the Palestinian members of Jordanian cabinets over the past two generations, shows that a preponderant number belong to families that constituted the core of the new composite elite which emerged during the nineteenth century. Their political discourse, from speeches to actions, has been encoded by the experiences they and their ancestors had under Ottoman rule. Finally, until we can chart the economic, social, and cultural relations between the inhabitants of the various regions of Palestine during the Ottoman period, we cannot have a clear understanding of the politics of identity, nor can we confidently answer the questions of when, how, why, and in what ways Palestine became a nation in the minds of the people who call themselves Palestinians today.

Appendix 1 Weights and Measures

There was no single system or standard of weights and measures in Greater Syria during the eighteenth and nineteenth centuries, and the value of units carrying the same name varied from region to region, town to town, village to village, and even from one soap factory or granary to the next. As seen in Chapter 3, a measuring container could also be made to yield different results depending on who was giving and who was taking. None of this was unusual in agricultural societies that enjoyed a degree of autonomy from central state control. Nevertheless, the shift in the economic center of gravity to the coastal cities, the increasing importance of international trade, and greater urban control over the rural surplus all militated for standardization in the weighing and measuring of agricultural products.[1] A more intrusive Ottoman state set in motion a process of "creeping" standardization in Palestine beginning in the 1840s. Its basic concern was to rationalize taxes on the movement of goods through ports and city gates and to control the units with which taxes collected in kind were measured.[2] Whenever possible, I have defined the value of units on the basis of contemporary local sources, such as records of the Nablus Advisory Council. All of the following units, unless otherwise cited, are for the city of Nablus.[3] Measures of weight, it should be noted, were based on one common denominator: a grain of wheat.[4]

MEASURES OF WEIGHT

Dirham	Equal to 64 grains of wheat, or 3.2 grams[5]
Mithqal	Equal to 1.5 *dirhams*, or 4.8 grams
Uqiyya	Equal to 75 *dirhams*, or 240 grams
Uqqa	Equal to 400 *dirhams*, or 5.3 *uqiyyas*, or 1.28 kilograms
Ratel	Equal to 900 *dirhams*, or 12 *uqiyyas*, or 2.88 kilograms
Wazna	Equal to 10 *ratels*, or 28.8 kilograms
Qintar	Equal to 100 *ratels*, or 225 *uqqas*, or one camel load, or 288 kilograms[6]

MEASURES OF CAPACITY

Sa	A dry measure the value of which differed depending on the type of grain as well as on the locale. A *sa* of wheat in the city of Nablus was equal to 3 *ratels* and 4 *uqiyyas*, or 9.6 kilograms; and a *sa* of barley equaled 2.5 *ratels*, or 7.2 kilograms. In the subdistrict of Bani Sa'b, the values were 7.2 kilograms and 5.76 kilograms, respectively.
Mudd	Equal to 2 *sa*[7]
Tabba	Equal to 2 *mudd*, or 4 *sa*[8]
Kayla Istanbuliyya (*Islambuliyya* in local sources)	Equal to 35.27 liters. This became the standard unit of the Ottoman Empire in 1841.[9] On June 3, 1850, the Nablus Advisory Council was notified that they would soon receive a standardized measuring container, called *kayla islambuliyya*, in three sizes: 1/8, 1/4, and 1/2. All other measuring containers, the order continued, must be destroyed, and henceforth no one was to use the *irdabb* as a unit of measure.[10]
Irdabb	In the eighteenth and nineteenth centuries, an *irdabb* equaled 182 liters, or about 133.7 kilograms of wheat.[11]
Jar of olive oil	Equal to 16 *uqqas*[12]

UNITS OF LENGTH

Dhira of fabric	Equal to 68 centimeters
Hindaza of fabric	Equal to 65.6 centimeters[13]
Dhira of builders	Equal to 75 centimeters[14]

Appendix 2 Court Records, Judges, and Private Family Papers

)

The Islamic court records (*sijills*) of Palestine began to be collected and bound in 1923 on the initiative of *Hajj* Amin al-Husayni, then both *mufti* of Jerusalem and head of the Islamic Higher Council.[1] The Nablus *sijills* are located in the Nablus Islamic Court, and the ones used in this study are listed in Table 10. As indicated below, few records from the sixteenth through the eighteenth centuries have survived. A flash flood near the end of the eighteenth century apparently destroyed all but five volumes, and these cover only a handful of years.[2] From 1798 onward, the records are complete.

JUDGES OF THE NABLUS ISLAMIC COURT

The autonomy of Jabal Nablus within the context of Ottoman rule was reflected by the fact that Nabulsi families provided the judges of the Nablus Islamic court. Jerusalem was the official center of Palestine's judicial system because of its religious significance.[3] Its Islamic court was consistently assigned a high-ranking judge with the rank of *mulla*, who was directly answerable to *shaykh al-Islam*, the highest religious authority in the Ottoman Empire.[4] Until the last quarter of the nineteenth century, the Jerusalem judge was empowered to assign a deputy (*na'ib*) to each of Palestine's districts by sending an appointment letter, a copy of which was faithfully recorded in each district's Islamic court records.[5] These appointment letters show that the Jerusalem judge, typically a person from outside Palestine who served for no more than one year, usually confirmed a choice that was locally made. They also show that Mustafa Khammash and Abd al-Wahid Khammash, father and son, respectively, dominated

Table 10. Islamic Court Records of Nablus, 1655–1865

Volume Number	Period Covered	Number of Pages
1	1655–1658	360
2	1685–1689	432
3	1689–1692	194
4	1722–1726	351
5	1728–1729	186
6	1798–1807	370
7	1808–1817	402
8	1817–1830	432
9	1831–1839	417
10	1840–1847	307
11	1847–1850	193
12	1850–1860	382
13A	1860–1863	378
13B	1863–1865	244

SOURCES: NICR, 1–13B.

Note: The period covered and the number of pages of each volume in this table differs from the ones provided in Muhammad Adnan al-Bakhit, et al., *Kashshaf ihsa'i zamani li-sijillat al-mahakem al-shar'iyya wa al-awqaf al-islamiyya fi Bilad al-Sham* (Statistical and Chronological Index of the Islamic Court Records and Muslim *waqfs* in Greater Syria) (Amman, 1984), p. 199. They also differ from the list in Ramini, *Nablus fi al-qarn al-tasi ashar*, pp. 7–9. Both calculated the period covered by looking at the first and last pages of each volume. These volumes, however, consist of two parts: a listing of cases brought before the court starting from the first page and a chronological listing of all administrative correspondence received, starting from the last page and moving inward. The range of years covered by the second part is substantially longer than that covered by the first. The most important miscalculation is for Volume 7, which they date from 1808–1809 but which in fact covers the years 1808–1817. For many of the volumes they also miscalculated the number of pages.

this position for roughly four of the most turbulent decades of the nineteenth century, hence providing some stability to this important institution.[6]

PRIVATE FAMILY PAPERS

All of the private family documents used in this study are photocopies I made of originals that remain in private hands. In the references, each document is identified by the name of the family and by a reference number. Here, only the family name, time span covered, and types of documents are identified.

1. *Nimr Family Papers.* This is the private collection of Ihsan Nimr. It

contains a few hundred documents dating from the seventeenth through the nineteenth centuries. They span a wide range, from personal letters and business contracts to property purchases and *timar* land grants. They also include some documents collected from other families.

2. *Smadi Family Papers.* 1637–1881. Most of the documents deal with urban properties, business contracts, or lawsuits.

3. *Arafat Family Papers.* 1874–1923. Almost all of the documents are business records and correspondence of *Hajj* Isma'il Arafat.

4. *Burqawi Family Papers.* 1807–1893. Most of the documents concern acquisitions of property in and around the village of Dayr al-Ghusun.

5. *Tuqan Family Papers.* 1689–1866. Most of the documents deal with the purchase of lands and urban properties, especially during the early 1790s.

6. *Jardana Family Papers.* 1745–1839. The documents deal with purchases of urban properties, lawsuits, and *waqf* exchanges.

7. *Abd al-Hadi Family Papers.* 1842–1852 (including the Advisory Council Records). The documents deal with tax collection and soap production in the early 1840s.

8. *Khammash Family Papers.* 1723–1868. Most of the documents are *waqf* endowments.

9. *Khalaf Family Papers.* 1844–1883. All of the documents pertain to the same property, a house.

10. *Ya'ish Family Papers.* 1674. A *waqf* endowment.

Appendix 3 Soap Factories and the Process of Production

The physical layout of soap factories, the types of raw materials used, and the process of production remained remarkably the same throughout the Ottoman centuries and varied little from city to city in Greater Syria. However, the number and price of soap factories in Nablus as well as the volume of soap production increased significantly during the nineteenth century.

PHYSICAL LAYOUT AND THE PROCESS OF PRODUCTION

A typical soap factory in Nablus during the Ottoman period was made up of three basic parts.[1] The first part consisted of wells, located beneath the ground floor, in which olive oil was stored. The number of wells ranged from three to seven, and their capacity varied from five to thirty or more tons each.[2] The largest well was called "the lake" (al-bahra); the smallest, "the adjacent one" (al-janibi, pronounced al-jnayb). The second part took up the entire ground floor, which had a high ceiling designed to absorb heat from the cooking process. In the back and along the sides of the ground floor were storage rooms for the other raw materials: qilw and lime (shid),[3] as well as wood and crushed olive pits (jift).[4] A small room in the front served as an office. The soap-cooking center was usually located in the large, open space in the middle of the ground floor. This section contained the furnace room (qamim), a large copper vat (qidra, or halla), the "adjacent" oil well, fermentation pits for the qilw/shid mixture, and a water tank. The furnace was located below the ground level and reached via a short set of stairs. On top of the furnace sat the copper vat which weighed about one ton.[5] (These vats were expensive and often jointly owned, and/or owned separately from the soap factory itself).

Next to the furnace room was the "adjacent" oil well, which held exactly one vat's worth of olive oil (250 jars, or approximately five tons). The location and size of this well were designed to save measuring time and to conserve energy: by the time the first batch was cooked, the second would already be warm and ready to go. The third part of the soap factory, called *al-mafrash*, took up the entire second floor. There the cooked soap was spread, cut, dried, and packaged.

Soap production took place in stages, each lasting longer than the previous one. The first stage was preparation of *qilw/shid* mixture. The *qilw* was put into a stone urn or mortar (*jurn*) and pounded into a fine powder with a wooden pestle (*mihbash*). Meanwhile, the *shid* was spread in a shallow pit and soaked in water until it coagulated and dried. Then it was rolled and crushed into a fine powder. The two powders were then combined and put into a row of fermentation pits (*ahwad*, usually three to six in number) that were raised from the floor. Each pit was about 1 meter long, 70 centimeters wide, and 20 centimeters deep. Hot water was then released from a small spigot (*mibzal*) in the bottom of the copper vat (the oil remained on top) and poured on top of the mixture in the pits. As the water absorbed the chemical content of the mixture, it was allowed to drip slowly into an identical, albeit deeper, series of pits located below. This was repeated until the chemical content of the water reached a certain strength. That water was then added to the vat, so that the oil would absorb the chemicals, closing the cycle. This cycle was repeated dozens of times (an average of forty times) while the hot, liquid soap in the vat was stirred continuously with a long, oarlike piece of wood called the *dukshab*.

Controlling the soda content of the liquid soap as well as the speed of the coagulation process was the all-important task of the supervisor (*raʿis*). Taken out too early, the soap would not dry well. Taken out too late, the soap would become very hard and difficult to cut. The critical decision of when to stop the cooking process was based largely on the sense of smell. A round, 60-centimeter-long wooden stick, called *al-shammama*, was dipped into the liquid soap and then sniffed. If the supervisor thought it was ready, he passed the stick to the soap-factory owner for consultation. In case of disagreement, an expert was called in to render an opinion.

The cooking process took about eight days. This is why the product was and still is referred to as the *tabkha*, which loosely translates as "a cooked batch."[6] Each *tabkha* consumed 250 jars of oil (5,128 kilograms).[7] The large amount and expense of the oil involved often forced oil merchants to pool their resources in order to commission just one batch of soap. The other raw materials, usually provided by the soap-factory owner, amounted to approximately 7 qintars of *qilw*,[8] 10 qintars of *shid*,[9] and about 25 jars of water per *tabkha*.[10]

When the liquid soap was ready, it was carried in wooden barrels up to the *al-mafrash* via a steep set of stairs. There the soap was poured on the large floor and was contained by planks of wood about 3–5 centimeters high. After the soap firmed up, the uneven top layer was shaved off with a scraper (*mabshara*) to smooth the surface. Then strings dusted with white powder were stretched across at regular intervals a few centimeters above the surface and plucked, so that the powder fell and formed lines on top of the soap. Following these lines, workers holding a long, wooden stick with a sharp metal piece attached at the bottom cut the soap into cubes, each called a *falqa*.[11] Later, other workers put the factory's mark on each cube of soap by stamping it with a metal seal attached to a wooden hammer. The soap was then stacked into tall, hollow structures, called *tananir*, which were shaped like inverted cones. A space was left between each cube of soap for ventilation. The *al-mafrash* usually had long, high windows to speed up the drying process, which, depending on type of soap and its destination, took anywhere from three months to a year. After it dried, the soap was put into sacks and loaded onto camels for shipment. Each *tabkha* netted anywhere from 20 to 22.5 qintars, or roughly six tons, of soap.[12]

NUMBERS AND PRICES OF SOAP FACTORIES

In eighteenth- and nineteenth-century Nablus, most soap factories were located in the Habala, Yasmina, and Gharb quarters. With the doubling of soap-factory buildings after the mid-nineteenth century, the number of operational soap factories in the Gharb and Yasmina quarters grew, and most of the production became concentrated in the southern and western parts of the city, near what is today known as "Soap-Factories Street" (*shari al-masabin*).

It is not clear how many soap factories existed in Nablus during the eighteenth century. The extant records of the Islamic court for that time are limited to less than ten years, and there were only a few transactions involving soap factories. Not so for the nineteenth century. The records are fairly complete, and because soap production began to increase significantly by the mid-1820s, references to soap factories became more frequent as they were renovated, rented, sold, endowed as *waqf*, and fought over. Judging from these records, there were at least 13 soap-factory

Table 11. Soap Factories in Nablus, Early Nineteenth Century

Name	Quarter	Status
Yusifiyya[1]	Habala	Renovated
Bashawiyya[2]	Habala	Renovated
Sawwariyya[3]	Habala	Renovated
Rukabiyya[4]	Habala	Not operational
Bishtawiyya[5]	Yasmina	Functional
Sultaniyya[6]	Yasmina	Functional
Shunnariyya[7]	Yasmina	Not operational
Husniyya[8]	Yasmina	Renovated
Hallaqiyya[9]	Yasmina	Functional
Gharzaniyya[10]	Gharb	Not operational
Shaytaniyya[11]	Qaryun	Functional
Uthmaniyya[12]	Qaryun	Renovated
Shafi'iyya[13]	Qaysariyya	Not operational

SOURCES: NICR, 4–13B.

1. NICR, 5:81–82; 6:324; 9:397–398; 12:67–70; 13B:189–190.

2. NICR, 7:69–70, 203, 363; 8:281–283, 316, 325.

3. NICR, 5:81–82; 8:329; 9:77, 78, 206–207, 254–255, 393.

4. NICR, 6:11; 12:175–176, 252, 306–307, 372. This factory was renovated in the 1850s and became known as the Tahiriyya, after As'ad al-Tahir.

5. NICR, 5:84–85; 7:40; 12:122.

6. NICR, 6:348.

7. NICR, 6:269.

8. NICR, 6:165; 7:84; 9:94; 10:83–85; 12:154, 243. This factory could also have been known as the Tbeiliyya and/or the Ya'ishiyya (NICR, 6:264).

9. NICR, 8:328, 361; 9:151; 10:267; 11:94–97; 12:48–50.

10. NICR, 4:39; 7:346.

11. NICR, 7:92–93; 13A:95–96. This factory was also known as the Jaytaniyya.

12. NICR, 6:23; 8:316; 9:95; 9:399.

13. NICR, 6:98, 107.

buildings at the turn of the nineteenth century. Of these, four were described as abandoned, ruined, and/or transformed into residences and warehouses. Five others, said to be in bad need of repairs, were renovated by the late 1820s. Only four factories seemed to be fully functional (see Table 11). By the late 1820s, therefore, there were at least nine operational soap factories.

By 1860, there were 15 fully functional soap factories in Nablus, according to Rosen,[13] and by 1882 30 factories, according to a British trade report.[14] Tamimi and Bahjat, in a visit to Nablus during World War I, noted that there were 29 fully operational soap factories in Nablus, 23 of them large and the rest small.[15] In sum, from 1800 to 1917, the number of soap-factory buildings in Nablus doubled, and that of operational soap factories more than tripled. The first major phase of expansion in terms of facilities began in the 1820s, when a number of already existing factories were renovated and put back into production. The second phase began in the 1850s, when a number of new soap factories were built and/or already existing structures—such as tanneries, pottery works, and warehouses—were converted into soap factories.[16]

The available information indicates that prices for fully operational soap factories appreciated significantly, although the exact rate cannot be established or adjusted for the rate of devaluation of the piaster.[17] The Husniyya soap factory, for instance, cost 900 piasters in November 1802,[18] 1,800 piasters in September 1811,[19] and 120,000 piasters in June 1856.[20] The Hallaqiyya soap factory (along with some adjacent property) jumped from 10,500 piasters in December 1829 to roughly 28,000 piasters in September 1835 and to 50,000 piasters in January 1840.[21] In October 1834 the Shaqrawiyya soap factory was bought from the survivors of the recently executed Qasim al-Ahmad (leader of the 1834 revolt against the Egyptian occupation) for 16,000 piasters,[22] but it was worth 132,000 when it was acquired a generation later by a rich merchant over a two-year period (1860–1862).[23]

The above examples are meant only as a rough approximation of trends. The range of prices differed during the same period, sometimes widely, depending on the size, condition, equipment, and properties attached to each soap factory. The relationship with the buyer and political leverage also played important roles. Still, it makes sense that there was a steep rise in prices between 1800 and 1860. First, real estate values in general increased during this period, due to the growing population and to heavy investment by merchants in urban properties, especially after they gained access to political office in the 1840s. Second, it was far quicker, less expensive, and more convenient to acquire existing soap factories then to expand and renovate them, rather than to construct new ones, or to attempt to buy a series of properties from a myriad of families in order to convert already existing structures into suitable soap factories. After the initial wave of renovations had run its course by the late 1820s, however, demand for facilities began to outstrip the supply of available factories. Over the next three decades the prices of existing soap factories

Table 12. Soap Production in the Levant, 1837

City/Town	Tabkha
Aleppo	200–250
Idlib	100–120
Kilis	10–15
Damascus	100
Dayr al-Qamar	200
Jerusalem, Nablus, Gaza, Lydda, Ramla	500
Latakia, Tarsous, Adana	?

SOURCE: Bowring, *Commercial Statistics,* p. 19.

rose very quickly and soon reached the point at which it became cost effective to construct new ones, especially because soap production doubled soon after the mid-nineteenth century (see below). It must also be remembered, furthermore, that soap factories, once acquired, were almost immediately endowed as family (*ahli*) *waqfs* and, technically, were excluded from the real estate market. It was this combination of factors that caused the number of factories in Jabal Nablus to double after the mid-nineteenth century.

VOLUME OF PRODUCTION

Far more difficult to estimate is the volume of production, although there is little doubt that output increased significantly. The first reliable set of figures available can be calculated from Bowring's report on soap production in Greater Syria as a whole (Table 12).

All of the figures in Table 12 are estimates for a good year.[24] Bowring does not mention Tripoli, although other sources cite it as an important soap-manufacturing city.[25] For Latakia, Tartous, and Adana, he mentioned only that they produced "some quantities," implying that it was not much.[26] Still, it is clear that Palestine was the largest single source of soap in the Fertile Crescent. Unfortunately, Bowring does not distinguish among the cities of Palestine, but there is no doubt that Nablus was by far the largest soap-production center. As Schölch shows, for example, the doubling of soap exports from Palestine during the 1860s and 1870s went hand in hand with the doubling of the soap factories in Nablus.[27] In addition, Nablus accounted for thirty of the forty factories in Palestine during this period.[28]

The few available clues as to the volume of soap production in Nablus are not very helpful, though they bear exploring. One set of figures, for 1842–1843, was found among the Abd al-Hadi family papers.[29] This document contains a list of taxes on soap manufacturers calculated according to the number of *tabkhas* they cooked that year. In all, 75,240 piasters were assessed on 10 producers who cooked a total of 90 *tabkhas*. This unusually small number, it must be immediately pointed out, does not include the production of at least two soap factories, both owned by the Abd al-Hadis. The precedent for this practice was set in 1838, when soap producers agreed among each other to assess taxes according to the number of *tabkhas* except for those produced in the Shaqrawiyya and the Sawwariyya soap factories, both owned by the Abd al-Hadis.[30] The Abd al-Hadis were the most powerful ruling family in Palestine throughout the 1830s, and they obviously used their political clout to exempt themselves from taxes. It is not clear whether any of their allies were also exempted. It is also not clear from the document whether these taxes were calculated for the entire production of that year or only for those batches that, for one reason or another, had not been taxed.

Another major reason why the figure of 90 *tabkhas* is artificially low is that this document was drafted in 1852–1853: ten years after the fact. Underreporting of both rural and urban production and of the amount of taxes collected were, as one would expect, favorite practices of Nabulsi leaders, because true accounts would leave less in their pockets after they paid the Ottoman government its dues. Also, this document was submitted to the Nablus Advisory Council, whose members, all soap manufacturers, were then embroiled in a battle with the customs officials over taxes on soap production and export.[31] In such circumstances, they would have every incentive to underestimate the true amount of production.

The second figure is from Tamimi and Bahjat's report in 1917. They estimated that Nablus's factories produced an average of 400 *tabkhas* annually.[32] This also might be a low number, because when the authors broke down the production figures on the basis of which family produced how much, they only listed 12 families who, together, produced 317 *tabkhas*. In any case, the best educated guess that can be made at this time is that the annual volume of production in Nablus increased from roughly an average of 100 *tabkhas* at the turn of the nineteenth century to approximately 400 *tabkhas* during the early twentieth century.

Glossary

The following brief definitions are based on the context in which these terms appeared in the local sources.

Afandi   An honorific indicating a learned person, especially a religious scholar who held an official position.

Agha   A military chief; in Nablus usually associated with the Nimr ruling family who were referred to as the *aghawat.*

Beik   The same as Bey: a military/administrative rank; in Nablus usually associated with the ruling Tuqan family who were referred to as the *beikawat.*

Firman   An imperial edict.

Hajj   A pilgrimage to Mecca; an honorific indicating one who made the pilgrimage.

Khawaja   A rich merchant, either Muslim or non-Muslim.

Mufti   A juriconsultant.

Mutasallim   The same as a *qaʾimmaqam:* an official appointed by a governor of a province to be in charge of a district within that province.

Nahiya   A subdistrict.

Salam   An advance-purchase moneylending contract.

Sanjaq   The same as *liwa:* a district within a province.

Sayyid   The same as *sharif* (pl. *ashraf*): an honorific indicating an officially recognized descendant of the family of the Prophet Muhammad.

Shariʿa   Body of Muslim law.

Shaykh   An elder. In the city, used for religious scholars and heads of Sufi orders, artisan guilds, and city quarters. In rural areas, used for subdistrict chiefs, clan leaders, or heads of villages.

Sufi	A Muslim mystic.
Ulama	Body of Muslim religious officials and scholars.
Urf	Unwritten customary law; prevalent in the countryside.
Waqf	A religious endowment, either charitable (*khayri*) or for the benefit of the family and descendants of the endower (*ahli*).
Wilaya	A province.

Notes

INTRODUCTION

1. There was no administrative unit called Palestine during the Ottoman period. This name is used to denote the territories defined as Palestine during the British Mandate (1920–1948). It is doubtful whether the name Palestine was commonly used by the native population to refer to a specific territory or nation before the late nineteenth century. In official correspondence and court cases registered in the Nablus Islamic court up to 1865 the word appeared only once, and the context precluded a nationalist meaning. This is not to say that the idea of Palestine as a territorial unit, once it emerged as part of everyday political discourse among the inhabitants, had no local or Ottoman roots. This issue still awaits a systematic investigation. For a preliminary discussion, see Beshara Doumani, "Rediscovering Ottoman Palestine: Writing Palestinians into History," JPS, 21:2 (Winter 1992), pp. 9–10; and Alexander Schölch, *Palestine in Transformation, 1856–1882: Studies in Social, Economic, and Political Development* (Washington, D.C., 1993), pp. 9–17.

2. Throughout this book the name Nablus is used to refer to the city alone; and the name Jabal Nablus, to the city and its hinterland combined.

3. For example, Halil İnalcik, *Studies in Ottoman Social and Economic History* (London, 1985); Huri İslamoğlu-İnan, ed., *The Ottoman Empire and the World Economy* (Cambridge, England, 1987); and I. Metin Kunt, *The Sultan's Servants: The Transformation of Ottoman Provincial Government, 1550–1650* (New York, 1983).

4. For example, in chronological order, Abdel-Karim Rafeq, *The Province of Damascus, 1723–1783* (Beirut, 1966); André Raymond, *Artisans et commerçants au Caire au XVIIIe siècle*, 2 vols. (Damascus, 1973–1974); Leila Fawaz, *Merchants and Migrants in Nineteenth-Century Beirut* (Cambridge, Mass., 1983); Linda Schatkowski Schilcher, *Families in Politics: Damascene Factions and Estates of the Eighteenth and Nineteenth Centuries* (Stuttgart, 1985); James Reilly, "Origins of Peripheral Capitalism in the Damascus Region, 1830–1914" (Ph.D. diss., Georgetown University, 1987); Bruce Masters, *The Origins of Western Economic Dominance in the Middle East: Mercantilism and the Islamic Economy in Aleppo,*

1600–1750 (New York, 1988); and Abraham Marcus, *The Middle East on the Eve of Modernity: Aleppo in the Eighteenth Century* (New York, 1989).

5. The following are but a few examples of a large body of literature that ranges from modernization, dependency, and world-system frameworks to works that draw on Marxist theories. They are listed in chronological order: H. A. R. Gibb and Harold Bowen, *Islamic Society and the West*, 2 vols. (Oxford, 1951, 1957); Bernard Lewis, *The Emergence of Modern Turkey* (Oxford, 1961); William R. Polk and Richard L. Chambers, eds., *Beginnings of Modernization in the Middle East: The Nineteenth Century* (Chicago, 1968); İnalcik, *Studies*; Samir Amin, *Accumulation on a World Scale* (New York, 1974); Çağlar Keyder, "The Dissolution of the Asiatic Mode of Production," *Economy and Society* 5 (May 1976), pp. 178–196; Peter Gran, *Islamic Roots of Capitalism, Egypt 1760–1840* (Austin, Tex., 1979); Bruce McGowan, *Economic Life in Ottoman Europe* (Cambridge, England, 1981); Immanuel Wallerstein and Reşat Kasaba, "Incorporation into the World Economy: Change in the Structure of the Ottoman Empire, 1750–1839," in J.–L. Bacqué-Grammont and Paul Dumont, eds., *Économie et sociétés dans l'Empire ottoman fin du XVII–début du XXe siècle* (Paris, 1983), pp. 335–354; Şevket Pamuk, *Ottoman Empire and the World Economy, 1820–1913: Trade, Capital, and Production* (Cambridge, England, 1987); İslamoğlu-İnan, ed., *Ottoman Empire*; I. Smilianskaya, *Al-Buna al-iqtisadiyya wa-al-ijtima'iyya fi al-mashriq al-arabi ala masharif al-asr al-hadith* (Social and Economic Structures in the Arab East on the Eve of the Modern Period) (Beirut, 1989); Rifa'at Ali Abou El-Haj, *Formation of the Modern State in the Ottoman Empire, Sixteenth to Eighteenth Century* (Albany, N.Y., 1991).

6. One of the most useful works outlining these issues is Roger Owen, *The Middle East in the World Economy, 1800–1914* (London, 1981).

7. See, for example, Roger Owen, "The Middle East in the Eighteenth Century—An 'Islamic' Society in Decline? A Critique of Gibb and Bowen's *Islamic Society and the West*," *Review of Middle East Studies*, 1 (1975), pp. 101–112. An overview of previous critiques as well as a useful bibliography can be found in Huri İslamoğlu-İnan, "Introduction: 'Oriental Despotism' in World System Perspective," in İslamoğlu-İnan, ed., *Ottoman Empire*, pp. 1–24.

8. As of late, these areas have become the object of intensive but still mostly unpublished research. By way of example, see Antoine Abdel Nour, *Introduction à l'histoire urbaine de la Syrie ottomane, XVIe–XVIIIe siècle* (Beirut, 1982); Suraiya Faroqhi, *Towns and Townsmen of Ottoman Anatolia: Trade, Crafts and Food Production in an Urban Setting, 1520–1650* (Cambridge, England, 1984); Lucette Valensi, *Tunisian Peasants in the Eighteenth and Nineteenth Centuries* (Cambridge, England, and New York, 1985); Ken Cuno, *The Pasha's Peasants: Land, Society, and Economy in Lower Egypt, 1740–1858* (Cambridge, England, 1992); Alixa Naff, "A Social History of Zahle, the Principal Market Town in Nineteenth-Century Lebanon" (Ph.D. diss., University of California, Los Angeles, 1972); Hala Fattah, "The Development of the Regional Market in Iraq and the Gulf, 1800–1900" (Ph.D. diss., University of California, Los Angeles, 1986); and Dina Khoury, "The Political Economy of the Province of Mosul: 1700–1850" (Ph.D. diss., Georgetown University, 1987).

9. Gabriel Baer, "The Impact of Economic Change on Traditional Society in

Nineteenth Century Palestine," in Moshe Maʿoz, ed., *Studies on Palestine during the Ottoman Period* (Jerusalem, 1975), p. 495.

10. Alexander Schölch, "European Penetration and the Economic Development of Palestine, 1856–1882," in Roger Owen, ed., *Studies in the Economic and Social History of Palestine in the Nineteenth and Twentieth Centuries* (London, 1982), pp. 10–87. Schölch expanded this article and incorporated it into his book, *Palestine in Transformation*. See also Yaʿakov Firestone, "Production and Trade in an Islamic Context: Sharika Trade Contracts in the Transitional Economy of Northern Samaria, 1853–1943," IJMES, 6 (1975), pp. 185–209; Marwan Buheiry, "The Agricultural Exports of Southern Palestine 1885–1914," JPS, 10:4 (Summer 1981), pp. 61–81; and Haim Gerber, "Modernization in Nineteenth-Century Palestine: The Role of Foreign Trade," MES, 18 (1982), pp. 250–264.

11. Schölch, "European Penetration," p. 55. By Greater Syria I mean here the areas today known as Syria, Lebanon, Jordan, and Israel/Palestine.

12. For a similar periodization, see Schilcher, *Families in Politics*, pp. 76–77.

13. For a concise and provocative statement of this issue, see Janet L. Abu-Lughod, *Before European Hegemony: The World System, A.D. 1250–1350* (Oxford, 1989). For the Ottoman period, see Çağlar Keyder and Faruk Tabak, eds., *Landholding and Commercial Agriculture in the Middle East* (Albany, N.Y., 1991). For Egypt, see Cuno, *Pasha's Peasants*.

14. For example, C. A. Bayly, *Rulers, Townsmen and Bazaars: North Indian Society in the Age of British Expansionism, 1770–1870* (Cambridge, England, 1983); David Ludden, *Peasant History in South India* (Princeton, N.J., 1985); and Sugata Bose, ed., *South Asia and World Capitalism* (Delhi, 1990).

15. Albert Hourani, "Ottoman Reform and the Politics of Notables," in Polk and Chambers, eds., *Beginnings of Modernization*, pp. 41–68.

16. For example, Philip Khoury, *Urban Notables and Arab Nationalism: The Politics of Damascus, 1860–1920* (Cambridge, England, 1983).

17. Owen, *Middle East*, pp. 52–53.

18. For a similar characterization of the role of merchants in Greater Syria, see Dominique Chevalier, "De la production lente à l'économie dynamique en Syrie," *Annales*, 21 (1966), p. 67; and Owen, *Middle East*, pp. 88–89.

19. For a detailed discussion of the points that follow and comprehensive references to the arguments made, see Doumani, "Rediscovering Ottoman Palestine: Writing Palestinians into History."

20. See, for example, George Adam Smith, *Historical Geography of Palestine* (London, 1894). Smith dwelt in great detail on the religious significance of the Holy Land and provided maps so accurate that they were consulted by the British government in defining the borders of Palestine during the Versailles Conference in 1919. As far as he was concerned, however, the history of Palestine stopped in A.D. 634 , with the Arab conquest, and did not resume until Napoleon's invasion in 1798 except for the brief interlude of the Crusades. Thirteen centuries of continuous settlement by an Arabized Palestinian population are barely mentioned, and when they are, it is only to stress the inferiority and irrationality of the Orient as compared to the Occident.

21. For example, Abd al-Wahab al-Kayyali, *Tarikh Filastin al-hadith* (The Modern History of Palestine) (9th ed.; Beirut, 1985).

22. For example, Moshe Ma'oz, *Ottoman Reform in Syria and Palestine, 1840–1861: The Impact of the Tanzimat on Politics and Society* (Oxford, 1968), p. v; and Yehoshua Ben-Arieh, "The Population of the Large Towns in Palestine during the First Eighty Years of the Nineteenth Century According to Western Sources," in Ma'oz, ed., *Studies on Palestine*, p. 49. For a general critique of Israeli nationalist historiography on the Ottoman period, see Doumani, "Rediscovering Ottoman Palestine: Writing Palestinians into History," pp. 18–22; David Myers, "History as Ideology: The Case of Ben Zion Dinur, Zionist Historian 'Par Excellence,'" *Modern Judaism* 8:2 (May 1988), pp. 167–193; and Edward Said and Christopher Hitchens, eds., *Blaming the Victims: Spurious Scholarship and the Palestinian Question* (London and New York, 1988).

23. This was especially true in travelers' accounts and photographic images, both of which constantly referenced the Biblical period. For an insightful discussion of the latter genre, see Sarah Graham-Brown, *Palestinians and Their Society, 1880–1946: A Photographic Essay* (London and New York, 1980). Also, see Annelies Moors and Steven Machlin, "Postcards of Palestine: Interpreting Images," *Critique of Anthropology*, 7 (1987), pp. 61–77. Still, the output was so prolific that a great deal of invaluable information about economic, social, and cultural life was gathered during this period. For examples, see M. Volney, *Travels through Syria and Egypt in the Years 1783, 1784, and 1785* (2 vols.; London, 1788); John Lewis Burckhardt, *Travels in Syria and the Holy Land* (London, 1822); Smith, *Historical Geography*; Elizabeth Anne Finn, *Palestine Peasantry: Notes on Their Clans, Warfare, Religion and Laws* (London, 1923); James Finn, *Stirring Times: Or Records from Jerusalem Consular Chronicles of 1853 to 1856* (ed. Elizabeth Anne Finn; 2 vols.; London, 1878); Mary Eliza Rogers, *Domestic Life in Palestine* (London, 1862; reprint, London and New York, 1989); and P. J. Baldensperger, *The Immovable East: Studies of the People and Customs of Palestine* (Boston, 1913).

24. For example, see NIMR, 1:139; and Aref al-Aref, "The Closing Phase of Ottoman Rule in Jerusalem," in Ma'oz, ed., *Studies on Palestine*, pp. 334–340.

25. Amnon Cohen, *Palestine in the Eighteenth Century: Patterns of Government and Administration* (Jerusalem, 1973); and Ahmad Hasan Joudah, *Revolt in Palestine in the Eighteenth Century: The Era of Shaykh Zahir al-Umar* (Princeton, N.J., 1987). Both books focus on high politics and Ottoman administration. In contrast, a number of authors have written on the period before the supposed era of Ottoman decline: the sixteenth century. For example, see Uriel Heyd, *Ottoman Documents on Palestine, 1552–1615: A Study of the Firman According to the Muhimme Defteri* (Oxford, 1960); Wolf-Dieter Hütteroth and Kamal Abdulfattah, *Historical Geography of Palestine, Transjordan and Southern Syria in the Late Sixteenth Century* (Erlangen, Germany, 1977); Amnon Cohen and Bernard Lewis, *Population and Revenue in the Towns of Palestine in the Sixteenth Century* (Princeton, N.J., 1978); and Amnon Cohen's two books on Jerusalem: *Jewish Life under Islam: Jerusalem in the Sixteenth Century* (Cambridge, Mass., and London, 1984), and *Economic Life in Jerusalem* (Cambridge, England, 1989).

26. Some of these lacunae are just beginning to be addressed. For example, see two articles by Judith Tucker, "Marriage and Family in Nablus, 1720–1856: To-

wards a History of Arab Muslim Marriage," *Journal of Family History*, 13 (1988), pp. 165–179; and "Ties That Bound: Women and Family in Late Eighteenth- and Nineteenth-Century Nablus," in Nikkie Keddie and Beth Baron, eds., *Women in Middle Eastern History: Shifting Boundaries in Sex and Gender* (New Haven, Conn., and London, 1991), pp. 233–253. Also, see Annelies Moors, "Women and Property: A Historical-Anthropological Study of Women's Access to Property Through Inheritance, the Dower and Labour in Jabal Nablus, Palestine" (Ph.D. diss., University of Amsterdam, 1992); Suad M. Amiry, "Space, Kinship and Gender: The Social Dimensions of Peasant Architecture in Palestine" (Ph.D. diss., University of Edinburgh, 1987); and Ruba Kanaʿan, "Patronage and Style in Mercantile Residential Architecture of Ottoman Bilad al-Sham: The Nablus Region in the Nineteenth Century" (M.Phil. thesis, University of Oxford, 1993).

27. Fernand Braudel, *The Mediterranean and the Mediterranean World in the Age of Philip II* (2d ed., 2 vols.; New York, 1976), 1:14.

28. They rarely spent more than one or two nights. Usually, their stories revolved around the same icons: Jacob's well at the entrance of the valley, the ancient scrolls of the Samaritan community, the lush canopy of orchards and gardens surrounding the city, and the Roman ruins in the nearby village of Sebastya. See, for example, Walter Keating Kelly, *Syria and the Holy Land: Their Scenery and Their People* (London, 1844), pp. 410–435.

29. Finn, *Stirring Times*, 2:154.

30. These records are privately owned. To my knowledge, they are the only ones of their kind that exist for the entire Fertile Crescent, other than a volume covering one year (1844–1845) for Damascus. I am indebted to Lubna Abd al-Hadi for kindly facilitating my access to them. They consist almost entirely of letters and reports, the overwhelming majority of which are responses to inquiries from the governors of Sidon and Jerusalem about fiscal, political, and administrative matters. Regular reports were also sent to the military commander of the region concerning the provisioning of troops and conscription. There are also copies of a number of petitions and letters from peasants, merchants, and employees addressed to the council. There are no records of direct communication between the council and the central government in Istanbul or any minutes of meetings.

31. For details on the types of cases to be found in the Nablus Islamic court records and the difficulties they pose in terms of quantification and interpretation, see Beshara Doumani, "Merchants, the State, and Socioeconomic Change in Ottoman Palestine: The Nablus region, 1800–1860" (Ph.D. diss., Georgetown University, 1990), chap. 3.

32. I am indebted to Arjun Appadurai for this concept. See his article, "Introduction: Commodities and the Politics of Value," in Arjun Appadurai, ed., *The Social Life of Things* (Cambridge, England, 1986), pp. 3–63. He argues (p. 13) that "the commodity situation in the social life of any 'thing' be defined as the situation in which its exchangeability (past, present, or future) for some other thing is its socially relevant feature."

33. Grains were also key products of Jabal Nablus and no doubt played a crucial role in urban-rural relations. Surprisingly, however, the sources contained very little information on the grain trade, forcing its exclusion from this study. Monographs focusing on a particular commodity are not new in Ottoman history. See,

for example, Roger Owen, *Cotton and the Egyptian Economy, 1820–1914* (Oxford, 1969); and Schilcher, *Families in Politics*. The latter deals primarily with the grain trade.

CHAPTER 1

1. A person appointed by the governor (*wali*) of a province (*wilaya*) to head a district within that province was given the title of *mutasallim* and, later on, *qa'immaqam*. To translate these words as deputy-governor would be technically correct, but because Jabal Nablus was ruled by native sons for most of the Ottoman period, this translation would not adequately reflect the large degree of authority and autonomy they enjoyed in practice. Therefore, the transliterated terms will be used throughout this study.

2. NIMR, 1:210–211.

3. Separate *firmans* were sent to Hasan *Agha* Nimr, Khalil *Beik* Tuqan, and Shaykh Isa Burqawi, among others: NICR, 6:337–339, 341, 351, 353–354, 356–360, 362, 365, 370; and NIMR, 1:119, 206, 208, 216, 217. *Beik*, from Bey, is a military/administrative rank. In Nablus the ruling Tuqan and Nimr families were commonly referred to as the *Beikawat* and the *Aghawat*, respectively.

4. For a discussion of Ottoman military garrisons in Palestine during the eighteenth century, see Cohen, *Palestine*, pp. 270–292.

5. The timing of the *dawra* was determined by the departure of the annual pilgrimage caravan to the Holy Cities of Mecca and Medina. For details, see Rafeq, *Province of Damascus*, pp. 21–22; Karl Barbir, *Ottoman Rule in Damascus, 1708–1758* (Princeton, N.J., 1980), pp. 122–125; and NIMR, 1:111. For an example of annual campaigns by the central authorities in North Africa during the eighteenth and early nineteenth centuries, see Valensi, *Tunisian Peasants*, p. 229.

6. For an example from the sixteenth century, see Heyd, *Ottoman Documents*, pp. 92–93. Even though the Ottoman government became more effective in the collection of taxes by the mid-nineteenth century, there were still villages in Jabal Nablus at that time which had not paid some or all of their taxes since the Egyptian occupation a decade earlier (NMSR, pp. 152, 155–156). Jabal Nablus's reputation was widespread. John Mills, writing in the 1860s, noted: "No district in Syria has been more turbulent and less manageable to the Turkish government, than that of Nablus and the surrounding villages" (John Mills, *Three Months' Residence at Nablus and an Account of the Modern Samaritans* (London, 1864), p. 95).

7. NICR, 6:370.

8. JICR, 281:130–136. Also see Adel Manna, "The *Sijill* as Source for the Study of Palestine during the Ottoman Period, with Special Reference to the French Invasion," in David Kushner, ed., *Palestine in the Late Ottoman Period: Political, Social, and Economic Transformation* (Jerusalem, 1986), pp. 351–362.

9. NICR, 6:351, 353.

10. Ibid., 6:337. This *firman* was registered on February 23, 1801.

11. Ibid., 6:351.

12. NIMR, 1:226–243.

13. Ibid., 1:222–223. No confirmation of this claim was found. In a footnote,

Nimr explicitly traced the genealogy of this story to eyewitness accounts. However, it is also possible that this story actually originated from a similar incident that took place in 1832, when 600 Nabulsi irregulars stormed through Egyptian lines and entered Acre when it was besieged by the forces of Ibrahim Pasha (Mikhayil Mishaqa, *Muntakhabat min al-jawab alaiqtirah al-ahbab* (Selected Answers to Inquiries from Loved Ones) [ed. Asad Rustum and Subhi *Abu* Shaqra; Beirut, 1955; reprint, Beirut, 1985], p. 112).

14. NIMR, 1:225–236.

15. Mills, *Three Months' Residence*, p. 88.

16. For a general discussion, see Immanuel Wallerstein, *The Modern World System* (2 vols.; New York, 1974, 1980); and Fernand Braudel, *Civilization and Capitalism, 15th–18th Century*, vol. 2, *The Perspective of the World* (New York, 1986). For a comparative perspective on the dynamics of Aleppo as a social space within the context of Ottoman rule, see Masters, *Origins*, chap. 1.

17. J. Thomas, *Travels in Egypt and Palestine* (Philadelphia, 1853), p. 113. On the next page Thomas noted that the hinterland, "although finely diversified with hills...is almost everywhere cultivable, and in fact highly cultivated."

18. By way of example, John Mills concluded a detailed description with the words, "one of the richest and most delightful scenes in the whole country" (*Three Months' Residence*, p. 6). Crosby wrote that the olive groves around the city were so thick that his party did not see the town until they arrived at the gate. He then noted: "Everywhere were running streams and fountains, by the side of which grew pomegranates, magnolias, figs, olives, oranges, and apricots, in the greatest luxuriance and profusion" (Crosby [El-Mukattem], *Lands of the Moslem: A Narrative of Oriental Travel* [New York, 1851], pp. 293–295).

19. Shams al-Din al-Ansari, *Nukhbat al-dahr fi aja'ib al-barr wa al-bahr* (Time's Selected Wonders in Land and Sea) (St. Petersburg, Russia, 1866), p. 201.

20. Mills, *Three Months' Residence*, pp. 27–28.

21. H. B. Tristram, *Pathways to Palestine* (2 vols.; London, 1881–1882), 2:31–32.

22. A few Jewish families undoubtedly lived in Nablus sometime in the past, for a small stairway near the middle of the central marketplace was referred to as "the Jews' stairs" (*daraj al-yahud*). Their number must have been very small, for it did not warrant a Jewish representative on the local city council alongside those representing the Christian and Samaritan communities. In fact, Jewish individuals appeared in only three out of the thousands of cases registered in the Nablus Islamic court records between 1798 and 1865.

23. Christians also lived in some villages in Jabal Nablus. One example is the village of Rafidya. Nimr names the Christian families in Jabal Nablus and claims that many were "brought over" from Damascus and Jerusalem by his ancestors to work, among other things, as tanners, weavers, carpenters, jewelers, or ironsmiths. He also claims that a great many of them moved to Jerusalem, Jaffa, Salt, and Egypt when the manufacturing sector in Nablus started to decline (NIMR, 2:272–273).

24. The Church Missionary Society was founded in 1799. The school, in which classes of Muslim boys were segregated from those of Christian boys, was funded by the Anglo-Prussian Episcopal See, established in Jerusalem in 1841. See Finn,

Stirring Times, 1:389–390; 2:74, 149–154, 368. Also, see Mills, *Three Months' Residence*, pp. 97–103. For background on missionary activities in Palestine, see Schölch, *Palestine in Transformation*, chap. 3.

25. NIMR, 2:50; Tuqan Family Papers, 1.16; and NICR, 6:283, 11:145, 12:90. Although the Samaritan community was very small and generally poor, some of its members—such as al-Abd al-Samiri, Abd al-Latif al-Shalabi al-Samiri, and his son Isra'il—practically monopolized the sensitive positions of scribe and treasurer of the Nablus city government throughout the first half of the nineteenth century, partly because of their expertise in accounting but mostly because they lacked natural local allies. Presumably they were at the mercy of their masters and incapable of crossing them.

26. By the time carriage roads and railroad lines were laid in the late nineteenth century, the economic center of gravity had already shifted from the interior to the coastal cities of Jaffa and Haifa as the latter became the points of departure for the burgeoning trade with Europe.

27. Not enough information has been unearthed thus far concerning the dynamics of these networks prior to 1850. The important question—How "national" was the economy of Palestine during the Ottoman period?—is one that has yet to be systematically investigated.

28. For a discussion of the commercial interdependence between Egypt and Greater Syria, see Asad Rustum, *The Struggle of Mehmet Ali Pasha with Sultan Mahmud II and Some of Its Geographical Aspects* (Cairo, 1925).

29. Nablus was also close to the Damascus–Cairo coastal highway on the west. The Ottoman government's concern that functioning outposts be maintained for the security of travelers led them to earmark some of the taxes of Jabal Nablus, at least until the mid-eighteenth century, for supplying and manning these posts (NICR, 4:340; Heyd, *Ottoman Documents*, pp. 45–46).

30. Abdul-Rahim Abu-Husayn, *Provincial Leadership in Syria, 1575–1650* (Beirut, 1985), pp. 175–177. In 1708 the Damascus governor became commander of the Damascus caravan. After the mid-nineteenth century, the Damascus caravan began to decline in size and importance. For an historical overview, see Abdul-Karim Rafeq, "Qafilat al-hajj wa ahimmiyatuha fi al-ahd al-uthmani" (The Pilgrimage Caravan and Its Importance in the Ottoman Era), *Dirasat Tarikhiyya*, 6 (1981), pp. 5–28.

31. NIMR, 1:77.

32. As early as 1572, orders were issued to use some revenues from Palestine for meeting the expenses of this caravan (Heyd, *Ottoman Documents*, p. 119).

33. Barbir, *Ottoman Rule in Damascus*, p. 124.

34. For example, see the registration of the payment of 2,412 piasters by the Nabulsi tax clerk to the head of the tanners' guild (*dabbaghin*), Hajj Mahmud Kalbuna, in 1822–1823 (NICR, 8:420).

35. Letters regarding payment for the leather pouches, prices, and amounts produced during the mid-nineteenth century can be found in NMSR, pp. 163, 295–296, 307. By the mid-nineteenth century, Hebron began to outproduce Nablus in this regard.

36. NMSR, p. 307. Nabulsi artisans were also commissioned to make woolen sacks, ropes, and other miscellaneous items for the pilgrimage caravan. See

NMSR, pp. 295–296; and Ibrahim Awra, *Tarikh wilayat Sulayman basha al-adil* (History of the Reign of Sulayman Pasha the Just) (ed. Constantine Pasha al-Mukhlasi; Sidon, 1936), p. 290.

37. Doumani, "Merchants," chap. 3.

38. Beshara Doumani, "The Political Economy of Population Counts in Ottoman Palestine: Nablus, circa 1850," IJMES, 26 (1994), pp. 1–17.

39. Ibid., p. 15, n. 8. Also, see Cohen and Lewis, *Population and Revenue*, p. 21; and Hütteroth and Abdulfattah, *Historical Geography*, pp. 45–47, 61.

40. Peasant weddings were the backbone of the local textile trade in Nablus (see Chapter 2). The types of products that artisans made for peasants included: plows, pickaxes, sickles, cowbells, winnowing forks, threshing boards, wedding chests, kitchen implements (made of clay, wood, or copper), leather shoes, saddles, and jewelry. See Shukri Arraf, *Al-Ard' al-insan' wa al-juhd: Dirasa li hadaratina al-madiya ala ardina* (Land, Man, and Effort: A Study of Our Past Civilization on Our Land) (Acre, 1982), pp. 132–160.

41. These same six names appear in the sixteenth-century Ottoman cadastral surveys of Nablus (Cohen and Lewis, *Population and Revenue*, p. 147). Al-Habala was the largest quarter. Population growth led to the development of two subquarters: al-Arda and Tal al-Kreim.

42. Amiry, "Space, Kinship and Gender," pp. 97–103.

43. For a discussion of *urf* in the context of Nablus, see NIMR, 2:494–509. See also Jamil al-Salhut, *Al-Qada al-asha'iri* (Clan Law) (Acre, 1987). Various aspects of customary law differed from one region to another. The inhabitants of Jabal al-Khalil, for example, had their own particular set of codes called Abraham's Law (*shari'at Ibrahim*). See Finn, *Stirring Times*, 1:216.

44. Finn, *Stirring Times*, 1:216.

45. NMSR, pp. 279–280.

46. Rosemary Sayigh's study of how refugee camps in Lebanon were socially and physically constructed along village and clan lines is a case in point (*Palestinians: From Peasants to Revolutionaries* (London, 1979).

47. I am indebted for this information to Shawki Kassis, from Rama village near Nazareth.

48. See the discussion in Owen, *Middle East*, pp. 41–42.

49. Marj Ibn Amir, the wide, fertile plain that separates the central and northern hill regions, formed a natural boundary to the north, as did the Mediterranean Sea and the River Jordan in the west and east, respectively. There was no natural boundary separating Jabal Nablus from Jabal al-Quds, but the line tended to be drawn through the lands of Kafr Malik, Sinjil, Dayr Ghassana, and Rantis from east to west. The villages of Sinjil, Turmus Ayya, Lubban al-Sharqiyya, and Rantis were at one point or another under the control of the Jamma'in subdistrict chiefs in Jabal Nablus. For example, see the petition presented to the Nablus council by the peasants of Rantis, who complained that Shaykh Sadiq Rayyan had taken over some of their lands (NMSR, pp. 209, 211).

50. There was, for example, a marked concentration of mills in Wadi al-Far'a in the sixteenth century (Hütteroth and Abdulfattah, *Historical Geography*, p. 33).

51. The increased demand for grain was driven by the general rise in popula-

tion and by European merchants who were willing to pay high prices, especially during the Crimean War. For a general overview of the grain trade, see Schilcher, *Families in Politics*, pp. 75–78. This expansion eventually reached beyond the east bank of the River Jordan, especially after the Ottoman government reimposed its control in the late nineteenth century. See the next section for details.

52. Mustafa Murad al-Dabbagh, *Biladuna Filastin* (Our Country, Palestine), 11 vols. (Beirut, 1988), 6:438–439.

53. NMSR, p. 34. Similarly, the inhabitants of the largest village in northeast Jabal Nablus, Tubas, spent much of their time every year living in tents in order to work on their distant lands and to graze their flocks of sheep and goats (Dabbagh, *Biladuna*, 6:444–445).

54. A sizable portion of Marj Ibn Amir was eventually sold to Jewish settlers by the Lebanese Sursuq family. The metamorphosis of Marj Ibn Amir sheds a great deal of light on the larger socioeconomic transformations of Palestine, and the area is deserving of further study.

55. NMSR, pp. 18–19.

56. Some of the more important mother villages in the Nablus region are Tubas, Bayta, Dayr al-Ghusun, Ya'bad, Qabatya, Aqraba, Kafr Qaddum, Dayr Istya, Kafr Thuluth, Attil, and Umm al-Fahm. See Shukri Arraf, *Al-Qarya al-arabiyya al-filastiniyya: Mabna wa isti'malat aradi* (The Palestinian-Arab Village: Structure and Land Use) (Jerusalem, 1986), pp. 144–162.

57. This was not a new phenomenon but, rather, a cyclical one coinciding with periods of increased cultivation and relative security. For a comparative study of one "mother" village during the Roman-Byzantine times and the modern era, see David Grossman and Zeev Safrai, "Satellite Settlements in Western Samaria," *The Geographical Review*, 70 (1980), pp. 446–461.

58. The best of these lands were described in land-sale documents as "good for winter and summer crops." On such lands, peasants would normally plant wheat and barley every other winter and sow sesame and corn (*dhurra*) during the summers. For details about agricultural practices, see Nabil Badran, "Al-Rif al-filastini qabl al-harb al-alamiyya al-ula" (The Palestinian Countryside before the First World War), *Shu'un Filastiniyya*, 7 (March 1972), pp. 116–129.

59. Valensi, *Tunisian Peasants*, pp. 116–120.

60. Braudel, *The Mediterranean*, 1:236.

61. For Tunisia, see Valensi, *Tunisian Peasants*, pp. 223–228.

62. One such story, told to me by the elders of Bayt Wazan village in July 1990, concerned the building of Ahmad al-Qasim's house in the middle of their village sometime in the 1820s. Similar stories about other houses of the powerful Qasim clan were told to me by the elders of Jamma'in and Salfit villages. It is not clear whether olive oil helped make a significantly better mortar. More likely, the use of olive oil in these instances was a calculated expression of power, wealth, and conspicuous consumption.

63. The most detailed and comprehensive source on the political history of Jabal Nablus during the Ottoman period is Ihsan Nimr's *Tarikh Jabal Nablus wa al-Balqa* (History of Jabal Nablus and al-Balqa) (4 vols.; Nablus, 1936–1961), especially the first volume. Based on a wide variety of sources, including family papers, Islamic court records, and oral history, it provides an intimate, albeit often

unreliable, narrative by a native son. A helpful political overview that relies extensively on Nimr's work can be found in two articles by Meriam Hoexter: "The Role of the Qays and Yaman Factions in Local Political Divisions: Jabal Nablus Compared with the Judean Hills in the First Half of the Nineteenth Century," AAS, 9:3 (1973), pp. 249–311; and "Egyptian Involvement in the Politics of Notables in Palestine: Ibrahim Pasha in Jabal Nablus," in Amnon Cohen and Gabriel Baer, eds., *Egypt and Palestine: A Millennium of Association (868–1948)* (New York, 1984), pp. 190–213. A detailed compilation of information on Jabal Nablus during the Ottoman period from published Arabic sources is Muhammad Izzat Darwaza, *Al-Arab wa al-uruba fi haqabat al-taqallub al-turki min al-qarn al-thalith hatta al-qarn al-rabi ashar al-hijri* (Arabs and Arabism during the Upheavals of the Turkish Era from the Thirteenth to the Fourteenth Islamic Centuries) (11 vols.; 2d ed.), vol. 5, *Fi sharq al-Urdun wa Filastin* (In East Jordan and Palestine) (Sidon, 1981). Three other helpful works are Akram al-Ramini, *Nablus fi al-qarn al-tasi ashar* (Nablus in the Nineteenth Century) (Amman, 1977); Mustafa al-Abbasi, *Tarikh al Tuqan fi Jabal Nablus* (History of the Tuqan Household in Jabal Nablus) (Shfa'amr, Israel, 1990); and Walid Al-Arid, "XIX. Yüzyilda Cebel-i Nablus" (Ph.D. diss., Istanbul University, 1992).

64. Abdul-Karim Rafeq, *Al-Arab wa al-uthmaniyun, 1516–1916* (The Arabs and the Ottomans, 1516–1916) (Damascus, 1974), pp. 95–100; Hütteroth and Abdulfattah, *Historical Geography*, pp. 17–20.

65. Hütteroth and Abdulfattah, *Historical Geography*, pp. 5, 125–141.

66. Heyd, *Ottoman Documents*, pp. 96–97, 99.

67. Some of these still stand, especially in Bayt Wazan (Qasim) and Kur (Jayyusi). The most famous was the Jarrar compound in Sanur village, which had towers. For more information, see NIMR, 1:197–198.

68. Attempts to choose different leaders inevitably led to rebellions and to refusal to pay taxes. Consequently, the Ottoman government's freedom of choice in this matter was limited to appointing a brother or a cousin instead.

69. NIMR, 1:86.

70. Officially, the former generated no more than 20,000 akjas (an old Ottoman currency) annually, whereas the latter could go up to 100,000. For a subtle discussion of this institution, see Kunt, *Sultan's Servants*, pp. 9–14. A fairly comprehensive list of names of *timar* and *za'ama* holders in Jabal Nablus during the early eighteenth century can be found in NICR, 4:342; 5:8, 36. Remarkably, this arrangement, at least in its outer form, survived well into the nineteenth century. For example, a document dated June 29, 1852, lists the *timar* holders in Jabal Nablus and indicates whether they served in the armed escort contingent (*jarda*) of the pilgrimage caravan (NMSR, p. 223–225). Additional information can be gleaned from NMSR, pp. 215–216, 231, 301–302, and 306.

71. NIMR, 2:224–227. Nimr's contention is borne out by a list of revenues from Lajjun district in the sixteenth century, according to Ottoman cadastral survey records. The list shows that individuals with *timar* revenues from more than one village had these villages dispersed at separate geographical ends of the district (Hütteroth and Abdulfattah, *Historical Geography*, p. 103).

72. The Nimr papers show that *timar* villages in southeastern Jabal Nablus remained within the Nimr household for more than 200 years. Some examples

which show the mechanics of this process during the early part of the eighteenth century can be found in NICR, 4:342; 5:106, 176.

73. For examples of sale and purchase, see NICR, 4:125, 226, 269; 5:36, 62, 173, 175, 181. An example of *timar* rentals is in NICR, 4:101. All of these cases date from between the years 1723 and 1730. For the nineteenth century, see NICR, 8:366; 9:343. The latter case is dated December 22, 1837.

74. For example, NICR, 4:58. This document, dated mid-January 1724, shows that a peasant actually lost his land to a middleman who paid out the peasant's dues to the *timar* holder in advance. For the interweaving of *timar* with *iltizam* (tax farming), see NICR, 4:314, dated early April 1726.

75. NIMR, 2:459–460.

76. Some of the new leading families—such as the Tamimis, Jawharis, Khammashs, and Mir'is—came to dominate important posts in the religious hierarchy. Others—such as the ancestors of the Bishtawi, Nabulsi, and Sadder families—joined the merchant elite. Still others—such as the Nimrs, Shafi'is, Sultans, Akhramis, Bayrams, and Asqalans—retained their military orientation (NIMR, 1:86–105).

77. Early on, most began to avoid military duty by paying for replacements when called upon. In 1724, for example, Muhammad *Agha* Nimr arranged for the payment of one lump sum (2,000 piasters) on behalf of all 52 *timar* and *za'ama* holders (NICR, 4:341).

78. NIMR, 1:159–160

79. For example, Shaykh Yusuf Jarrar, who wrote the poem discussed above, was *mutasallim* of Nablus in 1772 (NIMR, 1:202–203, 205).

80. I am referring primarily to the political branch of this family, whose ancestor is Salih Pasha Tuqan. This branch carried the appellation *beik*, as opposed, for example, to the *khawaja* branch, which was mainly involved in trade. For the origins and history of the Tuqan family, see al-Abbasi, *Tarikh al Tuqan*.

81. His grandfather, *Hajj* Mahmud, was a rich merchant (NICR, 2:395–397). His father, Ibrahim *Agha*, secured a *za'ama* and served as a commander in the military contingent of the pilgrimage caravan. Other members of the Tuqan family also became *timar* holders (NICR, 5:181).

82. Ibid., 4:5–6.

83. Ibid., 4:12–13, 171.

84. Ibid., 4:340. Al-Abbasi, referring to the same document, mistakenly omitted Bani Sa'b from this list (*Tarikh al Tuqan*, p. 20). Nimr was also mistaken in claiming that Umar *Agha* Nimr was the *mutasallim* of Nablus at that time (NIMR, 1:131–132). This document shows that he was appointed by Salih Pasha Tuqan as his deputy, although the official appointment letter might have been issued from Damascus.

85. Shaykh Mansur was a subdistrict chief who, most likely, belonged to the Mansur branch of the Hajj Muhammad clan, the dominant one in this area of Jabal Nablus (NIMR, 2:185). This subdistrict later became known as Mashariq al-Baytawi in reference to Bayta, its seat (*kursi*) village.

86. Abu-Husayn, *Provincial Leadership*, pp. 155, 168–169, 172, 175–177.

87. Ibid., pp. 183–198; Heyd, *Ottoman Documents*, pp. 45–46.

88. Cohen, *Palestine*, pp. 158–160.

89. Amnon Cohen, basing himself on central Ottoman archives, took Nimr to task for including the Sha'rawiyya subdistrict in the *sanjaq* of Nablus instead of Lajjun (Cohen, *Palestine*, p. 165, n. 202). This document shows that Nimr was right all along. In fact, it casts doubt on Cohen's entire discussion of the Lajjun district, which assumes its integrity throughout the eighteenth century even though its urban center, Jenin, had long been under the control of the Jarrars.

90. For example, some of the holders of *timar* and *za'ama* properties in the Lajjun district resided in Nablus, not Jenin (NICR, 4:179). The Turabays did not make Nablus their headquarters, but their close connections to the city, particularly its merchant community, were such that they were sometimes referred to in the central Ottoman archives as the "shaykhs of Nablus" (Abu-Husayn, *Provincial Leadership*, pp. 185–186).

91. NICR, 5:178. For historical context, see NIMR, 1:107, 114, 117, 119–123, 134–135, 143–146; and al-Abbasi, *Tarikh al Tuqan*, pp. 63–67.

92. Rafeq, *Province of Damascus*, p. 130.

93. Abd al-Aziz Muhammad Awad, *Al-Idara al-uthmaniyya fi wilayat Suriyya, 1864–1914* A.D. (Ottoman Administration in the Province of Syria, 1864–1914) (Cairo, 1969), pp. 62–66, 72, 78.

94. For background on Zahir al-Umar from secondary sources, see Cohen, *Palestine*; Joudah, *Revolt in Palestine*; and Tawfiq Mu'ammar, *Zahir al-Umar: Kitab yatanawal tarikh al-Jalil khassatan wa al-bilad al-suriyya ammatan min sanat 1698 hatta sanat 1777* (Zahir al-Umar: A Book Dealing with the History of the Galilee in Particular and the Syrian Lands in General from the Year 1698 to the Year 1777) (Nazareth, 1979).

95. Uthman Pasha (1760–1771) and the Azm household, which held the post of Damascus governor nine times between 1725 and 1808 (Schilcher, *Families in Politics*, p. 30).

96. According to Ibrahim Awra, head scribe of one of the Acre governors, Acre was considered a life-grant *(malikana)* by the Ottoman government (*Tarikh*, p. 308).

97. Ibid., pp. 303–316.

98. In 1830 the leaders of Nablus rebelled against attempts by Abdullah Pasha to collect more than what was demanded from them by the *mutasallim* of Nablus (Mishaqa, *Muntakhabat*, pp. 108–109).

99. Barbir, *Ottoman Rule*, pp. 3–10.

100. For a general overview, see Halil İnalcik, "Centralization and Decentralization in Ottoman Administration," in Thomas Naff and Roger Owen, eds., *Studies in Eighteenth Century Islamic History* (Carbondale, Ill., and London, 1977), pp. 27–52. For the province of Damascus, see Rafeq, *Province of Damascus*, pp. 4–10; and Barbir, *Ottoman Rule*, pp. 81–110.

101. Mu'ammar, *Zahir al-Umar*, pp. 62–65.

102. For examples, see Awra, *Tarikh*, pp. 305–317.

103. NIMR, 1:156, 239–241. The Jayyusis, torn by internal splits, were then the weakest link in the chain of subdistrict chiefs.

104. Nimr argues, for example, that the Tuqan's strong ties to the Ottoman government were in large part due to the clever way in which they claimed credit for the defense of Nablus during the sieges by Zahir al-Umar (NIMR, 1:183–196).

105. Cohen, *Palestine*, pp. 70–77.

106. NIMR, 1:252; al-Abbasi, *Tarikh al Tuqan*, p. 97.

107. Ahmad Haidar Shihab, *Tarikh Ahmad basha Jazzar* (History of Ahmad Pasha Jazzar) (ed. Antoine Chibli and Ignace-Abdo Khalife; 2 vols.; Beirut, 1955), 1:102, 447–448.

108. The Abd al-Hadis were chiefs of the Sha'rawiyya subdistrict. They increased their power during this period by representing themselves as a counterweight to the Jarrars, their distant cousins.

109. NIMR, 1:243–299.

110. Ibid., 1:238–239, 243.

111. Ibid., 1:291.

112. The struggle with the Tuqans clearly exposed the Nimrs' already very limited political role. The Nimrs were important only in the sense that they led the urban opposition to the Tuqans. After the Egyptian occupation the Nimrs quietly turned their attention to business and real estate.

113. For example, see William R. Polk, *The Opening of South Lebanon, 1788–1840: A Study of the Impact of the West on the Middle East* (Cambridge, Mass., 1963); Ma'oz, *Ottoman Reform*; and Shimon Shamir, "Egyptian Rule (1832–1840) and the Beginning of the Modern Period in the History of Palestine," in Cohen and Baer, eds., *Egypt and Palestine*, pp. 214–231.

114. The literature on these events is extensive. Two of the more useful works are Asad Rustum, *The Royal Archives of Egypt and the Disturbances in Palestine, 1834* (Beirut, 1938); and S. N. Spyridon, "Annals of Palestine, 1821–1841," JPOS, 18 (1938), pp. 63–132. Rustum notes that the 1834 conscription order demanded the largest share from Nablus (*Disturbances in Palestine*, p. 53). Also see Asad Rustum, *Bashir bayna al-sultan wa al-aziz: 1804–1841* (Bashir Between the Sultan and the Khedive) (2 vols.; Beirut, 1956).

115. NMSR, p. 170. These villages were Tayba, Na'ura, Nin, Shatta, Solem, Tamra, and Arrana.

116. Ibid., pp. 104–105.

117. Raouf Sa'd Abujaber, *Pioneers over Jordan: The Frontier of Settlement in Transjordan, 1850–1914* (London, 1989); and Eugene Rogan, "Incorporating the Periphery: The Ottoman Extension of Direct Rule over Southeastern Syria (Transjordan), 1867–1914" (Ph.D. diss., Harvard University, 1991).

118. They were: the *mutasallim*, Sulayman *Beik* Tuqan; the judge, Muhammad Sulayman Khalidi, from Jerusalem; the *mufti* (juriconsultant), Ahmad Abu al-Hida Khammash; the *naqib al-ashraf*, Muhammad Murtada Hanbali; Abd al-Wahid Khammash (longest-serving *qadi* in nineteenth-century Nablus and temporarily replaced by Khalidi); Muhammad Shehada Khammash (a former judge and cousin of Abd al-Wahid Khammash); Abd al-Fattah *Agha* Nimr; and As'ad al-Tahir (ally of the Abd al-Hadi family). See NMSR, p. 19.

119. Ibid., p. 19; recorded on December 18, 1849. The letter had been received nine months earlier, in mid-March 1849. It summarized the regulations governing the functions, jurisdiction, and composition of advisory councils in the provinces (NICR, 11:160–161). The Nablus Advisory Council was charged with carrying out the government's policies, overseeing administrative and fiscal matters in Jabal Nablus as a whole, maintaining law and order, and supervising public works. For

a detailed history of this council and changes in the social composition of its members, see Doumani, "Merchants," pp. 140–168.

120. This edict was drafted by Reshid Pasha, author of the Hatt-i-Sherif of Gulhane which proclaimed the 1839 reforms. See Halil İnalcik, *Application of the Tanzimat and Its Social Effects* (Lisse, 1976), pp. 6–7.

121. For example, in the twelve times that the names of the council members were listed up to June, 1850, not once were members of the Samaritan and Christian communities mentioned. They did, however, appear regularly after this date (NMSR, pp. 8, 10–13, 17, 23–24, 29, 43–45).

122. Ibid., p. 19.

123. Ibid., p. 46.

124. Ibid., pp. 126, 129, 249, 252.

CHAPTER 2

1. NICR, 7:64–68. The wife, *Sayyida* Salha, daughter of *Sayyid* Abd al-Wahhab *Afandi* Fityani, came from a family of important religious figures and established textile merchants. She was his second wife and probably bore him four children, because nine of the thirteen were already adults in 1810. In fact, Abd al-Razzaq's third-oldest son, Ahmad, was married on the same day that his father had been married, seven years earlier, to *Sayyida* Salluh, daughter of *Sayyida Hajj* Muhammad *Afandi* Hashim Hanbali. The Hanbali family (named after the school of law to which it belonged) routinely held high religious posts such as *naqib al-ashraf* and was heavily invested in the soap industry (NICR, 6:161, dated June-July, 1803).

2. Clifford Geertz uses the word "clientelization" to describe a somewhat similar situation in the context of market exchanges in the bazaar of Sefrou, Morocco. In this case, however, he was mainly referring to the tendency of urban customers to buy repeatedly from and to establish a personal connection with specific purveyors, hence becoming enmeshed in a "system in which exchange is mediated across a thousand webs of informal contract." See Clifford Geertz, Mildred Geertz, and Lawrence Rosen, *Meaning and Order in Moroccan Society: Three Essays in Cultural Analysis* (Cambridge, England, 1979), p. 220.

3. For a comparative perspective, see David Seddon, *Moroccan Peasants: A Century of Change in the Eastern Rif, 1870–1970* (Folkestone, England, 1981), p. 92. See also Ted Swedenberg, "The Role of the Palestinian Peasantry in the Great Revolt (1936–1939)," in Edmund Burke III and Ira Lapidus, eds., *Islam, Politics and Social Movements* (Berkeley, Calif., 1988), pp. 172–177.

4. For a discussion of this and other points regarding the importance of textiles, see S. D. Goiten, *A Mediterranean Society: The Jewish Communities of the Arab World as Portrayed in the Documents of the Cairo Geniza*, vol. 1, *Economic Foundations* (Berkeley, Calif., 1967), p. 101.

5. Goiten noted that in the Cairo Geniza documents during the medieval period clothes were labeled as washed or secondhand, both of which testify to their importance (ibid., vol. 4, *Daily Life* (Berkeley, Calif., 1983), pp. 183–184.

6. This was not unique to either Nablus or this period. Goiten, for example, reached similar conclusions for Cairo in the medieval period (ibid., pp. 184–185).

7. Parents were and still are usually referred to as *umm* (mother of) or *abu* (father of) the eldest son, even if the first-born was a female.

8. The entire episode is described by John Mills, who lived in Abdullah's house during his stay in Nablus. In fact, the negotiations took place on neutral ground: his room (*Three Months' Residence*, pp. 155–159). It is interesting to note that the division of the clothes followed Islamic law (*shari'a*) rules for inheritance even though this case did not come before the court and no Muslim officials were present. One can only surmise that, as far as inheritance practices were concerned, the rules of Islamic law were so ingrained in the population as a whole that they were followed by non-Muslims.

9. Usually, each household (*dar*) consisted of a number of *buyut* (NICR, 13A:74).

10. I am indebted for the insight on the political use of clothes as gifts to Bernard Cohn, "Cloth, Clothes, and Colonialism: India in the Nineteenth Century," in A. B. Weiner and J. Schneider, eds., *Cloth and Human Experience* (New York, 1989), pp. 303–353.

11. Malik Masri, *Nabulsiyat* (Amman, 1990), pp. 45, 55, 77–79, 129, 146, 166, 175, 179, 216.

12. Ibid., p. 166. Interviews I conducted with young men and women in Nablus in 1986–1987 and in 1990 suggest that this ritual continues in most households.

13. Masri, *Nabulsiyat*, p. 163.

14. Arafat Family Papers, 1:29 (emphasis added). The letter was written in the local dialect and contained many grammatical mistakes, reflecting the inadequate education of its writer. The translation is not literal. A *dimaya* was the principal form of outerwear, especially for rural men, and *surtali* was a cotton/silk mix with vertical black stripes. See Nimir Serhan, *Mawsu'at al-folklore al-Filastini* (Encyclopedia of Palestinian Folklore) (2d ed.; 3 vols.; Amman, 1989), vol. 3, pp. 650, 684. *Dima* cloth, developed by Damascene artisans in the late 1850s partly as a response to increased competition from Europe, was a cotton version of the *alaja*, historically one of Damascus's most famous silk/cotton textile products. For details, see Sherry Vatter, "Journeymen Textile Weavers in Nineteenth-Century Damascus: A Collective Biography," in Edmund Burke III, ed., *Struggle and Survival in the Modern Middle East* (Berkeley, Calif., 1993), p. 85.

15. Muhammad Izzat Darwaza, *Mi'at am filastiniyya: Mudhakkirat wa tasjilat* (One Hundred Palestinian Years: Memories and Notes) (Damascus, 1984), p. 19. Darwaza's recollections were independently confirmed in a number of interviews with *Hajj* Khalil Atireh, a long-time merchant and head (*mukhtar*) of the Gharb quarter, June 9, 1988; Hani Arafat, son of one of largest textile merchants in Nablus, March 14, 1989; and Najib Arafat (b. 1901), son of *Hajj* Isma'il and himself a life-long textile merchant (August 8, 1990).

16. Rogers, *Domestic Life*, p. 263.

17. Mills, *Three Months' Residence*, pp. 88–89 (emphasis added). This market was still dominated by textile merchants in the early 1920s (Masri, *Nabulsiyat*, pp. 85–86).

18. This division might be related to the long power struggle between the Nimrs, who controlled the eastern half, and the Tuqans, who controlled the western half during the late eighteenth and early nineteenth centuries (NIMR, 1:192–

202, 225–299). This explanation, however, cannot fully account for the persistence of this division in the popular consciousness.

19. For a history of the Nabi Musa festival, see Kamil J. al-Asali, *Mawsim al-nabi Musa fi Filastin: Tarikh al-mawsim wa al-maqam* (The Nabi Musa Feast in Palestine: History of the Feast and the Sanctuary) (Amman, 1990).

20. Masri, *Nabulsiyat*, pp. 154–155.

21. Ibid., p. 171.

22. Interview with Najib Arafat.

23. The majority of merchant estates were probably not registered in the Islamic court. Hence the results of any sample based on a small absolute number of cases must be treated with caution. The following percentages should be viewed as general indicators, not empirically accurate figures.

24. NICR, 6:52, 197–199, 237, 251, 253, 318, 364; 7:64, 72, 372, 375, 386, 392; 8:226, 242, 269, 285, 304, 309, 376–377, 382, 390, 409, 421; 9:37, 70, 73–74, 141, 149, 172, 279, 324, 377; 10:8, 103, 118, 140, 142, 161, 221, 301; 11:8, 47; 12:99, 169, 204, 233. Because inheritance estates, as a rule, did not mention the occupation of the deceased, I considered only estates in which the commodities listed came in large quantities that could only be stored in warehouses of wholesale merchants and in which the value of these commodities constituted the bulk of the value of the estate as a whole. Thus retailers and local traders were not included, nor were owners and operators of certain economic enterprises such as mills. To determine the primary specialization, the most important factor considered was the type of commodities that made up the largest share by far of the total goods (that is, items not for personal use) listed in the estate.

25. For example, *Hajj* Isma'il Arafat, in addition to being a textile merchant, was both a soap manufacturer and a landowner—olive groves, not surprisingly, constituted the bulk of his holdings (Arafat Family Papers 1.34–1.47).

26. Furthermore, in a sample of 26 inheritance cases of artisans for the same period, those involved in textile production constituted, along with those of shoemakers, the largest group in terms of numbers among the artisan community. NICR, 6:137; 7:384; 8:372, 412, 427, 431; 9:6, 16, 96–97, 103, 117, 128, 286; 10:34, 60, 174, 250; 11:33, 61, 156; 12:75, 93, 97, 169. Again, these percentages must be treated cautiously. There is no doubt that artisans who worked in textiles far outnumbered all other artisans, but the location of most production facilities in private homes and the prevalence of a putting-out system skewed the sample.

27. Interview with Najib Arafat. The bulk of information on the Arafat family was gathered from cases registered in the Islamic law court, such as inheritance estates, *waqf* endowments, lawsuits, and property transactions. This was supplemented by a collection of family papers, kindly provided to me by Saba Amr Isma'il Arafat, as well as by interviews with Najib Isma'il Muhammad Arafat, himself a long-time textile merchant; Hani Tawfiq Ahmad Arafat; and Ibtihaj Said Umar Arafat (January 10, 1993).

28. For a discussion of the "affirmation of identity" genre in Palestinian historiography, see Doumani, "Rediscovering Ottoman Palestine: Writing Palestinians into History," pp. 13–17.

29. For example, Abd al-Razzaq's nephew, Muhyi al-Din, bought a soap factory

in 1829 (NICR, 8:328, 361). One of his great-grandchildren, however, was an artisan who produced cords, braids, and other trimmings (NICR, 13B:218).

30. According to Saba Arafat (letter, April 4, 1993), this family produced the city's first professionally trained doctor (Nuʿman Saʿid), pharmacist (Nur al-Din Saʿid), and architect (Tawfiq Abd al-Fattah). All were educated in Istanbul early in the twentieth century. Masri refers to the "Arafat Pharmacy" in his neighborhood during the early Mandate period (*Nabulsiyat*, p. 92).

31. NICR, 6:198, 237, 251; 7:64–68, 109; 8:304; 9:70, 73, 141, 324; 10:8, 221, 301).

32. Ibid., 4:26, 161.

33. Ibid., 10:221.

34. He was also a landowner and founding member of the Mustashfa al-Watani (National Hospital), the first of its kind in Nablus (NIMR, 3:28, 80).

35. Interviews with Najib and Hani Arafat.

36. The second-oldest male child, Shaykh Amr, owned a soap factory (interview with Najib Arafat, son of Ismaʿil's second wife). His oldest half-brother, Ahmad, owned a textile shop on the western end of Khan al-Tujjar.

37. Letter to the author, April 4, 1993.

38. Interviews with Najib and Hani Arafat.

39. By the end of the nineteenth century, this practice was discontinued for the most part, and attaching a surname for individuals was slowly institutionalized. Among the causes of this development were urbanization, the breakup of clans and individuation of the family, the extension of central control to the rural areas, and the need of the new Ottoman bureaucracy to keep extensive records for social control.

40. Masri's memoirs contain many fascinating details about the dynamics of a typical textile-merchant household (*Nabulsiyat*, pp. 29–43, 75–77).

41. The Islamic court was often resorted to in order to prevent such instances from occurring. This is why most of the inheritance estates brought before the judge for resolution involved minors and/or other areas of real or potential dispute.

42. The most common reason for changing or adopting a family name is a change of location. Many Nablus families are called by the name of the village or town or county they originally came from. Other reasons, to the extent that they can be linguistically discerned, include a particular occupation, a prominent physical feature, or peculiar events.

43. The Khammashs, for example, share an ancestor with the Jawharis, but by the eighteenth century they had managed to carve a distinct place for themselves, and by the early nineteenth century they had come to dominate leading religious positions in Nablus.

44. NICR, 4:51.

45. Ibid., 4:51, 69.

46. See a dispute over this *waqf* in which Ammun, the granddaughter of Abd al-Razzaq's brother, Abd al-Ghani, wins a case against the *waqf* superintendent who had withheld her share (ibid., 13B:97–98).

47. The fact that his uncle died without male children may have contributed significantly to the concentration of the family's resources in his hand, for he was the oldest son of one of the three brothers (ibid., 4:51).

48. At least three of them were learned shaykhs.

49. Around the same time, other descendants retained the family name Shahid, which continues to the present. The infrequency of references to this family in the court records, at least in comparison with the Arafats, suggests that they were less wealthy.

50. The information contained in the family tree, including the religious titles, was gathered from the first fourteen volumes of the Nablus Islamic Court records. The Arafats' official family tree, as compiled by them, differs in some respects from the one used in this study. For consistency, I have relied solely on the court records.

51. Letter to the author, April 4, 1993.

52. For example, Shaykh Abd al-Rahim Arafat married his cousin, Khadija, daughter of Shaykh *Hajj* Abdullah Arafat (NICR, 8:233); and Khadija's brother, *Sayyid* Ibrahim, married his cousin, Aysha, daughter of Shaykh Abd Al-Razzaq Arafat (ibid., 6:198). Aysha, incidentally, was previously married to *Sayyid* Ibrahim's brother, *Sayyid* Ahmad (ibid.). It was not unusual for a man to wed his brother's widow in order to support his nephews and nieces and to keep the property within the household. For other examples of Arafat-Arafat marriages, see ibid., 6:71; 8:231; 11:6, 101; 12:23.

53. Ibid., 7:64, 171.

54. Ibid., 6:36, 171; 7:64–68. In the mid-1930s Shaykh Amr Arafat, son of *Hajj* Isma'il, supervised the reconstruction of the Nasr Mosque, which had suffered severe damage in a 1927 earthquake (letter from Saba Arafat, April 4, 1993).

55. NICR, 6:171; 7:307, 350, 375; 8:233; 9:96; 10:221; 12:99–100, 113; 13A:123. Examples of extensive economic and cultural ties among the Arafats and these families can be found in ibid., 6:260–264; 8:233, 281–283; 9:73, 393; 10:261; 11:6, 30, 101, 115, 172; 12:135, 242; 13B:141–143.

56. During the late nineteenth century, many Arafat males resumed their religious education.

57. This was confirmed in an interview with Najib Arafat.

58. For example, NICR, 6:64–65, 228, 250, 252; 7:109; 8:233, 304, 409; 9:96; 11:101; 12:99–100, 233; 13B:141–144. Some members of the Arafat family were also co-owners of property in the commercial center of Nablus with the Abd al-Hadi and Tuffaha families.

59. See, for example, the estates of merchants from Mosul, Beirut, and Aleppo who died in Nablus while on business (ibid., 7:395; 8:284; 9:75).

60. It must be noted here that the reliance on textiles as an example of regional and local trade networks can give the misleading impression that subregional trade networks were of little importance. The social life of grain, for example, would emphasize those connections.

61. After his oldest son, Ahmad, died during a pilgrimage to Mecca, *Hajj* Abdullah asked his wife and female children to choose legal agents. He then gathered them in court, along with his one remaining son, Ibrahim, in order to divide up his estate as if he had already died. This was done in the same manner as all other estates. He only asked that he receive a daily stipend from Ibrahim on behalf of himself, his wife, one of his daughters, and the two daughters of his deceased son. He died sometime between 1805 and 1812 (NICR, 6:193, 198). *Saya* is yet another

type of blended cotton/silk cloth with bright colors and vertical stripes used to make outergarments for men and women. *Thiyab* (sing. *thawb*) is a light cotton ready-made robe. *Baladi* means locally made. Darwaza notes that *malti* cloth was imported from England, probably via Malta (*Mi'at am*, p. 71).

62. In addition to the Arafats, some of the families of textile merchants who did business primarily with Egypt are: Fityan, Nabulsi, Abd al-Muhsin, Ghazzawi, Balbisi, Darwish-Ahmad, Kawkash, Bishtawi, Zu'aytar, Masri, Qutub, and Tuffaha (NICR, 6:198, 237; 7:64, 109, 386; 8:242; 9:212; 10:8; 221).

63. Ibid., 7:109.

64. They were *Sayyid Hajj* Hasan Tuffaha Husayni, *Sayyid* Muhammad Kawkash, Muhammad Bishtawi, Yusuf Murad Balbisi, and the beneficiaries of the deceased merchant, *Hajj* Abdullah Darwish-Ahmad.

65. NICR, 13B:125–127.

66. Ibid., 7:386.

67. Mikhayil Mishaqa, a well-known Lebanese contemporary chronicler, was for three years a member of this expatriate community of Levant merchants living in Damietta during the early nineteenth century and wrote about his experiences there (*Muntakhabat*, pp. 63–67).

68. NIMR, 2:296.

69. NICR, 9:212.

70. For example, in January 1806 a dispute arose over who was to be the legal guardian of the children of Husayn *Beik* Jurri, who died while conducting business in Egypt. Witnesses and business partners involved included members from the Arafat, Shahid, Tuffaha, Bashsha, and Kawkash families (ibid., 6:228).

71. Ibid., 13B:141–143. Settlements of very large estates in Nablus and elsewhere in Palestine were routinely referred to the Jerusalem Islamic court judge, who, because of his higher rank, had the prerogative in such matters.

72. Ibid., 6:198; 7:64; 10:221.

73. This included the soap production of Nablus, Gaza, Lydda, and Ramla. See John Bowring, *Report on the Commercial Statistics of Syria* (London, 1840; reprint, New York, 1973), p. 19.

74. The relationship was of long standing: in the sixteenth century, Egyptian merchants invested large amounts of capital in promoting local production and export of Jerusalem soap to Egypt (Cohen, *Jewish Life*, p. 193). Export statistics show that most of Palestine's soap was sent to Egypt in the second half of the nineteenth century (Schölch, "European Penetration," pp. 13, 50, 53; Buheiry, "Agricultural Exports," p. 73). Finally, Sarah Graham-Brown estimated that during the Mandate period Egypt consumed approximately one-half of the soap output of Nablus ("The Political Economy of Jabal Nablus, 1920–1948," in Owen, ed., *Studies*, p. 140).

75. He bought it sometime during the last quarter of the nineteenth century. This factory was later sold by his children from his second wife to the Abd al-Hadi family, in whose possession it remains (Saba Arafat, letters to the author, August 8 and December 12, 1993).

76. Interview, August 8, 1990.

77. Darwaza, *Mi'at am*, p. 71. Judging from the name, *mansuri* cloth must originally have been an imitation of an Egyptian cloth.

78. See, for example, Vatter, "Journeymen Textile Weavers."

79. Darwaza, *Mi'at am*, pp. 70–77.

80. They came from al-Arish (northern Sinai).

81. Interviews with Najib and Hani Arafat. Saba Arafat recalls that members of the Haffar and Mansur families visited Tawfiq Arafat's house in Nablus on more than one occasion (letter, April 4, 1993). Darwaza mentions the Haffars first in his list of Damascene agents and tells of the close relations between Damascene agents and Nabulsi merchants in general *(Mi'at am*, pp. 71, 74). Masri relates how *Hajj* Amin Haffar, a close friend of his father's, invited him for a feast in his house while he was visiting Damascus (*Nabulsiyat*, pp. 140–141).

82. In addition to the Haffars, they usually were members of the Mansur, Khattab, and Tuban families.

83. Arafat Family Papers, 1.1.

84. NICR, 13A:191. For similar examples, see ibid., 13A:237, 258.

85. Nimr Family Papers, 3.5.9.

86. Even in Egypt, soap was sometimes was used in lieu of money in commercial transactions and in the repayment of loans. For example, see Cuno, *Pasha's Peasants*, p. 58.

87. *Haddars* are usually remembered as owners of portable textile shops on donkeys who always appeared during the harvest season (for example, interviews with *Hajj* Sharif Kamil Jarrar [b. 1897], from the village of Burqin, July 17, 1990; and Muhammad Fayyad Muhammad Bushnaq [b. 1905], from the village of Rummana, July 17, 1990).

88. These were the most frequently mentioned among the more than thirty villages registered in Shaykh Abd al-Razzaq's inheritance estate. They are also mentioned in the estates of his brother, Abdullah, and his grandson, Sa'id (NICR, 6:198; 7:64–68; 10:221).

89. Arafat Family Papers, 1.5, 1.6, 1.11, 1.29.

90. Interview with Najib Arafat. Most of the business was with the village of Sanur. They also had occasional agents in the village of Qabatya.

91. Arafat Family Papers, 1.9, 1.19.

92. Ibid., 1.19.

93. Almost all of the sources mention these important outreach activities. See, for example, accounts of weddings in the villages of Qabalan and Tubas that were attended by Malik Masri and his father (*Nabulsiyat*, pp. 55–61, 203–204).

94. Arafat Family Papers, 1.1 (emphasis added). Haffari refers to cloth made in the factory of the Damascene Haffar family, as discussed above. A fixed color was one that would not bleed or run when the garment was washed. I have not been able to discover the meaning of *ibrim ansiri*.

95. For a discussion of the socioeconomic and cultural aspects of weddings in Palestinian villages, as well as of the importance of the village collective to marriage rituals, see Serhan, *Mawsu'at*, vol. 1, pp. 279–294.

96. Interview with Najib Arafat; Serhan, *Mawsu'at*, vol. 2, p. 293.

97. Darwaza, *Mi'at am*, p. 55.

98. Ibid., p. 70.

99. Thus one can speak of a *kiswa* as a wardrobe for a wedding, for a graduation, or for a pilgrimage or simply as a new set of clothes to replace one that is

worn out or no longer fits (interview with Najib Arafat). A detailed description of types of clothes for these special occasions can be gleaned from Malik Masri's description of the *kiswas* he acquired while growing up (*Nabulsiyat*, pp. 45, 55, 77–79, 129, 146, 166, 175, 179, 216).

100. Darwaza, *Mi'at am*, p. 70.

101. Masri, *Nabulsiyat*, pp. 209–210.

102. Ibid., pp. 207–210; Serhan, *Mawsu'at*, vol. 2, pp. 298–299.

103. Arafat Family Papers, 1.1–1.3, 1.5–1.6, 1.9, 1.11–1.13, 1.19, 1.21, 1.24, 1.28, 1.30.

104. Masri, *Nabulsiyat*, p. 209. Differences between these two local styles may have been due, among other things, to the topographical differences between the eastern and western slopes of Jabal Nablus (see Chapter 1) as well as to the desire to visually express discrete local identifications within Jabal Nablus as a whole.

105. In the late nineteenth and early twentieth centuries, Jenin grew in size, and large textile shops were established. All the peasants of the small village of Dayr Ghazala, for example, traveled to Jenin together to purchase the *kiswa* for a marriage ceremony. Members of the Atari and Naji families—from Arraba and Qabatya villages, respectively—usually supplied the peasants of Dayr Ghazala with their textile needs (interview with Awad Yusuf *Abu* Alayya [b. 1908], July 17, 1990).

106. Finn, 2:344–345. According to Najib Arafat, a typical procession in the early part of the twentieth century consisted of three or four women and five or six men, plus their children (interview).

107. Masri, *Nabulsiyat*, pp. 206–207.

108. Ibid., pp. 40, 123–127.

109. Interview with Najib Arafat; and Saba Arafat, letter to the author, April 4, 1993.

110. Interview with *Umm* Walid, August 8, 1990.

111. Arafat Family Papers, 1.30.

112. Interviews with Hani and Najib Arafat.

113. See a letter from Husayn Abdullah to *Hajj* Isma'il, in which he pleaded with the latter to accept payment in wheat instead of oil, as promised earlier (Arafat Family Papers, 1.8).

114. Darwaza, *Mi'at am*, pp. 70–71. Masri related similar stories and confirmed that interest was calculated into loan payments. He also quoted a rhymed satiric song (discussed at the end of this chapter), written by peasants from Talluza village, complaining about debt collectors (Masri, *Nabulsiyat*, pp. 204, 225–228).

115. Interviews with Hani and Najib Arafat.

116. Ihsan Nimr provided some examples of how ruling families spoke in two voices in a calculated carrot-and-stick policy (NIMR, 4:361–364).

117. Interview with Hani Arafat.

118. Arafat Family Papers, 1.6.

119. Ibid., 1.13.

120. Ibid., 1.5. Because the value of the currency fluctuated widely during this period, relational measures were often mentioned in loan contracts.

121. Interview with Mahmud Muhammad Abd al-Razzaq Abd al-Haqq (*Abu*

Adnan), who was born in Bayt Wazan at the turn of the century and has lived there all his life, July 22, 1990.

122. Interview with Sharif Kamil Jarrar, July 17, 1990.

123. According to Sharif Kamil al-Jarrar, most of the peasants in his village were indebted during the early part of the twentieth century (interview).

124. Interview with Khalid Qadri, July 16, 1990.

125. For a discussion of the term "middle peasant," see Chapter 4.

126. For more on this family, see Chapter 5.

127. Arafat Family Papers, 1.21. Ahmad al-Hijjawi was *Hajj* Ahmad's business agent. *Mukhkhamasat* were pentagon-shaped coins, often used for jewelry (see Arraf, *Al-Ard*, p. 159). *Majarrat* is the plural of *majaer*, a gold coin, probably from Hungary. This coin was also found in Gaza and Damascus in the mid-nineteenth century (see Abdul-Karim Rafeq, "Ghazza: Dirasa umraniyya wa iqtisadiyya min khilal al-watha'iq al-shar'iyya, 1273–1277/1857–1861" (Gaza: A Cultural and Economic Study Based on Islamic Court Documents, 1273–1277/1857–1861), in *Al-M'utamar al-duwali al-thalith li tarikh Bilad al-Sham (Filastin)* (The Third International Conference on Bilad al-Sham: Palestine), vol. 2, *Jughrafiyyat Filastine wa hadaratiha* (The Geography and Civilization of Palestine) (Amman, 1980), pp. 133–134.

128. Arafat Family Papers, 1.22, 1.24–1.25, 1.31.

129. Ibid., 1.22.

130. Ibid., 1.31, dated June 8, 1900.

131. Masri, *Nabulsiyat*, pp. 225–228.

CHAPTER 3

1. Al-Abbasi, *Tarikh al Tuqan*, pp. 83–86. For background, see Daniel Crecelius, *The Roots of Modern Egypt: A Study of the Regimes of Ali Bey al-Kabir and Muhammad Bey Abu al-Dahab, 1760–1775* (Minneapolis, Minn., and Chicago, 1981).

2. Ibrahim Danafi al-Samiri, *Zahir al-Umar wa hukkam Jabal Nablus, A.H. 1185–1187/A.D. 1771–1773* (Zahir al-Umar and the Rulers of Jabal Nablus, A.H. 1185–1187/A.D. 1771–1773) (ed. Musa Abu Dayya; Nablus, 1986), p. 35. This manuscript is privately owned and was first published in NIMR, 1:390–399. Ibrahim Danafi al-Samiri was a member of the Danafi family of the Samaritan community, whose members often served as scribes or treasurers of the rulers of Nablus and its rich merchants, including *Hajj* Isma'il Arafat, whom we met in Chapter 2. Ibrahim Danafi inherited this position from his grandfather, Marjan.

3. The word used for clothes is *atyab*, slang for *thiyab* (sing. *thawb*). See Chapter 2.

4. Al-Samiri, *Zahir al-Umar*, p. 35.

5. There is no agreement on Zahir al-Umar's exact date of birth. See Joudah, *Revolt*, p. 29, n. 2.

6. These generalizations are based on two articles by Eliyahu Ashtor ("The Venetian Cotton Trade in Syria in the Later Middle Ages" and "The Venetian Supremacy in Levantine Trade: Monopoly or Pre-colonialism?"), which were re-

printed in his *Studies on the Levantine Trade in the Middle Ages* (London, 1978), pp. 675–715 and 5–53, respectively. For historical context, see Abu-Lughod, *Before European Hegemony*, pp. 233–235.

7. Cohen, *Palestine*, p. 11; Owen, *The Middle East*, pp. 83–84.

8. Owen, *Middle East*, pp. 83–84. See also Charles Issawi, ed., *The Economic History of the Middle East, 1800–1914* (Chicago, 1966; reprint, Chicago, 1975), pp. 31–33.

9. For example, Elena Frangakis-Syrett, "The Trade of Cotton and Cloth in Izmir: From the Second Half of the Eighteenth Century to the Early Nineteenth Century," in Keyder and Tabak, eds., *Landholding*, pp. 97–111; Fariba Zarinebaf-Shahr, "Tabriz under Ottoman Rule (1725–1730)" (Ph.D. diss., University of Chicago, 1991), p. 178; and Frank Perlin, "Proto-Industrialization and Pre-Colonial South Asia," *Past and Present*, 98 (1983), pp. 30–95.

10. According to Cohen, an example for this strategy in northern Palestine was set by Paul Maashouk, who worked as consul for Britain and Holland in the port city of Acre (*Palestine*, p. 12). Cohen states that Maashouk was a Dutchman, but Bruce Masters persuasively argues that he was a local (*Origins*, p. 108, n. 78).

11. For a sketch of Ibrahim al-Sabbagh's economic and political role during his tenure as Zahir al-Umar's right-hand man, see Joudah, *Revolt*, pp. 127–134; and Cohen, *Palestine*, p. 16.

12. Cohen, *Palestine*, p. 16.

13. Ibid., pp. 21–22.

14. Quoted in Issawi, ed., *Economic History*, p. 33.

15. For example, see C. A. Bayly, *The Imperial Meridian: The British Empire and the World, 1780–1830* (London and New York, 1989), pp. 46–63.

16. See Owen, *Cotton*.

17. See Thomas Philipp, "Social Structure and Political Power in Acre in the 18th Century," in Thomas Philipp, ed., *The Syrian Land in the 18th and 19th Century* (Stuttgart, 1992), pp. 91–108.

18. A typical example is Shihab, *Tarikh Ahmad basha Jazzar.*

19. His two key appointees, *Abu* Nabut and Mustafa Barbar, became virtually autonomous rulers. The former ruled Jaffa and Gaza for years, and the latter had free rein over Tripoli and its hinterland. As for Jabal Nablus, it was largely left alone, with Sulayman Pasha playing a patriarchal peace-keeping role. For details, see Awra, *Tarikh*, pp. 318–321, 377–381, 476–478. This book was written in 1853. See pages 34–73 for a description of the differences between Ahmad Pasha and Sulayman Pasha.

20. Ibid., pp. 63, 326–328.

21. Ibid., pp, 73, 105.

22. Ibid., pp. 108–127, 144, 196–198, 431–433.

23. Mishaqa, *Muntakhabat*, p. 38. This translation was taken from Mikhayil Mishaqa, *Murder, Mayhem, Pillage, and Plunder: The History of the Lebanon in the 18th and 19th Centuries* (trans. Wheeler M. Thackston, Jr.; Albany, N.Y., 1988), pp. 56–57.

24. Awra, *Tarikh*, p. 165. Cotton was also appropriated from peasants through taxes-in-kind (ibid., p. 150).

25. For North Africa, see two works by Julia Clancy-Smith: *Rebel and Saint:*

Muslim Notables, Populist Protest, Colonial Encounters (Algeria and Tunisia, c. 1800–1904) (Berkeley, Calif., 1994), chap. 5; and "The Maghrib and the Mediterranean World in the Nineteenth Century: Illicit Exchanges, Migrants, and Social Marginals," in Kenneth J. Perkins and Michel Le Gall, eds., *Volume in Honor of L. Carl Brown* (Princeton, N.J., forthcoming).

26. In 1849, for example, the governor of Jerusalem expressed his concern to the Nablus Advisory Council that cash crops were leaving the country illegally and hence were undermining local needs (NMSR, p. 14). For more details, see below.

27. For example, in November 1832 Muhammad Ali informed his son Ibrahim Pasha, the commander of the Egyptian forces, that he had sent him 2,000 purses (*kis*, pl. *akyas*; each purse contained 500 piasters) of money and that he would send him the wages for the soldiers after he sold the cotton harvest (Asad Rustum, *Al-Mahfuzat al-malakiyya al-misriyya* (4 vols.; Beirut, 1940–1943; reprint, Beirut, 1986), 2:167.

28. Ibid., 2:357. Muhammad Ali Pasha's dismissal of the Palestinian cotton harvest as insignificant was probably the result of a (unfair but true) comparison with the huge amounts of cotton that Egypt produced, and of the fact that the largest Egyptian harvest ever had taken place just two years earlier. In addition, 1833 was preceded by the long siege of Acre, which must have certainly discouraged the cultivation of cotton, because many of the cotton-growing villages were adjacent to it.

29. Still, these reasons should not have prevented Muhammad Ali Pasha from imposing a monopoly in any case. The most likely explanation, therefore, is that he wanted to allay the European powers' concern that Greater Syria would be subjected to the same economic policies as Egypt, policies which they considered to be an obstacle to their access and control of the rural surplus.

30. Cohen, *Palestine*, pp. 13, 260. The dominant position of Nablus cotton by the early nineteenth century (see below) was perhaps due to this expansion, for it seems that little if any cotton was grown in this region during the sixteenth century. An Ottoman cadastral survey which listed the types of crops grown in the villages of Palestine in 1596, for example, shows that most of the cotton-growing villages were in the Acre region and listed none for the Nablus region. Hütteroth and Abdulfattah painstakingly compiled this information (*Historical Geography*, pp. 111–220; and the results can be clearly seen in the attached map, entitled "Agricultural Production in the Southern Syrian *Liwas* 1005 H./1596 A.D."). This information must be viewed with some caution, for this survey did not mention the soap industry in Nablus, even though it was vibrant at the time. In addition, we know from the same cadastral survey that Nablus was an important textile center (Cohen and Lewis, *Population and Revenue*, pp. 54–62). As Halil İnalcik reminded us, such centers were usually located in areas where cotton was cultivated on a significant scale ("When and How British Cotton Goods Invaded the Levant Markets," in İslamoğlu, ed., *Ottoman Empire*, p. 374).

31. For Latakia, Bowring mentions only that all of its production was usually consumed locally (*Commercial Statistics*, p. 13). For Acre and Jaffa he writes that they produced "some quantities" of cotton, the implication being that the amounts were not significant (ibid., p. 14.). Bowring's calculations are the most reliable

source we have for the early nineteenth century, because they were based on detailed reports gathered during a long field trip to the region on behalf of the British government.

32. Ibid., p. 13. Another observer, Julius Zwiedinek von Sudenhorst, was of the same opinion (*Syrien und seine Bedeutung für den Welthandel* [Vienna, 1873], p. 54). Nablus cotton found its way to many regional markets, large and small. Damascus was no doubt the largest market in the north, but even small market towns in Mount Lebanon bought their cotton supplies from Nablus. For example, John Burckhardt noted in 1810 that in Zahle, "cotton is brought from Belad Safad and Nablous" (*Travels*, p. 7).

33. The Ottoman government, in turn, was pressured by European textile manufacturers, business associations, and government officials to encourage the production of cotton. The Manchester Cotton Association, for example, promoted exhibitions of commodities in Istanbul and Izmir and urged landowners to focus on growing cotton. See Susan Lee Yeager, "The Ottoman Empire on Exhibition: The Ottoman Empire at International Exhibitions 1851–1867, and the *sergi-i umumi Osmani, 1863*" (Ph.D. diss., Columbia University, 1981), pp. 120–122.

34. NMSR, p. 89. Ten years later, in 1861, the Ottoman government made concerted efforts to encourage the planting of cotton all over its dominions in order to take advantage of the cotton famine caused by the civil war in the United States. For example, they called for annual cotton shows to be held in key cities, approved awards for outstanding cotton producers, and abolished taxes on imported cotton gins (Awad, *Al-Idara al-uthmaniyya*, p. 241).

35. NMSR, p. 89.

36. Ibid., pp. 108–114, 118–121, 124–125.

37. Ibid., p. 109. For each *wazna* of ginned cotton not returned they received approximately 46 piasters (ibid., p. 119).

38. Ibid., pp. 93, 108–114, 271, 306; NICR, 7:372.

39. Interview with Kamal Abdulfattah, March 3, 1990.

40. Cotton was usually ginned in shops owned by the same merchants. The estate of *Hajj* Badran, son of *Hajj* Muhammad Badran (d. 1799), for instance, shows that indebted peasants from the villages of Tanna, Maythalun, and Sir paid him in raw cotton and olive oil. His shop, meanwhile, contained ten cotton gins (NICR, 6:52).

41. That year Nablus exported 7,500 bales of 100 *uqqas* each to the port of Marseilles, or approximately 3,750 *qintars* (Bowring, *Commercial Statistics*, p. 14).

42. Ibid., pp. 9–10.

43. Owen, *Middle East*, p. 79.

44. In 1863, for example, the British Foreign Office reported that the Nablus region produced four times as much cotton as it had produced in previous years. For this and other details on the rise and fall of cotton production in Palestine, see Schölch, "European Penetration," pp. 12–21.

45. Owen, *Middle East*, p. 66.

46. For example, statistics for the years 1856–1862, provided by the British Foreign Office, show that the average proportion of northern Palestine's cultivated area devoted to cotton was only 6 percent, as compared with 40 percent for wheat,

14 percent for olives, 13 percent for sesame, and 9 percent for barley (Schölch, "European Penetration," p. 61).

47. İnalcik, "When and How," pp. 375, 380; Owen, *Middle East*, pp. 84–85.

48. For example, Nablus cotton was listed first among the goods traded in Nazareth's famous weekly market in the late nineteenth century (W. M. Thomson, *The Land and the Book* [London, 1894], pp. 442–443).

49. For a summary of the context and importance of the 1838 treaty, see Owen, *Middle East*, pp. 90–91.

50. Ibid., p. 88. For Beirut, see Charles Issawi, "British Trade and the Rise of Beirut, 1830–1860," IJMES, 8 (1977), pp. 98–99.

51. This success also increased competition from within, because anyone with access to capital sought a share in this profitable activity.

52. For British traders, an important moment was the abolition of the Levant Company monopoly in 1825, which increased the numbers of British merchants doing business in the Ottoman Empire and assured them of more vigorous and effective backing by the British government (A. G. Wood, *A History of the Levant Company* [Oxford, 1935], pp. 180–202). A similar set of developments took place in France (V. J. Puryear, *France and the Levant* [Berkeley, Calif., and Los Angeles, 1941], pp. 10–14).

53. NMSR, p. 258.

54. Ibid., pp. 191, 286, 312.

55. Ibid., p. 41.

56. For a comparative perspective, see Eugene Rogan, "Money-Lending and Capital Flows from Nablus, Damascus and Jerusalem to the *qada'* of al-Salt in the Last Decades of Ottoman Rule," in Philipp, ed., *Syrian Land*, pp. 239–260.

57. NMSR, p. 39. Transportation costs were calculated and detailed in further correspondence (ibid., p. 219).

58. Ibid., pp. 60, 258.

59. Ibid., pp. 286, 312.

60. Ibid., p. 43.

61. Ibid., p. 124.

62. Ibid., p. 192.

63. Ibid., pp. 200–201.

64. NMSR, p. 311. The Alami family has long held leading religious posts in the city of Jerusalem and has intermarried with the Nimr family in Nablus (NIMR, 1:91–92).

65. Doumani, "Population Counts," pp. 4–9.

66. This was the concern of the Jerusalem Advisory Council in 1855, for example (Finn, *Stirring Times*, 2:407–408).

67. NMSR, p. 242.

68. Ibid., p. 3.

69. NMSR, pp. 226–227. *Khawaja* is an honorific normally used to denote non-Muslim men of means, usually merchants. In Nablus, however, it was used to denote rich merchants, regardless of religion. Only in the mid-nineteenth century did its meaning narrow to non-Muslims.

70. Not all of the *zakhayir* were sold off. Part of the wheat, barley, oil, and clarified butter was used to supply soldiers of the central government who were

stationed in the Nablus region following the Egyptian invasion, as well as to the local militia (*nafir am*). See, for example, NMSR, pp. 57, 123, 143–144, 146–148, 178, 182, 216–217, 238, 241, 253, 268, 271–273, 276, 280–283, 288, 292–293, 297, 300.

71. NMSR, p. 215. The specific ports are not mentioned, the implication being that there was demand from all of them (Beirut, Acre, and Jaffa).

72. Ibid., pp. 215, 311–312.

73. Another example is the case of Darwish *Afandi* from Damascus, who, in 1851, successfully bid on 81 *kayla* of lentils and 3,103 *uqqas* of cotton-in-the-boll (ibid., pp. 161–162; both dated December 3, 1851).

74. Ibid., p. 38.

75. Ibid., p. 44.

76. NMSR, p. 56. The country the consul represented is not mentioned. In the absence of vowels, the transliteration of the consul's name is uncertain.

77. Schölch, *Palestine in Transformation*, pp. 13–17.

78. Similar examples can be found in NMSR, pp. 143, 147.

79. For example, auction bids recorded in ibid., pp. 8–9, 18–19, 25–26, 38, 40, 46–48, 57, 60, 67, 79, 82–84, 88, 98–99, 123, 131–132, 137–138, 142–144, 146–147, 158, 161–162, 164–165, 185–186, 191–192, 196, 200–201, 210, 215, 221–222, 248, 258, 277, 311–312, 318.

80. Owen, *Middle East*, p. 90.

81. Ihsan Nimr wrote that the first floor of most living quarters was reserved for the storage of looms and that both men and women worked together at home in the spinning and weaving of cotton or woolen thread. A husband and wife team working all day, according to Nimr, could make a piece (*shaqqa*) of cloth worth half a gold coin. The time period and actual worth of the gold coin are not specified (NIMR, 2:286).

82. NICR, 9:117.

83. For an overview, see Donald Quataert, "Ottoman Women, Households, and Textile Manufacturing, 1800–1914," in Keddie and Baron, eds., *Women in Middle Eastern History*, pp. 161–176.

84. Calculated from inheritance estate of a wool and cotton merchant who died a month later (NICR, 9:96).

85. Cohen and Lewis, *Population and Revenue*, pp. 54–62.

86. Schölch, "European Penetration," p. 50.

87. Shmuel Avitsur, "The Influence of Western Technology on the Economy of Palestine during the Nineteenth Century," in Maʿoz, ed., *Studies*, p. 485.

88. İnalcik, "When and How," pp. 374–383.

89. Ibid., pp. 380–381.

90. Owen, *Middle East*, p. 95.

91. Avitsur, "Western Technology," p. 486.

92. NIMR, 4:205–207. See below for a discussion of *bisht*. *Qilw* are the ashes of the barilla plant, used in soap production (see Chapter 5 and Appendix 3 for details).

93. Ibid., 4:213–214.

94. Ibid., 4:217–220.

95. Dominique Chevalier, "Un example de résistance technique de l'artisinat

syrien aux XIXe et XXe siècles: Les tissus ikates d'Alep et de Damas," *Syria*, 39:3–4 (1962).

96. Owen, *Middle East*, pp. 93–95.

97. Donald Quataert, "Ottoman Handicrafts and Industry in the Age of European Industrial Hegemony, 1800–1914," *Review*, 11 (1988), pp. 169–178. See also his books: *Social Disintegration and Popular Resistance in the Ottoman Empire, 1881–1908: Reactions to European Penetration* (New York, 1983); and *Ottoman Manufacturing in the Age of the Industrial Revolution* (Cambridge, England, 1993).

98. For example, the estate of Shaykh Abd al-Razzaq Arafat listed a number of women employed by him (NICR, 7:64). Shaykh Abd al-Razzaq Arafat and his brother Abdullah, for example, both invested heavily in the dyeing process (ibid. 6:198; 7:47).

99. Owen, *Middle East*, pp. 88, 90–91.

100. Gerber, "Modernization," pp. 250–264.

101. H. B. Tristram, *The Land of Israel: Journal of Travels in Palestine, Undertaken with Special Reference to Its Physical Character* (London, 1882), pp. 137–138.

102. Nimr mentioned that balsam seeds (*bizir al-balsam*), brazilwood (*baqam*), pomegranate skin (*qishr al-rumman*), and tumeric (*kurkum*) were also locally produced (NIMR, 2:284).

103. Rustum, *Al-Mahfuzat*, 1:164.

104. NICR, 6:237, 364; 9:75.

105. For example, ibid., 6:290; 9:70; 10:8.

106. James Silk Buckingham, *Travels among the Arab Tribes Inhabiting the Countries East of Syria and Palestine* (London, 1825), pp. 2, 15, 34–35.

107. NICR, 8:284.

108. Ibid., 10:8.

109. Interview with Awad Yusuf Abd al-Rahman *Abu* Ilaya (b. 1908), July 17, 1990.

110. Interview with Hamid *Abu* Aysha (b. 1902), August, 10, 1990.

111. Later on, this industry became concentrated in the Qaryun quarter.

112. NICR, 6:59, 290; 9:20, 117.

113. Vatter, "Journeymen," pp. 75–90.

114. Quataert, "Ottoman Handicrafts," p. 177. For examples, see Quataert, "Ottoman Women."

115. NIMR, 2:332. Weaving and spinning can be considered as one of the four major sources of income for women, the other three being moneylending, inheritance, and the marriage dowry.

116. For example, NICR, 6:251, 290; 9:20, 96.

117. Ibid., 6:251.

118. Ibid., 6:290.

119. Judith Tucker, *Women in Nineteenth-Century Egypt* (Cambridge, England, 1985), pp. 84–85. The absence of direct evidence is due to the fact that until the late 1850s, peasants in general were absent from the Islamic court records except in cases involving primarily moneylending and land. See Chapter 4 for details.

120. NMSR, p. 37.

121. Ibid.

1. Rogers, *Domestic Life*, p. 225.

2. NICR, 13A:151. Recall, from Chapter 2, that *Sayyid* Mahmud Hashim sold his soap factory to *Hajj* Isma'il Arafat and married his granddaughter to the latter's son, Amr.

3. The literature on the complexity of peasant societies and their role in shaping the modern period is extensive. For example, see Eric Wolf, *Peasant Wars of the Twentieth Century* (New York, 1969); James C. Scott, *The Moral Economy of the Peasant: Rebellion and Subsistence in Southeast Asia* (New Haven, Conn., 1976); Sydel Silverman, "The Peasant Concept in Anthropology," *Journal of Peasant Studies*, 7 (1979), pp. 49–69; Frank Perlin, "Precolonial South Asia and Western Penetration in the 17th–19th Centuries," *Review*, 4 (1980), pp. 267–306; Ludden, *Peasant History*; Jeffrey Paige, "One, Two, or Many Vietnams? Social Theory and Peasant Revolution in Vietnam and Guatemala," in Edmund Burke III, ed., *Global Crises and Social Movements* (Boulder, Colo., and London, 1988), pp. 145–179.

4. NICR, 13A:141, 146–148, 151, 155; 13B:41, 44, 47.

5. Tax-farming bids registered in the minutes of the Advisory Council during the 1848–1853 period show that urban merchants were making inroads into villages long considered to be within the sphere of influence of subdistrict chiefs. Many more served as financial backers of tax-farming bids by the subdistrict chiefs (NMSR, pp. 3, 30, 212–213, 226–227, 263).

6. One of four orthodox Sunni schools. All were recognized as valid by the Ottoman state, but the Hanafi school was the one officially adopted by the Ottoman religious bureaucracy.

7. Abdur Rahim, *The Principles of Muhammadan Jurisprudence According to the Hanafi, Maliki, Shafi'i and Hanbali Schools* (London, 1911; reprint, Westport, Conn., 1981), p. 281.

8. An exception, discussed below, is an unusual case registered in the Jerusalem Islamic court records (JICR, 318:9–10).

9. Nimr Family Papers, 2.2.12(B); 3.1.7, 3.3.8(B)–3.3.10, 3.4.5(B). Document 3.3.9 was reproduced in NIMR, 2:280.

10. Nimr Family Papers, 3.1.7(B).

11. This is according to Ahmad *Agha* Nimr's own soap-factory account sheets for the year 1825–1826 (Nimr Family Papers, 3.1.6).

12. For example, Nimr Family Papers, 3.3.10, dated September 3, 1851.

13. According to Awad Yusuf *Abu* Alayya (b. 1908), from the village of Dayr Ghazala, peasants sometimes made the better part of the bargain by delivering low-quality goods, particularly in the case of grain. Conflicts over these issues, he added, were not unusual.

14. NICR, 13B:136.

15. See, for example, ibid., 12:246; 13A:133, 136, 140, 146, 219, 257, 261; 13B:15, 25, 32, 38, 41–42, 44, 71.

16. Ibid., 13B:136.

17. This was a long-standing practice in Greater Syria. For example, Amnon Cohen notes that in the case of sixteenth-century Jerusalem the wish to ensure

future supplies was behind advance-purchase arrangements of olive oil by Jerusalemite merchants. He does not mention the *salam* system, however, and his description of the terms of advance purchase does not include the key provision of fixed prices (*Economic Life*, pp. 75–76).

18. Eugene Rogan describes a similar situation in the Salt region between 1885 and 1914 ("Incorporating the Periphery," chap. 6).

19. Masters, *Origins*, pp. 6, 146–185.

20. For example, a *timar* grant document (*bara'a*) dated December 18, 1723 (Nimr Family Papers, 1.1.13), a list of *timar* villages controlled by the Nimrs in the early nineteenth century (ibid., 2.2.13), and a list of villages included in the Nimr tax farm in the mid-nineteenth century (ibid., 2.2.8, 2.2.11).

21. The receipt for these taxes was reproduced in NIMR, 2:233–234.

22. For example, Ahmad *Agha* Nimr's son, Abd al-Fattah, received moneys from Shaykh Sufyan Bustami and Shaykh Sulayman Banna, to whom he promised delivery of thirty jars of olive oil—measured by the jar of the Qatqutiyya soap factory—within thirty days (Nimr Family Papers, 3.3.8(B), dated December 7, 1841).

23. NICR, 13A:121–122.

24. In Jabal Nablus the word *maris* usually refers to one thin strip of open agricultural land, devoid of trees, located in a valley, and used mainly to sow wheat and other grains. Normally, a small valley would be divided into numerous thin strips, each owned separately. For the use of this word in Gaza during the same period, see Rafeq, "Ghazza," p. 121.

25. NICR, 13A:114–115.

26. Ibid., 13A:224.

27. Ibid., 13B:83–84.

28. Nimr Family Papers, No. 3.3.9 (emphasis added).

29. Schölch, "European Penetration," p. 14.

30. The first contract, signed on September 8, 1851, had exactly the same terms and prices. The only difference was the added phrase: "this *salam* . . . is free from the vice of usury" (Nimr Family Papers, 3.3.10).

31. Schölch, "European Penetration," pp. 14–18; Buheiry, "Agricultural Exports," pp. 61–81.

32. For example, another Christian merchant from Jaffa, *Khwaja* Nicola Gharghur, was forced to turn to the Nablus council in order to enforce a *salam* contract he made with three shaykhs from Talluza village to deliver 24,375 piasters' worth of barley to Jaffa port in 1852 (NMSR, p. 161).

33. Elizabeth Anne Finn, *Home in the Holy Land: A Tale Illustrating Customs and Incidents in Modern Jerusalem* (London, 1866), pp. 350–353.

34. This was the title of one of the chapters in Consul James Finn's book, *Stirring Times* (2:266).

35. Similar examples from the hinterland of Damascus were detailed by Abdul-Karim Rafeq: "Land Tenure Problems and Their Social Impact in Syria around the Middle of the Nineteenth Century," in Tarif Khalidi, ed., *Land Tenure and Social Transformation in the Middle East* (Beirut, 1984), p. 389. (Rafeq uses the words *bay mu'jjal* (postponed purchase) to describe these contracts because this is how they are referred to in the Damascus Islamic Court records.)

36. Shaykh Husayn Abd al-Hadi was represented in court by a leading Jerusa-

lemite notable, *Sayyid* Ahmad *Agha* al-Alami (JICR, 318:9–10). I am indebted to Judith Mendelsohn Rood for kindly providing me with a copy of this document.

37. Cuno, *Pasha's Peasants*, pp. 125–129.

38. JICR, 319:84. I am indebted to Judith Mendelsohn Rood for kindly providing me with a copy of this document.

39. NMSR, p. 150.

40. Finn, *Stirring Times*, 1:239–240.

41. NICR, 12:65. The appointment letter was dated November 13, 1851.

42. Tamimi, born in Nablus (1303/1885–1886) to a notable family of ulama, merchants, and soap manufacturers, was educated in Istanbul and France and worked as director of the Ottoman commercial bureau in Beirut. Bahjat, born in Aleppo (1308/1890–1891), had a law degree from Istanbul and, before World War I, worked as a teacher of Turkish and philosophy.

43. Tamimi and Bahjat, *Wilayat Bayrut*, p. 89.

44. Ibid. p. 94.

45. Ibid., p 103.

46. Ibid., pp. 103, 122.

47. Ibid., p. 105. The 60–70 percent rate was probably applied for loans not secured against collateral. For similar rates in Egypt in the 1830s, see Cuno, *Pasha's Peasants*, p. 145.

48. Darwaza, *Mi'at am*, pp. 77–80.

49. The author was referring to all peasants in Greater Syria during the nineteenth century (Muhammad Kurd Ali, *Kitab khitat al-Sham* [The Plan of Damascus] [3d ed.; 6 vols.; Damascus, 1983], p. 249).

50. The only group that elicited unreserved praise were the Jewish European settlers they visited in Petah Tikvah. Despite ambivalent feelings toward their colonization project, Tamimi and Bahjat lauded their efficient organization, cleanliness, and sophisticated culture (*Wilayat Bayrut*, pp. 84–215).

51. The first peasant inheritance estate to be registered in the nineteenth century was in 1860 (NICR, 13A:17).

52. Land purchases involved a wide range of urban and rural groups, and for the first time, some peasants came to the court to register marriages, divorces, and inheritance estates.

53. Cuno, *Pasha's Peasants*, pp. 75–76.

54. For instance, in a theft lawsuit between two peasant clans, dated February 14, 1843, the judge disqualified one of the witnesses because, among other things, he was considered as "one of those who disinherit women" (*min al-ladhina la yuwarrithuna al-nisa*) (NICR, 10:89).

55. Moors, "Women and Property," pp. 76–77.

56. NICR, 12:339.

57. Ibid., 9:120, 375; 12:86, 277, 279–280, 286–287, 301, 309.

58. Ibid., 9:160.

59. For a discussion of the formation of the Ottoman view on state and private lands, see Baber Johansen, *The Islamic Law on Land Tax and Rent: The Peasants' Loss of Property Rights as Interpreted in the Hanafite Legal Literature of the Mamluk and Ottoman Periods* (London, 1988), especially chap. 4.

60. For more details, see Bernard Lewis, "Land Tenure and Taxation in Syria,"

Studia Islamica, 50 (1979), pp. 115–116. For the categories of landholding as outlined in Ottoman cadastral surveys of Palestine in the sixteenth century, see Cohen and Lewis, *Population and Revenue,* p. 42.

61. For this point in particular, and for a discussion of the military and fiscal imperatives behind the development of Ottoman policies regarding land tenure, see Halil İnalcik, "Land Problems in Turkish History," *The Muslim World,* 14 (1955), pp. 221–222. An example of a ruling along these lines by an Islamic court judge in Nablus can be found in NICR, 12:310.

62. Cuno, *Pasha's Peasants,* pp. 77–81. Cuno further elaborated this argument in regard to Greater Syria in his paper, "Was the Land of Ottoman Syria *miri* or *milk?* An Examination of Juridical Differences within the Hanafi School" (unpublished paper delivered to the PARSS Seminar on the Middle East, University of Pennsylvania, November 1993).

63. Cuno, *Pasha's Peasants,* pp. 81–84.

64. NICR, 4:58.

65. Ibid., 9:263, 326, 331–332; 12:303, 310, 353.

66. Ibid., 9:241.

67. Owen, *Middle East,* p. 34. Also see Naff, "Zahle," pp. 162–164; Iliya Harik, *Politics and Change in a Traditional Society: Lebanon, 1711–1845* (Princeton, N.J., 1968), pp. 27–28; and Cuno, *Pasha's Peasants,* pp. 81–84.

68. For similar reasons, peasant land purchases were also underrepresented in the Damascus court registers during this period, although, on the whole, they were still far more common there than in the Nablus court records (see Reilly, "Origins," pp. 192–193).

69. For a typical ruling on state ownership of land, rights of usufruct, and the application of Ottoman secular law, see NICR, 9:326.

70. Ibid., 12:324.

71. In most other cases of this sort, the status of land was simply left undefined although, judging from the description and location, they were clearly state lands. For example, the court accepted the argument of one peasant from the village of Marda that he bought several pieces of land, some clearly located far from the village, from a fellow peasant in 1835–1836 (ibid., 12:197–198). In another case, the court accepted the argument that a piece of flat land located between the villages of Bayta and Yasuf—that is, also clearly state land—was the private property of two peasants from Yutma village because they "legally" purchased it in 1800–1801 (ibid., 12:246). By leaving the status of these lands undefined, the presiding judge never put himself in a position where the contradiction between theory and practice was brought to the surface, allowing him to conveniently ignore this issue altogether when necessary. For other cases involving the sale of state-owned lands, see ibid., 12:60, 79, 284, 303. See also the sale of what may have been state lands in ibid., 7:232; 10:219; 12:92.

72. For a summary of the debate, see Peter Sluglett and Marion Farouk-Sluglett, "The Application of the 1858 Land Code in Greater Syria: Some Preliminary Observations," in Khalidi, ed., *Land Tenure,* pp. 409–421.

73. For example, Kayyali, *Tarikh Filastin,* p. 38.

74. A total of eleven purchases were registered: NICR, 9:241, 288, 349, 369; 10:20, 21, 22.

75. Ibid., 9:350–351, 379; 10:11–17, 51.

76. Ibid., 9:50; 10:4, 31, 48.

77. Ibid., 9:379.

78. Similar purchases of lands near Baqa al-Gharbiyya village were transacted during this period (Ibid., 9:349–350).

79. These purchases, too numerous to list, are dispersed in ibid., 10–13A, 13B. For typical examples, see ibid., 11:105; 12:80, 144–146, 185–190.

80. Ibid., 13B:64.

81. Ibid., 13A:225.

82. Over the course of the nineteenth century, more and more *salam* contracts started to list the names of one or more individuals who guaranteed, on pain of being personally liable, that the goods in question would be delivered.

83. NICR, 13B:188, dated April 25, 1865. If flight did not release debt obligations, neither did death. In a lawsuit registered on February 27, 1862, the survivors of a rich grain and oil merchant, Mas'ud Qaltaqji, brought the survivors of a peasant, As'ad al-Khadir, from the village of Dayr al-Ghusun, to court in order to enforce a *salam* contract signed by their parents which stipulated the delivery of eighty-eight and one-half jars of olive oil. As usual, the defendants lost the case but did not have the olive oil demanded from them. The judge then ordered that the lands, house, and immovable properties of the debtors be sold in order to satisfy the debt (NICR, 13A:151).

84. Nimr Family Papers, 5.2.43. *Mi'na* refers to the flat space between terraces. Qasim was a member of a rich merchant family that dealt primarily in soap.

85. Another document refers to these lands as "fit for planting winter and summer crops"; that is, flat valley lands (Nimr Family Papers, 5.2.44).

86. Ibid., 5.2.44, dated late May 1855. As mentioned above, most merchants were not keen on keeping lands they appropriated through enforcement of loan obligations and preferred to be more selective in their purchases. This particular case is a good example. The Jaffa merchant lived too far away and would have been considered a stranger in Jabal Nablus. The man to whom he sold the land, in contrast, belonged to one of Nablus's oldest ruling families and had the political influence, conveniently located infrastructure—such as shops, a soap factory, an olive press, and grain mills—and patronage relations that would allow him to capitalize on these lands much more efficiently. (The village of Aqraba had long been part of the Nimr's *timar* holdings.)

87. NMSR, p. 236.

88. NICR, 12:122.

89. A typical example is Ma'oz, *Ottoman Reform.*

90. For examples of *salam* contracts and other loan obligations between peasants, see NICR, 12:69, 103, 247, 256, 284, 303, 324, 345; 13A:92, 106, 136, 146, 149, 151, 155, 158, 162, 257; 13B:5, 15, 25, 33, 38, 41–42, 44, 47. For examples of land sales between peasants (including disputes over such sales), see ibid., 9:197–198, 331–332; 10:61, 219; 12:92, 94, 105–106, 109, 232, 237, 246, 286–287, 294, 301, 304–306, 309; 13A:28, 61–62, 141, 147–148; 13B:26–27, 29. For examples of business contracts and share-cropping agreements, see ibid., 11:152; 12:11, 345, 352; 13B:56, 73.

91. Naff, "Zahle," pp. 172–174. She based this observation on local sources, such as land records.

92. Dina Rizk Khoury, "The Introduction of Commercial Agriculture in the Province of Mosul and Its Effects on the Peasantry, 1750–1850," in Keyder and Tabak, eds., *Landholding*, pp. 155, 164, 171.

93. NICR, 11:142.

94. Kafr al-Labad is twenty kilometers northeast of Nablus on the way to Tulkarem. Burqa is sixteen kilometers north of Nablus on the way to Jenin.

95. For examples, see NICR, 13A:17, 180–181.

96. Ya'kov Firestone, "Production and Trade in an Islamic Context: Sharika Trade Contracts in the Transitional Economy of Northern Samaria, 1853–1943," IJMES, 6 (1975), pp. 185–209, 308–324.

97. For example, Shaykh Muhammad *Afandi* Husayni, a Jerusalemite, was appointed as judge of the subdistricts of Jamma'in al-Gharbiyya (NICR, 12:249, 251, 254).

98. Ibid., 13B:73.

99. This type of business venture between peasants was not a new development. A similar arrangement had been reached in 1842–1843 between a peasant from the village of Dayr al-Ghusun who had just moved to the city of Nablus and a fellow peasant from the village of Baqa al-Gharbiyya (ibid., 12:11).

100. For another example of how wealthy peasants established trading networks between villages and even between regions, see ibid., 12:352.

101. NICR, 13A:61–62. These lands were located in three different villages: Burqa, Kufr Lubbad, and Bazarya. Shaykh Burqawi headed the Sayf clan. Burqa was the seat village of the other ruling clan, al-Ahfa. For further details see Chapter 1.

102. Ibid., 12:249–251, 254.

103. NMSR, p. 30. The term *shaykh nahiya* did not disappear overnight. It was sometimes used in conjunction with *muhassil, mudir,* (manager), and *nazir* (supervisor). As a group, they and other appointed officials were most often referred to as *ma'murin* (employees; literally, those who are ordered) (NMSR, p. 76). The term for subdistrict also changed to *muqata'a* and, if it had a judge appointed to it, *qada*.

104. Ibid., p., 76.

105. Among other things, they were responsible for counting the adult males in the villages, for reporting numbers of births and deaths to the census bureau on a monthly basis, for overseeing the disarming and conscription of the peasants, and for abiding by the decisions of judges assigned to their subdistricts.

106. Tamimi and Bahjat, *Wilayat Bayrut*, p. 103.

107. Ibid., p. 93 (emphasis added).

108. For forms of peasant resistance in general, see James C. Scott, *Weapons of the Weak: Everyday Forms of Peasant Resistance* (New Haven, Conn., 1985).

109. Now known as Asira al-Shamaliyya. Both *sham* and *shamal* mean "north." The former has long been used to refer to Damascus or Greater Syria; hence the term Bilad al-Sham, meaning, presumably, the lands north of Egypt.

110. NMSR, p. 174 (emphasis added). Para was the smallest denomination of money used at that time. Forty paras equaled one piaster.

111. Ibid.

112. NMSR, pp. 174–175 (emphasis added). A *mashlah* was a long, flowing cloak made of wool or camel hair and usually embroidered with gold. The verb tenses used in the last part of this memorandum, when translated, give the impression that this was a live report being transmitted to the governor from the premises of the council.

113. NICR, 10:220.

114. Hafiz Pasha himself prepared the grounds for such a response by relegating the matter to his assistant whose terse communiqué, in turn, assumed the guilt of the peasants in this matter.

115. See Yehoshua Porath, "The Peasant Revolt of 1858–1861 in Kisrawan," AAS, 2 (1966), pp. 77–157; and Marwan Buheiry, "The Peasant Revolt of 1858 in Mount Lebanon: Rising Expectations, Economic Malaise and the Incentive to Arm," in Khalidi, ed., *Land Tenure*, pp. 291–301.

116. NMSR, p. 231.

117. Ibid., p. 242.

118. For a general discussion in the Ottoman context of the relationship between notions of political authority and agrarian production, see Huri İslamoğlu-İnan, "Peasants, Commercialization, and Legitimation of State Power in Sixteenth-Century Anatolia," in Keyder and Tabak, eds., *Landholding*, pp. 57–64.

119. He might have had the *salam* moneylending system in mind, though this was not spelled out.

120. NICR, 10:289–290.

121. NMSR, pp. 73–74.

122. The word *watan* could mean nation, homeland, country, or fatherland. The term "fatherland" is used to emphasize that they meant the Ottoman polity as a whole, not a specific nation or an ethnic homeland.

123. NMSR, pp. 76–77. See above for translation.

124. Ibid., p. 77.

125. It is not clear whether all the prisoners were freed, because the council members only referred to four prisoners in their letter, whereas the petition by Asira peasants mentioned ten.

126. Tamimi and Bahjat, *Wilayat Bayrut*, p. 95.

127. David Urquhart, *The Lebanon (Mount Souria): A History and Diary* (2 vols.; London, 1860), 1:5.

128. One fruitful area for further research would be an investigation of whether and to what degree peasants, judges, merchants, and others changed their attitudes and approach to law in general and to Islamic law in particular, and, if so, the role of these changing attitudes in constructing the meanings of modernity during the nineteenth century.

CHAPTER 5

1. NICR, 8:328. Each soap factory had a name and a personality, somewhat akin to famous skyscrapers of modern cities. This one was located in the Yasmina quarter.

2. He held the post of *mutasallim* for most of 1827 and 1828 (ibid., 8:289, 360–361). He and his two brothers, Abd al-Rahman and Abdullah, inherited the factory from their father, Muhammad *Beik* Tuqan (ibid., p. 328).

3. Muhyi al-Din had legitimate reasons to be afraid. The Tuqans had, on more than one occasion, used their political position to extort moneys and property from merchants. Nimr recounts some incidents of expropriation and murder of some merchants by the Tuqans during Musa *Beik* Tuqan's rule in the early nineteenth century (NIMR, 1:256). Two similar incidents that took place in the late eighteenth century were recounted by Ibrahim al-Danafi al-Samiri (al-Samiri, *Zahir al-Umar*, pp. 44, 47).

4. NICR, 8:361.

5. Ibid., 9:151. This form of loan, called *bay bi'l-wafa*, was widely resorted to. In case of default, she had the right to sell the property in order to collect the principal.

6. Ibid., 9:151. Loans by women, especially to relatives, were common in Nablus and other cities in the Ottoman Empire. It was not unusual for women to sue delinquent borrowers in court. For example, see Ronald Jennings, "Women in Early Seventeenth Century Ottoman Judicial Records: The Sharia Court of Anatolian Kayseri," JESHO, 18 (1975), pp. 53–114; Abraham Marcus, "Men, Women, and Property: Dealers in Real Estate in 18th Century Aleppo," JESHO, 26 (1983), pp. 138–163; Tucker, *Women*, chap. 4. Also, see Tucker's two articles on women in Nablus during the Ottoman period: "Marriage and Family," pp. 165–179, and "Ties That Bound," pp. 233–253.

7. NICR, 10:267.

8. Soap was produced in most cities and towns of the Fertile Crescent. In Palestine the most important was Nablus, followed by Jaffa (including Lydda and Ramla), Jerusalem, and Gaza. See Bowring, *Commercial Statistics*, pp. 19, 83; Kurd Ali, *Khitat al-Sham*, 4:159, 190; Schölch, "European Penetration," pp. 50–51; Graham-Brown, "Political Economy," pp. 138–141; and Gerber, "Modernization," p. 256. For further details, see Appendix 3. Tamimi and Bahjat (*Wilayat Bayrut*, p. 54) noted that the soap industry also expanded in Tripoli, but no other sources make mention of this point.

9. NIMR, 2:288; Dabbagh, *Biladuna*, 6:198.

10. Al-Ansari, *Nukhbat al-dahr*, pp. 200–201.

11. Bowring, *Commercial Statistics*, p. 19.

12. Kurd Ali, *Khitat al-Sham*, 4:159.

13. A copy of the advertisement can be found in Graham-Brown, *Palestinians*, p. 115.

14. NIMR, 1:291.

15. Nimr claimed that these properties were taken over by the people of Nablus (ibid., 1:295).

16. NICR, 8:225, dated October, 1830.

17. He came from a family of rich peasants based in the large village of Ya'bad, though it had branches in the villages of Misilya and Qabatya as well (ibid., 7:78–79; 13A:174). The latter was one of the two largest olive-producing villages in Jabal Nablus. He moved to Nablus before the Abd al-Hadis and, along with his father, helped the Abd al-Hadis to locate and purchase dozens of prime commercial

properties. Many of these properties were jointly owned with them, and Shaykh Yusuf often acted as the agent of Husayn Abd al-Hadi and his children in property purchases (for example, ibid., 9:85–86, 247, 249–251, 281–283). A relative, Abdullah *Afandi* Zayd al-Qadri, was appointed as a guardian over Abd al-Rahman, son of Husayn Abd al-Hadi, who was then governor of Sidon province (ibid., 10:240).

18. This jibes with Nimr's assessment (NIMR, 2:291). Kurd Ali stated that soap produced in Damascus was allowed to dry for three years in special places before being sold (*Khitat al-Sham*, 4:159).

19. NIMR, 1:95–105.

20. Also located in the Habala quarter. The other half of this soap factory was already endowed as *waqf* by Khalil *Beik* Sawwar; hence its name.

21. NICR, 5:81–82. This *waqf* was later voided with a note saying that it had been replaced by the 1161/1748 version. Unfortunately, the Islamic court records for that year are lost.

22. NIMR, 1:120–121.

23. Ibid., 1:121–122, 130–142. Nimr claimed that the golden age of Nablus was during the time of Umar *Agha* Nimr's rule. He also credited him with initiating the commercial trade in soap with the Arabian Gulf (ibid., 2:288).

24. His grandfather had two sons, and his father had two sons. If there were only male children, and if they all inherited, the most that *Hajj* Umar could receive would be exactly one-quarter. Apparently, however, the whole soap factory was passed to his father from his grandfather, and his father, in turn, divided half of it equally between his two sons and kept the other half (NICR, 5:81–82; and Nimr Family Papers, 3.1.8).

25. Nimr Family Papers, 3.1.8.

26. Ibid., 3.1.5. See also NICR, 8:276. Renovation began in May 1825.

27. They were built in 1830/1831 (NICR, 8:276).

28. Nimr Family Papers, 3.1.5.

29. Ibid., 3.1.6. This document was reproduced in NIMR, 2:opposite p. 288.

30. NIMR, 1:290.

31. Ibid., 2:301–302.

32. NICR, 8:281.

33. Ibid., 8:316.

34. NICR, 8:281–283, 316, 325. The Amrs were, and continue to be, one of the most important families in the Hebron area. *Hajj* Ahmad Qaddumi was a leading religious figure originally from the village of Qaddum, southwest of Nablus.

35. Ibid., 8:283.

36. The other half of the Uthmaniyya factory was part of the Tuqan family *waqf*. It must be assumed that they were also coordinating this program of expansion with Ahmad Fakhr al-Din, because it made little sense to renovate only one-half of a factory.

37. NICR, 8:316.

38. Ibid., 8:329.

39. Umar *Agha* Nimr, whom we met previously, endowed one-quarter of this soap factory as a family *waqf* on January, 18, 1729 (ibid., 5:81–82). See also ibid., 8:329. The Abd al-Hadis gained portions of this factory through *waqf* exchanges

with the Sawwar and Fakhr al-Din Akhrami families in the 1830s (ibid., 9:77–78, 254–255).

40. Nimr Family Papers, 3.1.6.

41. Ibid., 3.1.2. The implication that labor became more expensive is misleading, because some labor costs were included in the miscellaneous column of the 1825–1826 account sheet.

42. The *jift* was supplied by a merchant, by the "people of Asira," by the Qaryun quarter, and "from outside."

43. Nimr Family Papers, 3.1.2. This document shows continuity in the patterns of partnerships, but with even greater fragmentation. This situation, as we shall see below, was the exception that proved the rule, for it had more to do with the declining power of the Nimr family than with the overall trends.

44. Tamimi and Bahjat, *Wilayat Bayrut*, p. 120. In calculating the costs of production and sale prices of soap, they came up with three possible margins of profit, all of which were between 20 and 30 percent.

45. Calculated at 250 jars of oil per *tabkha* at a market price of 23 piasters per jar. The price per jar was determined from the account sheet.

46. In 1825/1826 and 1842/1843 taxes on each *tabkha* of soap were 614 and 836 piasters, respectively (Nimr Family Papers, 3.1.6; Abd al-Hadi Family Papers, 1.1.4).

47. NICR, 12:205–206. The family name suggests that they were, at one time, makers and sellers of *bishts* (see Chapter 3).

48. This degree of concentration of an extended family's resources was not necessarily typical just a few decades earlier. The four sons of Arafat Abd al-Majid Shahid, discussed at length in Chapter 2, each established their own household and did not centralize the extended family's resources. When one of the sons, Abd al-Razzaq Arafat, died indebted in 1810, his property was sold to other rival families even though his brothers were rich at the time.

49. Some examples of the dozens of purchase cases can be found in NICR, 12:73, 208, 216, 218, 229–231, 235–236, 263. The first document cited, for instance, was a purchase of oil presses in the nearby villages of Rafidiya and Bayt Wazan.

50. Ibid., 12:207. It is important to note here that the inheritance estate, like all others in the Nablus Islamic Court, did not include immovable properties.

51. Ibid., 12:207.

52. Deniz Kandiyoti, "Islam and Patriarchy: A Comparative Perspective," in Keddie and Baron, eds., *Women in Middle Eastern History*, p. 33. See also her article, "Bargaining with Patriarchy," *Gender and Society*, 2 (1988), pp. 274–290.

53. NICR, 12:208, 210.

54. Ibid., 12:162–165. On July 23, 1856, they endowed this factory as a family *waqf*. The Asaliyya, as it came to be called, was located in the Aqaba quarter.

55. Ibid., 10:83–85.

56. Interview with Hasan Fihmi Masri, July 20, 1990. Born in 1933, he started working in soap factories at the age of nine, and at the time of this writing, was operating the Yusufiyya soap factory.

57. In the early twentieth century *Hajj* Isma'il Arafat's son, Shaykh Amr, was considered to be the local authority on this subject (see Chapter 2).

58. Interviews with Hasan Masri; and with Husam Sharif, November 29, 1987. Nimr provided an almost identical list but did not mention the specializations (NIMR, 2:292).

59. For example, Salah Tbeila, identified as "the pride of merchants," bought more than two-thirds of the Gharzaniyya soap factory in late November 1723 (NICR, 4:39); and in February 1726 Abd al-Wahid Khammash's grandfather married the daughter of *Khawaja* Salih Tbeila (ibid., 4:308).

60. Interview with Hasan Masri. Masri's father was one of the Egyptian artisans recruited to Nablus for this purpose. Ironically, his father tried to form a soap-workers' union in 1958, and he also became active in the union movement in the late 1970s.

61. Ma'oz, *Ottoman Reform*, p. 9 (emphasis added).

62. Ibid., p. 12.

63. Hütteroth and Abdulfattah, *Historical Geography*, p. 62; and David H. K. Amiran, "The Pattern of Settlement in Palestine," *Israel Exploration Journal*, 3 (1953), p. 69.

64. For example, Cynthia Nelson, ed., *The Desert and the Sown: Nomads in a Wider Society* (Berkeley, Calif., 1974).

65. Talal Asad, "The Bedouin as a Military Force: Notes on Some Aspects of Power Relations between Nomads and Sedentaries in Historical Perspective," in Nelson, ed., *Desert*, p. 71.

66. Volney, *Travels*, 1:382–383.

67. Ibid., p. 391.

68. Burckhardt, *Travels*, pp. 344, 346.

69. NIMR, 2:361, 365; Finn, *Stirring Times*, 1:241.

70. For example, see Finn, *Stirring Times*, 1:252, 2:42.

71. NIMR, 2:543.

72. For an example, see Finn, *Stirring Times*, 1:317.

73. Raouf Sa'd Abujaber, whose ancestors worked in the *qilw* trade, argues that this trade was no longer an important source of income for bedouins by the 1860s due to the introduction of industrially produced caustic soda, which was both cleaner and cheaper (Abujaber, *Pioneers*, p. 135).

74. NIMR, 2:289. Sometimes the barilla plants were sent directly to the soap factories and burned there.

75. Burckhardt, *Travels*, pp. 354–355.

76. Indicative of the importance of the *qilw* trade was the attempt by the Egyptian government to monopolize it during the occupation in the 1830s. The Egyptian commanders forced the Bani Sakhr and other Arab tribes to bring all their *qilw* to Gaza, where the government bought and stored it. The soap merchants in Nablus and Jerusalem were obliged to buy their provisions from government offices in Gaza at a higher price. Both the bedouins and the soap-factory owners, however, complained bitterly about this arrangement and the extra costs involved, especially in transportation. The Egyptians quickly realized that this monopoly caused a drop in soap production and, consequently, in taxes on soap. Therefore, after only one year, they rescinded the order and allowed bedouins to deliver the *qilw* directly to Nablus and Jerusalem (Asad Rustum, *Al-Usul al-arabiyya li-tarikh Suriyya fi ahd Muhammad Ali basha* [Materials for a Corpus of Arabic

Documents relating to the History of Syria under Mehemet Ali Pasha] [5 vols.; Beirut, 1933–1936], 2:133–134).

77. NIMR, 2:289. As usual, he does not specify the period.

78. For a detailed account, see Rogan, "Incorporating the Periphery," part 2. In the mid-nineteenth century, Palestinian merchants exerted pressures on the Ottoman governor of Jerusalem to facilitate cultivation of the Jordan plain and to undertake infrastructural projects (Finn, *Stirring Times*, 2:17).

79. NICR, 6:260–263.

80. The deceased was married to the daughter of the *naqib al-ashraf* of Jerusalem.

81. His was only a temporary appointment, and the deceased's son, Muhammad Murtada, took his father's position when he reached his legal majority. Muhammad Murtada went on to become not only a soap factory owner but also the longest-serving religious official in Nablus: he held the position of *naqib al-ashraf* for forty consecutive years (1823–1863). For the first and last documents which mention him in this capacity, see ibid., 8:238, 311; 13A:239. For details, see Doumani, "Merchants," chap. 3.

82. In the seventeenth and eighteenth centuries the Bishtawis were important *timar* holders, but they shifted gradually to trade and soap production. In January 1729 Muhammad *Beik* Nasrallah Bishtawi and his wife, Aysha, daughter of Ibrahim Tuqan, endowed a soap factory as a family *waqf* (NICR, 5:84–85). In April 1810 a member of the Bishtawi family purchased approximately 1/12 of this factory from the Shafi'i family (ibid., 7:40). By the late 1850s, it seems that this factory was entirely in the hands of *Sayyid* As'ad Bishtawi, whose inheritance case was discussed in the previous section (ibid., 12:122).

83. Muhammad Salih *Afandi* Hanbali owned a soap factory, or part of one, in 1213/1798–1799 (ibid., 6:24). Hasan *Agha* Nimr's recently deceased brother, Abd al-Latif *Agha*, also owned a soap factory (ibid., 6:324).

84. Ibid., 6:260–264.

85. Ibid., 6:264, 269–273.

86. A *waqf* endowment by Abd al-Wahid's father and paternal uncle—Mustafa and Hasan, respectively—mentions that they had renovated the Sultaniyya factory, located in the Yasmina quarter, sometime before 1806 (ibid., 6:348).

87. *Sayyid* Muhammad Hashim Hanbali bought shares in the Tbeiliyya soap factory between 1802 and 1811, and it does not seem that the Tbeila family held any more shares after that point (ibid., 6:165, 7:84). In the early eighteenth century the Bustami family owned a soap factory, but they had no shares left by 1825 (ibid., 4:307). The fate of the Sawwar, Shafi'i, and Akhrami families were discussed earlier. Members of the Qaddumi, Qadi-Shwayka, and Tuffaha Husayni families also operated soap factories at this time, but as renters, not owners. The first two rented part of the Bashawiyya soap factory from a charitable *waqf* (ibid., 7:363, 8:281), and *Sayyid* Hasan Tuffaha Husayni was a financial backer of the Nimr family's soap factory (ibid., 6:324). For more details, see below.

88. To the above list of merchants one must also add the Ya'ish family, one of the few merchant families to own a soap factory in the eighteenth century. There is no evidence that they remained soap owners at the turn of the nineteenth cen-

tury, however. The Ya'ishiyya soap factory, named after them, was already the property of the deceased.

89. NICR, 6:98; located in the Qaysariyya quarter. The same sum was paid by Muhammad, son of Ali Tuqan, for a small, ruined shop next to the soap factory (ibid., 6:107).

90. Ibid., 6:11, 18, 48; located in the Habala quarter. The purchase of this soap factory was quite complicated, and it changed hands a number of times during that year.

91. Ibid., 6:23; located in the Qaryun quarter.

92. Ibid., 6:260–264. It is not clear where this factory was located, and it could possibly be the same as the Husniyya or Ayshiyya factory.

93. Ibid., 7:92–93; located in the Qaryun quarter, next to the Nasr mosque.

94. Ibid., 7:363.

95. Ibid., 7:346; located in Spinner's Street, Gharb quarter.

96. Both served briefly as *mutasallims* of Nablus. Qasim al-Ahmad even moved his residence to the city proper, purchasing a large complex which included an entire soap factory called the Shaqrawiyya.

97. Asa'd Mansur, *Tarikh al-Nasira*, p. 70. Descendants of Qasim al-Ahmad claim that his son planned the assassination.

98. NICR, 9:180. The house, which still stands, is very large, and the soap factory was considered but a part of it. The other half of the property was sold to a rich merchant, *Hajj* Dawud, son of *Hajj* Mahmud Kan'an, for 55,000 piasters on May 3, 1860 (ibid., 12:334–335).

99. Ibid., 9:77–78, 206–207, 254–255, and ibid., 9:85–86, respectively.

100. Between 1830 and 1864 he served for a total of 28 years. He died in 1876. For more details, see Doumani, "Merchants," chap. 3.

101. The petition was signed on April 20, 1840. For the text and context of the petition, see NIMR, 1:338–341.

102. Located in the Yasmina quarter, adjacent to the family's residence, it was endowed as a private family *waqf*, along with a substantial number of other properties (NICR, 11:121–123; dated September 1848). This was not a new departure for the Khammash family: Abd al-Wahid's father and uncle had invested in the renovation of the Sultaniyya factory in 1806 (ibid., 6:348).

103. Ibid., 9:206–207.

104. Nimr Family Papers, 3.1.1.

105. NIMR, 1:333.

106. As mentioned earlier, a close relative, *Sayyid* Hasan Tuffaha Husayni, was a partner of Ahmad *Agha* Nimr's cousin in a soap factory during the first decade of the nineteenth century.

107. Nimr Family Papers, 3.1.4(A). Also reproduced in NIMR, 2:292–293.

108. NIMR, 1:341.

109. Ibid., 1:341–342.

110. Nimr Family Papers, 3.1.1. For the *waqf* document, see NICR, 12:67–70.

111. NICR, 9:393; dated January 14, 1839.

112. Two other allies of the Abd al-Hadis who acquired shares in soap factories at this time, but who were not mentioned in the list, are Tahir al-Musa and

Shaykh Salah al-Baqani. For example, in September 1839 Tahir al-Musa purchased one-sixth of the Uthmaniyya factory from Salah al-Baqani (NICR, 9:399). The former came from Arraba, the hometown of the Abd-Hadis, and he was appointed deputy to the *mutasallim* of Nablus in early May 1836 (ibid., 9:174). Salah al-Baqani served briefly as a judge and signed the petition against Ahmad *Agha* Nimr (NIMR, 1:340).

113. He endowed two-thirds of the Shaytaniyya factory as a private family *waqf* in mid-December 1811 (NICR, 7:92–93).

114. The name of the third soap factory, added to their holdings sometime between 1839–1841, is not known, but it was located in the Habala quarter. It was endowed as a family *waqf* by Mahmud *Beik* Abd al-Hadi in late June 1841 (ibid., 12:48–50).

115. *Hajj* Anabtawi, originally a wealthy peasant from Anabta, was a business partner with the Abd al-Hadis and jointly owned a number of properties with them, such as a flour mill in Wadi al-Tuffah (Apple Valley), which extends westward from the city (ibid., 9:172). He also represented them frequently in court (for example, ibid., 9:191, 253, 259, 262, 273). In 1852 a letter by the Nablus Advisory Council claimed that he and Shaykh Yusuf Zayd Qadri were two pillars of the merchant community. This was part of an application to have them approved as the financial backers of Mahmud *Beik* Abd al-Hadi's reappointment as the *mutasallim* of Nablus (NMSR, p. 249).

116. NICR, 13A:162. In 1856 he endowed 80 percent of this factory as a private family *waqf* (NICR, 12:175–176, 306–307, 372).

117. Ibid., 9:399.

118. Ibid., 10:267; 12:48–50.

119. Ibid., 11:121–123.

120. Ibid., 13A:220, 265; 13B:7, 115, 128.

121. NMSR, p. 293; dated May 1, 1853.

122. Respectively, NICR, 13B:144, 164–165; 13B:115; 13B:19–20; 13A:30–36, 74–75, 110–111.

123. Ibid., 12:162–165. This factory was endowed as a family *waqf* on July 23, 1856. Fourteen years earlier, in August 1842, they endowed a small share of the Husayniyya soap factory as a family *waqf* (ibid., 10:83–85).

124. Tamimi and Bahjat, *Wilayat Bayrut*, p. 119.

125. Ibid., p. 119; Darwaza, *Mi'at am*, p. 77.

126. Tamimi and Bahjat, *Wilayat Bayrut*, p. 120. Darwaza noted that they outdistanced by far all other merchants in Jabal Nablus *(Mi'at am*, pp. 77–79).

127. On April 30, 1850, for instance, four soap producers—*Hajj* As'ad Tahir, *Sayyid* Mahmud Tamimi, *Hajj* Amin Hashim Hanbali, and Abd al-Fattah *Agha* [Nimr]—were appointed as new members of the council. The other members at this time included the *qa'immaqam*, Sulayman *Beik* Tuqan; the *qadi*, Abd al-Wahid Khammash; the *naqib al-ashraf* Muhammad Murtada *Afandi* Hanbali; and the *mufti Sayyid Abu* al-Hida Khammash—all of whom were soap-factory owners (NMSR, p. 46). For background and details, see Doumani, "Merchants," chap. 3.

128. NMSR, p. 186 (emphasis added).

129. Ibid., p. 196.

130. Ibid., p. 210. His letter is summarized in the council's answer detailed below.

131. Ibid., p. 210.

132. Ibid., pp. 221–222.

133. Ibid.

134. Ibid., pp. 53, 66, 72–73, 94.

135. The central government condemned smuggling and threatened violators on a number of occasions (ibid., pp. 12, 14, 41, 56). See also below for a discussion of the smuggling of oil from Jabal Ajlun into Nablus.

136. They were spelled out in NICR, 10:199–200, 289–290; 11:141–142, 180.

137. An Arabic translation of the *firman* issued by the sultan was registered in the Nablus Islamic Court on May 7, 1846 (ibid., 10:199–200). The officials addressed specifically included governors, head scribes, judges, customs officials, Advisory Council members, and *muftis* in the two provinces and their districts.

138. Ibid., 11:141–142, 180.

139. Further detailed clarifications, sent between 1849–1851, can be found in NMSR, pp. 38, 92, 132.

140. See Ibid., pp. 92 and 304 for the first and last cases.

141. For example, ibid., p. 227.

142. Ibid., p. 235.

143. Fiscal years began in March and were calculated on the basis of a solar calendar. This calendar was first introduced in 1740, and by 1794 it was applied to all financial matters (Kemal Karpat, *Ottoman Population, 1830–1914: Demographic and Social Characteristics* [Madison, Wis., 1985], pp. xi–xiii).

144. NMSR, pp. 132–133.

145. Ibid., pp. 38, 304; NICR, 11:141.

146. NMSR, pp. 153–154, 183, 221, 227, 235–236. The soap merchants also claimed that some of the 1851/1852 soap was made from old 1266/1849–1850 stocks, so they really had a double grievance (ibid., pp. 153–154).

147. Ibid., pp. 264–265, 304.

148. Ibid.

149. Ibid., p. 153. Apparently there was some truth to this allegation, for the customs officials were warned not to do so by the central government (ibid., pp. 132–133).

150. Ibid., p. 153.

151. Ibid., pp. 92, 195, 202, 221, 227, 235–236, 275, 293, 304.

152. Soap exported to Safad, on the other hand, was taxed at the very light rate of 8 paras per load, and perfumed soap manufactured in Jerusalem and on its way to Damascus paid 1 piaster in customs for each load when passing through Nablus. The very low taxes on soap are more readily apparent when compared, for example, with tobacco and garlic, which were assessed 1 and 5.5 piasters per load, respectively (NICR, 8:389).

153. NMSR, p. 50.

154. Ibid., p. 227. The anger of the central government is also transparent in ibid., p. 70.

155. NICR, 10:289–290.

156. NMSR, pp. 259, 274–275. This means that at least 1.5 million piasters' worth of soap was exported during this period.

157. Ibid., p. 240.

158. Ibid., p. 227.

159. Ibid., pp. 226–227.

160. Ibid., pp. 11, 153, 240, 242, 294, 313.

161. Ibid., pp. 226–227, 274.

162. Ibid., p. 293.

163. Ibid., p. 304.

164. Ibid., p. 38.

165. Ibid., pp. 259, 274–275, 304.

CONCLUSION

1. Rogers, *Domestic Life*, p. 389 (emphasis in original).

2. By uttering these words, and later by refusing to eat or drink until they received a favorable answer to their request for asylum, the young boys correctly followed established customary procedures for protection.

3. Rogers, *Domestic Life*, pp. 214–235, 351–359, 360, 361–370, 372–373, 389–394.

4. NIMR, 1:380–383; Schölch, *Palestine in Transformation*, p. 225.

5. The future exclusion of Nablus's leading families from the post of *mutasallim* did not mean the complete imposition of central Ottoman control. Real influence over the daily affairs of the city would now be shared between the revolving door of annually appointed Ottoman governors, on the one hand, and by the city council, dominated by the wealthy merchant families, on the other.

6. The difference between the two families did not fail to attract the attention of two keen contemporary observers: the British consul in Jerusalem, James Finn, and Mary Rogers herself. (The following observations must, of course, be treated cautiously, for they reduced a complicated reality into a simplistic Eurocentric vision of tradition versus modernity.) Finn, for example, claimed that the Abd al-Hadis were "cunning at keeping up with Constantinople progress, and bidding for popularity with the European Consuls. They were, however, not to be trusted" (Finn, *Stirring Times*, 2:239). Meanwhile, Ahmad Jarrar, immediately after Finn entered his house in the village of Jaba: "growled out, 'so the Sultan is giving away all the land of Islam, bit by bit, to the Christians'" (ibid., 1:263). Mary Rogers, in a similar vein, was awed by what she perceived to be the manly beauty, courage, daring, strength, and straightforwardness of the Jarrar leaders. But after spending a day in their residence in the village of Sanur, she wrote: "I never heard of a Jerrar who could read or write, or even sign his name. On the other hand, many of the men of the Abdul Hady family are well educated, and set a high value on *book* learning: and the ladies of Arrabeh are somewhat polished, and look very different to the simple rustic women of Senur" (Rogers, *Domestic Life*, p. 239 [emphasis in original]).

7. NMSR, pp. 19, 46, 126, 129, 249, 252. See Chapter 1 for details.

8. Doumani, "The Political Economy of Population Counts," pp. 5–9.

APPENDIX 1

1. For example, in 1735 the French consul in Sidon urged Zahir al-Umar to impose a uniform standard of weights for the Galilee (Cohen, *Palestine*, p. 14).

2. Invariably, units of weights and measures appeared in local sources within the context of letters about taxes (NMSR, pp. 43, 50, 132; NICR, 11:18).

3. Unless otherwise cited, the following is based on NIMR, 2:275–277. For a detailed survey of weights and measures used in Palestine as a whole, see Arraf, *Al-Ard*, pp. 224–229.

4. NIMR, 2:275.

5. Arraf, *Al-Ard*, p. 224.

6. A *qintar* of Nablus soap was defined as equal to 225 *uqqas* in NMSR, p. 132; dated August 19, 1851.

7. Arraf, *Al-Ard*, p. 226.

8. Ibid.

9. Walther Hinz, *Al-Makayil wa al-awzan al-islamiyya wa ma yuʿadiluha fi al-nizam al-mitri* (Islamic Weights and Measures and Their Metric Equivalent) (trans. Kamil al-Asali; Amman, 1970), pp. 72–73.

10. NMSR, p. 43.

11. Hinz, *Al-Makayil*, pp. 58–59.

12. NMSR, p. 50; dated July 28, 1852. That same year, another customs document defined a jar of oil destined for soap making in the Jerusalem region as containing 13.5 *uqqas* (NMSR, p. 132; dated August 15, 1852).

13. Hans Wehr, *A Dictionary of Modern Written Arabic* (ed. J. Milton Cowan; 3d ed.; New York, 1976), p. 1036.

14. Arraf, *Al-Ard*, p. 226.

APPENDIX 2

1. For details on the records of the Nablus Advisory Council, see the discussion in and notes to the Introduction. For a comprehensive overview of these records, see Beshara Doumani, "Palestinian Islamic Court Records: A Source for Socioeconomic History," *MESA Bulletin*, 19 (1985), pp. 155–172. Internal records of the Nablus Islamic Court show that all the volumes known to exist today were accounted for in that period.

2. Interview with Nazih al-Sayih, head scribe of the Nablus Islamic Court for the past three decades, according to stories that were passed to him (February, 1987). Nimr, writing in the 1930s, made the same claim (NIMR, 1:6).

3. For a general overview, see Gibb and Bowen, *Islamic Society*, 2:86–93. For Palestine, see Doumani, "Palestinian Islamic Court Records," pp. 155–161.

4. According to Gibb and Bowen, there were only 27 *mullas* in the Ottoman Empire in the second half of the eighteenth century. In rank, Istanbul came first, followed by the Holy Cities of Mecca and Medina, then Cairo and Damascus, followed by Jerusalem, along with three suburbs of Istanbul, Smyrna, Aleppo, Salonika, and Yeni-shehir (*Islamic Society*, pp. 89, 121).

5. No appointment letters were registered for the years 1829, 1831, 1837, 1845,

1852–1853, or 1856–1857. All of these gaps occurred during the long tenures of Abd al-Wahid Khammash and his father, Mustafa Khammash. Most likely, they served during those years.

6. A full list of Nablus judges during the 1799–1860 period, as well as the exact dates of their appointment, can be found in Doumani, "Merchants," pp. 409–411.

APPENDIX 3

1. A detailed description can be found in NICR, 12:154. This account is also based on personal visits. Often, soap factories had residential apartments built above the second floor; that is, buildings were three or sometimes four stories high. Most of the soap factories discussed in Chapter 5 are still standing.

2. For example, the al-Qadi soap factory had four wells, each with a capacity of 750 jars of olive oil (about 15 tons), enough for three cooked batches of soap (*tabkhas*). This soap factory is one of the smaller ones in Nablus. Larger ones have wells with at least twice this capacity. This information is based on a visit to the factory and on a conversation with Husni Ali Abd al-Haq (b. 1922), who, at the time of the interview (August 1, 1990), supervised soap production in this facility.

3. Limestone is abundant in the hill regions of Palestine. To make *shid*, soft limestone is piled in a large pit, covered with wood, and burned. Produced mostly in villages, *shid* was also used in construction.

4. After the oil is pressed, the crushed olive pits are sun dried, then packed for use as fuel. They retain heat and burn for a long time, like small coals.

5. NIMR, 2:290.

6. Bowring refers to it as a "copper" (*Commercial Statistics*, p. 19).

7. NIMR, 2:291. Tamimi and Bahjat, *Wilayat Bayrut*, p. 120. Their accounts were confirmed by the account-books of the Yusifiyya soap factory and the inheritance estate of the Bishtawi brothers. See Chapter 5.

8. Nimr claims that 10 qintars of qilw went into each *tabkha* (NIMR, 2:291).

9. This figure was calculated using a log of expenses and profits for the Yusifiyya soap factory (see Chapter 5). According to this log, dated 1826, approximately 147 qintars of *shid* were used for 21 batches of soap. See below for details.

10. Not a single source mentions the amount of water, and some ignore it altogether. The figure of 25 jars is calculated from the formula provided in Muhammad Sa'id al-Qasimi, *Qamus al-sina'at al-shamiyya* (2 vols.; Paris, 1962), 2:268.

11. The size of each *falqa* differed, depending on the destination. Those exported to Egypt measured about 3 by 5 by 5 centimeters and were twice as large as the ones cut for local consumption.

12. NIMR, 2:291; Tamimi and Bahjat, *Wilayat Bayrut*, p. 120.

13. G. Rosen, "Über Nablus und Umgegend," *Zeitschrift der Deutschen Morgenländdischen Gesellschaft*, 14 (1860), p. 638; cited in Schölch, "European Penetration," p. 50.

14. Cited in ibid.

15. Tamimi and Bahjat, *Wilayat Bayrut*, p. 119.

16. Some of the new names were Shaqrawiyya, Salihiyya, Khayyatiyya, Asaliyya, Ayshiyya, and al-Qadi. See Chapter 5.

17. Soap factories were rarely sold as a whole. The following prices were calculated from the sale of shares.

18. NICR, 6:165.

19. Ibid., 7:84. A year earlier the Bishtawiyya soap factory had sold for 900 piasters (ibid., 7:40), but five years later, in January 1816, another factory, the Bashawiyya soap factory, sold for 9,000 piasters (ibid., 7:363).

20. Ibid., 12:154.

21. Respectively, ibid., 8:328, 361; 9:151; 10:267. In September 1839 the Uthmaniyya soap factory sold for roughly 33,556 piasters (ibid., 9:399).

22. Ibid., 9:180.

23. Ibid., 13A:31–36, 74–75, 110–111.

24. Olive trees produce abundantly only every other year.

25. For example, Kurd Ali, *Khitat al-Sham*, 4:159; Tamimi and Bahjat, *Wilayat Bayrut*, p. 54.

26. Bowring, *Commercial Statistics*, p. 19. There is also some confusion concerning the size of each *tabkha*. Bowring gives the figure of 20 to 22 *qintars* of soap each for Aleppo, Idlib, and Kilis but specifies 3,200 *uqqas*, which only comes to 16 *qintars*, for all other cities and towns. As we have seen, however, in Nablus each *tabkha* produced about 20–22.5 *qintars* of dry soap.

27. Schölch, "European Penetration," p. 50.

28. Ibid.

29. Abd al-Hadi Family Papers, 1.1.4.

30. NICR, 9:393.

31. For example, NMSR, pp. 221–222.

32. Tamimi and Bahjat, *Wilayat Bayrut*, p. 119.

Select Bibliography

The titles of books written in Arabic are translated for the benefit of readers who do not know Arabic. Where authors include an English translation of the title, that translation is used. All translations appear between parentheses after the original title.

ARCHIVAL SOURCES

Jerusalem Islamic Court, East Jerusalem, Palestine. *Sijillat mahkamat al-Quds al-shar'iyya* (The Islamic Court Records of Jerusalem). Vols. 280–349. 1798–1865.
Nablus, Palestine. The Nablus Advisory Council Records (*Sijillat majlis shura Nablus*). 1848–1853. The original is privately owned.
Nablus Islamic Court, Nablus, Palestine. *Sijillat mahkamat Nablus al-shar'iyya* (The Islamic Court Records of Nablus). Vols. 1–13B. 1665–1865.

FAMILY PAPERS

Nablus, Palestine. Documents from the Nimr, Smadi, Arafat, Burqawi, Tuqan, Jardana, Abd al-Hadi, Khammash, Khalaf, and Ya'ish families.

UNPUBLISHED MANUSCRIPTS

Amiry, Suad M. A. "Space, Kinship and Gender: The Social Dimensions of Peasant Architecture in Palestine." Ph.D. diss., University of Edinburgh, 1987.
Al-Arid, Walid. "XIX. Yüzyilda Cebel-i Nablus." Ph.D. diss., Istanbul University, 1992.
Cuno, Ken. "Was the Land of Ottoman Syria *miri* or *milk*? An Examination of Juridical Differences within the Hanafi School." Unpublished paper delivered to the PARSS Seminar on the Middle East, University of Pennsylvania, November 1993.

Doumani, Beshara. "Merchants, the State, and Socioeconomic Change in Ottoman Palestine: The Nablus Region, 1800–1860." Ph.D. diss., Georgetown University, 1990.

Fattah, Hala. "The Development of the Regional Market in Iraq and the Gulf, 1800–1900." Ph.D. diss., University of California, Los Angeles, 1986.

Kanaʿan, Ruba. "Patronage and Style in Mercantile Residential Architecture of Ottoman Bilad al-Sham: The Nablus Region in the Nineteenth Century." M.Phil. thesis, University of Oxford, 1993.

Khoury, Dina. "The Political Economy of the Province of Mosul: 1700–1850." Ph.D. diss., Georgetown University, 1987.

Manna, Adel. "The Sancak of Jerusalem between Two Invasions (1798–1831): Administration and Society." Ph.D. diss., Hebrew University of Jerusalem, 1986. (Hebrew).

Meriwether, Margaret Lee. "The Notable Families of Aleppo, 1770–1830: Networks and Social Structure." Ph.D. diss., University of Pennsylvania, 1981.

Moors, Annelies. "Women and Property: A Historical-Anthropological Study of Women's Access to Property through Inheritance, the Dower and Labour in Jabal Nablus, Palestine." Ph.D. diss., University of Amsterdam, 1992.

Naff, Alixa. "A Social History of Zahle, the Principal Market Town in Nineteenth-Century Lebanon." Ph.D. diss., University of California, Los Angeles, 1972.

Reilly, James. "Origins of Peripheral Capitalism in the Damascus Region, 1830–1914." Ph.D. diss., Georgetown University, 1987.

Rogan, Eugene. "Incorporating the Periphery: The Ottoman Extension of Direct Rule over Southeastern Syria (Transjordan), 1867–1914." Ph.D. diss., Harvard University, 1991.

Sabri, Bahjat. "Liwa al-Quds fi al-qarn al-tasi ashar, 1840–1873." M.A. thesis, Ayn al-Shams University, 1973.

Yeager, Susan Lee. "The Ottoman Empire on Exhibition: The Ottoman Empire at International Exhibitions 1851–1867, and the *sergi-i umumi Osmani*, 1863." Ph.D. diss., Columbia University, 1981.

Zarinebaf-Shahr, Fariba. "Tabriz under Ottoman Rule (1725–1730)." Ph.D. diss., University of Chicago, 1991.

PUBLISHED WORKS

Al-Abbasi, Mustafa. *Tarikh al Tuqan fi Jabal Nablus* (History of the Tuqan Household in Jabal Nablus). Shfaʿamr, Israel, 1990.

Abdel-Karim, Ahmad. *Al-Taqsim al-idari li Suriyya* (Administrative Structure of Syria). Cairo, 1961.

Abdel Nour, Antoine. *Introduction a l'histoire urbaine de la Syrie ottomane, XVIe–XVIIIe siècle.* Beirut, 1982.

Abir, Mordechai. "Local Leadership and Early Reforms in Palestine, 1800-1834." In Moshe Maʿoz, ed., *Studies on Palestine during the Ottoman Period.* Jerusalem, 1975, 284–310.

Abou El-Haj, Rifaʿat Ali. *Formation of the Modern State in the Ottoman Empire, Sixteenth to Eighteenth Century.* Albany, N.Y., 1991.

Abu-Husayn, Abdul-Rahim. *Provincial Leadership in Syria, 1575–1650.* Beirut, 1985.
Abu Izz al-Din, Sulayman. *Ibrahim basha fi Suriyya* (Ibrahim Pasha in Syria). Beirut, 1929.
Abujaber, Raouf Sa'd. *Pioneers over Jordan: The Frontier of Settlement in Transjordan, 1850–1914.* London, 1989.
Abu-Lughod, Janet L. *Before European Hegemony: The World System, A.D. 1250–1350.* Oxford, 1989.
———. "The Islamic City: Historic Myth, Islamic Essence, and Contemporary Relevance." IJMES, 19 (1987), 155–176.
Adas, Michael. "From Avoidance to Confrontation: Peasant Protest in Precolonial and Colonial Southeast Asia," *Comparative Studies in Society and History,* 23 (1981), 217–247.
Amin, Samir. *Accumulation on a World Scale.* New York, 1974.
Amiran, D. H. K. "The Pattern of Settlement in Palestine." *Israel Exploration Journal,* 3 (1953), 65–78, 192–209, 250–260.
Amiry, Suad, and Vera Tamari. *The Palestinian Village Home.* London, 1989.
Al-Ansari, Shams al-Din. *Nukhbat al-dahr fi aja'ib al-barr wa al-bahr* (Time's Selected Wonders in Land and Sea). St. Petersburg, Russia, 1866.
Antoun, Richard, and Iliya Harik. *Rural Politics and Social Change in the Middle East.* Bloomington, Ind., 1972.
Appadurai, Arjun. "Introduction: Commodities and the Politics of Value." In Arjun Appadurai, ed., *The Social Life of Things* (Cambridge, England, 1986), 3–63.
———, ed. *The Social Life of Things.* Cambridge, England, 1986.
Al-Aref, Aref. "The Closing Phase of Ottoman Rule in Jerusalem." In Moshe Ma'oz, ed., *Studies on Palestine during the Ottoman Period.* Jerusalem, 1975, 334-340.
———. *Al-Muffassal fi tarikh al-Quds* (A Detailed History of Jerusalem). Jerusalem, 1961.
Arraf, Shukri. *Al-Ard, al-insan', wa al-juhd: Dirasa li hadaratina al-madiya ala ardina* (Land, Man, and Effort: A Study of Our Past Civilization on Our Land). Acre, 1982.
———. *Al-Qarya al-arabiyya al-filastiniyya: Mabna wa isti'malat aradi* (The Palestinian-Arab Village: Structure and Land Use). Jerusalem, 1986.
Asad, Talal. "The Bedouin as a Military Force: Notes on Some Aspects of Power Relations between Nomads and Sedentaries in Historical Perspective." In Cynthia Nelson, ed., *The Desert and the Sown: Nomads in a Wider Society.* Berkeley, Calif., 1974, 61–74.
Al-Asali, Kamil J. *Mawsim al-nabi Musa fi Filastin: Tarikh al-mawsim wa al-maqam* (The Nabi Musa Feast in Palestine: History of the Feast and the Sanctuary). Amman, 1990.
Ashtor, Eliyahu. *Studies on the Levantine Trade in the Middle Ages.* London, 1978.
Aston, T. H., and C. H. E. Philpin, eds. *The Brenner Debate: Agrarian Class Structure and Economic Development in Pre-Industrial Europe.* Cambridge, England, 1985.

Avitsur, Shmuel. "The Influence of Western Technology on the Economy of Palestine during the Nineteenth Century." In Moshe Maʿoz, ed., *Studies on Palestine during the Ottoman Period*. Jerusalem, 1975, 485–494.

Awad, Abd al-Aziz Muhammad. *Al-Idara al-uthmaniyya fi wilayat Suriyya, 1864–1914 A.D.* (Ottoman Administration in the Province of Syria, 1864–1914). Cairo, 1969.

Awra, Ibrahim. *Tarikh wilayat Sulayman basha al-adil* (History of the Reign of Sulayman Pasha the Just). Edited by Constantine Pasha al-Mukhlasi. Sidon, 1936.

Badran, Nabil. "Al-Rif al-filastini qabl al-harb al-alamiyya al-ula" (The Palestinian Countryside before the First World War). *Shuʾun Filastiniyya*, 7 (March 1972), 116–129.

Baer, Gabriel. "The Dismemberment of Awqaf in Early 19th Century Jerusalem." *AAS*, 13:3 (1979), 220–241.

———. *Fellah and Townsman in the Middle East: Studies in Social History*. Totowa, N.J., 1982.

———. "The Impact of Economic Change on Traditional Society in Nineteenth Century Palestine." In Moshe Maʿoz, ed., *Studies on Palestine during the Ottoman Period*. Jerusalem, 1975, 495–498.

———. "Jerusalem Families of Notables and the Wakf in the Early 19th Century." In David Kushner, ed., *Palestine in the Late Ottoman Period*. Jerusalem and Leiden, 1986, 109–122.

———. "Village and City in Egypt and Syria." In A. L. Udovitch, ed., *The Islamic Middle East, 700–1900: Studies in Economic and Social History*. Princeton, N.J., 1981, 595–652.

Bakhit, Muhammad Adnan. *The Ottoman Province of Damascus in the Sixteenth Century*. London, 1972.

———, et al. *Kashshaf ihsaʾi zamani li-sijillat al-mahakam al-sharʿiyya wa al-awqaf al-islamiyya fi Bilad al-Sham* (Statistical and Chronological Index of the Islamic Court Records and Muslim *waqfs* in Greater Syria). Amman, 1984.

———, and Noufan Raja Hmuod, eds. *Daftar muffasal liwa Ajlun: Tapu defter-i raqam 970* (The Detailed Defter of Ajlun District: Tapu Deferti No. 970). Amman, 1989.

———. *Daftar muffasal nahiyat Marj Ibn Amir wa tawabiʿiha wa lawahiquha al-lati kanat fi tassaruf al-amir Tarabay sanat 945 h/1538 m* (Muffasal Defteri of Marj Ibn Amir and Its Territories That Were Entrusted to Amir Tarabay, A.H. 945/A.D. 1538). Amman, 1989.

Baldensperger, P. J. *The Immovable East: Studies of the People and Customs of Palestine*. Boston, 1913.

Barbir, Karl. *Ottoman Rule in Damascus: 1708–1758*. Princeton, N.J., 1980.

Bargouthi, Omar Saleh. "Traces of the Feudal System in Palestine." *JPOS*, 9 (1929), 70–79.

———, and Khalil Totah. *Tarikh Filastin* (History of Palestine). Jerusalem, 1923.

Barker, Edward B. *Syria and Egypt under the Last Five Sultans of Turkey*. 2 vols. London, 1876. Reprint, New York, 1973.

Barnes, John. *An Introduction to the Religious Foundations of the Ottoman Empire*. Leiden, 1986.

Bayly, C. A. *The Imperial Meridian: The British Empire and the World, 1780–1830.* London and New York, 1989.

———. *Rulers, Townsmen and Bazaars: North Indian Society in the Age of British Expansionism, 1770–1870.* Cambridge, England, 1983.

Bekawi, Sobhi M. *English Travel Literature Dealing with Palestine from 1800–1850.* Cairo, 1978.

Ben-Arieh, Yehoshua. "The Population of the Large Towns in Palestine during the First Eighty Years of the Nineteenth Century According to Western Sources." In Moshe Ma'oz, ed., *Studies on Palestine during the Ottoman Period.* Jerusalem, 1975, 49–69.

Bishawi, Said Abdullah Jibril. *Nablus: Al-awda al-siyasiyya wa al-ijtima'iyya wa al-thaqafiyya wa al-iqtisadiyya fi asr al-hurub al-salibiyya, 492–690/1099–1291* (Nablus: Political, Social, Cultural, and Economic Conditions during the Crusader Wars, 492–690/1099–1291). Amman, 1991.

Blumberg, Arnold, ed. *A View from Jerusalem, 1849–1858: The Consular Diary of James and Elizabeth Anne Finn.* London, 1980.

Bodman, H. L. *Political Factions in Aleppo, 1760–1826.* Chapel Hill, N.C., 1963.

Bose, Sugata, ed. *South Asia and World Capitalism.* Delhi, 1990.

Bowring, John. *Report on the Commercial Statistics of Syria.* London, 1840. Reprint, New York, 1973.

Braudel, Fernand. *Civilization and Capitalism, 15th–18th Century.* 3 vols. New York, 1986.

———. *The Mediterranean and the Mediterranean World in the Age of Philip II.* 2 vols., 2d ed. New York, 1976.

Breik, Mikha'il. *Tarikh al-Sham, 1720–1780* (History of Damascus). Edited by Qustantine al-Basha. Harissa, Lebanon, 1930.

Buckingham, James Silk. *Travels among the Arab Tribes Inhabiting the Countries East of Syria and Palestine.* London, 1825.

Al-Budayri, al-Hallaq Ahmad. *Hawadith Dimashq al-yawmiyya, 1154–1175/1741–1762* (Daily Events in Damascus, 1154–1175/1741–1762). Edited by Ahmad Izzat Abd al-Karim. Cairo, 1959.

Buheiry, Marwan. "The Agricultural Exports of Southern Palestine, 1885–1914." *JPS*, 10:4 (Summer 1981), 61–81.

———. "The Peasant Revolt of 1858 in Mount Lebanon: Rising Expectations, Economic Malaise and the Incentive to Arm." In Tarif Khalidi, ed., *Land Tenure and Social Transformation in the Middle East.* Beirut, 1984, 291–301.

———, and Leila Buheiry, eds. *The Splendor of the Holy Land: Artisans, Geographers, and Travellers.* New York, 1978.

Burckhardt, John Lewis. *Travels in Syria and the Holy Land.* London, 1822.

Canaan, Tawfiq. *Mohammedan Saints and Sanctuaries in Palestine.* London, 1927.

Chevalier, Dominique. "De la production lente a l'économie dynamique en Syrie." *Annales,* 21 (1966), 59–70.

———. "Un example de résistance technique de l'artisinat syrien aux XIXe et XXe siècles: Les tissus ikates d'Alep et de Damas," *Syria,* 39:3–4 (1962), 300–324.

Clancy-Smith, Julia. "The Maghrib and the Mediterranean World in the Nineteenth Century: Illicit Exchanges, Migrants, and Social Marginals." In Kenneth J. Perkins and Michel Le Gall, eds., *Volume in Honor of L. Carl Brown.* Princeton, N.J., forthcoming.

———. *Rebel and Saint: Muslim Notables, Populist Protest, Colonial Encounters (Algeria and Tunisia, c. 1800–1904).* Berkeley, Calif., 1994.

Cohen, Amnon. *Economic Life in Jerusalem.* Cambridge, England, 1989.

———. *Jewish Life under Islam: Jerusalem in the Sixteenth Century.* Cambridge, Mass., and London, 1984.

———. "Local Trade, International Trade and Government in Jerusalem during the Early Ottoman Period." AAS, 12:1 (1978), 5–12.

———. "Ottoman Rule and the Re-Emergence of the Coast of Palestine." *Cathedra,* 34 (January 1985), 55–74.

———. *Palestine in the Eighteenth Century: Patterns of Government and Administration.* Jerusalem, 1973.

———, and Gabriel Baer. *Egypt and Palestine: A Millennium of Association (868–1948).* New York, 1984.

———, and Bernard Lewis. *Population and Revenue in the Towns of Palestine in the Sixteenth Century.* Princeton, N.J., 1978.

Cohn, Bernard. "Cloth, Clothes, and Colonialism: India in the Nineteenth Century." In A. B. Weiner and J. Schneider, eds., *Cloth and Human Experience.* New York, 1989, 303–353.

Crecelius, Daniel. *The Roots of Modern Egypt: A Study of the Regimes of Ali Bey al-Kabir and Muhammad Bey Abu al-Dahab, 1760–1775.* Minneapolis, Minn., and Chicago, 1981.

Croly, George. *The Holy Land: Syria, Iduma, Arabia, Egypt & Nubia, From Drawings Made on the Spot by David Roberts.* 2 vols. London, 1842, 1849.

Crosby (El-Mukattem). *Lands of the Moslem: A Narrative of Oriental Travel.* New York, 1851.

Cuno, Ken. "Egypt's Wealthy Peasantry, 1740–1820: A Study in the Region of al-Mansura." In Tarif Khalidi, ed., *Land Tenure and Social Transformation in the Middle East.* Beirut, 1984, 303–332.

———. "The Origins of Private Ownership of Land in Egypt: A Reappraisal." IJMES, 12 (1980), 245–275.

———. *The Pasha's Peasants: Land, Society, and Economy in Lower Egypt, 1740–1858.* Cambridge, England, 1992.

Al-Dabbagh, Mustafa Murad. *Biladuna Filastin* (Our Country, Palestine). 11 vols. Beirut, 1988.

Darwaza, Muhammad Izzat, *Al-Arab wa al-uruba fi haqabat al-taqallub al-turki min al-qarn al-thalith hatta al-qarn al-rabi ashar al-hijri* (Arabs and Arabism during the Upheavals of the Turkish Era from the Thirteenth to the Fourteenth Islamic Centuries). 11 vols., 2d ed.. Vol. 5, *Fi sharq al-Urdun wa Filastin* (In East Jordan and Palestine). Sidon, 1981.

———. *Mi'at am filastiniyya: Mudhakarat wa tasjilat* (One Hundred Palestinian Years: Memories and Notes). Damascus, 1984.

DeJong, F. "Sufi Orders in Nineteenth and Twentieth Century Palestine." *Studia Islamica,* 58 (1983), 149–181.

Dols, Michael W. "The Second Plague Pandemic and Its Recurrences in the Middle East: 1347–1894." JESHO, 22 (1979), 162–189.

Doumani, Beshara. "Palestinian Islamic Court Records: A Source for Socioeconomic History." *MESA Bulletin*, 19 (1985), 155–172.

———. "The Political Economy of Population Counts in Ottoman Palestine: Nablus, circa 1850." IJMES, 26 (1994), 1–17.

———. "Rediscovering Ottoman Palestine: Writing Palestinians into History." JPS, 21:2 (Winter 1992), 5–28.

Farah, Bulos. *Min al-uthmaniyya ila al-dawla al-ibriyya* (From the Ottoman to the Hebrew State). Nazareth, 1985.

Farah, Caesar E. "The Quadruple Alliance and Proposed Ottoman Reform in Syria, 1839–1841." IJTS, 2 (1981), 101–127.

Faroqhi, Suraiya. *Men of Modest Substance: House Owners and House Property in Seventeenth-Century Ankara and Kaysari.* Cambridge, England, 1987.

———. "Notes on the Production of Cotton and Cotton Cloth in Sixteenth- and Seventeenth-Century Anatolia." In Huri İslamoğlu-İnan, ed., *The Ottoman Empire and the World Economy.* Cambridge, England, 1987, 262–270.

———. *Towns and Townsmen of Ottoman Anatolia: Trade, Crafts and Food Production in an Urban Setting, 1520–1650.* Cambridge, England, 1984.

Farraj, Nicola. *Qissat al-shaykh Zahir* (The Story of Shaykh Zahir). Beirut, 1926.

Fawaz, Leila. *Merchants and Migrants in Nineteenth-Century Beirut.* Cambridge, Mass., 1983.

Finn, Elizabeth Anne. *Home in the Holy Land: A Tale Illustrating Customs and Incidents in Modern Jerusalem.* London, 1866.

———. *Palestine Peasantry: Notes on Their Clans, Warfare, Religion and Laws.* London, 1923.

Finn, James. *Stirring Times: Or Records from Jerusalem Consular Chronicles of 1853 to 1856.* Edited by Elizabeth Anne Finn. 2 vols. London, 1878.

Firestone, Yaʿakov. "Crop-Sharing Economics in Mandatory Palestine." MES, 11 (1975), 2–23, 175–194.

———. "Production and Trade in an Islamic Context: Sharika Trade Contracts in the Transitional Economy of Northern Samaria, 1853–1943." IJMES, 6 (1975), 185–209, 308–324.

Fisher, Stanley. *Ottoman Land Laws.* London, 1919.

Fox-Genovese, Elizabeth, and Eugene Genovese. *Fruits of Merchant Capital: Slavery and Bourgeois Property in the Rise and Expansion of Capitalism.* Oxford, 1983.

Frangakis-Syrett, Elena. "The Trade of Cotton and Cloth in Izmir: From the Second Half of the Eighteenth Century to the Early Nineteenth Century." In Çağlar Keyder and Faruk Tabak, eds., *Landholding and Commercial Agriculture in the Middle East.* Albany, N.Y., 1991, pp. 97–111.

Frantz-Murphy, Gladys. "A New Interpretation of the Economic History of Medieval Egypt: The Role of the Textile Industry, 254–567/868–1171." JESHO, 24 (1981), 274–297.

Geertz, Clifford, Mildred Geertz, and Lawrence Rosen. *Meaning and Order in Moroccan Society: Three Essays in Cultural Analysis.* Cambridge, England, 1979.

Gerber, Haim. "Modernization in Nineteenth-Century Palestine: The Role of Foreign Trade." MES, 18 (1982), 250–264.

———. *Ottoman Rule in Jerusalem, 1890–1914.* Berlin, 1985.

———. "Sharia, Kanun and Custom in the Ottoman Law: The Court Records of 17th-Century Bursa." IJTS, 3 (1984/1985), 131–147.

———. *The Social Origins of the Modern Middle East.* Boulder, Colo., 1987.

Gharayba, Abdel-Karim Mahmud. *Suriyya fi al-qarn al-tasi ashar* (Syria in the Nineteenth Century). Cairo, 1961.

Gibb, H. A. R., and Harold Bowen. *Islamic Society and the West.* 2 vols. Oxford, 1951, 1957.

Gilsenan, Michael. "Against Patron-Client Relations." In Ernest Gellner and John Waterbury, eds., *Patrons and Clients.* London, 1977, 167–183.

Goiten, S. D. *A Mediterranean Society: The Jewish Communities of the Arab World as Portrayed in the Documents of the Cairo Geniza.* Vol. 1, *Economic Foundation.* Berkeley, Calif., 1967. Vol. 4, *Daily Life.* Berkeley, Calif., 1983.

Goldstone, Jack. "East and West in the Seventeenth Century: Political Crises in Stuart England, Ottoman Turkey, and Ming China." *Comparative Studies in Society and History,* 30 (1988), 103–142.

Gozanski, Tamar. *Tatawur al-ra'smaliyya fi Filastin* (Capitalist Development in Palestine). Haifa, 1987.

Graham-Brown, Sarah. *Palestinians and Their Society, 1880–1946: A Photographic Essay.* London and New York, 1980.

———. "The Political Economy of Jabal Nablus, 1920–1948." In Roger Owen, ed., *Studies in the Economic and Social History of Palestine in the Nineteenth and Twentieth Centuries.* London, 1982, 88–176.

Gran, Peter. *Islamic Roots of Capitalism, Egypt 1760–1840.* Austin, Tex., 1979.

———. "Political Economy as a Paradigm for the Study of Islamic History." IJMES, 11 (1980), 511–526.

Grant, Elihu. *The People of Palestine.* London, 1921.

Grossman, David, and Zeev Safrai. "Satellite Settlements in Western Samaria." *The Geographical Review,* 70 (1980), 446–461.

Haddad, Yusuf. *Al-Mujtama wa al-turath fi Filastin: Qaryat al-Bassa* (Society and Folklore in Palestine: A Case Study of Al-Bassa Village). Acre, 1987.

Hanna, Abdullah. *Harakat al-amma al-dimashqiyya fi al-qarnayn al-thamin-ashar wa al-tasi ashar* (Damascene Popular Movements in the Eighteenth and Nineteenth Centuries). Damascus, 1985.

———. *Al-Qadiyya al-zira'iyya wa al-harakat al-fallahiyya fi Suriyya wa Lubnan, 1820–1920* (The Agricultural Question and Peasant Movements in Syria and Lebanon, 1820–1920). Beirut, 1975.

Harik, Iliya F. *Politics and Change in a Traditional Society: Lebanon, 1711–1845.* Princeton, N.J., 1968.

Heyd, Uriel. *Ottoman Documents on Palestine, 1552-1615: A Study of the Firman According to the Muhimme Defteri.* Oxford, 1960.

Hill, Enid. *Mahkama! Studies in the Egyptian Legal System.* London, 1979.

Hilton, Rodney, ed. *The Transition from Feudalism to Capitalism.* London, 1984.

Al-Hilu, Mussallam. *Qissat madinat Nablus* (Story of the City of Nablus). Tunis, n.d.

Hindess, Barry, and Paul Q. Hirst. *Pre-Capitalist Modes of Production.* London, 1975.

Hinz, Walther. *Al-Makayil wa al-awzan al-islamiyya wa ma yu'adiluha fi al-nizam al-mitri* (Islamic Weights and Measures and Their Metric Equivalent). Translated by Kamil al-Asali. Amman, 1970.

Hoexter, Meriam. "Egyptian Involvement in the Politics of Notables in Palestine: Ibrahim Pasha in Jabal Nablus." In Amnon Cohen and Gabriel Baer, eds., *Egypt and Palestine: A Millennium of Association (868–1948).* New York, 1984, 190–213.

———. "The Role of the Qays and Yaman Factions in Local Political Divisions: Jabal Nablus Compared with the Judean Hills in the First Half of the Nineteenth Century." AAS, 9:3 (1973), 249–311.

Hofman, Yitzhak. "The Administration of Syria and Palestine under Egyptian Rule, 1831-1840." In Moshe Ma'oz, ed., *Studies on Palestine during the Ottoman Period.* Jerusalem, 1975, 311-333.

Holt, P. M. *Egypt and the Fertile Crescent, 1516–1922: A Political History.* Ithaca, N.Y., 1966.

Homsi, Mahdi S. *Tarikh Tarablus min khilal watha'iq al-mahkamah al-shar'iyya fi al-nisf al-thani min al-qarn al-sabi ashar* (The History of Tripoli According to Islamic Court Records during the Second Half of the Seventeenth Century). Tripoli, 1985.

Hourani, Albert. "The Changing Face of the Fertile Crescent in the Eighteenth Century." *Studia Islamica,* 8 (1957), 89–122.

———. "Ottoman Reform and the Politics of Notables." In W. R. Polk and Richard L. Chambers, eds., *Beginnings of Modernization in the Middle East.* Chicago, 1968.

Hunayti, Harb. *Qissat madinat Jenin* (The Story of the City of Jenin). Tunis, n.d.

Hurub Ibrahim basha al-masri fi Suriyya wa al-Anadol (The Battles of Ibrahim Pasha the Egyptian in Syria and Anatolia). Edited by Asad Rustum. Cairo, 1927.

Al-Husayni, Muhammad As'ad. *Al-Manhal al-safi fi al-waqf wa ahkamihi, wa al-watha'iq al-tarikhiyya lil-aradi wa al-huquq al-waqfiyya al-islamiyya fi Filastin* (The Pure Spring Concerning *waqf* and Its Conditions, and the Historical Documents of the Islamic Lands and *waqf* Rights in Palestine). Jerusalem, 1982.

Hütteroth, Wolf-Dieter. "Ottoman Administration of the Desert Frontier in the Sixteenth Century." AAS, 19:2 (1985), 145–155.

———, and Kamal Abdulfattah. *Historical Geography of Palestine, Transjordan and Southern Syria in the Late Sixteenth Century.* Erlangen, Germany, 1977.

Ibn al-Siddiq. *Ghara'ib al-bada'i wa aja'ib al-waqa'i* (The Strange Wonders and Mysterious Events). Edited by Yusuf Na'isa. Damascus, 1988.

İnalcik, Halil. *Application of the Tanzimat and Its Social Effects.* Lisse, 1976.

———. "Centralization and Decentralization in Ottoman Administration." In Thomas Naff and Roger Owen, eds., *Studies in Eighteenth Century Islamic History.* Carbondale, Ill., and London, 1977, 27–52.

———. *Ottoman Empire: Conquest, Organization and Economy.* London, 1978.

———. *Studies in Ottoman Social and Economic History.* London, 1985.

————. "When and How British Cotton Goods Invaded the Levant Markets." In Huri İslamoğlu-İnan, ed., *The Ottoman Empire and the World Economy.* Cambridge, England, 1987, 374–383.

İslamoğlu-İnan, Huri. "Introduction: 'Oriental Despotism' in World System Perspective." In Huri İslamoğlu-İnan, ed., *The Ottoman Empire and the World Economy.* Cambridge, England, 1987, 1–24.

————. "M. A. Cook's Population Pressure in Rural Anatolia: A Critique of the Present Paradigm in Ottoman History." *Review of Middle East Studies,* 3 (1976), 120–135.

————. "Peasants, Commercialization, and Legitimation of State Power in Sixteenth-Century Anatolia." In Çağlar Keyder and Faruk Tabak, eds., *Landholding and Commercial Agriculture in the Middle East.* Albany, N.Y., 1991, pp. 57–76.

————, ed. *The Ottoman Empire and the World Economy.* Cambridge, England, 1987.

Issawi, Charles. "British Trade and the Rise of Beirut, 1830–1860." IJMES, 8 (1977), 91–101.

————. *The Fertile Crescent, 1800–1914: A Documentary Economic History.* Oxford, 1988.

————. "The Trade of Jaffa, 1825–1914." In Hisham Nashabe, ed., *Studia Palaestina: Studies in Honor of Constantine K. Zurayk.* Beirut, 1988, 42–51.

————, ed. *The Economic History of the Middle East, 1800–1914.* Chicago, 1966. Reprint, Chicago, 1975.

Jaussen, J. A., *Coutumes Palestiniennes: Napulouse et son district.* Paris, 1927.

Jennings, Ronald. "Women in Early Seventeenth Century Ottoman Judicial Records: The Sharia Court of Anatolian Kayseri." JESHO, 18 (1975), 53–114.

Johansen, Baber. *The Islamic Law on Land Tax and Rent: The Peasants' Loss of Property Rights as Interpreted in the Hanafite Legal Literature of the Mamluk and Ottoman Periods.* London, 1988.

Joudah, Ahmad Hasan. *Revolt in Palestine in the Eighteenth Century: The Era of Shaykh Zahir al-Umar.* Princeton, N.J., 1987.

Kandiyoti, Deniz. "Bargaining with Patriarchy." *Gender and Society,* 2 (1988), 274–290.

————. "Islam and Patriarchy: A Comparative Perspective." In Nikkie Keddie and Beth Baron, eds., *Women in Middle Eastern History: Shifting Boundaries in Sex and Gender.* New Haven, Conn., and London, 1991, 23–42.

Karpat, Kemal. *Ottoman Population, 1830–1914: Demographic and Social Characteristics.* Madison, Wis., 1985.

————. *The Ottoman State and Its Place in World History.* Leiden, 1974.

Kasaba, Reşat. *The Ottoman Empire and the World Economy: The Nineteenth Century.* Albany, N.Y., 1988.

Al-Kayyali, Abd al-Wahab. *Tarikh Filastin al-hadith* (The Modern History of Palestine). 9th ed. Beirut, 1985.

Kelly, Walter Keating. *Syria and the Holy Land: Their Scenery and Their People.* London, 1844.

Kerr, Malcolm. *Lebanon in the Last Years of Feudalism, 1840-1868: A Contemporary Account by Antun Dahir al-Aqiqi and Other Documents.* Beirut, 1959.

Keyder, Çağlar. "The Dissolution of the Asiatic Mode of Production." *Economy and Society*, 5 (May 1976), 178–196.

————, and Faruk Tabak, eds. *Landholding and Commercial Agriculture in the Middle East*. Albany, N.Y., 1991.

Khalidi, Ahmad Samih. *Ahl al-ilm wa al-hukm fi rif Filastin* (Scholars and Rulers in Rural Palestine). Amman, 1968.

Khalidi, Tarif, ed. *Land Tenure and Social Transformation in the Middle East*. Beirut, 1984.

Khalidi, Walid. *Before Their Diaspora: A Photographic History of the Palestinians*. Washington, D.C., 1984.

Khatib, Alia. *Arab al-Turkman: Abna Marj Ibn Amir* (The Turkman Arabs: Sons of Marj Ibn Amir). Amman, 1987.

Khoury, Dina Rizk. "The Introduction of Commercial Agriculture in the Province of Mosul and Its Effects on the Peasantry, 1750–1850." In Çağlar Keyder and Faruk Tabak, eds., *Landholding and Commercial Agriculture in the Middle East*. Albany, N.Y., 1991, 155–171.

Khoury, Philip. *Urban Notables and Arab Nationalism: The Politics of Damascus, 1860–1920*. Cambridge, England, 1983.

Kunt, I. Metin. *The Sultan's Servants: The Transformation of Ottoman Provincial Government, 1550–1650*. New York, 1983.

Kurd Ali, Muhammad. *Kitab khitat al-Sham* (The Plan of Damascus). 3d. ed., 6 vols. Damascus, 1983.

Kurmus, Orhan. "The Cotton Famine and Its Effects on the Ottoman Empire." In Huri İslamoğlu-İnan, ed., *The Ottoman Empire and the World Economy*. Cambridge, England, 1987, 160–169.

Kushner, David, ed. *Palestine in the Late Ottoman Period: Political, Social and Economic Transformation*. Jerusalem, 1986.

Lawson, Fred. "Rural Revolt and Provincial Society in Egypt, 1820–1824." IJMES, 13 (1981), 131–153.

Levy, Avigdor. "Military Reform and the Problem of Centralization in the Ottoman Empire in the Eighteenth Century." MES, 18 (1982), 227–249.

Lewis, Bernard. *The Emergence of Modern Turkey*. Oxford, 1961.

Li Causi, Luciano. "Anthropology and Ideology: the Case of 'Patronage.'" *Critique of Anthropology*, 4/5 (1975), 90–110.

Littlewood, Paul. "Patronage, Ideology and Reproduction," *Critique of Anthropology*, 15 (1980), 29–45.

Ludden, David. *Peasant History in South India*. Princeton, N.J., 1985.

McCarthy, Justin. *The Population of Palestine*. New York, 1990.

McGowan, Bruce. *Economic Life in Ottoman Europe*. Cambridge, England, 1981.

————. "The Study of Land and Agriculture in the Ottoman Provinces within the Context of an Expanding Economy in the Seventeenth and Eighteenth Centuries." IJTS, 3 (1984/1985), 57–63.

Manna, Adel. *A'lam Filastin fi awakhir al-ahd al-uthmani, 1800–1918* (Notables of Palestine in the Late Ottoman Period). Jerusalem, 1986.

————. "The *Sijill* as Source for the Study of Palestine during the Ottoman Period, with Special Reference to the French Invasion." In David Kushner, ed.,

Palestine in the Late Ottoman Period: Political, Social, and Economic Transformation. Jerusalem, 1986, 351–362.

Mansur, As'ad. *Tarikh al-Nasira min aqdam azmaniha ila ayamina al-hadira* (The History of Nazareth from Ancient Times until the Present). Cairo, 1924.

Ma'oz, Moshe. *Ottoman Reform in Syria and Palestine, 1840–1861: The Impact of the Tanzimat on Politics and Society.* Oxford, 1968.

———, ed. *Studies on Palestine during the Ottoman Period.* Jerusalem, 1975.

Marcus, Abraham. "Men, Women, and Property: Dealers in Real Estate in 18th Century Aleppo." JESHO, 26 (1983), 138–163.

———. *The Middle East on the Eve of Modernity: Aleppo in the Eighteenth Century.* New York, 1989.

Masri, Malik. *Nabulsiyat.* Amman, 1990.

Masson, Paul. *Histoire du commerce français dans le Levant au XVIIIieme siècle.* New York, 1967.

Masters, Bruce. "The 1850 Events in Aleppo: An Aftershock of Syria's Incorporation into the Capitalist Economy." IJMES, 22 (1990), 3–20.

———. *The Origins of Western Economic Dominance in the Middle East: Mercantilism and the Islamic Economy in Aleppo, 1600–1750.* New York, 1988.

Mills, John. *Three Months' Residence at Nablus and an Account of the Modern Samaritans.* London, 1864.

Mishaqa, Mikhayil. *Muntakhabat min al-jawab ala iqtirah al-ahbab* (Selected Answers to Inquiries from Loved Ones). Edited by Asad Rustum and Subhi Abu Shaqra. Beirut, 1955. Reprint, Beirut, 1985.

———. *Murder, Mayhem, Pillage, and Plunder: The History of the Lebanon in the 18th and 19th Centuries.* Translated by Wheeler M. Thackston, Jr. New York, 1988.

Moors, Annelies, and Steven Machlin. "Postcards of Palestine: Interpreting Images." *Critique of Anthropology,* 7 (1987), 61–77.

Mu'ammar, Tawfiq. *Zahir al-Umar: Kitab yatanawal tarikh al-Jalil khasattan wa al-bilad al-suriyya ammatan min sanat 1698 hatta sanat 1777* (Zahir al-Umar: A Book Dealing with the History of the Galilee in Particular and the Syrian Lands in General from the Year 1698 to the Year 1777). Nazareth, 1979.

Mudhakkirat tarikhiyya an hamlat Ibrahim basha ala Suriyya (Historical Memoirs of Ibrahim Pasha's Campaign in Syria). Edited by Ahmad Ghassan Sabano. N.p., n.d.

Myers, David. "History as Ideology: The Case of Ben Zion Dinur, Zionist Historian 'Par Excellence.'" *Modern Judaism,* 8:2 (May 1988), 167–193.

Naff, Thomas, and Owen, Roger, eds. *Studies in Eighteenth Century Islamic History.* Carbondale, Ill., and London, 1977.

Nelson, Cynthia, ed., *The Desert and the Sown: Nomads in a Wider Society.* Berkeley, Calif., 1974.

Nimr, Ihsan. *Tarikh Jabal Nablus wa al-Balqa* (History of Jabal Nablus and al-Balqa). 4 vols. Nablus, 1936–1961.

Owen, Roger. *Cotton and the Egyptian Economy, 1820–1914.* Oxford, 1969.

———. "The Middle East in the Eighteenth Century—An 'Islamic' Society in Decline? A Critique of Gibb and Bowen's *Islamic Society and the West.*" *Review of Middle East Studies,* 1 (1975), 101–112.

———. *The Middle East in the World Economy, 1800–1914.* London, 1981.

———, ed. *Studies in the Economic and Social History of Palestine in the Nineteenth and Twentieth Centuries.* London, 1982.

Paige, Jeffrey. "One, Two, or Many Vietnams? Social Theory and Peasant Revolution in Vietnam and Guatemala." In Edmund Burke III, ed., *Global Crises and Social Movements.* Boulder, Colo., and London, 1988, 145–179.

Pamuk, Şevket. "Decline and Resistance of Ottoman Cotton Textiles, 1820–1913." *Explorations in Economic History,* 23 (1986), 200–225.

———. *Ottoman Empire and the World Economy, 1820–1913: Trade, Capital and Production.* Cambridge, England, 1987.

———. "The Ottoman Empire in Comparative Perspective." *Review* (Binghamton, N.Y.), 11 (1988), 127–150.

Perlin, Frank. "Precolonial South Asia and Western Penetration in the 17th–19th Centuries." *Review* (Binghamton, N.Y.), 4 (1980), 267–306.

———. "Proto-Industrialization and Pre-Colonial South Asia." *Past and Present,* 98 (1983), 30–95.

Philipp, Thomas. "Class, Community and Arab Historiography in the Early Eighteenth Century—The Dawn of a New Era." IJMES, 16 (1984), 161–175.

———. "Social Structure and Political Power in Acre in the 18th Century." In Thomas Philipp, ed., *The Syrian Land in the 18th and 19th Century.* Stuttgart, 1992, 91–108.

Pierotti, Ermete. *Customs and Traditions of Palestine.* Cambridge, England, 1864.

Polk, William R. *The Opening of South Lebanon, 1788–1840: A Study of the Impact of the West on the Middle East.* Cambridge, Mass., 1963.

———, and Richard L. Chambers, eds. *Beginnings of Modernization in the Middle East: The Nineteenth Century.* Chicago, 1968.

Porath, Yehoshua. "The Peasant Revolt of 1858–1861 in Kisrawan." AAS, 2 (1966), 77–157.

Puryear, V. J. *France and the Levant.* Berkeley, Calif., and Los Angeles, 1941.

Al-Qasimi, Muhammad Sa'id. *Qamus al-sina'at al-shamiyya.* 2 vols. Paris, 1962.

Quataert, Donald. "Ottoman Handicrafts and Industry in the Age of European Industrial Hegemony, 1800–1914." *Review* (Binghamton, N.Y.), 11 (1988), 169–178.

———. *Ottoman Manufacturing in the Age of the Industrial Revolution.* Cambridge, England, 1993.

———. "Ottoman Women, Households, and Textile Manufacturing, 1800–1914." In Nikkie Keddie and Beth Baron, eds. *Women in Middle Eastern History: Shifting Boundaries in Sex and Gender.* New Haven, Conn., and London, 1991, 161–176.

———. *Social Disintegration and Popular Resistance in the Ottoman Empire, 1881–1908: Reactions to European Economic Penetration.* New York, 1983.

Rafeq, Abdul-Karim. *Al-Arab wa al-uthmaniyun, 1516–1916* (The Arabs and the Ottomans, 1516–1916). Damascus, 1974.

———. *Buhuth fi al-tarikh al-iqtisadi wa al-ijtima'i li Bilad al-Sham fi al-asr al-hadith* (Studies in the Social and Economic History of Greater Syria in the Modern Period). Damascus, 1985.

———. "Changes in the Relationship between the Ottoman Central Administration and the Syrian Provinces from the Sixteenth to the Eighteenth Centuries." In Thomas Naff and Roger Owen, eds., *Studies in Eighteenth Century Islamic History.* Carbondale, Ill., and London, 1977, 53–73.

―――. "Economic Relations between Damascus and the Dependent Countryside, 1743–71." In A. L. Udovitch, ed., *The Islamic Middle East, 700–1900.* Princeton, N.J., 1981, 653–686.

―――. "Al-Fi'at al-ijtima'iyya wa masader al-tharwa wa al-sulta fi Ghazza fi awakher al-khamsinat min al-qarn al-tasi ashar" (Social Groups and the Sources of Wealth and Power in Gaza during the late 1850s). In Hisham Nashabe, ed., *Studia Palaestina: Studies in Honor of Constantine K. Zurayk.* Beirut, 1988, 83–126.

―――. "Ghazza: Dirasa umraniyya wa iqtisadiyya min khilal al-watha'iq al-shar-'iyya, 1273–1277/1857–1861" (Gaza: A Cultural and Economic Study Based on Islamic Court Documents, 1273–1277/1857–1861). In *Al-M'utamar al-duwali al-thalith li tarikh Bilad al-Sham (Filastin)* (The Third International Conference on Bilad al-Sham: Palestine). Vol. 2, *Jughrafiyyat Filastin wa hadaratiha* (The Geography and Civilization of Palestine). Amman, 1980, 68–157.

―――. "Land Tenure Problems and Their Social Impact in Syria around the Middle of the Nineteenth Century." In Tarif Khalidi, ed., *Land Tenure and Social Transformation in the Middle East.* Beirut, 1984, 371–408.

―――. "The Local Forces in Syria in the Seventeenth and Eighteenth Centuries." In V. J. Parry and M. E. Yapp, eds., *War, Technology and Society.* London, 1975, 277–307.

―――. *The Province of Damascus, 1723–1783.* Beirut, 1966.

―――. "Qafilat al-hajj wa ahimmiyatuha fi al-ahd al-uthmani" (The Pilgrimage Caravan and Its Importance in the Ottoman Era). *Dirasat Tarikhiyya,* 6 (1981), 5–28.

Rahim, Abdur. *The Principles of Muhammadan Jurisprudence According to the Hanafi, Maliki, Shafi'i and Hanbali Schools.* London, 1911. Reprint, Westport, Conn., 1981.

Al-Ramini, Akram. *Nablus fi al-qarn al-tasi ashar* (Nablus in the Nineteenth Century). Amman, 1977.

Raymond, André. *Artisans et commerçants au Caire au XVIIIe siècle.* 2 vols. Damascus, 1973–1974.

Reilly, James. "Status Groups and Property-Holding in the Damascus Hinterland, 1828–1880." IJMES, 21 (1989), 517–539.

Rogan, Eugene. "Money-Lending and Capital Flows from Nablus, Damascus and Jerusalem to the *qada'* of al-Salt in the Last Decades of Ottoman Rule." In Thomas Philipp, ed., *The Syrian Land in the 18th and 19th Century.* Stuttgart, 1992, 239–260.

Rogers, Mary Eliza. *Domestic Life in Palestine.* London, 1862. Reprint, London and New York, 1989.

Rustum, Asad. *Bashir bayna al-sultan wa al-aziz: 1804–1841* (Bashir between the Sultan and the Khedive). 2 vols. Beirut, 1956.

―――. *Al-Mahfuzat al-malakiyya al-misriyya* (A Calendar of State Papers from the Royal Archives of Egypt relating to the Affairs of Syria). 4 vols. Beirut, 1940–1943. Reprint, Beirut, 1986.

————.*Notes on Akka and Its Defenses under Ibrahim Pasha.* Cairo, 1926.

————. *The Royal Archives of Egypt and the Disturbances in Palestine, 1834.* Beirut, 1938.

————. *The Royal Archives of Egypt and the Origins of the Expedition to Syria.* Beirut, 1936.

————. *The Struggle of Mehmet Ali Pasha with Sultan Mahmud II and Some of Its Geographical Aspects.* Cairo, 1925.

————. *Al-Usul al-arabiyya li-tarikh Suriyya fi ahd Muhammad Ali basha* (Materials for a Corpus of Arabic Documents relating to the History of Syria under Mehemet Ali Pasha). 5 vols. Beirut, 1933–1936.

Sabri, Bahjat. *Al-Sijillat al-uthmaniyya li baladiyyat Nablus* (Ottoman Records on the Municipality of Nablus). Jerusalem, 1982.

Said, Edward, and Christopher Hitchens, eds. *Blaming the Victims: Spurious Scholarship and the Palestinian Question.* London and New York, 1988.

Al-Salhut, Jamil. *Al-Qada al-asha'iri* (Clan Law). Acre, 1987.

Al-Samiri, Ibrahim Danafi. *Zahir al-Umar wa hukkam Jabal Nablus, A.H. 1185–1187/A.D. 1771–1773* (Zahir al-Umar and the Rulers of Jabal Nablus, A.H. 1185–1187/A.D. 1771–1773). Edited by Musa Abu Dayya. Nablus, 1986.

Sayigh, Rosemary. *Palestinians: From Peasants to Revolutionaries.* London, 1979.

Schilcher, Linda Schatkowski. *Families in Politics: Damascene Factions and Estates of the Eighteenth and Nineteenth Centuries.* Stuttgart, 1985.

————. "The Huran Conflicts of 1860's: A Chapter in the Rural History of Modern Syria." IJMES, 13 (1981), 159–179.

Schölch, Alexander. "The Emergence of Modern Palestine (1856–1882)." In Hisham Nashabe, ed., *Studia Palaestina: Studies in Honor of Constantine K. Zurayk.* Beirut, 1988, 69–82.

————. "European Penetration and the Economic Development of Palestine, 1856–1882." In Roger Owen, ed., *Studies in the Economic and Social History of Palestine in the Nineteenth and Twentieth Centuries.* London, 1982, 10–87.

————. *Palestine in Transformation, 1856–1882: Studies in Social, Economic, and Political Development.* Translated by William C. Young and Michael C. Gerrity. Washington, D.C., 1993.

Scott, James C. *The Moral Economy of the Peasant: Rebellion and Subsistence in Southeast Asia.* New Haven, Conn., 1976.

————. *Weapons of the Weak: Everyday Forms of Peasant Resistance.* New Haven, Conn., 1985.

Seddon, David. *Moroccan Peasants: A Century of Change in the Eastern Rif, 1870–1970.* Folkestone, England, 1981.

Seger, Karen, ed. *Portrait of a Palestinian Village: The Photographs of Hilma Granqvist.* London, 1981.

Serhan, Nimir. *Mawsu'at al-folklore al-Filastini* (Encyclopedia of Palestinian Folklore), 2d ed., 3 vols. Amman, 1989.

Shamir, Shimon. "Egyptian Rule (1832–1840) and the Beginning of the Modern Period in the History of Palestine." In Amnon Cohen and Gabriel Baer, eds., *Egypt and Palestine: A Millennium of Association (868–1948).* Jerusalem, 1984, 214–231.

Sharif, Maher. *Tarikh Filastin al-iqtisadi al-ijtimaʻi* (The Economic and Social History of Palestine). Beirut, 1985.

Shihab, Amir Haidar. *Tarikh Ahmad basha Jazzar* (History of Ahmad Pasha Jazzar). Edited by Antoine Chibli and Ignace-Abdo Khalife. Beirut, 1955.

Silverman, Sydel. "The Peasant Concept in Anthropology." *Journal of Peasant Studies*, 7 (1979), 49–69.

Sluglett, Peter, and Marion Farouk-Sluglett. "The Application of the 1858 Land Code in Greater Syria: Some Preliminary Observations." In Tarif Khalidi, ed., *Land Tenure and Transformation in the Middle East*. Beirut, 1984, 409–424.

Smilianskaya, I. *Al-Buna al-iqtisadiyya wa-al-ijtimaʻiyya fi al-mashriq al-arabi ala masharif al-asr al-hadith* (Social and Economic Structures in the Arab East on the Eve of the Modern Period). Beirut, 1989.

Smith, George Adam. *Historical Geography of Palestine*. London, 1894.

Spyridon, S. N. "Annals of Palestine, 1821–1841." JPOS, 18 (1938), 63–132.

Swedenberg, Ted. "The Role of the Palestinian Peasantry in the Great Revolt (1936–1939)." In Edmund Burke III and Ira Lapidus, eds., *Islam, Politics and Social Movements*. Berkeley, Calif., 1988, 169–203.

Tabak, Faruk. "Local Merchants in Peripheral Areas of the Empire: The Fertile Crescent during the Long Nineteenth Century." *Review* (Binghamton, N.Y.), 11 (1988), 179–214.

Tamimi, Muhammad Rafiq, and Muhammad Bahjat. *Wilayat Bayrut*. Beirut, 1916–1917.

Thomas, J. *Travels in Egypt and Palestine*. Philadelphia, 1853.

Thomson, W. M. *The Land and the Book*. London, 1894.

Tibawi, A. L. *A Modern History of Syria including Lebanon and Palestine*. London, 1969.

Tristram, H. B. *The Land of Israel: Journal of Travels in Palestine, Undertaken with Special Reference to Its Physical Character*. London, 1882.

———. *Pathways to Palestine*. 2 vols. London, 1881–1882.

Tucker, Judith. "Marriage and Family in Nablus, 1720–1856: Towards a History of Arab Muslim Marriage." *Journal of Family History*, 13 (1988), 165–179.

———. "Problems in the Historiography of Women in the Middle East: The Case of Nineteenth-Century Egypt." IJMES, 15 (1983), 321–336.

———. "Ties That Bound: Women and Family in Late Eighteenth- and Nineteenth-Century Nablus." In Nikkie Keddie and Beth Baron, eds., *Women in Middle Eastern History: Shifting Boundaries in Sex and Gender*. New Haven, Conn., and London, 1991, 233–253.

———. *Women in Nineteenth-Century Egypt*. Cambridge, England, 1985.

Tuma, Emile. *Filastin fi al-ahd al-uthmani* (Palestine during the Ottoman Period). Jerusalem, 1983.

Turner, Bryan. *Marx and the End of Orientalism*. London, 1978.

Udovitch, A. L., ed. *The Islamic Middle East, 700–1900*. Princeton, N.J., 1981.

———. *Partnership and Profit in Medieval Islam*. Princeton, N.J., 1970.

Urquhart, David. *The Lebanon (Mount Souria): A History and Diary*, 2 vols. London, 1860.

Valensi, Lucette. *Tunisian Peasants in the Eighteenth and Nineteenth Centuries*. Cambridge, England, and New York, 1985.

Vatter, Sherry. "Journeymen Textile Weavers in Nineteenth-Century Damascus: A Collective Biography." In Edmund Burke III, ed., *Struggle and Survival in the Modern Middle East*. Berkeley, Calif., 1993, 75–90.

Volney, M. *Travels through Syria and Egypt in the Years 1783, 1784, and 1785*. 2 vols. London, 1788.

Wallerstein, Immanuel. *The Modern World System*. 2 vols. New York, 1974, 1980.

———, and Reşat Kasaba. "Incorporation into the World Economy: Change in the Structure of the Ottoman Empire, 1750–1839." In J. L. Bacqué-Grammont and Paul Dumont, eds., *Économie et sociétés dans l'Empire ottoman fin du XVII–début du XXe siècle*. Paris, 1983, 335–354.

Warburg, Gabriel, and Gad Gilbar, eds. *Studies in Islamic Society: Contributions in Memory of Gabriel Baer*. Haifa, 1984.

Wehr, Hans. *A Dictionary of Modern Written Arabic*. Edited by J. Milton Cowan. 3d ed. New York, 1976.

Wilson, Charles Williams, ed. *Picturesque Palestine, Sinai and Egypt*. 2 vols. New York, 1881, 1884.

Wolf, Eric. *Peasant Wars of the Twentieth Century*. New York, 1969.

Wood, A. G. *A History of the Levant Company*. Oxford, 1935.

Wright, G. Ernest. *Shechem: The Biography of a Biblical City*. New York and Toronto, 1965.

Zwiedinek von Sudenhorst, Julius. *Syrien und seine Bedeutung für den Welthandel*. Vienna, 1873.

Index

(V) denotes villages.